PAYMENT SYSTEMS

PROBLEMS, MATERIALS, AND CASES

Third Edition

By

Linda J. Rusch

Frederick N. and Barbara T. Curley
Professor of Commercial Law
Gonzaga University School of Law

AMERICAN CASEBOOK SERIES®

THOMSON
™
WEST

Mat #40498016

American Casebook Series and West Group are trademarks
registered in the U.S. Patent and Trademark Office.

© West, a Thomson business, 2000, 2003
© 2007 Thomson/ West
     610 Opperman Drive
     P.O. Box 64526
     St. Paul, MN 55164–0526
     1–800–328–9352

Printed in the United States of America

ISBN: 978–0–314–16932–7

TEXT IS PRINTED ON 10% POST
CONSUMER RECYCLED PAPER

To my husband, Doug.

LJR

Preface

    This book is designed to help the student learn the law of payment systems as well as the art and skill of statutory reading. Most law school fare, at least in the first year, is based upon teaching the skill of case analysis and the art of argument using analogy and distinction from cases. This book seeks to facilitate teaching the skills necessary to engage in statutory reading and analysis. This set of skills requires close attention to each word of the statute or regulation, reading the applicable commentary to the statute or regulation, and learning the interaction between statutory sections. Reading and rereading the text and comments of a statute is critical to this process of statutory interpretation. Whenever this text cites a statutory section, you are expected to read the section and its commentary provided in the statutory supplement.

    The student is then expected to use what he or she has learned through careful reading of the statutory material and commentary to solve the problems posed. Solving the problems requires the student to map out their reasoning based upon the statutory language or commentary to come to the result. As in case analysis and reasoning, the final result is not nearly as important to learning the skill of statutory reading and analysis as is the method of arriving at the result. Thus to completely answer any problem in this book the student should write down all of the analytical steps taken to arrive at the answer, including reference to the precise language from the relevant statutes or comments that the student used to arrive at the result. To that end, significant white space is provided in this text to enable the student to record his or her analysis next to each problem.

    The problem-solving orientation of this book is based upon the perspective that most law students will use the skills developed in law school to solve problems. These problems may be from clients in a law firm or other practice setting, from constituents in a legislative setting, from executives in a corporate setting, or from policy makers in an administrative setting. Using the tools of critical analysis and linear logical thinking to solve problems is the hallmark of a lawyer. Thus, this book provides repeated opportunities for students to practice their problem-solving skills.

    Confronting a complex and interrelated statutory regime can be daunting. First, it is necessary to learn little parts, while at the same time, it is necessary to have a big picture to understand how the little parts fit together. Unfortunately, it is difficult to learn both the big picture and the little parts at the same time. This book attempts to address that difficulty by using textual overviews to give a sense of the big picture and then moving on to the little parts in solving problems that are structured like building blocks. Finally, the use of review problems allows an integration of the little parts into the big picture.

Another daunting feature of a statutory regime is that students approach the material with the perspective of a novice while the teacher approaches the material with the perspective of an expert. The challenge for any set of materials used to teach any subject is to go in small enough steps to allow the novice to understand the basic material while providing enough advanced material to allow the expert to challenge the student to think about the gray areas where the rules or results are not clear. This book attempts to mediate that difficult challenge by using building block problems that allow the student to understand the basic concepts, using text or cases to give examples of analysis, and then using more complex problems to approach more advanced discussions.

Finally, in confronting a statutory regime, it is important to remember that the reader must not only read the sections that seem the most relevant to the issue, the reader must look for other sections that impact the situation and must remember to look up the defined terms in the statute. Many students are frustrated with the time it takes to thoroughly read the necessary sections and prepare the problems for the day. All I can say is that it will get easier with practice. Some of us even learn to prefer statutes to cases.

Acknowledgments

Thank you to the students who endured these materials and to my colleagues who have used the book and provided many helpful suggestions.

Thank you to the following publishers and authors for granting permission to reprint portions of the material in this book.

Gustavus, Joseph D., *Letter of Credit Compliance Under Revised UCC Article 5 and UCP 500*, 114 BANKING L. J. 55 (1997). Copyright © 1997 Warren, Gorham & Lamont. Reprinted with permission of A.S. Pratt & Sons, successor in interest to Warren, Gorham and Lamont.

Heller, Stephanie, and Baxter, Jr., Thomas C., Reporters, *A Commercial Lawyer's Take on the Electronic Purse: An Analysis of Commercial Law Issues Associated with Stored-Value Cards and Electronic Money*, 52 BUS. LAW. 653 (1997). Copyright © 1997 by the American Bar Association. Reprinted by permission of the American Bar Association.

Summary of Contents

PREFACE v

ACKNOWLEDGMENTS vii

TABLE OF CASES xvii

TABLE OF STATUTES AND REGULATIONS xix

Chapter 1 Introduction to Payment Systems 1
    A. Overview 1
    B. Currency 5
    C. Credit Cards 14

Chapter 2 Introduction to Negotiable Instruments as a Payment
    System 37
    A. Overview 37
    B. How Do Negotiable Instruments Transfer Value 40
    C. Negotiability Concepts 42
    D. Requisites of a Negotiable Instrument Under U.C.C. Article 3 47

Chapter 3 Contract Liability on a Negotiable Instrument 55
    A. Overview 55
    B. Incurring the Obligation to Pay 57
    C. To Whom the Obligation is Owed: Person Entitled to Enforce 63
    D. When the Obligation is Due 71
    E. To Whom the Obligation is Owed:
       Persons Not "Entitled to Enforce" 78
    F. Enforcement of the Obligation: Defenses,
       Claims in Recoupment, and Holder in Due Course 79
    G. Discharge of the Obligation 109
    H. Suretyship Defenses 118

Chapter 4 Negotiable Instruments as Personal Property 133
    A. Claims to the Instrument 133
    B. Warranty Liability 166

Chapter 5 Collection Through the Banking System 173
    A. Overview 173

B. Payor/Drawee Bank and Customer Relationship 180
C. The Collection Process: Overview 202
D. Collecting Bank: Forward Collection 203
E. Payor Bank: Settlement and Final Payment 209
F. Item Return and Chargeback 216
G. Funds Availability 222
H. Check 21 and Substitute Checks 227

Chapter 6 Forgery and Fraud in the Use of Negotiable Instruments ... 235
A. Introduction 235
B. Unauthorized Signatures 237
C. Incomplete Instruments and Alterations 268
D. Lost or Stolen Instruments 270

Chapter 7 Letters of Credit 277
A. Overview 277
B. Mechanics of Value Transfer 277
C. Incurring, Satisfying and Enforcing the Obligation to Pay 281
D. Allocation of the Risk of Errors and Wrongdoing 289

Chapter 8 Electronic Funds Transfer 325
A. Overview 325
B. EFTA and Regulation E 327
C. U.C.C. Article 4A 336
D. Regulation of Evolving Payment Systems 371

Table of Contents

PREFACE v

ACKNOWLEDGMENTS vii

TABLE OF CASES xvii

TABLE OF STATUTES AND REGULATIONS xix

Chapter 1 Introduction to Payment Systems 1

  A. Overview 1

  B. Currency 5

        UNITED STATES CONSTITUTION, Article I 6

        A COMMERCIAL LAWYER'S TAKE ON THE ELECTRONIC PURSE:

          AN ANALYSIS OF COMMERCIAL LAW ISSUES ASSOCIATED

          WITH STORED-VALUE CARDS AND ELECTRONIC MONEY 7

        City of Portland v. Berry 10

  C. Credit Cards 14

    1. A Short History of the Development of the Credit Card 14

    2. How the Credit Card System Works or How Value is

       Transferred from the Cardholder to the Merchant 14

    3. The Cardholder's Obligation to Pay: Creation,

       Satisfaction, and Enforcement 17

       Problem 1-1 19

       Problem 1-2 20

    4. Errors and Wrongdoing 21

       Problem 1-3 21

       Stieger v. Chevy Chase Savings Bank 22

       Problem 1-4 35

    Review 35

**Chapter 2 Introduction to Negotiable Instruments as a Payment
          System** 37

  A. Overview 37

  B. How Do Negotiable Instruments Transfer Value 40

  C. Negotiability Concepts 42

    1. Assignment of Contract Rights and

       Delegation of Contract Duties 43

    2. Contract Rights as Property 46

    3. Negotiable Instruments and Holder in Due Course 47

  D. Requisites of a Negotiable Instrument Under U.C.C. Article 3 47

       Problem 2-1 50

       Problem 2-2 51

       Problem 2-3 52

       Problem 2-4 54

Chapter 3 Contract Liability on a Negotiable Instrument **55**

  A. Overview 55

  B. Incurring the Obligation to Pay 57

       Problem 3-1 59

  C. To Whom the Obligation is Owed: Person Entitled to Enforce 63

       Problem 3-2 67

       Problem 3-3 70

  D. When the Obligation is Due 71

       Problem 3-4 72

       Problem 3-5 75

  E. To Whom the Obligation is Owed:
      Persons not "Entitled to Enforce" 78

       Problem 3-6 78

  F. Enforcement of the Obligation: Defenses, Claims in
      Recoupment, and Holder in Due Course 79

      Maine Family Federal Credit Union v. Sun Life Assurance
       Company of Canada 82

       Problem 3-7 97

       Problem 3-8 101

       Problem 3-9 104

       Problem 3-10 106

  G. Discharge of the Obligation 109

    1. Contract Obligation on the Instrument 109

       Problem 3-11 109

       Problem 3-12 111

    2. Underlying Obligation 112

       Problem 3-13 114

       Problem 3-14 115

    3. Accord and Satisfaction 116

       Problem 3-15 117

      4. Conclusion 118
   H. Suretyship Defenses 118
      1. Defining a Secondary Obligor 118
      2. Secondary Obligor's Liability to Obligee 120
      3. Rights of the Secondary Obligor
          Against the Principal Obligor 122
      4. Rights of Secondary Obligors as
          Against Other Secondary Obligors 123
          Problem 3-16 123
          Problem 3-17 126
          Problem 3-18 127
     Review 129
          Problem 3-19 129

Chapter 4 Negotiable Instruments as Personal Property 133
   A. Claims to the Instrument 133
      1. How Claims to an Instrument Arise 133
      2. Asserting Claims to an Instrument 135
          Problem 4-1 139
          Problem 4-2 140
          Mutual Service Casualty Insurance Company v.
          Elizabeth State Bank 145
          Problem 4-3 164
   B. Warranty Liability 166
          Problem 4-4 168
          Problem 4-5 169
     Review 170
          Problem 4-6 170

Chapter 5 Collection Through the Banking System 173
   A. Overview 173
   B. Payor/Drawee Bank and Customer Relationship 180
      1. Properly Payable 180
          Problem 5-1 181
      2. Paying an Item that is Not Properly Payable 183
          Problem 5-2 184
      3. Wrongful Dishonor 186

	Problem 5-3	195
	Problem 5-4	197
4.	Stop Payment Orders	198
	Problem 5-5	199
5.	Customer Death or Incompetence	201
	Problem 5-6	201
C.	The Collection Process: Overview	202
D.	Collecting Bank: Forward Collection	203
	Problem 5-7	205
	Problem 5-8	206
E.	Payor Bank: Settlement and Final Payment	209
	Problem 5-9	213
F.	Item Return and Chargeback	216
	Problem 5-10	219
	Problem 5-11	220
G.	Funds Availability	222
	Problem 5-12	225
H.	Check 21 and Substitute Checks	227
	Problem 5-13	230
	Problem 5-14	231
	Review	231
	Problem 5-15	232

Chapter 6 Forgery and Fraud in the Use of Negotiable Instruments . . . **235**

A.	Introduction	235
B.	Unauthorized Signatures	237
1.	Unauthorized Maker's Signature	237
2.	Unauthorized Drawer's Signaure	239
	Problem 6-1	241
	Problem 6-2	245
3.	Unauthorized Indorsements	247
	Problem 6-3	250
	Problem 6-4	253
	King v. White	255
	Problem 6-5	264
	Problem 6-6	267
C.	Incomplete Instruments and Alterations	268

            Problem 6-7 269
   D. Lost or Stolen Instruments 270
            Problem 6-8 271
      Review 272
            Problem 6-9 272
            Problem 6-10 274
            Problem 6-11 275
            Problem 6-12 276

Chapter 7 Letters of Credit **277**
   A. Overview 277
   B. Mechanics of Value Transfer 277
   C. Incurring, Satisfying, and Enforcing the Obligation to Pay 281
        JOSEPH D. GUSTAVUS, LETTER OF CREDIT COMPLIANCE UNDER
          REVISED UCC ARTICLE 5 AND UCP 500 282
        Voest-Alpine Trading USA Corp. v. Bank of China 284
            Problem 7-1 287
   D. Allocation of the Risk of Errors and Wrongdoing 289
        Intraworld Industries, Inc. v. Girard Trust Bank 290
        Mid-America Tire, Inc. v. PTZ Trading Ltd. 301
            Problem 7-2 323
      Review 324
            Problem 7-3 324

Chapter 8 Electronic Funds Transfer **325**
   A. Overview 325
   B. EFTA and Regulation E 327
     1. Scope 327
            Problem 8-1 328
     2. Regulation of the Bank-Customer Relationship 330
            Problem 8-2 332
            Problem 8-3 333
     3. Unauthorized Transfers 334
            Problem 8-4 335
   C. U.C.C. Article 4A 336
     1. Scope 336
     2. Incurring the Obligation to Pay 337

a. Obligations of a Receiving Bank
Other Than a Beneficiary Bank 339
Problem 8-5 339
b. Beneficiary Bank's Obligations 341
Problem 8-6 342
c. Canceling or Amending a Payment Order 343
Problem 8-7 343
3. Satisfying the Obligation to Pay 345
a. Payment of Accepted Payment Orders 345
Problem 8-8 345
b. Satisfying the Underlying Obligation 346
Problem 8-9 346
4. Funds Transfers and Rights Related to the Deposit Account . . . 347
Problem 8-10 347
Problem 8-11 348
5. Funds Transfer Through Fedwire 349
Problem 8-12 349
6. Allocation of the Risks of Error and Wrongdoing 350
a. Unauthorized Transfers 350
Problem 8-13 351
b. Errors in Transmission 352
First National Bank & Trust Co. v. Brant
(In re Calumet Farm, Inc.) 353
Problem 8-14 360
Problem 8-15 361
Problem 8-16 361
Problem 8-17 362
Regatos v. North Fork Bank 363
Problem 8-18 369
Problem 8-19 369
Problem 8-20 370
Problem 8-21 370
D. Regulation of Evolving Payment Systems 371
Problem 8-22 372
Review 372
Problem 8-23 372

Table of Cases

The principal cases are in **bold** type. Cases cited or discussed in the text are roman type. References are to pages. Cases cited in principal cases and within other quoted materials are not included.

American Airlines Employees Federal Credit Union v. Martin 243

Amzee Corp. v. Comerica Bank-Midwest 244

Atherton v. FDIC 106

Auto-Owners Ins. Co. v. Bank One 248

Carrier v. Citibank (South Dakota), N.A. 35

Cassello v. Allegiant Bank 244

City of Portland v. Berry **10**

Clean World Engineering, Ltd. v. MidAmerica Bank 239

Cohen, In re 271

Condor v. Union Planters Bank, N.A. 244

Cumberland Bank v. G & S Implement Co. 109

DBI Architects, P.C. v. American Express Travel-Related Services Co. 35

D'Oench, Duhme & Co. v. FDIC 106

First National Bank in Harvey v. Colonial Bank 212

First National Bank & Trust Co. v. Brant (In re Calumet Farm, Inc.) . . **353**

Fitts v. AmSouth Bank 350

Flatiron Linen, Inc. v. First American State Bank 271

Ford Motor Credit Co. v. Milhollin 17

Frost National Bank v. Midwest Autohous, Inc. 212

Gentner and Company Inc. v. Well Fargo Bank 271

Halifax Corp. v. Wachovia Bank 244

Heche v. Chase Manhattan Bank 244

Hedged Investment Partners, L.P. v. Norwest Bank Minnesota, N.A. 351

IBP, Inc. v. Mercantile Bank of Topeka 180

Intraworld Industries, Inc. v. Girard Trust Bank 278, **290**

King v. White **255**

Maine Family Federal Credit Union v. Sun Life
      Assurance Company of Canada **82**, 97, 138

Maryott v. First National Bank of Eden 186

Messing v. Bank of America 74

Mercantile Bank of Arkansas v. Vowell 239

Mid-America Tire Inc. v. PTZ Trading Ltd. **301**
Mid-Continent Specialists, Inc. v. Capital Homes 244
Mid Wisconsin Bank v. Forsgard Trading, Inc.......................... 97
Mutual Service Casualty Insurance Company v.
      Elizabeth State Bank **145**, 244
National Title Insurance Corp. v. First Union National Bank 243
O'Melveny & Meyers v. FDIC 106
Oak Brook Bank v. Northern Trust Co. 211
QAD Investors, Inc. v. Kelly 59
Regatos v. North Fork Bank **363**, 368
Regions Bank v. The Provident Bank, Inc. 350
Rodrique v. Olin Employee's Credit Union 249
Rogers v. Jackson 48
Schlegel v. Bank of America, N.A. 350
Schrier Bros. v. Golub 248
Security First Network Bank v. C.A.P.S., Inc. 331
Spacemakers of America, Inc. v. SunTrust Bank 243
Spear Ins. Co. v. Bank of America, N.A. 183
Stieger v. Chevy Chase Savings Bank **22**
Stowell v. Cloquet Co-op Credit Union 243
Union Planters Bank, Nat. Ass'n v. Rogers 243
United Catholic Parish Schools of Beaver Dam
      Educational Association v. Card Services Center 244
Voest-Alpine Trading USA Corp. v. Bank of China **284**
White Sands Forest Products, Inc. v. First National Bank of Alamorgordo .. 244

Table of Statutes and Regulations

United States Constitution
Article I

sec.	Page
8	5, 6
10	5, 6

United States Code
11 U.S.C.

362	344

12 U.S.C.

1823(e)	106

Expedited Funds Availability Act
(12 U.S.C.)

generally	3, 39, 174, 216

Check Clearing for the
21st Century Act
(12 U.S.C.)

generally	3, 39, 174, 175, 227

Truth in Lending Act
(15 U.S.C.)

generally	3, 15, 17
1601	17
1602	18, 19
1603	18
1631	19
1632	19
1637	19
1640	19
1642	20
1643–45	21

1666–66i	20, 21

Electronic Funds Transfer Act
(15 U.S.C.)

generally	4, 326

18 U.S.C.

470–92	10

Code of Federal Regulations

Reg. E
(12 C.F.R.)

Part 205	326
205.2	327
205.3	327
205.4	331
205.5	331
205.6	334
205.7	331
205.8	331
205.9	331
205.10	333
205.11	331, 334
205.12	329, 331
205.16	331
205.17	331

Reg. J
(12 C.F.R.)

Part 210	4, 39, 175
Subpart B	349
210.3	205
210.4	205
210.5	205, 228, 268

210.6 . . . . 205, 228, 268
210.7 205
210.9 211
210.12 . . . . 211, 212, 220
210.13 220
210.14 220
210.25 337

Reg. Z
(12 C.F.R.)

Part 226 . . . . 3, 17, 331
226.1 . . . . 17, 18
226.2 . . . . 18, 19
226.3 . . . . 18, 21
226.5 19
226.5a 19
226.6 19
226.7 19
226.8 19
226.9 19
226.10 20
226.11 20
226.12 . . . . 20, 21, 22
226.13 21
226.36 19
Appendix G 19
Supplement I 17, 19

Reg. CC
(12 C.F.R.)

Part 229 . . . . 3, 39, 175, 202
229.2 . . . . 224, 227, 229, 245
229.10 . . . . 223, 224, 330,
                                333, 342
229.12 . . . . 223, 224
229.13 225
229.15 through 229.18 224

229.19 224
229.20 222
229.21 225
229.30 . . . . 211, 218
229.31 218
229.32 218
229.33 218
229.34 . . . . 205, 212, 218,
                                245, 269
229.36 . . . . 203, 204, 217, 218
229.38 218
229.51 227
229.52 . . . . 228, 229
229.53 229
229.54 229
229.55 230
229.56 229

16 C.F.R.

Part 433 105

31 C.F.R.

100.5–100.7 10

Uniform Commercial Code

Rev. Article 1

1-102 38
1-103 . . . . 122, 133, 238, 350
1-201 . . . . 5, 38, 48, 49, 50,
                        58, 63, 64, 69, 81,
                        205, 211, 243
1-202 . . . . 76, 81, 101, 137,
                        143, 211, 243
1-308 117

Article 2

2-312 through 2-315 166
2-403 . . . . 10, 43, 137
2-507 42

Former Article 3

3-511 76

Rev. Article 3

3-102 37
3-103 . . . . 38, 48, 50, 56, 58,
81, 101, 118, 180,
204, 271
3-104 . . . . 37, 38, 47, 49, 50,
51, 58, 71, 133, 271
3-105 . . . . 49, 50, 56, 58,
63, 64, 133
3-106 . . . . 48, 50
3-107 . . . . 48, 50, 71
3-108 . . . . 49, 50, 56, 71
3-109 . . . . 49, 50, 63, 64
3-110 . . . . 49, 50, 64, 65
3-111 . . . . 49, 50, 71
3-112 . . . . 48, 50, 71
3-113 . . . . 49, 50, 180
3-115 268
3-116 . . . . 119, 123
3-117 . . . . 48, 50
3-118 . . . . 166, 250
3-201 . . . . 63, 64
3-202 . . . . 134, 136, 245
3-203 . . . . 64, 69, 106, 134,
166, 167
3-204 . . . . 56, 58, 64, 66, 247
3-205 . . . . 64, 66, 119, 247
3-206 . . . . 64, 136, 142, 144,
165, 208, 257

3-301 . . . . 56, 63, 64, 69, 136,
237, 247, 270, 271
3-302 . . . . . 57, 81, 101, 106, 109,
137, 139, 142, 143,
238, 239, 268, 271
3-303 . . . . 81, 101, 166
3-304 . . . . 81, 101
3-305 . . . . 57, 80, 106, 109,
121, 134, 138, 143,
199, 238, 239, 271
3-306 . . . . 57, 80, 133, 134,
136, 137, 138, 142,
143, 249
3-307 . . . . 142, 143, 144
3-308 . . . . 57, 59, 79, 237
3-309 . . . . 70, 111, 134, 270
3-310 . . . . 41, 112, 113, 116,
118, 181, 183, 210,
238, 240
3-311 . . . . 116, 117
3-312 271
3-401 . . . . 57, 237, 242
3-402 . . . . 56, 57, 58, 237, 242
3-403 . . . . 57, 58, 59, 136,
237, 240, 242, 248,
266
3-404 . . . . 248, 249, 254,
264, 269
3-405 . . . . 248, 249, 266,
267, 269
3-406 . . . . 59, 238, 239, 242,
247, 248, 249, 269
3-407 268
3-408 . . . . 58, 186, 197
3-409 . . . . 58, 72, 75, 167,
183, 186, 271
3-410 75

3-411 271
3-412 .... 56, 58, 63, 71, 72,
78, 120, 122, 237,
247, 268, 271
3-413 .... 58, 63, 71, 72, 75,
78, 122, 186, 268,
271
3-414 .... 56, 58, 63, 71, 72,
75, 78, 119, 122, 134,
199, 239, 240, 242,
268, 271
3-415 ..... 56, 58, 63, 64, 71, 72,
75, 78, 119, 120, 122,
123, 218, 239, 248,
268
3-416 .... 166, 167, 202, 204,
218, 238, 239, 240,
243, 245, 249, 255,
266, 268
3-417 .... 167, 183, 236, 243,
245, 268
3-418 ..... 70, 184, 199, 212, 243
3-419 .... 119, 122
3-420 .... 135, 136, 142, 244,
245, 249
3-501 .... 56, 72, 167, 237
3-502 .... 56, 72, 75, 186,
210, 217, 237, 240
3-503 .... 75, 101, 239
3-504 .... 75, 76, 218, 239
3-601 .... 81, 109
3-602 .... 109, 139, 180, 181,
183, 184, 210
3-603 109
3-604 .... 109, 113
3-605 .... 118, 120, 121, 122

Rev. Article 4
4-101 174
4-102 .... 38, 173
4-103 .... 39, 175, 179, 183, 204
4-104 .... 38, 173, 179, 180,
204, 210, 228
4-105 175
4-107 .... 204, 210
4-108 .... 204, 210
4-109 .... 204, 210
4-110 .... 205, 227
4-111 250
4-201 203
4-202 .... 204, 217
4-203 204
4-204 204
4-205 .... 204, 208, 222
4-206 204
4-207 ... 167, 202, 204, 218, 238,
239, 240, 243, 245, 255,
266, 268
4-208 .... 168, 183, 184, 199,
212, 236, 240, 243,
245, 268
4-209 .... 205, 218
4-210 .... 143, 222
4-211 .... 143, 222
4-213 203
4-214 .... 202, 203, 217, 223, 239
4-215 .... 202, 203, 209, 210,
220, 222, 242
4-301 ... 202, 203, 209, 210, 211,
217, 221, 240
4-302 .... 210, 212, 240
4-303 .... 197, 198, 200
4-401 .... 180, 183, 202, 210,
221, 242, 269

4-402 186

4-403 198

4-404 . . . . 180, 196

4-405 201

4-406 . . . . 59, 180, 243, 246,
250, 269, 368

4-407 . . . . 184, 198, 199, 201,
212, 240, 243

Article 4A

generally 327, 336

4A-102 . . . . 328, 336, 350

4A-103 . . . . 328, 338, 339

4A-104 . . . . 327, 328, 338

4A-105 338

4A-106 339

4A-107 . . . . 336, 349

4A-108 . . . . 327, 336

4A-201 . . . . 350, 353

4A-202 . . . . 339, 350

4A-203 350

4A-204 350

4A-205 353

4A-206 349

4A-207 353

4A-208 353

4A-209 . . . . 339, 342

4A-210 . . . . 339, 342

4A-211 343

4A-212 . . . . 339, 342

4A-301 339

4A-302 339

4A-303 353

4A-304 353

4A-305 . . . . 339, 353

4A-401 345

4A-402 345

4A-403 345

4A-404 . . . . 342, 345

4A-405 . . . . 342, 345

4A-406 346

4A-501 . . . . 337, 338, 349

4A-502 347

4A-503 347

4A-504 347

4A-505 353

Former Article 5

5-114 290

Rev. Article 5

5-101 277

5-102 . . . . 279, 280, 281

5-103 . . . . 277, 281

5-104 281

5-105 281

5-106 282

5-107 . . . . 280, 288

5-108 . . . . 282, 287, 289

5-109 289

5-110 287

5-111 287

5-112 287

5-114 287

5-117 287

Rev. Article 9

9-310 135

9-312 135

9-313 135

9-406 through 9-409 44

PAYMENT SYSTEMS
PROBLEMS, MATERIALS, AND CASES
THIRD EDITION

CHAPTER 1
INTRODUCTION TO PAYMENT SYSTEMS

A. Overview

A payment system is a mechanism for moving value from one place to another and from one person to another in payment for goods, services, real estate, or other items that we desire to have or use. Easily moving value from one place to another is essential to the functioning of a commercial society which is based upon the exchange of value in return for property and services. A payment system seeks to transfer value from one person to another at the lowest possible cost with an acceptable level of risk of error and wrongdoing. In a law and economics sense, the payment system is one of the "transaction costs" in any payment of an obligation. So it makes sense that the focus of developing a mechanism for payment is on lowering the cost of processing, increasing the ease of use, and protecting against errors in processing and wrongdoing in using the mechanism.

The number and features of mechanisms used to transfer value are limited only by the imagination of those engaging in the transactions where such movement is desired. For example, to buy your morning cup of coffee, you could have used dollar bills and coins, otherwise known as currency. Alternatively, you could have used a card you had previously purchased from the coffee shop. When you present the card in payment for the purchase, the clerk deducts the amount of your purchase from the credit amount associated with the card. This is a type of stored value card. Perhaps you used a credit card. The coffee shop will have obtained the purchase price when it forwarded the charge to its bank and the charge will be reflected on your next monthly statement from your card issuer. Alternatively, you could have used a debit card where the amount of the purchase is deducted directly from your bank account. Perhaps, to your surprise, the clerk allowed you to write a check to the coffee shop for the amount of the purchase. This simple example demonstrates the myriad of different payment mechanisms you could use to pay an obligation, in this case, the obligation to pay for your morning coffee. The mesh of imagination and electronics will certainly lead to other mechanisms evolving to facilitate commerce over the coming years.

One of the challenges of this diversity of mechanisms is that each one has different legal rules to allocate the risks associated with the mechanism. Each mechanism also has different types of risks that are more or less likely to occur. In addition, the legal rules governing each mechanism have often been promulgated by different governmental authorities and at different points in history. This state of affairs contributes to a complex collection of rules that can challenge a student beginning the study of payment systems. This overview is designed to present several overarching themes in payment systems in order to provide a broader perspective as we learn the details of the different legal systems governing each payment mechanism.

As you can see from the simple example of the purchase of a cup of coffee, you may use currency, a stored value card, a credit card, a debit card, or a check to pay for that purchase. With the exception of currency, what all of these payment systems have in common is that a device is used that in and of itself is not valuable but rather represents an obligation to pay something that is considered valuable. In commercial societies, the ultimate token of value is currency, such as dollar bills and coins in the United States or the Euro in the European Union. Currency is valuable because of society's faith in those tokens of value and because of the government's obligation and promise to support those tokens as a medium of exchange. Tokens used as a medium of exchange facilitate commercial transactions in a very cost-effective manner. Using a stored value, credit or debit card, or a check, ultimately results in debits or credits in amounts that represent the value in currency–the standard token.

What are the primary concerns in a payment system? First, each system needs to be understood in a mechanical sense of how value actually gets transferred from one person to another. This mechanical transfer may be easy, as in the case of dollar bills and coins that are transferred by one person handing possession of the currency to another. It may be more complicated, such as in the case of check collection where the check has to travel to the drawee bank, the bank holding the account on which it was drawn, and the system's operation results in a credit to the payee and a debit to the drawer of the check. Second, because payment systems involve obligations to pay in standard tokens, each system has rules about how a person incurs the obligation to pay, when the person is obligated to pay, and how the obligation is satisfied. Third, the obligation to pay is owed to someone else, an obligee. Each payment system has rules regarding who can enforce the obligation, when the obligation can be enforced, what defenses to the enforcement obligation will be recognized, and the relationship among multiple obligors and obligees regarding the obligation to pay. Finally, each payment system has rules allocating the risks of errors and wrongdoing such as theft, fraud, and forgery. We will return repeatedly to these four concerns as we work our way through the various payment systems.

As noted above, the legal rules governing the various payment systems have been promulgated by different government bodies, at different times in history. For example, the law governing checks is primarily found in the Uniform Commercial Code (U.C.C.) Articles 3 and 4 (law enacted by state legislatures) and two federal statutes: the Expedited Funds Availability Act (codified at 12 U.S.C. §§ 4001–4010) and the Check Clearing for the 21st Century Act (codified at 12 U.S.C. §§ 5001–5018). Each of the federal acts has spawned regulations promulgated by the Federal Reserve Board and found for the most part in Regulation CC (12 C.F.R. pt. 229). The rules governing checks now found in U.C.C. Article 3 are built upon common law principles developed over several hundred years and previously codified in the Uniform Negotiable Instruments Act. The two federal acts were enacted in 1987 and 2004 respectively. In comparison, the law governing credit cards is primarily state common law contract principles because the relationships between the players in the system are governed by contractual agreements. Some issues that arise in the functioning of the credit card system are regulated by the federal Truth in Lending Act (codified at 15 U.S.C. §§ 1601–1667f) and the implementing regulation, Regulation Z (12 C.F.R. pt. 226). With the increasing use of electronics and the continuing development of payment mechanisms, it is likely there the legal rules will continue to evolve in the piecemeal fashion that has been characteristic of the history of payment systems regulation.[*]

So what course of action is open to students of payment systems in light of the diversity of legal rules? First, the student needs to acquire a thorough understanding of the legal rules that govern each payment system. Second, the student needs to be aware of the policies and practices that form the foundation of

---

[*] Some commentators have engaged in a fair amount of criticism of this diversity of rules and results. *See* Clayton P. Gillette, *Rules, Standards, and Precautions in Payment Systems*, 82 VA. L. REV. 181 (1996). The one modern attempt, however, to change that diversity and promulgate a more unified system of rules collapsed under a storm of protest. *See* Fred H. Miller, *A Report on the New Payments Code*, 39 BUS. LAW. 1215 (1984); Edward Rubin, *Efficiency, Equity and the Proposed Revision of Articles 3 and 4*, 42 ALA. L. REV. 551, 557–58 (1991). For some examples of recent articles on issues raised by evolving payment mechanisms see, Mark E Budnitz, *Consumer Payment Products and Systems: The Need for Uniformity and the Risk of Political Defeat*, 24 ANN. REV. BANKING & FIN. L. 247 (2005); Bradley Crawford, *New Methods of Payment and New Forms of Money*, 20 BANKING & FINANCE L. REV. 393 (2005); Ronald J. Mann, *Regulating Internet Payment Intermediaries*, 82 TEX. L. REV. 681 (2004); Ronald J. Mann, *Making Sense of Payments Policy in the Information Age*, 93 GEO. L.J. 633 (2005); James Stevens Rogers, *The New Old Law of Electronic Money*, 58 SMU L. REV. 1253 (2005).

each payment system's set of legal rules. Third, the student needs to be able to conceptualize the principles that cut across the payment system lines in order to have a better perspective on the application of payment rules in a particular context.

The major bodies of law involved in providing legal rules for the various types of payment systems involve the common law of contracts, property, agency, and suretyship as well as state and federal statutes and regulations. The state statutes are primarily found in the U.C.C.* The federal statutes and regulations are part of the federal government's regulation of financial institutions and monetary policy. Three of them have already been mentioned above. In addition, we will also study Regulation J, 12 C.F.R. pt. 210 (which governs collection of payments through the Federal Reserve Banks) and the Electronic Funds Transfer Act (codified at 15 U.S.C. §§ 1693–1693r) and its implementing regulation, Regulation E (12 C.F.R. pt. 205). As we proceed through the various types of payment systems, pay attention to the source of the rules and whether there is a conflict between the U.C.C. rules and the federal statutes and rules.

This book is organized to address the following payment mechanisms: currency (Chapter 1), credit cards (Chapter 1), drafts and notes (Chapters 2 through 6), letters of credit (Chapter 7), and funds transfers (Chapter 8). Chapter 8 also presents an opportunity to think about the four concerns of payment systems identified earlier in the context of evolving payment systems.

---

* The Uniform Commercial Code is a uniform act developed by the National Conference of Commissioners on Uniform State Laws and the American Law Institute. The Uniform Commercial Code is divided into several different substantive articles: Article 1 General Provisions [Revised]; Article 2 Sales; Article 2A Leases; Article 3 Negotiable Instruments [Revised]; Article 4 Bank Deposits and Collections; Article 4A Funds Transfer; Article 5 Letters of Credit [Revised]; Article 6 Repealer of Article 6—Bulk Transfers and [Revised] Article 6—Bulk Sales; Article 7 Documents of Title [Revised]; Article 8 Investment Securities [Revised]; and Article 9 Secured Transactions [Revised]. The Uniform Commercial Code is designed to be enacted at the state, not federal, level. Thus each state has to decide whether to enact an article of the U.C.C. and whether to enact the article in its uniform form or to make non-uniform amendments. Although the U.C.C. is studied in its uniform version in law school, you should always look at the version as enacted within the state whose law governs the transaction in order to determine whether the state has made non-uniform amendments to the provision at issue. All references to the U.C.C. in this book are to the uniform 2006 version of the U.C.C.

B. Currency

Currency (government sanctioned bills and coins) commonly called "cash" or "money" is the most basic of payment mechanisms. **Read the definition of "money" in U.C.C. § 1-201(b)(24).** As briefly mentioned above, money is a token used to facilitate several different functions, only one of which, a medium of exchange, is incorporated into the U.C.C. definition. As a medium of exchange, money is used to facilitate exchanges of commodities, items of value, or services, as in the coffee shop example given earlier.

In addition to a medium of exchange, money serves as a standard of value, a store of value, and a standard for deferred payments. A "standard of value" means that we use money tokens to measure the value of other things. A "store of value" means that we use money in order to hoard value. A "standard for deferred payments" means that money is used as a measurement when borrowing value. What determines the value of money is ultimately a matter of public confidence in the token as a means of performing these three functions.[*]

How does it come to be that any particular token is recognized as money and suitable for fulfilling these purposes? The history of money in the United States is interesting for its approach to developing a medium of exchange to facilitate commerce. In its early history, the United States relied on gold and silver coinage of other countries as well as coining its own money out of those metals. Standards were set prescribing the quantity of gold or silver in each coin. Later, the government issued coins that contained less gold or silver but redeemable for a set amount of gold or silver. Banks also issued notes that were redeemable in gold or silver. These notes circulated as mediums of exchange and were valued based upon the level of confidence in the bank that issued the notes. Today, United States currency is not redeemable for a set amount of gold or silver.[**]

The federal government's power to deal with monetary concerns is prescribed in the U.S. Constitution, Article I, sec. 8 and sec. 10. The federal government was given the power to develop the currency for the nation and the states were prohibited from coining money.

---

[*] *See* THOMAS MAYER, JAMES S. DUESENBERRY, AND ROBERT Z. ALIBER, MONEY, BANKING AND THE ECONOMY 6–10 (5th ed. 1993); HIRAM JOME, PRINCIPLES OF MONEY AND BANKING 4 (1957); JAMES WILLARD HURST, A LEGAL HISTORY OF MONEY IN THE UNITED STATES, 1774-1970, at 34–35 (1973).

[**] *See generally* ARTHUR NUSSBAUM, A HISTORY OF THE DOLLAR (1957).

UNITED STATES CONSTITUTION, ARTICLE I

Section 8. The Congress shall have Power to lay and collect Taxes, Duties, Imposts and Excises, to pay the Debts and provide for the common Defence and general Welfare of the United States; but all Duties, Imposts and Excises shall be uniform throughout the United States;

To borrow money on the credit of the United States;

To regulate Commerce with foreign Nations, and among the several States, and with the Indian Tribes;

To establish an uniform Rule of Naturalization, and uniform Laws on the subject of Bankruptcies throughout the United States;

To coin Money, regulate the Value thereof, and of foreign Coin, and fix the Standard of Weights and Measures;

To provide for the Punishment of counterfeiting the Securities and current Coin of the United States;

* * * * *

To make all Laws which shall be necessary and proper for carrying into Execution the foregoing Powers, and all other Powers vested by this Constitution in the Government of the United States, or in any Department or Officer thereof.

* * * * *

Section 10. No State shall enter into any Treaty, Alliance, or Confederation; grant Letters of Marque and Reprisal; coin Money; emit Bills of Credit; make any Thing but gold and silver Coin a Tender in Payment of Debts; pass any Bill of Attainder, ex post facto Law, or Law impairing the Obligation of Contracts, or grant any Title of Nobility.

No State shall, without the Consent of the Congress, lay any Imposts or Duties on Imports or Exports, except what may be absolutely necessary for executing its inspection Laws: and the net Produce of all Duties and Imposts, laid by any State on Imports or Exports, shall be for the Use of the Treasury of the United States; and all such Laws shall be subject to the Revision and Controul of the Congress.

No State shall, without the Consent of Congress, lay any Duty of Tonnage, keep Troops, or Ships of War in time of Peace, enter into any Agreement or Compact with another State, or with a foreign Power or engage in War, unless actually invaded, or in such imminent Danger as will not admit of delay.

A COMMERCIAL LAWYER'S TAKE ON THE ELECTRONIC PURSE: AN ANALYSIS OF COMMERCIAL LAW ISSUES ASSOCIATED WITH STORED-VALUE CARDS AND ELECTRONIC MONEY, 52 BUS. LAW. 653, 665–70 (1997)[*]

In the seventy years following the American revolution, the federal government had only a limited role in the issuance of paper currency. Instead, notes issued by banks chartered under the laws of the states served as a form of private "money" or currency. These notes represented promises to pay, or monetary obligations, of the banks that issued them. Ordinarily, state bank notes were not payable at par and the discount rate for such notes usually varied with their perceived creditworthiness.

Because information during this period was communicated inefficiently and imperfectly, a person deciding whether to take a state bank note might find himself in a difficult position. To assist with the decision-making, this person might consult one of the "bank note reporters" that circulated and contained valuation amounts for the notes of various issuers. There also existed an active brokerage market, with brokers buying notes at a steep discount and then attempting to sell them at a more modest rate. Even in this early period of our national history, arbitrage was alive and well.

During this period, bank failures were common. When a bank failed that had issued circulating notes, the holders of such notes often sustained considerable losses. Counterfeit notes were also a problem, which was exacerbated by the inefficient means of communicating financial information during the period; malefactors were able to cheat people with counterfeits because the victims would be duped into taking the bad paper without having a means to communicate with the purported issuer to determine whether it was authentic. The absence of uniformity in state bank notes also added to the problem; the more different bank notes crossed an individual's hand, the less likely that individual would know that a particular bank note conformed to type.

One serious attempt to respond to these problems was the so-called "free banking movement." Supporters of this movement demanded that free banks support their note issuances with state or federal securities. A well-run issuer whose notes were backed by collateral might find that its notes traded at or near par with

---

[*]   Footnotes omitted. Report of the Task Force on Stored-Value Cards, American Bar Association, Business Law Section, Stephanie Heller and Thomas C. Baxter, Jr., Reporters. © 1997 by the American Bar Association, reprinted by permission.

gold. On the other hand, if a bank were poorly run, or if word leaked out that its notes were not sufficiently supported by collateral, this could lead to a run on the bank and a reluctance on the part of commercial counterparties to take the paper of an impugned issuer. By many accounts, the free-banking movement was a successful attempt at stabilizing the value of bank notes.

The federal government did not become involved in money matters until 1861. In an effort to finance the Civil War, the federal government began to issue its own currency. These federal notes were called "greenbacks" because of their distinctive color. The greenbacks were issued in denominations of $5, $10, and $20, and were redeemable by the government in coin on demand at designated subtreasuries.

In 1862, the greenbacks took a new form: a currency that was "legal tender" for all debts, with the notable exception of import duties and interest on the public debt. These notes were the first federal experience with legal tender currency. Initially, $150 million of these notes were issued.

The greenbacks did not displace privately issued notes in the nation's money supply. Instead, the government paper and the private paper coexisted from the time of the Civil War to 1913, when the Federal Reserve Act (FRA) was enacted. It took approximately twenty more years before national bank notes were no longer in circulation.

The FRA was, in part, a response to the Panic of 1907. Immediately after that financial crisis but before enactment of the FRA, the Aldrich-Vreeland Act came into force. This legislation permitted associations of national banks to issue a temporary currency (Aldrich-Vreeland notes) that would expand the money supply during financial crises, with the approval of the Treasury Department. Notes of this kind, however, did not constitute legal tender. When the FRA displaced the Aldrich-Vreeland Act, its supporters considered the FRA to be a "currency bill." The federal reserve note occupied a central part of the statutory scheme, revealing the importance of the currency issue at this time.

The new federal reserve currency caught on quickly and, by 1920, comprised about half of the currency in circulation. Like the Aldrich-Vreeland note, it was an elastic asset-backed currency, not legal tender. Unlike the Aldrich-Vreeland note, the federal reserve note was a direct obligation of the U.S. government as well as an obligation of the issuing federal reserve bank. In 1933, the federal reserve note was made legal tender. Today, the federal reserve note remains the only circulating form of legal tender. It is regarded both in the United States and worldwide as the money of the United States. . . .

"Legal tender" is a concept, not a thing. When legislation of a sovereign government provides that only certain types of paper or objects, if tendered to an obligor, will discharge indebtedness, that concept is known as legal tender. The weakest form of legal tender laws merely oblige the government to accept a particular media of exchange in satisfaction of taxes. Such laws enhance the acceptability of the paper, commonly known as money, because almost all persons will eventually be indebted to the tax collector and will, therefore, need money to discharge such indebtedness. Stronger forms of legal tender laws provide that certain media of exchange, if presented to a private party, will be deemed to satisfy debts denominated in such currency. These laws may apply unless the party specifically objects or even if the party objects. The strongest legal tender laws contain criminal sanctions against a transactor who refuses to accept the tender.

Congress first authorized notes issued by the United States as legal tender for the payment of all debts, both private and public, as an emergency measure to raise funds during the Civil War (Legal Tender Act). In 1869, the U.S. Supreme Court determined that the Legal Tender Act could not be applied retroactively to contracts executed before its enactment but left undecided whether the statute was constitutional if applied prospectively. In a series of later federal court cases based upon the Legal Tender Act (Legal Tender Cases), decided between 1870 and 1884, the U.S. Supreme Court held that Congress had the power, under the necessary and proper clause of the Constitution, to establish as legal tender a medium other than gold or silver coin. The Court stated that legal tender could be used to satisfy both public and private debts and to discharge a contract by tendering whatever constitutes legal tender *at the time of payment*. Although the Legal Tender Cases focused ostensibly on whether Congress had the authority to establish paper as a national currency and to make that currency lawful for all purposes, the collective opinions can be interpreted more broadly. One can read these cases as authorizing Congress to designate *any* money as legal tender which directly or indirectly enables Congress to exercise its express power to borrow on the credit of the United States and to coin money and regulate the value thereof.

Currently, for dollar-denominated indebtedness governed by U.S. law, "United States coins and currency (including federal reserve notes and circulating notes of federal reserve banks and national banks) are legal tender for all debts, public charges, taxes, and dues. Foreign gold or silver coins are not legal tender for debts." Tender of U.S. coin or currency in an amount equivalent to the dollar-denominated indebtedness will, therefore, work a discharge.

Find the notation on a dollar bill stating that it is legal tender. Is it important that the bill have that notation?

What risk does one have in taking a Federal Reserve Note as payment for an obligation? How do you know that the bills and coins that you are taking are valid? What happens if the bill or coin is a counterfeit? What recourse do you have? *See* 18 U.S.C. §§ 470–492. Who bears the risk of loss if the currency is destroyed? *See* 31 C.F.R. §§ 100.5–100.7. Who bears the risk if the coins or currency are lost or stolen? If you are the victim of the theft, can you retrieve the currency from the thief? From the person to whom the thief transferred the currency? Consider the following case. Compare U.C.C. § 2-403.

CITY OF PORTLAND V. BERRY
739 P.2d 1041 (Or. Ct. App. 1987)

Rossman, Judge

Plaintiff brings this interpleader action to determine which of the defendants is entitled to $18,000 in $1,000 and $500 bills that its Bureau of Police acquired for use as evidence in the criminal prosecution of the thief who stole them. Defendants Berry and Kelly (appellants) seek return of the bills.[1] The trial court awarded them to defendant United States National Bank of Oregon (Bank). Berry and Kelly appeal, and we affirm.

This dispute arose after appellants' live-in attendant, Wetzel, stole nine $1,000 bills and 18 $500 bills from them.[2] Over the course of three months, Wetzel took the bills to Bank, where she converted them into smaller denominations of cash, travelers' checks, a cashier's check, savings bonds and savings accounts. During the course of its investigation and preparation for prosecution of Wetzel for theft,

---

[1] Throughout the trial and in their briefs, Berry and Kelley refer to their theory as replevin. That confuses the issue. The City's interpleader action sought a determination of who was entitled to possession of the bills. Although replevin principles are useful as a basis for analysis, we do not rely on replevin to reach the result in this case.

[2] The $1,000 and $500 bills recovered from the bank were only a part of the valuables that were stolen. In January, 1986, Berry and Kelly obtained a default judgment against Wetzel for $131,085.50 on a complaint that alleged that Wetzel took silver certificates, 50, 20, ten and two dollar bills, coins and ingots valued at $54,834 and that she failed to repay a $4,100 loan. Berry and Kelly sought to recover the value of the stolen items, repayment of the loan and $100,000 in punitive damages.

the Bureau of Police subpoenaed and obtained the bills.[3] After Wetzel was convicted of theft,[4] plaintiff initiated this action to determine whether they should be returned to the appellants as victims of the theft or to Bank.

Appellants' assignments of error raise an issue of first impression in this state. First, they argue that the trial court should have applied the general rules of replevin to reach its disposition. Bank successfully argued below that the applicable rule is the "money rule,"[5] which provides that a third party who takes stolen money in good faith and for valuable consideration obtains good title and prevails over the victim of the theft. Appellants contend that the "money rule" should not apply here, because the bills are not "money" in the sense that they are not normal cash and that, even if they are "money," the policy reason for the rule does not apply when the bills in question are of $500 and $1,000 denominations.

We reject appellants' contention that the bills are not "money." Although the United States Treasury has not printed $500 and $1,000 bills since 1945 and has been systematically taking them out of circulation and destroying them since 1969, their rarity does not affect the fact that the bills continue in circulation and are legal tender.

As a general rule, an action for replevin will lie for recovery of personal property to which the plaintiff has the right to immediate possession. Money is personal property. If the action for recovery of money fails, it is usually because the specific money is not sufficiently identifiable as the plaintiff's property. When, however,

> "specific bills and coins are identifiable because of serial numbers or special markings, or because they are located uncommingled at a specific exclusive place or contained within a [sic] identifiable container, the bills and coins, so identifiable, can be replevied." *Williams Management*

---

[3] When the police first requested the bills, Bank retained four $1,000 bills and 14 $500 bills in its vault. The other bills had been purchased by bank employees and customers. Bank repurchased the bills and turned them over to the police pursuant to the subpoena.

[4] She was convicted in a stipulated facts trial to the court and was sentenced to five years in prison with a 14-month minimum and ordered to pay full restitution of $48,934.00. In addition, a default judgment was entered against her for $31,085.50 on a breach of contract and conversion action brought by Berry and Kelley.

[5] Each party asserts that the rule which it espouses is the general rule to which the opposing party's "rule" is the exception. We do not think that either rule is an exception but simply that the rules apply to different situations.

Enterprises v. Buonauro, 489 So 2d 160, 164 (Fla App 1986). (Citations omitted).

Even assuming that the particular bills are sufficiently identifiable, appellants' argument nevertheless fails. Although generally the owner of stolen property can recover it from anyone who acquires it, because a thief cannot pass title to stolen property, title to currency passes with delivery to a good faith purchaser for value. *Transamerica Insurance Company v. Long*, 318 F.Supp. 156, 160 (W.D.Pa.1970). Thus, as against the thief, appellants can assert their right of ownership. However, a third party who takes stolen money "in good faith and for good consideration will prevail over the unfortunate victim of the thief." *Kelley Kar Company v. Maryland Casualty Company*, 142 Cal.App.2d 263, 298 P.2d 590, 592 (1956); (citations omitted). A similar rule applies when bearer paper is lost or stolen. The victim of the loss or theft cannot recover from a good faith purchaser for value who takes the instrument in the ordinary course of business, because the purchaser is a holder in due course. *See* ORS 71.2010(20); 73.3020(1); 73.3050; 73.3060; White and Summers, UNIFORM COMMERCIAL CODE § 14-3 (1980). Although at least one state requires that the purchase be made in the ordinary course of business before a person who takes money in good faith and for value can obtain good title, *Sinclair Houston Federal Credit Union v. Hendricks*, 268 S.W.2d 290, 295 (Tex.Civ.App.1954), because of the necessity that currency be readily acceptable as payment for debts, we conclude that the good faith and valuable consideration requirements provide ample protection from pretextual transfers of stolen money from a thief to a third party. Accordingly, if Bank took the money in good faith and for good consideration, appellants have no ownership rights that can be asserted.

Appellants argue that the policy behind the rule, that there is a "necessity that money pass freely in commercial transactions," *Sinclair Houston Federal Credit Union v. Hendricks, supra*, 268 S.W.2d at 295, would not be furthered by its application when, as here, bills of these denominations are unusual and relatively rare. We do not agree. So long as the United States Treasury has not removed the bills from circulation and considers them to be legal tender, the policy underlying the rule remains viable. We do not accept appellants' argument that, because these specific bills were not freely flowing in commerce, the policy justification for the rule ceased to exist. Legal tender must continue to be freely acceptable without inquiry as to its source.

Appellants also challenge the trial court's factual determination that the bills "were received by the bank in good faith [and] for good consideration."[6] In *Community Bank v. Ell*, 278 Or. 417, 564 P.2d 685 (1977), the Supreme Court considered the Uniform Commercial Code good faith requirement of ORS 71.2010(19): "honesty in fact in the conduct or transaction concerned." The court's interpretation, which we adopt in this case, is that "[t]he appropriate standard is a subjective one, looking to the intent or state of mind of the party concerned." 278 Or. at 428, 564 P.2d 685. (Footnote omitted.) The trial court heard evidence that the large denomination of the bills aroused the interest of Bank employees, that they asked Wetzel where she got them, to which she replied that the money was an inheritance, and that the employees considered the answer believable. The employees testified that they did not suspect that the money was stolen and we find nothing in the record that would lead us to conclude that Bank was not acting in good faith.

Appellants argue that Bank did not give consideration for the bills, because it paid only the face value, not the price for which they could have been purchased on the open market. Face value of legal tender is valuable consideration.

Affirmed.

Consider the following questions. What risks do you bear in using currency? Should the rules allocating those risks in the use of currency be altered? If so, how so? Are there other risks to using currency that we have not considered? Consider why the value of a currency as measured against other types of currency may fluctuate.   See the following website which provides exchange rates, http://www.x-rates.com/. As a user of currency, how do you mitigate those risks? Are you likely to alter your behavior concerning the use of currency now that you know the risks and how the risks are allocated?

As we study the use of other payment mechanisms and the legal rules that apply to each one, consider the extent to which those rules should mimic the rules we have learned about currency.

---

[6] The trial court also determined that Bank had received the bills in the ordinary course of business. Because we do not require such a finding, we will not review the evidence supporting it.

C. Credit Cards

1. A Short History of the Development of the Credit Card

Using a credit card to pay obligations incurred in the purchase of goods and services is a commonplace phenomenon. Those of us who have grown up with the credit card system in place have difficulty imagining a time when you could not pull a piece of plastic from your wallet to pay for your purchases. It has not always been so.

Credit cards evolved from the practice of retailers issuing charge plates to customers in order to encourage the customers to shop at the retailer's store. This practice spread to the oil companies and airlines. The formation of the Diners Club® in the late 1940s allowed food, lodging ,and other travel and entertainment retailers to accept the Diners Club® card in payment for those services. Cardholder fees and a merchant discount (the merchant accepting less from Diners Club® than the cardholder was charged) funded Diners Club® services.

In the 1960s, Bank of America launched its card (precursor to Visa®) and the Interbank Card Association launched its card (precursor to MasterCard®). Throughout the years, there has been competition among credit card companies for customers. In the early years, each major issuer mailed unsolicited credit cards to potential customers. In more recent times, credit card companies have used fees, finance charges and expanding customer bases as the key to profitability. Universal credit cards (such as Visa® or MasterCard®) compete with travel and entertainment charge cards such as American Express®, and retailer's cards, such as J.C. Penney®. Much of the regulation of credit cards that we are about to consider can be explained by the historical development of the credit card market.[*]

2. How the Credit Card System Works or How Value is Transferred from the Cardholder to the Merchant

The credit card system is a system of payment governed in large part by contractual agreements between the parties to the system. A cardholder who makes a charge on a credit card is incurring an obligation to the issuer of the credit card to pay the issuer when the issuer bills the cardholder. The relationship between the

___

[*] For more on the history of credit cards, see LEWIS MANDELL, THE CREDIT CARD INDUSTRY: A HISTORY (1990).

issuer and the cardholder is governed by the contract between the parties and has been regulated in part by provisions of federal law such as the Consumer Credit Protection Act, Title I (incorporating the Truth in Lending Act and codified at 15 U.S.C. §§ 1601–1667f) and banking statutes, and by various state statutes such as the Uniform Consumer Credit Code and usury laws. The card issuing entity has a contractual relationship with a clearinghouse such as Visa® or MasterCard®. The clearinghouse has a contractual relationship with the merchant's bank and the merchant has a contractual relationship with its bank. The relationships can be diagramed as follows:

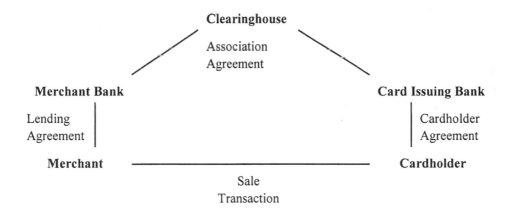

A typical credit card transaction starts with the cardholder using the credit card to pay for goods or services purchased from a merchant. Information on the card, about the merchant, and the transaction is communicated electronically through the network maintained by a clearinghouse (such as Visa® or MasterCard®) for approval. Once the transaction is approved and finalized, the merchant communicates the transaction information to its bank–the merchant bank. The merchant's bank has generally agreed to make funds available to the merchant based on the transaction information. The merchant's bank generally does so at a discounted amount so that the merchant receives less than the full amount that has been charged. For example, assume the cardholder made a $100 purchase at the merchant's business and the merchant bank charges a 2% fee. The merchant would receive a credit for $98 to its bank account at the merchant bank.

The merchant's bank then sends the transaction information to the clearinghouse association, which directs the transaction information to the entity that issued the credit card to the cardholder. There is a fee charged for this information exchange–an interchange fee. The merchant bank pays this interchange fee to the issuing bank. Assume that the interchange fee in our hypothetical transaction is 1.5%. The issuing entity would pay the merchant bank $98.50 instead of $100. The issuing entity then issues a bill in the form of a periodic statement to the cardholder. On the bill, the transaction with the merchant is reflected as a $100 charge. The cardholder then pays the issuing entity $100.

Out of that $100 in our hypothetical transaction, the merchant bank will net $.50, the issuing entity will net $1.50, and the merchant will net $98. Both the merchant bank and the issuing bank belong to the association and will pay fees to the association as required in the agreements with the association. The amount of the interchange fee is set by the association. The merchant discount will capture at least as much as the interchange fee and will vary from merchant bank to merchant bank. There have been unsuccessful antitrust challenges to the interchange fee.[*] While all of the transaction information used to be communicated using paper "charge slips," in the electronic age, much of the transaction information is transmitted electronically even if the merchant collects a paper charge slip.

In the event a cardholder disputes a charge on her credit card, the transaction is "charged back" through the system to the merchant. Thus the merchant has an incentive to employ security procedures, including obtaining a signed charge slip or its equivalent, to verify that the cardholder in fact made the charge.

Based upon a study of payment methods used in 2003, approximately 19 billion of 81 billion noncash payment transactions in the United States were made using credit cards. However, credit card transactions represented only 1.7 trillion dollars out of 66 trillion dollars transferred in noncash payment transactions. The average dollar value of a credit card transaction was 89 dollars.[**] Thus, credit card transactions are a high volume (23.4% of total number of transactions) of a relatively small dollar value (2.6% of total value of transactions) method of

---

[*] For a more in-depth treatment of these multi-party relationships, see BARKLEY CLARK AND BARBARA CLARK, THE LAW OF BANK DEPOSITS, COLLECTIONS AND CREDIT CARDS, Chap. 15 (Revised ed.1995 & Supp. 2006). For an explanation of the antitrust concerns, see Avril McKean Dieser, *Antitrust Implications of the Credit Card Interchange Fee and an International Survey*, 17 LOY. CONSUMER L. REV. 451 (2005); Adam J. Levitin, *The Antitrust Super Bowl: America's Payment Systems, No-surcharge Rules, and the Hidden Costs of Credit*, 3 BERKELEY BUS. L.J. 265 (2005).

[**] Geoffrey R. Gerdes et al., *Trends in the Use of Payment Instruments in the United States*, FEDERAL RESERVE BULLETIN 180, 181, 184 (Spring 2005).

transferring value.

As you think about this system, ask yourself what risks each participant in the system is taking when a credit card is used. If you were representing a party in the system, what would you recommend the party do to lessen those risks? How does the fact that on average the transactions are for low dollar values factor into what you might be willing to do to lessen the risks?

3. The Cardholder's Obligation to Pay: Creation, Satisfaction, and Enforcement

As can be seen from the above description, the legal rules that govern credit cards are based in large part on contract law. Unlike some payment mechanisms that we will study in later chapters, no comprehensive statutory or regulatory scheme exists which governs the various parties' rights and liabilities concerning the transfer of value from one entity to another.

Federal regulation of credit cards is contained in the Truth in Lending Act (TILA) which is Title I of the Consumer Credit Protection Act (CCPA) (codified at 15 U.S.C. §§ 1601–1667f). The Federal Reserve Board of Governors has issued Regulation Z, 12 C.F.R. part 226, to implement TILA. You should consult both the relevant section of TILA as well as Regulation Z. In addition, the Division of Consumer and Community Affairs of the Federal Reserve Board issues staff commentaries on Regulation Z. These commentaries are collected in Supplement I to Regulation Z. The Supreme Court has indicated a high degree of deference to the staff commentaries to Regulation Z. *Ford Motor Credit Co. v. Milhollin*, 444 U.S. 555, 565–66 (1980) ("deference is especially appropriate in the process of interpreting the Truth in Lending Act and Regulation Z. Unless demonstrably irrational, Federal Reserve Board staff opinions construing the Act or Regulation should be dispositive").

TILA and Regulation Z are based on the philosophy that disclosure of terms and conditions of credit will facilitate a consumer's ability to compare terms and be protected against unfair credit terms and practices. TILA § 102 (15 U.S.C. § 1601); Reg. Z, 12 C.F.R. § 226.1(b). Look at the titles of the sections of Regulation Z, 12 C.F.R. §§ 226.5 through 226.30. Most of the titles indicate regulation of the disclosure of credit cost information or the debtor's rights in the use of the credit.

The Federal Reserve Board periodically conducts studies regarding the effectiveness of TILA provisions to meeting its purpose. The latest study reports that consumers look frequently at the information on periodic statements regarding the cost of the credit. Those who maintain revolving balances tend to look at the statements more frequently than those who pay the balance in full.* In addition, the Federal Reserve Board has published two advance notices of proposed rulemaking that asks for public comment on the functioning and effectiveness of the current regulation in order to determine if any changes need to be made. *See* Federal Reserve Board, Truth in Lending, 69 Fed. Reg. 70925 (Dec. 8, 2004) and Federal Reserve Board, Truth in Lending, 70 Fed. Reg. 60235 (Oct. 17, 2005). There may be changes to Regulation Z in the near future after that review is completed.**

Although TILA and Regulation Z apply to many types of credit, the focus of these materials will be those rules that apply to extensions of credit using credit cards. **Read the definitions of "credit card," "cardholder," "credit," "creditor," and "person" in TILA § 103 (15 U.S.C. § 1602) and Reg. Z, 12 C.F.R. § 226.2.** Keep those definitions in mind as we determine the application of TILA and Regulation Z to credit card transactions.

Notice that in reading the definition of "creditor," it refers to "consumer credit." **Read the definition of "consumer" in TILA § 103 (15 U.S.C. § 1602) and Reg. Z, 12 C.F.R. § 226.2 and of "consumer credit" in Reg. Z, 12 C.F.R. § 226.2. Now read TILA § 104 (15 U.S.C. § 1603) and Reg. Z, 12 C.F.R. § 226.1(c), 226.3.** What credit card transactions are governed by TILA and Regulation Z? Do TILA and Regulation Z apply to credit cards issued to an individual for any purpose or to a business entity for any purpose? Do all of TILA and Regulation Z apply to credit cards used for non-consumer purposes?

---

* Thomas A. Durkin, *Credit Card Disclosures, Solicitations, and Privacy Notices: Survey Results of Consumer Knowledge and Behavior*, FEDERAL RESERVE BULLETIN A109, A115 (Aug. 7, 2006).

** Several commentators have written about perceived abuses card issuer and cardholder contractual relationship. *See, e.g.*, Oren Bar-Gill, *Seduction by Plastic*, 98 NW. U. L. REV. 1373 (2004); Carolyn Carter, et al., *The Credit Card Market and Regulation: In Need of Repair*, 10 N.C. BANKING INSTITUTE 23 (2006); Samuel Issacharoff and Erin F. Delaney, *Credit Card Accountability*, 73 U. CHI. L. REV. 157 (2006); Ronald J. Mann, *"Contracting" For Credit*, 104 MICH. L. REV. 899 (2006).

Problem 1-1

To solidify your understanding of the scope of the application of TILA and Regulation Z to credit cards, write in your own words a paragraph that describes that application. Make sure that your written paragraph takes into account the scope provisions and the definitions you have studied so far.

TILA and Regulation Z divide credit transactions into two types, closed end credit and open end credit. **Read the definitions of "open end credit" and "closed end credit" in Reg. Z, 12 C.F.R. § 226.2, and "open end credit plan" in TILA § 103 (15 U.S.C. § 1602).** Is the use of a credit card or charge card more likely to be an open end or a closed end credit plan? (The staff commentary indicates that a charge card is a card in which balances cannot be carried over from one billing cycle to another. Reg. Z, Supp. I, comment to 12 C.F.R. § 226.2(2)(a)(15) definition of "credit card.") The focus of TILA is on disclosure of credit terms and conditions. Based upon this initial classification as either open or closed end credit, and the definitions you have studied so far, identify the disclosure provisions in TILA and Regulation Z that are likely to apply to credit cards.

As you can see by looking at the types of disclosures required, the card issuer must make different types of disclosures to the cardholder at various points in time. If you put the disclosures on a timetable, you would look at disclosures that must be made in the solicitation/application process, after card issuance and before first usage, periodically during the time of usage, and annually. **Read TILA §§ 121, 122, and 127 (15 U.S.C. §§ 1631, 1632, and 1637) and Reg. Z, 12 C.F.R. §§ 226.5, 226.5a, 226.6, 226.7, 226.8, 226.9 and 226.36.** As you can see from reading through these disclosure requirements, the focus is not only on the timing of the disclosures, but also on the types of information related to the cost and terms of credit, and the form in which the information is provided. Lawyers who represent card issuers will periodically review the disclosure information and process for disclosure that the card issuer has instituted in order to make sure there is compliance with TILA and Regulation Z. Appendix G to Regulation Z contains model forms of disclosure.

Why is it important to a card issuer that it comply with the requirements of TILA and Regulation Z? **Read TILA § 130 (15 U.S.C. § 1640).**

Problem 1-2

a) Advise an issuer what information it must put in an ad in a magazine soliciting applications for a credit card. Can it provide any of the required information by referring the potential applicant to a website?

b) If the issuer has not followed the requirements of Regulation Z, what is its potential liability?

c) The card issuer you work for has asked you if it can send credit cards to persons who have sufficient credit worthiness to get a card without a further credit approval process. What problems do you see with that marketing plan? TILA § 132 (15 U.S.C. § 1642) and Reg. Z, 12 C.F.R. § 226.12(a).

Once you have obtained a credit card, use of that card and its terms and conditions govern your obligation to pay. If you fail to pay, the issuer has an action against you for breach of contract. TILA and Regulation Z regulate the card issuer's crediting of payments, refunds of a credit balance, and refunds based on return of property or cancellation of an obligation. **See TILA §§ 163 through 169 (15 U.S.C. §§ 1666b–1666h) and Reg. Z, 12 C.F.R. §§ 226.10, 226.11, 226.12(d) through (f).**

4. Errors and Wrongdoing

A cardholder usually has several concerns regarding credit card usage. First, are the transactions the card holder has engaged in accurately reflected and billed to the cardholder? Second, what are the cardholder's rights and obligations if the card is used to engage in a transaction that the cardholder has not authorized? Third, by usage of the card in the transactions, does the cardholder have the ability to assert rights against the card issuer if the merchant that took payment by charging the card has failed to perform in some manner? **Read TILA §§ 133–135, 161–170 (15 U.S.C. §§ 1643–1645, 1666–1666i) and Reg. Z, 12 C.F.R. §§ 226.12, 226.13.** How do these provisions deal with each of the three concerns of a cardholder as identified above?

Problem 1-3

Notes

a) In January you used the Internet website of a retailer to order $500 worth of clothing to be shipped to you. You used your credit card to pay for the clothing. It is now two weeks later and you have not yet received the clothing but your credit card has been charged for the purchase price. Your credit card payment is due in two weeks. What are your options?

b) Do your options differ if the card was used to order $500 worth of tee shirts for your employees to wear? Review Reg. Z, 12 C.F.R. § 226.3.

c) Under the facts of part (a) of this problem, what are the obligations of the card issuer when you complain to it that you have not yet received the clothing? Does TILA or Regulation Z govern your rights as against the merchant?

d) Would your analysis of part (a) of this problem differ if you received the clothing but were not happy with its quality and the merchant refused to take the clothing back and give you a refund?

If the use of the card is "unauthorized," what is the liability of the cardholder? **Review the definition of "unauthorized use" in footnote 22 to Regulation Z, 12 C.F.R. § 226.12 and the following case.** What must a card issuer prove to hold a cardholder liable for a purported unauthorized use of a credit card? **Review the requirements of Reg. Z, 12 C.F.R. § 226.12(b).** What incentive does the cardholder have to give notice of an unauthorized use to the card issuer?

STIEGER V. CHEVY CHASE SAVINGS BANK
666 A.2d 479 (D.C. Ct. App. 1995)

Pryor, Senior Judge

For the first time we are asked to determine whether a credit cardholder who permits use of the card by another for a specific purpose is liable for other uses not specifically authorized. The precise issue is whether, in such circumstances, the card user had "apparent authority" to use the card in the context of the provisions of the Truth-in-Lending Act, 15 U.S.C.A. §§ 1601 *et seq*. (1988). We agree with the Superior Court that for thirteen of the fifteen disputed charges the matching of the signature, combined with the cardholder's voluntary relinquishment of the card for a third party's use, constitutes such "apparent authority" under the Act, thereby making appellant liable for the full amount of the thirteen charges. We, therefore, affirm the decision of the Superior Court.

I.

On November 10, 1992, appellant brought suit against Chevy Chase Bank, F.S.B. ("Chevy Chase") claiming he should not be held liable for certain charges credited to his Chevy Chase Visa card. Appellant voluntarily gave his credit card to a Ms. Garrett for the limited purpose of renting a car and for hotel lodging during a business trip. Appellant contacted both the car rental agency and the hotel to determine what type of authorization would be needed for Ms. Garrett to use his Visa card. Both companies informed him that he must write a letter authorizing the charges. Appellant asserts that he wrote both companies, but was unable to produce a copy of the letter to the hotel, which he contends limited his liability to $350.00.

Shortly after the conclusion of Ms. Garrett's business trip, appellant learned that she had made several other charges he had not specifically authorized. His signature apparently had worn off the back of his credit card, and Ms. Garrett signed it as "P. Stieger" rather than Paul Stieger. On thirteen of the fifteen charges in dispute, Ms. Garrett had signed the charge slip "P. Stieger," and on the other two she signed her own name.[1] Appellant has obtained a judgment against Ms. Garrett for $3200.00, but only $750.00 has been collected, and Ms. Garrett can no longer be located. Therefore, this action was brought to contest Chevy Chase's refusal to dismiss the charges as unauthorized.

Commissioner Diaz ruled in favor of Chevy Chase on all fifteen charges. Appellant appealed to the Superior Court asserting that the charges were unauthorized under the Truth-In-Lending Act. After review of the case, a judge of the Superior Court held that the Commissioner "had a factual and legal basis upon which she could properly decide that the voluntary relinquishment of the cardholder's credit card for one purpose gives the bearer apparent authority to make additional charges." (*Citing Martin v. American Express, Inc.*, 361 So.2d 597, 599-600 (Ala.Civ.App.1978)).

The Superior Court judge also considered the Commissioner's reasonableness analysis. The Superior Court found that the merchants acted reasonably in

---

[1] Twenty-two charges were made by Ms. Garrett, of which seven were dropped by the Bank prior to trial.

accepting appellant's credit card in thirteen of the fifteen charges where the name signed ("P. Stieger") matched the signature on the card. However, the court reversed the two charges where Ms. Garrett had signed her own name. Appellant filed an application for allowance of appeal, and on April 29, 1994 we granted the application.

II.

In a broad sense, the resolution of this matter involves an economic consideration of whether the cardholder, card issuer, or merchant should bear the financial responsibility in the circumstances presented. The Truth-In-Lending Act was enacted "in large measure to protect credit cardholders from unauthorized use perpetrated by those able to obtain possession of a card from its original owner." *Towers World Airways Inc. v. PHH Aviation Systems, Inc.*, 933 F.2d 174, 176 (2nd Cir.), *cert. denied,* 502 U.S. 823, 112 S.Ct. 87, 116 L.Ed.2d 59 (1991). The Act specifically limits liability for the cardholder to a maximum of $50 for charges made by third parties that are "unauthorized." 15 U.S.C.A. § 1643(a). However, the Act does not limit liability for the cardholder for third party charges made with "actual, implied or apparent authority." 15 U.S.C.A. § 1602(o).

The essential question on appeal is whether the disputed charges were incurred by an "unauthorized user" under the Act. The statute specifically incorporates agency concepts by defining "unauthorized use" as "a use of a credit card by a person other than the cardholder who does not have actual, implied, or *apparent* authority for such use and from which the cardholder receives no benefit." 15 U.S.C.A. § 1602(o) (emphasis added); see also 12 C.F.R. § 226.12(b)(1) n. 22 (stating same). Thus, our inquiry focuses on whether the relinquishment of a credit card to another for a limited purpose, which is then expanded by the user to make additional charges not authorized by the cardholder, is an "unauthorized" use under 15 U.S.C.A. § 1602(o), thereby limiting cardholder liability. Since actual or implied authority are not alleged in this case, the narrower issue is whether Ms. Garrett had apparent authority to use the card.

Our cases reveal that "[a]pparent authority arises when a principal places an agent 'in a position which causes a third person to reasonably believe the principal had consented to the exercise of authority the agent purports to hold. This falls short of an overt, affirmative representation by a principal....'" *Insurance Management of Washington, Inc. v. Eno & Howard Plumbing Corp.*, 348 A.2d 310, 312 (D.C.1975) (*quoting Drazin v. Jack Pry, Inc.,* 154 A.2d 553, 554 (D.C.1959)); *see also Feltman v. Sarbov*, 366 A.2d 137, 139 (D.C.1976) (stating same).

Specifically, in this jurisdiction "apparent authority of an agent arises when the principal places the agent in such a position as to *mislead* third persons into believing that the agent is clothed with authority which in fact he does not possess." *Jack Pry, Inc. v. Harry Drazin*, 173 A.2d 222, 223 (D.C.1961) (footnote omitted) (emphasis added).

"Though a cardholder's relinquishment of possession may create in another the appearance of authority to use the card, the statute clearly precludes a finding of apparent authority where the transfer of the card was without the cardholder's consent as in cases involving theft, loss, or fraud." *Towers, supra*, 933 F.2d at 177. As one court has stated:

> Where a credit cardholder, who was under no compulsion by fraud, duress, or otherwise, voluntarily permits the use of his or her credit card by another person, the cardholder has authorized the use of that card and is thereby responsible for any charges as a result of that use, even if he or she requested that the other person not charge over a certain amount or make charges on it for specified purposes. The user has apparent authority to use the card even after actual authority ceases; provided, however, that the cardholder is not liable for use of the card after the issuer has been notified that actual authority for others to use the card no longer exists.

Standard Oil Co. v. Steele, 22 Ohio Misc.2d 27, 489 N.E.2d 842, 844 (Ohio Mun.Ct.1985).

Nearly every jurisdiction that has addressed a factual situation "where a cardholder voluntarily and knowingly allows another to use his card and that person subsequently misuses the card," *Martin, supra*, 361 So.2d at 601, has determined that the agent had apparent authority, and therefore was not an "unauthorized" user under the Act limiting liability for the cardholder. *See Towers, supra*, (concluding that Towers was liable for charges because Towers' consent and other conduct revealed the pilot's unrestricted access to the PHH card); *Martin, supra* (holding cardholder responsible for charges of business associate despite oral limitation of $500.00); *American Express Travel Related Serv. Co., Inc. v. Web, Inc.*, 261 Ga. 480, 405 S.E.2d 652 (1991) (concluding that company is responsible for employee's misuse of the credit card resulting in charges of $27,000.00); *Oclander v. First Nat'l Bank of Louisville*, 700 S.W.2d 804 (Ky.Ct.App.1985) (holding wife responsible for estranged husband's almost $12,000.00 in charges when wife mistakenly advised the bank that she had both cards in possession and the bank removed the "block" from the account); *Cities Serv. Co. v. Pailet*, 452 So.2d 319 (La.Ct.App.1984) (concluding that defendant liable for employee's charges outside the scope of the limited business trip); *Standard Oil, supra,* (holding company responsible for employee's charges); *Walker Bank & Trust Co. v. Jones,* 672 P.2d 73 (Utah 1983) (concluding that spouse was responsible for husband's charges despite notifying bank of intention not to be responsible for husband's charges when husband still maintained apparent authority to use the cards because cards had not been returned to the bank or the account closed), *cert. denied,* 466 U.S. 937, 104 S.Ct. 1911, 80 L.Ed.2d 460 (1984); *MasterCard, Consumer Credit Div. of First Wisconsin Nat'l Bank of Milwaukee v. Town of Newport,* 133 Wis.2d 328, 396 N.W.2d 345 (Ct.App.1986) (holding town responsible for town clerk's personal charges); *cf. Michigan Nat'l Bank v. Olson,* 44 Wash.App. 898, 723 P.2d 438 (1986) (reversing summary judgment where factual dispute over whether husband's girlfriend had been given card to use or husband had used the card himself).

However, when a voluntary relinquishment of the card to a third party who returns it after its use is then followed by an involuntary surrender, i.e. stolen, of the card to the same third party, there is an "unauthorized" use under the Act. *Blaisdell Lumber Co., Inc. v. Horton,* 242 N.J.Super. 98, 575 A.2d 1386 (App.Div.1990) (holding that plaintiff had not established card user as agent with express, implied or apparent authority to use credit card when lover stole card and used it without authorization); *Vaughn v. United States Nat'l Bank of Oregon,* 79 Or.App. 172, 718 P.2d 769 (1986) (affirming jury verdict finding cardholder not liable to bank when, although previously giving his credit card and personal identification number to a third party for specific purchases, subsequent automatic teller withdrawal was the result of the third party stealing the card). No liability can attach to the cardholder when the card was not voluntarily relinquished, but rather was stolen. *Thomas v. Central Charge Serv., Inc.,* 212 A.2d 533 (D.C.1965); *cf. Fifth Third Bank/Visa v. Gilbert,* 17 Ohio Misc.2d 14, 478 N.E.2d 1324 (Ohio Mun.Ct.1984) (concluding that bank did not prove that unemancipated daughter was given access to credit card to make charges and therefore father not liable). In addition, if the cardholder notifies the card issuer that the card is being used in an unauthorized manner, the cardholder will not be liable for any charges made by the third party after the notice. *See Cities Serv., supra, Standard Oil, supra, but see American Express, supra,* (concluding that Act does not limit liability where notice is given to the issuer of the credit card).

We agree with these general principles because the voluntary relinquishment of the credit card, as distinguished from the stolen card situation, can often "mislead third persons into believing the agent is clothed with authority which in fact he does not possess." *Drazin, supra,* 173 A.2d at 223.

III.

Appellant argues that he had the right to expect Ms. Garrett to use the credit card only for the charges he authorized, and that he cannot be held liable for his agent acting beyond the scope of her authority. Appellant also asserts that Ms. Garrett could not reasonably present herself as Paul Stieger, and that a merchant should be required to give greater scrutiny to the person using the card.

Turning to the specific facts in this case, appellant gave Ms. Garrett his credit card to use. As the Superior Court noted, thirteen of the charges had the same signature as appeared on the back of the card. Appellant placed Ms. Garrett, by voluntarily giving her the card, "in such a position as to mislead third persons into believing that the agent is clothed with authority which in fact [s]he does not possess." *Jack Pry, Inc., supra*, 173 A.2d at 223. To a merchant, voluntary relinquishment combined with the matching of a signature is generally a reasonable indication of apparent authority to utilize the credit card. See 15 U.S.C.A. § 1643(a)(1)(F); 12 C.F.R. § 226.12(b)(2)(iii) & Supp. I at 341 (requiring the card issuer to provide a means of verifying the authority of the card bearer such as a signature, photograph, fingerprint or electronic or mechanical confirmation).

We agree with the Superior Court that the Commissioner "could properly conclude that the third-party merchants' actions were reasonable," and that the "voluntary relinquishment of the cardholder's credit card for one purpose gives the bearer apparent authority to make additional charges." However, we agree with the Superior Court that the same cannot be said of the two charges where Ms. Garrett signed her own name rather than "P. Stieger." It is an unreasonable extension of the apparent authority provided to Ms. Garrett for a merchant to accept charges, where the signatures do not match, without any additional factors to mislead the merchant into believing that the person presenting the card is the agent of the cardholder.

Appellant attempted to limit his authorization exclusively to the hotel and car rental company, and to a specific dollar amount for each. He testified he did this by writing letters to the two companies limiting the amount Ms. Garrett could charge. These letters to the two companies would limit his liability to the amounts stated in the letters if they were in fact received by the companies when the credit card was offered as payment. Mr. Stieger was able to produce only a copy of the letter to the car company. The charge to the car company did not exceed the limit in the letter. However, Mr. Stieger was unable to produce a copy of the letter to the hotel that he asserts limited the amount Ms. Garrett could charge to $350. By testifying that he voluntarily gave his credit card to Ms. Garrett and wrote the hotel to authorize the charge, the bank has met its burden of showing apparent authority.[2] Since Mr. Stieger has not submitted a copy of the letter limiting his exposure to $350, we agree with the Superior Court that the Commissioner did not err in concluding that Mr. Stieger is liable for the full amount of the hotel charge in excess of the $350.

In sum, Mr. Stieger was in the best position to control the uses of his credit card by not relinquishing it to a third party he could not trust, by notifying the card issuer that his credit limit should be lowered to a specific dollar amount, thereby limiting his exposure, or by notifying the card issuer upon becoming aware of certain unapproved purchases that any further purchases are unauthorized. As one court has noted "[i]n four-party arrangements of this sort [cardholder, issuer, third party and merchant], it is totally unrealistic to burden the card issuer with the obligation to convey to numerous merchants whatever limitation the cardholder has placed on the card user's authority." *Towers, supra*, 933 F.2d at 179 (footnote omitted). The Truth-In-Lending Act, although generally designed to protect credit cardholders, specifically reveals a congressional preference that where apparent authority exists, under the circumstances, the cardholder should bear the financial responsibility. Mr. Stieger voluntarily relinquished his credit card to an unreliable person, and thereby put Ms. Garrett in a position to mislead merchants to believe that she possessed apparent authority to utilize the card. Under the circumstances, Mr. Stieger should bear the financial responsibility for the unauthorized charges made by Ms. Garrett as determined by the trial court.

Affirmed.

Ruiz, Associate Judge, dissenting:

I agree with the majority that under the Truth-in-Lending Act the focus of our inquiry must be on whether Garrett had "apparent authority" to make the contested charges. I part company with the majority at the point that it decides that Garrett's act of forging Stieger's signature can be used to establish apparent authority. I also disagree with the majority's conclusion that the Bank's burden of proving Garrett's authority was discharged by Stieger's inability to produce a copy of the document the Bank relies upon for that authority. Therefore, I respectfully dissent.

---

[2] This fact was uncontroverted, and thus under settled concepts, appellant created an apparent authority in Ms. Garrett to reasonably use the card. It sometimes happens, as here, that appellant provided the factual basis for appellee's burden to proceed. A remand on this point would be futile.

I.

As the majority observes, a principal purpose of the Truth-in-Lending Act is to protect credit cardholders from unauthorized use. The Act seeks to achieve that objective by limiting the liability of credit cardholders to $50 for "unauthorized" charges to their accounts. 15 U.S.C. § 1643(a)(1) (1988). (footnote omitted) For the cardholder to have any liability at all for unauthorized use of her card, however, the card issuer must have undertaken to establish procedures to guard against unauthorized use, including providing "a method whereby the user of such card can be identified as the person authorized to use it." *Id.* § 1643(a)(1)(F).

The term "unauthorized" is defined to mean "use of a credit card by a person other than the cardholder who does not have actual, implied, or apparent authority for such use and from which the cardholder receives no benefit." 15 U.S.C. § 1602(o). The parties do not appear to dispute that Stieger received no benefit from the impugned charges. Other than with respect to one charge, a hotel charge in Oklahoma as to which Stieger testified he had authorized Garrett to charge up to $350, there is no dispute as to the existence of actual or implied authority. Therefore, the threshold legal question in determining Stieger's liability is whether Garrett was an unauthorized user or had "apparent authority" within the meaning of the statute to use Stieger's credit card.

Congress' reference to "actual, implied or apparent authority" would appear to necessarily incorporate some manner of common-law definition, whether by reference to state law or federal common law. The Federal Reserve Board, which has authority to promulgate regulations implementing the Truth-in-Lending Act, 15 U.S.C. § 1604(a), in its "Official Staff Interpretations" of Regulation Z, section 12(b) of which implements § 1643, states that "[w]hether such authority exists must be determined under state or other applicable law."[2] 12 C.F.R. pt. 226, supp. I, at 341 (1995). Consequently, it seems appropriate to look to common-law rules of agency, both generally and in the states in which Garrett made the contested charges, which are Oklahoma, Texas, Virginia and the District of Columbia.

---

[2] The Staff Interpretations do not appear intended to have legally binding effect, however. The introduction to the interpretations states that "[g]ood faith compliance with this commentary affords protection from liability under [a provision] of the Truth-in-Lending Act [that] protects creditors from civil liability for any act done or omitted in good faith in conformity with any interpretation issued by a duly authorized official or employee of the Federal Reserve System." Thus, the interpretations provide a safe harbor for creditors, but do not bind the courts (or other agencies) in their interpretation of the Act. Nevertheless, reference to the interpretation should serve as persuasive authority.

The common-law rule permits only the acts of the putative principal to be used in establishing apparent agency. For example, the RESTATEMENT (SECOND) OF AGENCY provides:

> Apparent authority is the power to affect the legal relations of another person by transactions with third persons, professedly as agent for the other, *arising from and in accordance with the other's manifestations to such third persons.*

RESTATEMENT (SECOND) OF AGENCY § 8 (1958) (emphasis added).

Both Oklahoma and Texas have cited that provision of the RESTATEMENT with approval. *Stephens v. Yamaha Motor Co.*, 627 P.2d 439, 441 (Okla.1981) (noting that "the elements that must be present before a third person can hold the principal liable for the acts of the agent on the theory of apparent authority are (a) *conduct of the principal*, (b) reliance *thereon* by the third person, and (c) change of position by the third person to his detriment" (*quoting Rosser-Moon Furniture Co. v. Oklahoma State Bank*, 135 P.2d 336 (Okla.1943) (emphasis added)))[3]; *Ames v. Great Southern Bank*, 672 S.W.2d 447, 450 (Tex.1984) ("Apparent authority in Texas is based on estoppel. It may arise either from a *principal knowingly permitting an agent* to hold herself out as having authority or by a *principal's actions* which lack such ordinary care as to clothe an agent with the indicia of authority, thus *leading a reasonably prudent person to believe that the agent has the authority* she purports to exercise." (emphasis added)). The Supreme Court of Virginia has cited a comment to section 8 of the RESTATEMENT with approval, *Equitable Variable Life Ins. Co. v. Wood*, 234 Va. 535, 362 S.E.2d 741, 744 (1987), but it has not adopted the black-letter provision.

This court has never expressly adopted the RESTATEMENT definition; we have however, defined apparent authority in similar terms:

> "Apparent authority arises when a principal places an agent 'in a position which causes a third person to *reasonably believe that the principal had consented* to the exercise of authority the agent purports to hold. This falls short of an overt, affirmative representation by a principal.'"

Feltman v. Sarbov, 366 A.2d 137, 139 (D.C.1976) (*quoting Insurance Management v. Eno & Howard Plumbing Corp.*, 348 A.2d 310, 312 (D.C.1975) (*quoting Drazin v. Jack Pry, Inc.*, 154 A.2d 553, 554 (D.C.1959))) (emphasis added). For example, in *Jack Pry, Inc. v. Drazin*, 173 A.2d 222 (D.C.1961), relied upon by the majority,

---

[3] It should be noted that *Stephens* involved an attempt to impose vicarious tort liability on the principal based on the apparent agency of the tortfeasor.

the facts that we found to be sufficient to establish apparent agency were all acts of the putative principal, not of the apparent agent.

Thus, courts have repeatedly said that the third party must reasonably rely upon the conduct of the putative principal and not the putative agent in concluding that the putative agent had authority to bind the principal. Over a hundred years ago, the Supreme Court of the District of Columbia, sitting in general term, said that "if the fraud consists in the agent's pretending to have the authority for that which he does, the principal is not affected." *Brooke v. Barnes*, 12 D.C. (1 Mackey) 5, 11 (1880).

In the present case, Stieger, the putative principal, gave his credit card, embossed with his name, to Garrett, the putative agent. In accordance with instructions he received from the merchants for which he authorized her to use his credit card, he provided written authorization for two particular uses, and no others. He did not permit Garrett to sign the card. Thus, the question is whether a merchant, having knowledge of the putative principal's actions, could reasonably conclude that the putative agent had *carte blanche* to make charges to the credit card.

Stieger took care to find out how to authorize Garrett to make limited use of his charge card and followed the instructions given to him. The majority focuses primarily on Stieger's action in turning over the card to Garrett as if, instead of having provided the card so that she could use it only for such limited purposes, he had given her a master key that, without more, can open all doors. In this respect, however, it is important to remember that a credit card is *not* a bearer instrument. Were it otherwise, the result might be different. *See Henry v. Auchincloss, Parker & Redpath*, 193 F.Supp. 413, 415 (D.D.C.1961) (holding that by conferring control over stock certificates on son, mother gave him apparent authority to dispose of the stock certificates, notwithstanding forgery of some endorsements), *aff'd*, 305 F.2d 753, 113 U.S.App.D.C. 84; RESTATEMENT (SECOND) OF AGENCY § 195A ("A special agent for an undisclosed principal has no power to bind his principal by contracts or conveyances which he is not authorized to make unless: ... the agent is given possession of goods or commercial documents with authority to deal with them.").[4]

---

[4] In this respect, it is interesting to note that "apparent authority exists only with regard to those who believe and have reason to believe that there is authority; there can be no apparent authority created by an undisclosed principal." RESTATEMENT (SECOND) OF AGENCY § 8 cmt. a. In the instant case, it appears that with respect to the thirteen charges signed "P. Stieger," it is at least arguable that Garrett did not purport to act as an agent for Stieger, but

(continued...)

As the majority recognizes, however, because a credit card is not a bearer device, a third party is not reasonable in treating it as such by failing to check the identity of the user against the identity of the cardholder by at least matching the signature of the bearer with the signature on the card. *Ante* at 485. This point was reinforced by the evidence adduced by Stieger regarding the industry practice of requiring written authorization of the cardholder for use by an agent.[5] The majority holds Stieger liable for those charges where Garrett signed Stieger's name, but not those for which she signed her own name. According to the majority, the merchants reasonably relied on her signature for the former because it matched the signature on the back of the card. However, there is no dispute that Stieger did not permit Garrett to sign his card; her signing of the card was an act of forgery, compounded each of the thirteen times that she signed the charge slips as "P. Stieger". Under the common law, the principal's liability for acts within the apparent authority of an agent is based on the merchants' reasonable reliance on an action of the principal. That was not the case here, where the merchants relied on Garrett's forgeries. Thus,

---

[4] (...continued)
instead acted on her own behalf. If so, then she could not have bound Stieger, for his existence remained undisclosed to the merchants. The point does not appear to have been argued, however.

[5] At the hearing on his claim, Stieger testified regarding his experience with and investigation into the practices of merchants in accepting credit cards from persons other than the cardholder. The record does not reflect any objection to Stieger's testimony; in any event, Super.Ct.Sm.Cl.R. 12 provides that the trial shall be conducted "in such manner as to do substantial justice between the parties according to the rules of substantive law, and shall not be bound by the provisions or rules of practice, procedure, pleading or evidence, except such provisions relating to privileged communications." The record contains no evidence rebutting Stieger's claims; indeed, if the Bank presented any evidence at all, it has not been made a part of the record before us.

Specifically, Stieger testified about his experiences with the car rental company and the hotel, which required written authorization when he called about what he should do to permit Garrett to use his card. He also testified that a hotel in California required written authorization from him before they would charge his father's room to his credit card. He testified that merchants have often required him to prove his identity in connection with his use of his own credit card. He testified that his own investigation of local merchants disclosed that several never honor credit cards presented by one other than the cardholder, and that of the remainder, all but one require a written authorization. The one exception is a drug store chain, which will accept a credit card presented by one other than the cardholder without written authorization only if it is used to pay for a drug prescription which matches the name of the cardholder.

Garrett did not have apparent authority, within the meaning of 15 U.S.C. § 1643(a), to bind Stieger for the thirteen charges that she unlawfully signed "P. Stieger."

I believe that this result is consistent with the purpose of the rules of agency, which as Blackstone observed, is to further commerce. *See* 1 WILLIAM BLACKSTONE, COMMENTARIES ON THE LAWS OF ENGLAND *418 (1765) ("[W]ithout such a doctrine as this, no mutual intercourse between man and man could subsist with any tolerable convenience."). In the furtherance of commerce through the use of agents, there are two interests to be balanced. The rules should not make it too risky for a principal to employ agents. But the rules also should not make the dealings of third persons with agents so uncertain of their validity that third persons will refuse to deal with agents. The law of agency balances those interests by charging the principal only with her own acts, while demanding only that third persons behave reasonably in relying upon those acts. After those rules have been exhausted, the law places the burden of fraudulent conduct outside the scope of actual agency upon the party defrauded, whether it is the principal or a third party. That is logical, because each member of society participating in commerce is charged with looking out for his or her own interests, and when those interests are wrongfully infringed, is given the right to proceed against at least the primary wrongdoer.

In my view, the majority's opinion upsets the balance of interests in the common law of agency by making the credit cardholder bear a disproportionate share of the risk from an activity furthering commerce that clearly benefits the card issuer and the merchants who accept the card. I disagree that the cardholder is in a better position to prevent fraud by a user with limited authority, such as Garrett perpetrated in this case. As the Truth-in-Lending Act makes clear, it is the duty of the card issuer to "provide[ ] a method whereby the user of such card can be identified as the person authorized to use it." 15 U.S.C. § 1643(a)(1)(F). Currently, it appears that most card issuers rely on a combination of embossed name and a signature provided by the cardholder. If those means of identification are too easily avoided or defeated by persons intent on fraud, it would seem that it is the card issuer that bears the burden of either improving the system or absorbing the loss.

II.

Stieger argues that the Bank had the burden of proving that Garrett had authority to incur the entire hotel charge. The Bank denies that it had the burden, citing the "general rule" that the plaintiff bears the burden of proving his case. The Bank may be correct with respect to the general rule, but the more relevant specific rule is that the burden of proof regarding authority is on the one asserting authority, not the one denying the authority, regardless of whether the one asserting it is the defendant. *See, e.g., Rustler's Steak House v. Environmental Assocs.*, 327 A.2d 536, 539 (D.C.1974) (allocating burden to defendant alleging authority); *Bayless v. Christie, Manson & Woods Int'l*, 2 F.3d 347, 352 (10th Cir.1993) (applying Oklahoma law to allocate burden to defendant alleging authority); *Abbott v. Earl Hayes Chevrolet Co.*, 384 S.W.2d 782, 784 (Tex.Civ.App.1964) (allocating burden to defendant alleging authority); *Raney v. Barnes Lumber Corp.*, 195 Va. 956, 81 S.E.2d 578, 584 (1954) (allocating burden to plaintiff alleging authority).

Garrett signed the disputed hotel charge in her own name. Thus, even under the majority's analysis, because the hotel would have been unreasonable in accepting the charge on Stieger's card, there was no apparent authority. Therefore, to prevail, the Bank had to produce some evidence of Garrett's actual authority. The only evidence of Garrett's actual authority was Stieger's testimony that he wrote a letter to the hotel authorizing her to charge up to $350; neither Stieger nor the Bank produced a copy of Stieger's letter to the hotel. The Bank sought to meet its burden of proving Garrett's authority to make charges at the hotel by using that part of Stieger's testimony that established he had authorized her to use his credit card at the hotel, but ignoring the part of Stieger's testimony that placed a $350 limitation on the authority to make charges over $350.00. In those circumstances, I disagree with the majority's holding that the Bank met its burden of proving Garrett's authority. A party may not meet its burden by taking but one portion of a statement of the opposing party, while ignoring the rest. That is little different from saying that had Stieger testified that he had not authorized Garrett, the trial court may credit the "authorized" part of the statement, but discredit the "not" and declare the Bank's burden met. Moreover, the record contains nothing to indicate that the commissioner discredited anything Stieger said. Therefore, on this point at the least, the case should be remanded.

———————————

Compare the majority and dissent's discussion of apparent authority with this formulation found in the RESTATEMENT (THIRD) OF AGENCY § 2.03 (2006): "Apparent authority is the power held by an agent or other actor to affect a principal's legal relations with third parties when a third party reasonably believes the actor has authority to act on behalf of the principal and that belief is traceable to the principal's manifestations." Would there be a different result if the new Restatement formulation applied?

Another court has held that a corporate employer gave apparent authority to an employee to make charges on a corporate credit card when the employer had repeatedly paid the employee's charges on the card over a period of time, not merely by failing to complain about the charges made on the card. The court stated mere silence in the face of the charges on the periodic statement was not sufficient to create apparent authority. The court remanded for factual findings as to the point in time that the employer's course of conduct of payment resulted in apparent authority for the employee to make the charges. *DBI Architects, P.C. v. American Express Travel-Related Services Co.*, 388 F.3d 886 (D.C. Cir. 2004). *Compare Carrier v. Citibank (South Dakota), N.A.*, 383 F. Supp. 2d 334 (D. Conn. 2005), *aff'd*, 180 Fed. Appx. 296 (2d Cir. 2006).

Problem 1-4

Notes

You are the managing partner in a law firm. Some employees have credit cards issued to them under the law firm's name to pay for travel expenses incurred in the course of their employment. What processes would insure that the firm is not liable for charges made on those cards that the law firm does not intend to pay for?

Review

1. Summarize the rules regarding the allocation of the risk of errors and fraud in the use of credit cards. What risks does the card issuer bear? What risks does the merchant bear? What risks does the cardholder bear?
2. Compare and contrast the rules regarding errors and fraud in the use of credit cards with the rules regarding errors and fraud in the use of currency.
3. Why have different rules for two different types of payment mechanisms?

CHAPTER 2
INTRODUCTION TO NEGOTIABLE INSTRUMENTS AS A PAYMENT SYSTEM

A. Overview

In Chapter 1, we discussed generally the functioning of a payment system in a modern commercial society and considered the relatively simple payment systems represented by currency and credit cards. In this Chapter we start our consideration of a considerably more complicated payment system, payments made by means of a specialized type of contract called a negotiable instrument. Without realizing it, many of you use negotiable instruments on a regular basis. The most common usage of a negotiable instrument to make a payment is giving a payee a check as a means of paying for goods or services. In most circumstances, a check will qualify as a negotiable instrument.

Negotiable instruments are governed by state law, Uniform Commercial Code Article 3. U.C.C. § 3-102(a).* Negotiable instruments are writings that have certain characteristics as defined in U.C.C. § 3-104(a). Those characteristics are discussed in Section D of this Chapter. Drafts and notes are the two big categories of negotiable instruments. Drafts embody orders to pay and notes embody promises to pay. U.C.C. § 3-104(e).

A check is a type of a draft. Various types of checks exist: ordinary checks that are drawn on business and personal accounts at a bank or other financial institution, U.C.C. § 3-104(f); cashier's checks that are issued by a bank and drawn on the same bank, U.C.C. § 3-104(g); or teller's checks that are drawn by a bank on another bank, U.C.C. § 3-104(h). Drafts may also be drawn on non-bank entities. A traveler's check is a negotiable instrument that has additional characteristics specified in U.C.C. § 3-104(i). A traveler's check may be either a draft or a note. U.C.C. § 3-104, comment 4. A certificate of deposit is a note of a bank as defined

---

* The Uniform Commercial Code was drafted by the National Conference of Commissioners on Uniform State Laws ("NCCUSL") and the American Law Institute ("ALI"). The drafts as promulgated by NCCUSL and ALI are proposed for enactment by each state. The drafts may or may not be enacted in their uniform form. U.C.C. Articles 3 and 4 were revised in 1990 and then amended in 2002. This text refers to Articles 3 and 4 as revised in 1990 and amended in 2002. As of the time this text was printed, all states but two have enacted the 1990 revisions, and five states have enacted the 2002 revisions.

in U.C.C. § 3-104(j). **Read U.C.C. § 3-104(e) through (j).**

Read the definitions of "order" and "promise" in U.C.C. § 3-103. Notice that each requires that the instruction or undertaking be "written" and "signed." In addition, the instruction or undertaking must be to pay "money." Now read U.C.C. § 3-103(d). It refers you to Article 1 of the U.C.C. for general definitions.[*] **Read the definitions of "written," "signed," and "money" in U.C.C. § 1-201.**

Now look at a typical check blank. The payee line contains the pre-printed phrase "Pay to the order of." There is a place for putting an amount of money in both numerical and written form and a place to be signed on the bottom right hand side. The instruction to pay is to the financial institution whose name is preprinted on the lower left hand side, above the line entitled "memo." When the blank form is filled out, this is an example of an "order" under U.C.C. § 3-103(a)(8), a "draft" under U.C.C. § 3-104(e), and a "check" under U.C.C. § 3-104(f). A "draft" need not be a check. In reading the definitions we have already studied, what is the critical factual difference between a "draft" and a "check"? Now compare the definition of "check" in U.C.C. § 3-104(f) to the definition of "cashier's check" and "teller's check" in U.C.C. § 3-104(g) and (h). Articulate the difference between these three types of "drafts."

Now consider the other major type of negotiable instrument, a note. Reread the definition of "promise" in U.C.C. § 3-103. Notice that the major distinction between an "order" and a "promise" is the difference between an "instruction" and an "undertaking" to pay money. **Draft an undertaking to pay that would satisfy the requirements of a "promise" under U.C.C. § 3-103.** Now look at the definition of "certificate of deposit" in U.C.C. § 3-104(j). A certificate of deposit is a "note" of the bank.

Keep these two concepts of "order" and "promise" in mind as we continue the overview of negotiable instruments as a payment system. We will consider the rest of the requirements of a negotiable instrument in Section D of this Chapter.

If a draft or note is collected through the banking system, U.C.C. Article 4 will govern the process. *See* U.C.C. § 4-102 and § 4-104(a)(9) (definition of "item"). All of the rules regarding collection through banks, however, are not found in Article 4. Banks are regulated entities. The Federal Reserve Board, the

---

[*] U.C.C. Article 1 applies to any transaction covered by another Article of the U.C.C. U.C.C. § 1-102. Article 1 contains definitions and other general rules. You should make it a habit to always consult Article 1 to see if it has any sections relevant to the problem at hand. This text will refer to the provisions of Revised Article 1 as promulgated in 2001.

Comptroller of Currency and the Federal Deposit Insurance Corporation are only three of the major federal agencies that regulate banks. The Federal Reserve Board has promulgated regulations pursuant to congressional enacted statutes that regulate some aspects of the collection process. In 1987, Congress enacted the Expedited Funds Availability Act ("EFAA") (codified at 12 U.S.C. §§ 4001–10) to provide for limitations on how long a bank could take to give a depositor access to funds in the bank account when funds were deposited to that account. Pursuant to the EFAA, the Federal Reserve Board promulgated Regulation CC found at 12 C.F.R. pt. 229. In order to facilitate the check collection process in light of developments in electronic methods of communicating data, in 2004, Congress enacted the Check Clearing for the 21st Century Act (commonly called "Check 21") (codified at 12 U.S.C. §§ 5001–18). The Federal Reserve Board promulgated amendments to Regulation CC to implement Check 21.

These two Acts and Regulation CC govern some aspects of the check collection process and the availability of funds in banks subject to the regulation. In addition, if checks are collected through the Federal Reserve system, Regulation J, 12 C.F.R. pt. 210 will govern some aspects of the collection process. The relationship between Article 4 and applicable federal regulations is that the federal regulation controls the issue when it conflicts with the Article 4 rule. *See* U.C.C. § 4-103, cmt. 3. If there is not a conflict between the Article 4 rule and the federal regulation on a particular issue, both govern the issue.

Articles 3 and 4 have a relationship to other articles of the Uniform Commercial Code.   The other articles in the Code govern specific types of transactions. Article 3 and 4 could apply to one part of the transaction and another article could govern other parts of the transaction. For example, Article 2 governs transactions in goods. Suppose you buy a washing machine at your local department store and pay the store with a personal check. Article 2 will apply to disputes with the department store about the quality of the washing machine or other obligations under the contract for sale. Articles 3 and 4 will apply to the obligations and liabilities related to the check as it travels from your hands, to the store's hands, to the store's bank, to your bank, and finally back to you in your checking account statement. Because Articles 3 and 4 are part of a set of articles governing various types of transactions, various sections or concepts from other articles might be relevant to the issues under Articles 3 and 4. Familiarity with the other articles of the U.C.C. is essential for a well rounded view of commercial law.

Article 3 is based in part upon a prior uniform act called the Negotiable Instruments Act. Prior to that uniform act, the common law of contracts evolved special rules to facilitate commerce concerning bills of exchange (drafts in today's terminology) and notes.* These special rules were designed to make rights of holders of bills and notes easier to enforce and transfer than an assignment of contract rights. The rules about transfer of rights and enforceability of rights after transfer is a concept of negotiability. Negotiability has differing shades of strength depending on the type of transaction. The negotiability concept is discussed in Section C of this Chapter.

B. How Do Negotiable Instruments Transfer Value

As with other payment systems, one of the primary uses of negotiable instruments today is as a mechanism to transfer value to another person. What follows is a simplistic illustration of how drafts and notes are used to transfer value to another person.

Assume that you want to buy a car. In addition to the information that you might need to select a model suitable for you, you need to consider how you are going to pay for the car. In a barter economy you might find that the person who wants to sell the car is interested in obtaining something you have and you could work out a swap. Perhaps it would require several swaps with several people before you could obtain the item you needed to use to trade with the car seller. In an economy that uses money tokens, you could obtain sufficient tokens to give to the car seller in exchange for the car. In common parlance, you would have paid cash for the car. Actually obtaining possession of enough tokens to pay for the car may not be practical. There may also be safety concerns in carrying around so much currency given the ease of transferring rights to the currency. You could also use a credit card as discussed in Chapter 1. That may not be feasible depending upon your credit limit on the credit card and the interest rate that the issuer charges you for the extension of credit.

Having considered and rejected the types of payment systems that we have studied so far, we can now consider using a negotiable instrument as a payment mechanism. Assume that you have a checking account at State Bank. You have a sufficient balance in that account to cover the price of the car you wish to purchase. You write a check drawn on the account, payable to the car seller. The car seller deposits the check in the seller's account at a bank. The seller's bank gives the

---

*   *See* JOHN BARNARD BYLES, A TREATISE ON THE LAW OF BILLS OF EXCHANGE: PROMISSORY NOTES, BANK-NOTES AND CHEQUES (1891).

seller a credit in the seller's account in the amount of the check deposited. The seller's bank then transfers the check to a clearinghouse which credits the seller's bank's account with the clearinghouse. The clearinghouse transfers the check to your bank and debits your bank's account with the clearinghouse. Your bank then debits your checking account and returns the check to you in your bank statement for the month. The transaction can be represented graphically as follows:

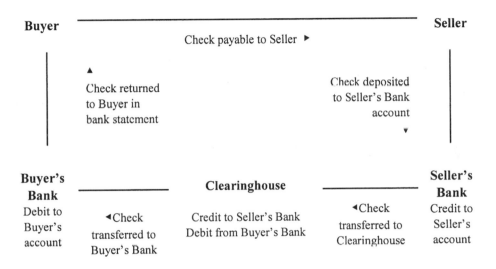

Thus the check has been used as a mechanism to transfer value from the buyer to the seller through a series of debits and credits in the collection system. The issuance of the check suspends any further obligation to pay for the car. If the check is not dishonored but is paid by the buyer's bank, the obligation to pay for the car is satisfied. *See* U.C.C. § 3-310. This scenario will be discussed in greater depth in Chapter 3.

Assume that you do not have enough credits in your checking account to pay for the car. Another option for paying for the car is to borrow the funds from someone willing to lend. Assume that the car seller is willing to lend you the money. The car seller has you sign a promissory note in which you promise to pay the seller or the holder of the note the amount lent in installments over a set period of time. By signing that note and giving it to the car dealer in payment for the car, you have incurred an obligation to pay the note which suspends your obligation to pay for the car. Assuming you make all of the payments on the note, the obligation to pay for the car will have been satisfied. *See* U.C.C. § 3-310. That promissory note is an asset of the seller and may be transferred by the seller in exchange for other assets such as money. The note may be enforced against you by people to whom the seller has transferred the note. Thus the note is a payment mechanism that transfers value to the car seller.

Those two simple examples allow a glimpse at the complicated world of negotiable instruments as a payment system. Unlike the relatively simple rules we have encountered in looking at currency and credit cards, the rules of negotiable instrument land are more complex and some would say archaic and unnecessary.[*] In fact, it will take the next several chapters to flesh out those rules and how they work. So far, nothing that we have discussed about how checks and notes transfer value has been keyed to the negotiability concept. It is to that concept that we now turn.

C. Negotiability Concepts

What is negotiability? The concept of negotiability has at its heart the idea that an item, including a representation of an obligation, can be transferred from one person to another with the transferee of that item having rights to that item that are free from claims to that item or defenses to the enforcement of the obligation the item represents. The legal rules about transfers of items and the relative degree of freedom that the transferee obtains differs depending upon what type of item is transferred. The idea of negotiability is contained in many systems of property transfer but in varying degrees of strength.[**]

Consider the following example from the law governing the sale of goods, U.C.C. Article 2. Assume that you purchase a new television set from a retailer. Assume the retailer paid for the television set from its supplier with a check that was dishonored. As between the retailer and the supplier, the supplier may have a right to recover the television set from the retailer because the check bounced. U.C.C. § 2-507. One could say that the retailer has a voidable title to the television set subject to being defeated due to the supplier's right to reclaim the television set. If the concept of derivative title is used, the retailer could sell the television set to

---

[*] *See* Ronald J. Mann, *Searching for Negotiability in Payment and Credit Systems*, 44 UCLA L. REV. 951 (1997); James Steven Rogers, *The Myth of Negotiability*, 31 B.C.L. REV. 265 (1990); Edward L. Rubin, *Learning from Lord Mansfield: Toward a Transferability Law for Modern Commercial Practice*, 31 IDAHO L. REV. 775 (1995).

[**] *See* Curtis Nyquist, *A Spectrum Theory of Negotiability*, 78 MARQUETTE L. REV. 897 (1995).

a purchaser, but the purchaser's title would be subject to being defeated by the supplier who wants the television set returned due to the failure of the payment (i.e. the bounced check). This derivative title concept is well entrenched in commercial law.

You may also see references to an aspect of derivative title called the shelter rule. What this means is that a transferee of property receives the same title, no more and no less, that its transferor had.[*] This derivative title rule is codified in the first sentence to U.C.C. § 2-403(1). The second sentence of that section, however, codifies an exception to the derivative title rule that reflects an idea of negotiability of goods. In the example given above, if the purchaser is a good faith purchaser for value and has taken delivery of the television set, the purchaser receives good title to the television set. The purchaser's right to the television set is not subject to being defeated by the supplier's attempt to repossess the television set. The purchaser has received transfer of the item free of the supplier's claim to the item. This is a type of "negotiability of goods" rule.

Transferability of rights is essential to a commercial society. The above example is an illustration of transferability of rights to tangible property we call "title." We can also transfer rights that have to do with intangible obligations, such as rights and duties created by contract. The rules governing assignment and delegation in contract law are concerned with the rights and obligations of both the transferor and transferee of the rights and duties created by contract.

1. Assignment of Contract Rights and Delegation of Contract Duties

In your contracts class you may have studied the idea of assignment and delegation of a contract. Assignment of a contract right is generally thought of as transferring to a person not a party to the contract the right to receive the other party's performance under the contract. Delegation of a contract duty is generally thought of as transferring to a person not a party to the contract the obligation to perform a contractual duty. Thus, whenever thinking about the ideas of assignment of a contract right or delegation of a contract duty, there are at least three actors in the situation: the original parties to the contract and a third party.

---

[*] *See* John F. Dolan, *The U.C.C. Framework: Conveyancing Principles and Property Interests*, 59 B.U.L. REV. 811 (1979); Steven L. Harris, *Using Fundamental Principles of Commercial Law to Decide U.C.C. Cases*, 26 LOY. L.A.L. REV. 637 (1993).

Assignment of a contract right can be illustrated as follows:

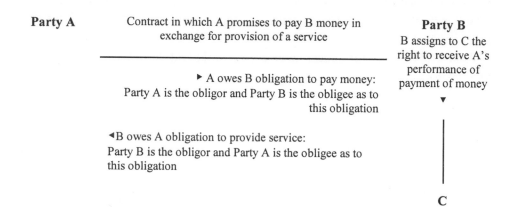

In order for B to assign its right to receive A's performance to C, B must manifest its intent to transfer the rights and generally the assignee, C in this example, must assent to the assignment for the assignment to be effective. *See* RESTATEMENT (SECOND) CONTRACTS §§ 324, 327. Once B has effectively assigned to C the right to receive A's performance, B no longer has a right to receive A's performance. *See* RESTATEMENT (SECOND) OF CONTRACTS § 317. C's rights against A to enforce the right to payment that has been assigned are the same as whatever B's rights were prior to the assignment. If A had a defense to payment that could be asserted against B that accrued prior to the assignment from B to C, A can generally assert that defense as against C as long as A has not waived that right to assert defenses. *See* RESTATEMENT (SECOND) OF CONTRACTS §§ 336, 337. Once A is notified of the assignment to C, A is obligated to render its performance to C and cannot discharge its obligation by rendering performance to B. *See* RESTATEMENT (SECOND) OF CONTRACTS § 338. In some rare circumstances, A may be able to effectively preclude B from validly assigning B's right to receive A's performance if the contract between A and B so provides or other principles of law make B's right not assignable. *See* RESTATEMENT (SECOND) OF CONTRACTS § 317, 322. *But see* U.C.C. §§ 9-406 through 9-409.

A negotiable instrument is a type of contract. An issuer of a negotiable instrument makes a promise to pay the amount of the instrument. That contract (the negotiable instrument) may be assigned and rights under that contract transferred to transferees. An obligor on an instrument may have defenses to payment of the instrument that are similar to defenses an obligor would raise to a breach of contract suit. Unlike the simple assignment of a contract described above, a transferee of a negotiable instrument may obtain greater rights than the transferor had to enforce the promise against the obligor on the negotiable instrument even if the negotiable instrument does not contain a waiver of defenses clause. In many circumstances, the transferee obtains these greater rights because it qualifies as a holder in due course, a concept that will be discussed in Chapter 3. Those greater rights mean that the transferee who is a holder in due course may not be subject to the defenses the obligor raises to making payment of the negotiable instrument. A person who does not qualify as this special type of transferee, that is, is not a holder in due course, obtains rights similar to the rights an assignee of a contract right obtains under the above-described scheme for assignment of contract rights. Thus, the transferee who is not a holder in due course would be subject to the defense if the transferor would be subject to the defense. What defenses may be asserted against both a holder in due course and a person who is not a holder in due course of a negotiable instrument are discussed in Chapter 3.

One of the primary effects of a writing that qualifies as a negotiable instrument is to utilize this holder in due course doctrine to transfer the right to receive the obligor's obligation to pay money free of the defenses the obligor may raise to that obligation to pay. Contracts that do not qualify as negotiable instruments do not get the benefit of the holder in due course doctrine.

Delegation of contract duties can be illustrated as follows:

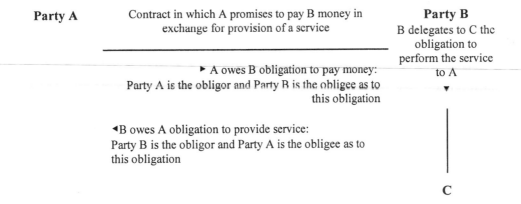

B delegates its duty to perform to C by manifesting an intent to do so and obtaining C's consent to the delegation. *See* RESTATEMENT (SECOND) OF CONTRACTS §§ 318, 328. If C consents to the delegation, C must perform the duties under the contract but the delegation does not discharge the duty of B under the contract with A, unless A releases B from its obligation. *See* RESTATEMENT

(SECOND) OF CONTRACTS § 318. Generally A can preclude B from delegating its duties under the contract if a contract term prohibits such delegation or if A has a substantial interest in having B perform the obligation. *See* RESTATEMENT (SECOND) OF CONTRACTS §§ 318, 322.

The law of negotiable instruments does not alter these contract rules governing delegation of contractual duties.

2. Contract Rights as Property

Another consequence of the negotiability concept as applied to negotiable instruments is to provide special protection from property-based claims to the instrument. We will consider this in Chapter 4, but a short preview is important to understanding how negotiable instruments differ from other types of contracts.

A contract right is also an intangible form of personal property.[*] Thus persons other than an assignee may assert property claims to those contract rights. The common law approach is to follow a derivative rights concept in most situations. A subsequent assignee is subject to the rights of a first assignee in many situations. Return to the example above. Assume that B has assigned its right to C to receive A's performance. Subsequent to that assignment to C, B assigns the same right to D to receive A's performance. In many situations, D's right under the second assignment would be inferior to C's rights under the first assignment.[**]

In some situations, however, a subsequent assignee from the obligor may obtain superiority over the rights of a first assignee. For example, if the first assignment is voidable or revoked, the subsequent assignee may have rights superior to the first assignee. If the subsequent assignee acquires its rights in good faith, without knowledge of the first assignee's rights, and for value and in addition, obtains payment, a judgment against the obligor, a new contract with the obligor, or possession of a writing that is customarily accepted as the evidence of the right assigned (i.e. a negotiable instrument), the subsequent assignee may prevail over the first assignee. RESTATEMENT (SECOND) OF CONTRACTS § 342.

If the contract right is represented by a negotiable instrument, the obligation to pay is reified in the instrument. An assignee of that instrument that is a holder in

---

[*] E. ALLAN FARNSWORTH, CONTRACTS § 11.9 (4th ed. 2004).

[**] To the extent U.C.C. Article 9 on secured transactions applies to the priority contest, the Article 9 rules would also trump the normal first in time contract assignment rule.

due course takes that instrument free of another's property-based claim to the instrument, even if that property-based claim arose prior to the holder in due course's rights to the instrument. A transferee of a negotiable instrument that does not qualify as a holder in due course is not able to take the instrument free of pre-existing property claims to the instrument. We will consider this aspect of a negotiable instrument in Chapter 4. A transferee of a contract that does not qualify as a negotiable instrument is not able to assert the rights of a holder in due course and will be able to take free of pre-existing assignee's right to the contract right only if it qualifies for one of the exceptions to the general rule as set forth above.

3. Negotiable Instruments and Holder in Due Course

This special status of a holder in due course who takes free of claims and defenses enables the negotiable instrument to be freely transferable and enforceable without having to litigate claims and defenses that might preclude payment of the instrument. Thus, a negotiable instrument in the hands of a holder in due course is a powerful mechanism for transferring value from one person to another. This ability to create a special type of contract that allows this freedom from claims and defenses is the hallmark of the concept of negotiability.

As we continue our exploration of the rules governing negotiable instruments, keep in mind the law of assignment of contracts as set forth above and ask yourself how the rules for negotiable instruments are both the same and different than the rules regarding contract assignment.[*]

D. Requisites of a Negotiable Instrument Under U.C.C. Article 3

In order to know whether the specialized rules briefly described above come into play, you must determine whether the piece of paper you have in hand is a negotiable instrument. If it is not a negotiable instrument, it may still be a contract and enforceable under the general rules governing enforcement and transfer of contract rights. **Read U.C.C. § 3-104 and the comments**. Subsection (a) sets forth the requirements for a negotiable instrument. All of the requirements stated in that section must be met. If even one requirement is not met, the instrument is not a negotiable instrument. Each of the words or phrases in U.C.C. § 3-104(a) is further

---

[*] *See* Gregory E. Maggs, *The Holder in Due Course Doctrine as a Default Rule*, 32 GA. L. REV. 783 (1998).

defined in other sections of Article 3 or Article 1. The first step in statutory analysis is breaking the statutory section down into its component parts. Then it is necessary to find out if the statute further defines or explains the meaning of each component part. When you read the sections, also *read the comments*. These comments are not enacted law but are treated as persuasive authority as to the meaning of the statutory text and are often very helpful in trying to understand what the statutory text means.

We have already looked at one of the elements of a negotiable instrument. The negotiable instrument must be a "promise" or an "order." **Review the definitions in U.C.C. § 3-103 ("promise" and "order") and § 1-201 ("written", "signed" and "money").**

That promise or order must be "unconditional." What does that mean? **Read U.C.C. § 3-106.** As you can see by reading U.C.C. § 3-106, there are three ways to make a writing conditional. What is the difference between an express condition and an implied condition? What is the difference between a writing that is "subject" to another writing and one that "refers" to another writing? **Read U.C.C. § 3-117.** How does that section relate to the effect of a separate agreement on the obligation to pay represented by an instrument? What contract doctrine does the phrase "subject to applicable law regarding exclusion of proof of contemporaneous or previous agreements" in U.C.C. § 3-117 refer to? For an example of an analysis of the application of U.C.C. § 3-117, see *Rogers v. Jackson*, 804 A.2d 379 (Me. 2002). Are the rules in U.C.C. § 3-106(c) and (d) exceptions to the principle of an "unconditional" promise or order?

Why might it be important for the promise or order to not have any conditions to it stated in a separate writing? Why might it be important for the promise or order to not have any conditions stated in the same writing that contains the promise or order? How might this requirement of unconditional be related to the idea of transferring the instrument free of claims and defenses to payment?

The promise or order must be to "pay a fixed amount of money, with or without interest or other charges described in the promise or order." We have already looked at the definition of "money" in U.C.C. § 1-201. A negotiable instrument may be payable in U.S. dollars or other currency that qualifies as "money." **Read U.C.C. § 3-107.**

What does it mean that the amount must be fixed? Is it referring to the principal amount, interest, or the costs of collecting the obligation? **Read U.C.C. § 3-112.** Does that help your understanding of this requirement?

The fourth requirement is that the promise or order must be "payable to bearer or order at the time it is issued or first comes into possession of a holder." This requirement is initially confusing because it uses the word "order" in a different sense than the word "order" has been used so far. This requirement also contains two concepts: a statement of how the instrument is payable ("payable to bearer or order") and a timing rule (as of time of "issue" or first in possession of a "holder"). Start with the concept of how the instrument has to be payable. Payable to bearer or order is explained in U.C.C. § 3-109. **Read U.C.C. § 3-109.**

Payable to order or to bearer language is akin to "magic words." For the language to make an instrument payable to bearer or to order, the form and syntax of the language in U.C.C. § 3-109 must be followed. **Read U.C.C. § 3-104(a)(1) and (c) and comment 2 to that section.** The payable to bearer or order language must be on the instrument at the time the instrument is first issued, U.C.C. § 3-105, or at the time the instrument first comes into possession of a holder. U.C.C. § 1-201(b)(21).

A promise or order that is payable to order requires that there be an "identified person" named in the instrument. U.C.C. § 3-110 provides rules for determining who is the person identified in the instrument. This section is very important in determining how the instrument may be negotiated (necessary to make someone a holder in due course) and who is the person entitled to payment of the instrument.

The fifth requirement is that the instrument must be "payable on demand or a definite time." These phrases are further defined in **U.C.C. § 3-108.**

Finally, the last requirement is that the instrument state no "other undertaking or instruction by the person promising or ordering payment to do any act in addition to payment of money" except as allowed in U.C.C. § 3-104(a)(3). How is this different from the requirement that the promise or order be "unconditional?"

Other terms may be included in an instrument without affecting negotiability. *See* **U.C.C. §§ 3-111, 3-113**. What terms might you want in a negotiable instrument if you were the person to whom the payment of money would be made? What about a promise to pay costs and fees for collection? How about a promise by the person to whom payment is made to apply the payments first to interest and then to principal?

An instrument that does not meet the U.C.C. § 3-104 requirements cannot be made negotiable by declaration. U.C.C. § 3-104, comment 2. Why is there this restriction on the idea of freedom of contract? Why is it important that parties not be able to opt into the rules governing negotiable instruments unless all of the requirements of U.C.C. § 3-104(a) are met? Why have an exception to this idea in U.C.C. § 3-104(c)? In some circumstances, the parties may make an instrument non-negotiable even if it meets these requirements. U.C.C. § 3-104(d). Why should we let parties opt out of the rules governing negotiable instruments?

Problem 2-1

At this point, you have read a base section, U.C.C. § 3-104, and a myriad of sections that give further content to the meaning of words and phrases contained in that base section. Construct a list of questions you must ask and answer to determine if a particular writing is a negotiable instrument, incorporating all of the sub-rules we have read in the text and comments of U.C.C. §§ 1-201, 3-103, 3-105 through 3-113, 3-117, as those sections relate to the six requirements of a negotiable instrument. This is an important skill to develop when working with a statutory scheme.

Notes

Now try your hand at these problems to determine in each instance whether there is a negotiable instrument. Remember, **ALL** of the requirements of U.C.C. § 3-104(a) (as further refined through the other sections we have looked at) must be met in order to have a negotiable instrument.

Problem 2-2

Evaluate whether each example meets the requirements of a negotiable instrument. In each case, Marla sent the following note to Pete on a piece of paper. If the item is a negotiable instrument, identify whether it is a draft or a note.

Notes

a) I agree to pay $100 to Pete in the event Pete needs money for his rent.
    Marla

b) I promise to pay Betty or her order on January 10, 2008, 10,000 euros with interest at the 90-day Treasury Rate adjusted monthly plus all costs of collection. This obligation is secured as stated in a security agreement dated January 5, 2006. This amount is payable at the residence of Marla.
    Marla

c) To: Pete
    From: Marla Rhodes
    Pay to bearer $1,000 30 days after sight.

d) I promise to pay to the order of Pete $1,000 on January 10, 2008, subject to prepayment without penalty at any time, as soon as Pete transfers his Sony high definition TV to me.

Marla

e) Pete, I would appreciate it if you would pay the $400 you owe me to the order of George on July 5, 2006.

Marla

Problem 2-3

Determine whether each communication is a negotiable instrument. If the item is a negotiable instrument, identify whether it is a note or a draft.

a) Fred sent the following email to Jane to pay a debt that Fred owed Jane:

From: Fred@abc.org
To: Jane@xyz.org

Pay to the order of Jane or bearer $1,000 on January 10, 2008, subject to acceleration in the event the holder deems itself insecure.

b) Alvin sent the following writing to Beth:

I promise to pay to Beth $1,000 on April 3, 2008, subject to an extension of time at the option of the holder hereof.
Alvin

Alvin and Beth had an agreement that Alvin would pay Beth pursuant to the terms of the writing only when Alvin had sufficient funds to make the payment.

c) Carl wrote the following on a napkin while drinking in a bar and gave the napkin to Sherry:

I promise to pay to the order of Santa Claus $1,000. I also agree to grant a security interest in my car to secure this obligation and to execute all documents necessary for that purpose. I waive presentment and notice of dishonor.
Carl

d) Jane wrote a note to Bill that stated:

I promise to pay Bill all amounts I owe Bill on January 3, 2008. The amounts owed to Bill shall be calculated based upon a contract dated July 1, 2004.
Jane

e) Betty signed a paper document that provided the following:

> The undersigned promises to pay to First Bank or bearer $10,000 plus 5% per annum interest on February 12, 2007 or on demand made before that time. This obligation is secured by collateral as stated in a security agreement dated July 2, 2003. All payments will be credited first to interest and then to principal.
>
> *Betty*

Problem 2-4

Draft a negotiable promissory note that encompasses the following terms. The borrower is John and the lender making the loan is State Bank.

- Principal: $15,000 payable in five years
- Interest: 2% over prime as set by the federal funds rate
- Acceleration in the event the holder deems itself insecure
- Prepayment with a 1% fee based upon the outstanding principal balance at time of prepayment
- All amounts owed secured by a security interest in the obligor's inventory
- Obligor agrees to pay all costs of collection, including attorney's fees
- Waiver of presentment and notice of dishonor
- Payable at the holder's offices on the due date

Notes

CHAPTER 3
CONTRACT LIABILITY ON A NEGOTIABLE INSTRUMENT

A. Overview

The payment system of negotiable instruments addresses the same four issues we have considered in the payment systems of currency and credit cards: (i) the mechanics of value transfer; (ii) incurring and satisfying the obligation to pay; (iii) enforcing the obligation to pay; and (iv) allocating the risks of errors and wrongdoing. While the discussion in Chapter 2 touched briefly on three of the four issues, we will now turn to these issues in greater detail in this Chapter and the chapters that follow.

Chapter 2 briefly discussed the treatment of a negotiable instrument as both a type of contract and as a type of property. We now turn to those issues in greater depth. This Chapter addresses a negotiable instrument as a type of contract. Chapter 4 addresses the negotiable instrument as a type of property. Contract liability on a negotiable instrument is concerned with the issues of incurring, satisfying, and enforcing the obligation to pay that the instrument represents. This contract liability is often referred to as "liability on the instrument" as opposed to other types of liability we will learn about that are referred to as "liability off the instrument." This concept is referred to as "contract" liability because many of the concepts that we will talk about are derived from principles of contract law. After all, as we learned in Chapter 2, if a writing is not a negotiable instrument, it may still qualify as an enforceable promise to pay money based on contract principles.

To provide an organized approach to these issues, the following questions will be addressed in this Chapter. First, how is the contract liability on the instrument incurred? Second, when is the person who incurred the contract liability on the instrument obligated to pay and to whom is that liability owed? Third, how does the person to whom the obligation is owed enforce the contract liability on the instrument? Fourth, how is the obligation to pay the contract liability discharged?

To answer these questions one must work through many sections of Article 3 of the U.C.C. To help you keep the details straight as we cover these sections, it is helpful to have in mind a big picture construct of the way that Article 3 addresses these four questions when the writing is a negotiable instrument. We have already learned that a negotiable instrument must be "signed" by the person ordering or promising payment. The person who signs a negotiable instrument will incur contract liability to pay the instrument, that is, will have liability "on the instrument."

In some circumstances, based upon agency law principles, a person signing a negotiable instrument results in binding a person that has not signed the instrument. For example, a corporate officer, acting within the scope of the officer's agency authority on behalf of the corporation to borrow money for corporate purposes, will bind the corporation to an obligation to pay the note when the corporate officer signs the note using the officer's own name. *See* U.C.C. § 3-402(a).

When a person signs a negotiable instrument, the person will sign it in a particular capacity. These capacities have names: "maker" U.C.C. § 3-103(a)(7); "drawer" U.C.C. § 3-103(a)(5); and "indorser" U.C.C. § 3-204. The capacity in which the person signs the negotiable instrument determines the liability of that person on the instrument. For example, a person that signs a negotiable note as a maker will incur liability on the note as stated in U.C.C. § 3-412 (a maker is an issuer of a note, U.C.C. § 3-105).

A person that signs a negotiable instrument will incur liability on the instrument to a particular person. Liability will be owed to "the person entitled to enforce" the instrument, U.C.C. § 3-301, and in some circumstances to an "indorser who has paid" the instrument. *See* U.C.C. § 3-414 (drawer's liability). It is these persons to whom the liability is owed who will be the proper plaintiffs to bring a lawsuit to enforce the signer's liability on the instrument.

The liability will also be owed at a particular time as determined by the terms of the instrument and the terms of the Article 3 section setting forth the liability owed. Consider what we learned in Chapter 2 regarding "payment on demand or at a definite time" as one of the requirements for a negotiable instrument. U.C.C. § 3-108. If a negotiable note is payable on demand, for example, in order to have the liability come due there must be a demand for payment. That demand for payment is called a "presentment." U.C.C. § 3-501. If the negotiable instrument is not paid when due, the instrument has been "dishonored." U.C.C. § 3-502. In some circumstances, in order to enforce a person's liability on an instrument, the person seeking enforcement must have given timely "notice of dishonor" to the person that signed the instrument. *See* U.C.C. § 3-415 regarding the liability of an indorser.

Assume a person entitled to enforce a negotiable instrument is seeking to enforce the terms of the instrument against the person who has signed the instrument. The plaintiff's case consists of proving that (i) the instrument is a negotiable instrument, (ii) the defendant is obligated on the instrument because of the signature, and (iii) the plaintiff is entitled to enforce the obligation. The defendant of course may try to challenge any aspect of the plaintiff's case and if the defendant is successful, the plaintiff will not win its case based on Article 3 principles. (But remember, the plaintiff may have a viable breach of contract case against the defendant.)

But suppose the defendant has a different type of defense, such as an argument that the obligation to pay should not be enforced because the defendant has a complaint about what was provided to the defendant when it issued the negotiable instrument. The plaintiff may respond to that defense by asserting that the defense may not be raised as against the plaintiff because the plaintiff qualified as a holder in due course. While the holder in due course idea is a complex concept (*see* U.C.C. § 3-302), the essence is that the holder in due course has taken the instrument for value, in good faith, and without notice of claims to the instrument and defenses to payment of the instrument. If the person entitled to enforce has the rights of a holder in due course, that person will take free of many defenses to payment and will take free of claims to the instrument. U.C.C. §§ 3-305, 3-306. A person who is entitled to enforce, but does not have the rights of a holder in due course, will be subject to all claims to the instrument and all defenses to payment of the instrument.

This litigation-oriented construct is set forth in U.C.C. § 3-308. **Read that section and its comments.** Compare that section and the comments with the overview given above of the typical plaintiff's claim and the defendant's response to that claim.

This introduction has set forth a schematic that addresses three of the four big picture questions posed at the beginning of this Chapter: (i) how is contract liability on an instrument incurred; (ii) when is the person with the contract liability obligated to pay and to whom is the obligation owed; and (iii) how is the contract liability enforced. The fourth question, how the contract liability is discharged, will be addressed after the details of the enforcement scheme as outlined above are explored in more detail.

B. Incurring the Obligation to Pay

As stated above, a person is not liable on a negotiable instrument unless the person has signed the instrument or is responsible for the signature. **Read U.C.C. §§ 3-401, 3-402, 3-403.** A person signs an instrument in a particular capacity. **Read the definitions of "maker," "drawer," "drawee," and "acceptor" in**

U.C.C. § 3-103. Read the definition of "acceptance" in U.C.C. § 3-409(a) and the rule on the liability of a drawee that does not sign an instrument, U.C.C. § 3-408. Read the definitions of "indorsement" and "indorser" in U.C.C. § 3-204(a) and (b).

As we learned in Chapter 2, a negotiable instrument is either a "note" or a "draft." U.C.C. § 3-104(e). A maker signs a note and is referred to as an "issuer" of the note. **Read U.C.C. § 3-105.** A maker's liability on a note is stated in U.C.C. § 3-412. **Read U.C.C. § 3-412** and review the overview describing the elements of the plaintiff's case for proving contract liability on the note. U.C.C. § 3-412 sets out the elements of a plaintiff's case in a suit against a maker. Now **review U.C.C. § 3-413(a)** on the contract liability of an acceptor, **U.C.C. § 3-414(b)** on the contract liability of a drawer of drafts that are not drawn on the drawer, and **U.C.C. § 3-415(a)** on the contract liability of an indorser. Each of these sections follow the same construct for the plaintiff's case to prove contract liability on the instrument as described in the introduction to this Chapter.

As you study the provisions of these sections and the comments, think about the following questions. What qualifies as a signature? Who incurs contract liability on an instrument by virtue of a signature? What if the person signing the instrument is an agent of a principal and the agent is signing the instrument on behalf of the principal? We briefly considered the principles of agency in Chapter 1 when we discussed authority for purposes of determining an "unauthorized use" when using a credit card.

Article 3 refers to the agent as a "representative" and the principal as the "represented person." When a representative signs a negotiable instrument, there are two separate questions: (i) is the representative bound by the signature; and (ii) is the represented person bound by the signature. U.C.C. § 3-402(b) and (c) address the first question. U.C.C. § 3-402(a) addresses the second question by reference to common law principles of agency. The representative's liability is determined in part by the form in which the representative signed the instrument. **Read U.C.C. § 3-402.**

What if the signature on the negotiable instrument is unauthorized, that is, a forgery or outside the scope of authority for an agent? **Read the definition of "unauthorized signature" in U.C.C. § 1-201(b)(41).** Who should be liable on an instrument if the signature is unauthorized? An unauthorized signature results in the unauthorized signer incurring liability. **Read U.C.C. § 3-403.** For example, if X signs Y's name to an instrument and that signature is not authorized under U.C.C. § 3-402(a), Y is not liable on the instrument but X is liable on the instrument to a person who in good faith paid or took the instrument for value. An unauthorized signature, however, may be ratified by post-signing words or conduct. U.C.C. § 3-403(a). Thus Y could ratify X's signing of Y's name. Generally ratification would require that Y act with knowledge of X's signing of the instrument and Y retaining the benefits received in the transaction in which X signed Y's name. *See QAD Investors, Inc. v. Kelly*, 776 A.2d 1244 (Me. 2001).

In order to raise the issue of whether the signature on a negotiable instrument is authentic or made with the requisite authority, the defendant in an action to enforce the defendant's contract liability on an instrument must specifically deny in the pleadings that the signature was authentic or made with authority. **Reread U.C.C. § 3-308(a).** Thus, to continue the example above, if the person entitled to enforce sues Y on the basis of X's signature of Y's name on a negotiable instrument, Y must specifically deny in the answer to the complaint that it is Y's signature and that X was authorized to sign Y's name. Once a defendant puts the signature's validity into question by the specific denial, the person entitled to enforce must prove that the signature is valid. As we will study in Chapter 6, in some circumstances a defendant may be precluded from raising the invalidity of a signature. *See* U.C.C. §§ 3-406, 4-406.

The first step in analyzing contract liability on an instrument is to identify the type of instrument (a note or a draft). The second step is to identify the capacity in which the potential defendant has signed the instrument: drawer, maker, acceptor, or indorser. The third step is to determine if the signature is authentic and authorized. To test your understanding of these concepts, try your hand at the following problem.

Problem 3-1

Identify the type of instrument (note or draft), whether the instrument is "signed," the capacity of the person signing (maker, drawer, acceptor, indorser), and who has contract liability on the instrument.

Notes

a)
| January 5, 2006 |
| I, Martin Best, promise to pay to the order of Jane Doe, the sum of $2000 on demand. |
| *Martin Best* |

b)

> January 5, 2006
> I, Martin Best, promise to pay to the order of Jane Doe, the sum of $2000 on demand.
>
>   *M*

Any change in analysis from part (a) above?

c)

> January 5, 2006
> To: Acme Co.
> Pay to the order of Finance Co. the sum of $2000.
>
>   *Bill Dunn*

Assume that Bill Dunn did not sign the instrument, Ed Johnston signed Bill's name.

d)

> January 5, 2006
> To: Acme Co.
> Pay to the order of Finance Co. the sum of $2000.
>
>   *Bill Dunn by Ed Johnston, agent*

Assume that Bill authorized Ed to sign the instrument. Would it make any difference in your analysis if Bill did not authorize Ed to sign the instrument?

e)
> January 5, 2006
> To: Acme Co.
> Pay to the order of Finance Co. the sum of $2000.
> *Bill Dunn*

Bill signed his own name to the writing. After delivery of the writing to Finance Co., Finance Co.'s treasurer applied the following stamp to the back of the writing as follows:
FINANCE CO.

f)
> Bill Dunn
> 123 Main St.
> Evans, OH　　　　Jan. 5, 2006
>
> Pay to the order of Finance Co. $2000.
>
> First Bank
> 456 Johnson St.
> Evans, OH
> 　　　　　　*Ed Johnston*

Does it make any difference if Bill authorized Ed to sign the writing on behalf of Bill?

g)

> January 5, 2006
> To: Acme Co.
> Pay to the order of Finance Co. the sum of $2000.
>
> *Bill Dunn*

Bill Dunn signed his own name. After Bill Dunn delivered the writing to Finance Co., Finance Co. took the writing to Acme Co. and asked Acme's president to sign the writing. Acme's president, Sue Acme, signed the writing on the back as follows:

Acme Corp. by Sue Acme, President

h)

> January 5, 2006
> The undersigned promises to pay to the order of First Bank or bearer the sum of $20,000 plus interest at 5% per annum one year from the date hereof.
>
> *Tool Supply Co., Jane Tool, President*

This writing was executed in return for a loan of $20,000 from First Bank. Would your analysis change if Jane Tool also signed the writing on the back as follows:

Jane Tool

Notes

i)
> January 5, 2006
> To: First State Bank
> Pay to the order of Acme Co.
> $20,000.
>
> *First State Bank*

Would it change your analysis if the clerk that signed First State Bank's name was not authorized to do so?

j) Would it make any difference in your analysis of part (h) above who received the proceeds of the loan, Tool Supply Co. or Jane Tool?

C. To Whom the Contract Obligation is Owed: Person Entitled to Enforce

Sections 3-412 through 3-415 each set forth to whom the contract obligations are owed. In each case, the obligation is owed, among others, to the person entitled to enforce the instrument. It is to that concept we now turn. **Read U.C.C. § 3-301.** A person will be entitled to enforce the instrument if that person falls within one of the three categories set forth in that section.

The first category is a holder. Holder is defined in U.C.C. § 1-201(b)(21). Whether someone is a holder of an instrument depends upon whether the instrument is payable to bearer or payable to order. U.C.C. § 3-109. A person may become a holder of an instrument in one of two ways: issuance of the instrument (**U.C.C. § 3-105**) or negotiation of the instrument (**U.C.C. § 3-201**). **Read U.C.C. §§ 3-301, 1-201(b)(21), 3-105, and 3-201.**

To illustrate the concept of a "holder," consider the following example. Assume the drawer of a check makes a check payable to the order of cash. This check would be a bearer instrument. When the drawer gives that check to someone else, the check is issued under U.C.C. § 3-105 but not negotiated under U.C.C. § 3-201. Do you see why from reading those two sections? The person in possession is a holder under U.C.C. § 1-201(b)(21) and a person entitled to enforce under

U.C.C. § 3-301. Continue the example. Assume that the initial transferee of the check gave possession of the check to another person. That transfer would be a negotiation under U.C.C. § 3-201. Mere transfer of possession, even if involuntary, is a negotiation of a bearer instrument. **Compare U.C.C. § 3-203**.

If the instrument is an order instrument, a different analysis applies. Assume the drawer of a check makes a check payable to the order of Ned Smith. Under U.C.C. § 3-109 the check is an order instrument. When the drawer of the check gives that check to anyone, either Ned Smith or someone else, that is an issuance under U.C.C. § 3-105, but not a negotiation under U.C.C. § 3-201. Do you see why?

Assume that the issuance of the check was to Ned Smith, the named payee, and the drawer intended that Ned be the payee of the check. *See* U.C.C. § 3-110(a). Ned is a holder under U.C.C. § 1-201(b)(21) and thus a person entitled to enforce under U.C.C. § 3-301. If the issuance was not to Ned Smith, such as if the drawer gave the check to Barb Jones even when the check was made out to Ned Smith, Barb Jones would not be a holder under U.C.C. § 1-201(b)(21). Do you see why?

Now assume Ned Smith has possession of the check in which he is the named payee. In order for him to make anyone else a holder of the instrument, he has to transfer possession and also indorse the instrument. Do you see why?

Indorsement is defined in **U.C.C. § 3-204**. There are several different types of indorsement:

    (i) special or blank;

    (ii) qualified or unqualified; and

    (iii) restricted or unrestricted.

Section 3-205 defines special and blank indorsements. Notice that a special indorsement need not use the "magic words" we encountered in evaluating whether an instrument was payable to order under U.C.C. § 3-109. Section 3-415(b) allows an indorsement without recourse, which usually is identified as a qualified indorsement. Restrictive indorsements come into play most often in the bank collection process for instruments and will be taken up more fully when that process is discussed. *See* U.C.C. § 3-206. A person may not indorse an instrument in such a way as to attempt to restrict further transfer or negotiation of that instrument or to condition the right of the indorsee to receive payment. Attempts to do so will be unsuccessful. U.C.C. § 3-206(a), (b). **Read U.C.C. §§ 3-204, 3-205 and 3-206.**

Given that there are six categories of indorsement types, the indorsement must be evaluated to determine what type it is. To continue the example above, assume a check states "pay to the order of Ned Smith." The six categories of indorsement for that check are illustrated by the following chart. For each type of indorsement, determine the steps the current holder needs to take after the indorsement is placed on the check in order to negotiate the check to so that the next person is a holder of the check.

Also think about who must indorse the instrument in each example so as to make the next person a holder. **Read U.C.C. § 3-110.**

Manner in which instrument payable	Type of indorsement	Action needed for further negotiation
(a) Pay to the order of Ned Smith	Blank, unqualified, unrestricted Indorsement: Ned Smith	
(b) Pay to the order of Ned Smith	Blank, qualified, unrestricted Indorsement: Ned Smith, without recourse	
(c) Pay to the order of Ned Smith	Blank, qualified, restricted Indorsement: Ned Smith, without recourse, for deposit only	
(d) Pay to the order of Ned Smith	Special, unqualified, unrestricted Indorsement: Pay to Alice Jones, Ned Smith	
(e) Pay to the order of Ned Smith	Special, qualified, unrestricted Indorsement: Pay to Alice Jones, Ned Smith without recourse	

Manner in which instrument payable	Type of indorsement	Action needed for further negotiation
(f) Pay to the order of Ned Smith	Special, qualified, restricted Indorsement: Pay to Alice Jones in trust for Carrie Bonds, Ned Smith without recourse	
(g) Pay to the order of Ned Smith/John Smith	Indorsement: John Smith	
(h) Pay to the order of Spiderman (Spiderman is Ned Smith's nickname.)	Indorsement: Spiderman without recourse	
(i) Pay to the order of the CFO of General Mills Co.	Indorsement: Bill Jones, CFO	

An instrument payable to bearer may also be indorsed, even though it need not be, to be negotiated to the next person. When a bearer instrument is indorsed, it is often for the purpose of obtaining the indorser's contract obligation on the instrument. Thus sometimes an instrument will be indorsed by someone even if that person is not a holder. This is called an "anomalous" indorsement. **Reread U.C.C. § 3-204 and § 3-205.**

Even though there are two other methods for becoming a person entitled to enforce, what we have discussed above is geared toward identifying who is the "holder" of an instrument. Being able to recognize who is a "holder" is critical to determining whether someone qualifies as that special type of holder–a holder in due course. A holder in due course must, first of all, be a "holder."

Problem 3-2

Identify whether the instrument has been issued or negotiated and whether the person in possession of the instrument is a holder. If someone is not a holder, what should have been done to make that person a holder?

Notes

a) Abby wrote a check for $10 payable to the order of "Bill or bearer" and signed by Abby as drawer. Abby gave the check to Carl. Has the check been issued or negotiated to Carl? Is Carl a holder of the check?

b) Abby wrote a check for $10 payable to the order of "Bill" and signed by Abby as drawer. Abby gave the check to Carl. Has the check been issued or negotiated to Carl? Is Carl a holder of the check?

c) Abby wrote a check for $10 payable to the order of "Bill" and signed by Abby as drawer. Abby gave the check to Bill. Bill gave the check to Carl. When Abby gave the check to Bill, was that an issuance or a negotiation of the check? When Bill gave the check to Carl, was that a negotiation of the check? Is Carl a holder of the check?

d) Abby wrote a check for $10 payable to the order of "Bill" and signed by Abby as drawer. Abby gave the check to Bill. Bill wrote on the back of the check "Bill" and lost the check. Carl picked up the check. Is Carl a holder? When the check moved from Bill to Carl, was that a negotiation?

e)   Abby wrote a check for $10 payable to the order of "Bill" and signed by Abby as drawer. Bill wrote on the back of the check "Bill without recourse." Bill gave the check to Carl. Is Carl a holder? What is Bill's contract liability on the check?

f)   Abby wrote a check for $10 payable to the order of "Bill" and signed by Abby as drawer. Abby wrote "without recourse" next to her signature on the bottom right hand corner of the check. What is Abby's contract liability on the check? Same answer if the instrument is a draft but not a check?

g)   Abby wrote a check for $10 payable to the order of "Bill" and signed by Abby as drawer. Bill wrote on the back of the check "Bill without recourse." Bill gave the check to Carl. Carl delivered the check to Dan. Is Dan a holder? Does Carl have any contract liability on the instrument?

h)   Abby wrote a check for $10 payable to the order of "Bill" and signed by Abby as drawer. Bill wrote on the back of the check "Pay to Carl, Bill." Bill gave the check to Carl. Is Carl a holder? What must Carl do to further negotiate the check?

Notes

i)   Abby wrote a check for $10 payable to the order of "Bill" and signed by Abby as drawer. Bill wrote on the back of the check, "Pay to Carl if Carl paints my house, Bill" and gave possession of the check to Carl. Is Carl a holder? How can Carl transfer the check to someone else and make that next person a holder?

j)   Abby wrote a check for $10 payable to the order of "Bill and Ted" and signed by Abby as drawer. She gave the check to Bill. What must Bill do to negotiate the check to Carl? Would it make any difference if the check was payable to the order of "Bill or Ted"? What if the check was payable to the order of "Bill/Ted"?

So far, the focus has been on the first category of persons listed in U.C.C. § 3-301 as a person entitled to enforce, the holder. The second category of person entitled to enforce is a nonholder in possession of an instrument who has the rights of a holder. This person may obtain the rights of a holder based upon a voluntary transfer of possession of the instrument as provided in **U.C.C. § 3-203**, or by other principles of law. **Read that section and the definition of "delivery" in U.C.C. § 1-201.** Section 3-203 is an expression of the concept of derivative title, a person may transfer only the rights that person has under the instrument. What does it mean to have the "rights of a holder" even if the person in possession is not a holder in its own right? For example, assume that Jane wrote a check for $20 payable to the order of Ben. Jane delivered the check to Ben. Without indorsing the check in any manner, Ben delivered the check to Scott. By now you should recognize that Scott would not be a "holder" of the check. If you are not sure why, review the material we have just covered. Is Scott a "nonholder in possession with the rights of a holder"? What do you need to know in order to answer that question? **Review U.C.C. § 3-203.**

The third category of a person who is "entitled to enforce" is a person not in possession of an instrument who is entitled to enforce the instrument in the situations provided in U.C.C. §§ 3-309 and 3-418(d). At this point, we will concentrate on the requirements of U.C.C. § 3-309 concerning lost or stolen instruments. **Read U.C.C. § 3-309**. We will consider U.C.C. § 3-418 in Chapter 6 when we consider recovery when there are errors or wrongdoing concerning a negotiable instrument.

Problem 3-3

Notes

a) Ann signed a negotiable note as maker for $100, payable to the order of "Brad." Brad gave the note to Candy without indorsing the note. Is Candy a person entitled to enforce Ann's contract liability on the instrument against Ann?

b) Ann signed a negotiable note as maker for $100, payable to the order of "Brad." Brad wrote on the back of the note, "Pay to Doug, Brad." Brad then delivered the note to Candy. Is Candy a person entitled to enforce Ann's contract liability against Ann? Is Candy a person entitled to enforce Brad's contract liability against Brad?

c) Ann signed a negotiable note as maker for $100, payable to the order of "Brad." Brad wrote on the back of the note, "Pay to Doug, Brad." Brad then delivered the note to Candy. Candy gave the note to Doug. Doug then gave the note to Ernie. Is Ernie a person entitled to enforce Ann's

Notes

contract liability against Ann? Is Ernie a person entitled to enforce Brad's contract liability against Brad? Does Doug have any contract liability on the instrument?

d) Alvin signed a negotiable note for $100 as maker, payable to the order of "Betty." Betty had possession of the note but then misplaced it. If Betty cannot find the note, may Betty be a person entitled to enforce Alvin's contract liability against Alvin? What would Betty have to prove to be able to enforce the note even though she no longer has possession of it? Same analysis if the note is stolen from Betty? Same analysis if Betty gave the note to Carl instead of misplacing the note?

D. When the Obligation is Due

Once the proper plaintiff is determined (that is, who is entitled to enforce) and the proper defendant is determined (that is who is responsible for the signature and in what capacity), the issue is when is the contract obligation due. **Reread U.C.C. § 3-412, liability of an issuer of a note.** The maker is obligated to pay according to the terms of the note. We have already discussed the terms of the note regarding time of payment. A negotiable instrument must be payable either on demand or at a definite time. **Review U.C.C. § 3-108.** It may also state the place of payment. *See* U.C.C. § 3-111. The instrument will also state how much is payable. **Review U.C.C. §§ 3-104, 3-107, 3-112. Now look at U.C.C. §§ 3-413(a), 3-414(b), and 3-415(a).** Each of these sections specifies that the obligation of the relevant "signer" of the instrument is to pay according to the terms of the instrument.

Each of these sections also specifies the time the terms of the instrument are to be determined. For the obligation of a maker of a note or a drawer of a draft, the terms of the instrument are determined as of the time the instrument was issued, or if not issued, when it first came into possession of a holder. If the issuer or drawer signed an incomplete instrument, in some circumstances the maker or the drawer may be liable based on the terms of the writing as completed. **Review U.C.C. § 3-412 and § 3-414 and find these principles stated in those sections.**

An acceptor's liability on the instrument is determined by the terms of the instrument at the time it was accepted or if the acceptor signed the draft while it was incomplete, in some circumstances by the terms at the time of completion. U.C.C. § 3-413. An indorser's liability on an instrument is determined by the terms of the instrument at the time of indorsement, or if the indorser signed the instrument while it was incomplete, in some circumstances by the terms of the instrument as completed. U.C.C. § 3-415.

Now take a closer look at the obligation of a drawer as stated in U.C.C. § 3-414. Notice that the obligation of a drawer of a draft that the drawee has not "accepted" (review U.C.C. § 3-409 on the meaning of "acceptance") is owed upon dishonor of the draft. If the draft is not dishonored, the drawer's obligation on an unaccepted draft is not yet due. **Read U.C.C. § 3-502(b) on dishonor of an unaccepted non-documentary draft.** Notice that when that type of draft is dishonored depends upon whether the draft is a check, how the draft is presented to the drawee, and whether the draft is payable at a definite time or on demand. Section 3-502(b) defines dishonor by referring to a "presentment," which can either be a presentment for payment or a presentment for "acceptance." **Read U.C.C. § 3-501 which defines presentment and sets forth rules regarding the process of presentment.** If the drawee has "accepted" the draft, the accepted draft is dishonored as stated in U.C.C. § 3-502(d). Notice that U.C.C. § 3-501 applies to either a presentment for payment or a presentment for acceptance. Based upon these two sections, consider the following problem.

Problem 3-4

Notes

a) Acme Co. is the payee of a negotiable nondocumentary draft payable on demand. Bill is the drawer of the draft. Craig is the drawee. Acme Co. sent an e-mail message to Craig demanding payment of the draft. Has Acme Co. made a proper presentment?

Notes

b) Allison is a payee of a check. Bank is the drawee and has established a cutoff hour of 3 p.m. for presentment of instruments. Allison presented the check at 4 p.m. to the teller at Bank. The teller told Allison that it will pay the check by the end of the next business day. Has Bank dishonored the check?

c) Acme Co. is the payee of a negotiable nondocumentary draft payable on demand. Bill is the drawer of the draft. Craig is the drawee. Acme transferred the draft for value to Doug without signing the draft. To negotiate the draft to Doug, Acme should have indorsed the draft. Doug presented the draft to Craig, demanding payment. Craig refused to pay because Acme had not signed the draft. Has Craig dishonored the draft?

d) Acme Co. is the payee of a negotiable nondocumentary draft payable on May 3. Bill is the drawer of the draft. Craig is the drawee. May 3 comes and goes. Has Craig dishonored the draft? Would your answer change if the instrument was a negotiable note?

e) John is the payee of a check drawn on Bank. John goes to Bank and exhibits the check to the teller, asking Bank to pay him the funds represented by the check. The teller informs John that in order to cash the check he must place his thumbprint on the back of the check in addition to signing the check on the back. John signs the check on the back but refuses to place his thumbprint on the check. Bank teller refuses to pay the amount of the check to John. Has Bank dishonored the check? *See Messing v. Bank of America, N.A.*, 821 A.2d 22 (Md. 2003).

f) John is the payee of a negotiable nondocumentary draft payable on May 3. Acme Co. is the drawer and National Insurance is the drawee. On April 3, John presented the draft to National Insurance and asked National Insurance to "accept" the draft. If National Insurance refused to "accept" the draft, is there a dishonor?

g) Assume in part (f) above, that National Insurance signed the front of the draft when John presented it. John then signed the draft and transferred it to ABC Corp. ABC Corp. then took the draft to National Insurance on May 1, demanding payment of the draft. On May 2, National Insurance refused to pay. Has National Insurance dishonored the draft?

h) Would your analysis of parts (f) and (g) above change if the draft was payable on demand?

Now consider the liability of an indorser as stated in U.C.C. § 3-415. Not only must the instrument be dishonored (U.C.C. § 3-502) for the indorser's liability to arise, in most cases the indorser must also be given notice of dishonor. Notice of dishonor is governed by U.C.C. § 3-503. In some circumstances, notice of dishonor may be excused as stated in U.C.C. § 3-504. **Read U.C.C. §§ 3-503 and 3-504.**

Section 3-504 also allows for waiver of presentment by the terms of the instrument. **Read U.C.C. § 3-502(e).** If the terms of the instrument waive presentment and the instrument is a demand instrument, when will the instrument be considered dishonored?

A drawee that accepts the draft has the liability stated in U.C.C. § 3-413. Review the meaning of acceptance as stated in U.C.C. § 3-409. Now consider the effect of an "acceptance" of the draft by the drawee on the obligation of the drawer of the draft or an indorser of the draft. **Read U.C.C. §§ 3-414(d) and (e), 3-415(d), and 3-410.**

Problem 3-5

Notes

a) Alice is the payee of a negotiable note payable on demand. Brett is the maker of the note. The note contains the following clause: "All parties to this instrument waive presentment and notice of dishonor." Must Alice make a presentment to Brett and Brett refuse to pay before the note is dishonored?

b) Ann is the payee of a negotiable note payable on demand. Brad is the maker of the note. Ann indorsed the note in blank and delivered the note to Candy. Candy presented the note to Brad. Brad refused to pay. What does Candy have to do in order to enforce Ann's indorsement contract? How is notice of dishonor given? When must notice of dishonor be given? If a notice of dishonor is timely mailed to

Notes

Ann but she does not receive it, is notice of dishonor effective? *See* U.C.C. § 1-202.

c) Ann is the payee of a negotiable note payable on May 3. Brad is the maker of the note. Ann indorsed the note in blank and delivered the note to Candy. Candy presented the note to Brad on May 3. Brad refused to pay. The note provides that "presentment of this instrument is not required." What does Candy have to do in order to enforce Ann's indorsement contract?

d) Same facts as (b) above, except that prior to Candy presenting the note to Brad, Brad told Ann that he would not pay the note. Does that change your analysis of problem (b)? *See* Comment to U.C.C. § 3-504 and former U.C.C. § 3-511. What is the difference between "waiver" and "excuse?"

e) Same facts as (b) above. Candy gave Ann notice of dishonor 40 days after Brad's dishonor of the instrument. The reason that Candy waited so long was that Candy was in a location that suffered an earthquake and resulting in an interruption in mail service. Can Candy enforce Ann's indorsement contract?

f)   John is the payee of a negotiable nondocumentary draft payable on May 3. Acme Co. is the drawer and First Bank is the drawee. John presented the draft to First Bank on May 1. First Bank signed the draft on the front. John then indorsed the draft in blank and transferred the draft to Amy. If First Bank refuses to pay the draft when Amy presents it on May 3, against whom will Amy be able to enforce contract liability on the draft? Does she need to give notice of dishonor to anyone? Would your analysis change if John indorsed the draft before First Bank signed the draft? What if the drawee is National Insurance Co., does that change your analysis?

g)   John is the payee of a check drawn on State Bank and issued by Mary, the drawer. John indorses the check in blank and deposits the check in his checking account at Commerce Bank and Commerce Bank forwards the check for collection to State Bank. State Bank dishonors the check and returns the check to Commerce Bank the next day. What must Commerce Bank do to be able to enforce John's indorsement contract?

We will return to presentment, dishonor, and notice of dishonor when we study the check collection system in Chapter 5.

E. To Whom the Obligation is Owed: Persons Not "Entitled to Enforce"

Reread U.C.C. §§ 3-412, 3-413, 3-414, and 3-415. In each section, the contract obligation of the relevant signer is also owed to a person that is not entitled to enforce. Each section states that the obligation defined in the section is owed to "an indorser who paid the instrument." In the case of the indorser's contract liability, that obligation is owed to "a subsequent indorser who has paid the instrument." U.C.C. § 3-415. Finally, an acceptor also has contract liability to a drawer who has paid the draft. U.C.C. § 3-413.

The following example illustrates this concept. Assume a negotiable note payable to the order of P and signed by M as maker. P indorsed the note in blank and transferred the note to T. T demanded M pay the note (presentment). M refused to pay (dishonored) the note. T gave P notice of dishonor and demanded P pay the note. P did so. P now demands M pay the note. Under U.C.C. § 3-412, M owes its contract liability on the note to P, an indorser who has paid the note.

Problem 3-6

Notes

a) Ari issued a negotiable demand draft for $10 payable to the order of "Bruce" and signed by Ari as drawer. Bruce indorsed the draft, "Pay Chris, Bruce." Bruce gave the draft to Chris. Chris indorsed the draft, "Pay Darla, Chris" and delivered the draft to Darla. Darla presented the draft to the drawee Xavier. Xavier refused to pay.   What does Darla do next? Against whom can Darla enforce a contract liability on the draft?

b) Assume in part (a) above that Darla gave timely notice of dishonor to Chris and demanded that Chris pay the draft. Chris did so. Against whom may Chris enforce the contract liability on the draft? To whom must Chris give notice of dishonor? How long does Chris have to give notice of dishonor?

c) Ari issued a negotiable draft payable on May 3 for $10 and payable to the order of "Bruce." Ari signed the draft as the drawer. Bruce indorsed the draft, "Pay Chris, Bruce." Bruce gave the draft to Chris. Chris indorsed the draft, "Pay Darla, Chris" and delivered the draft to Darla. Darla presented the draft to the drawee Xavier on May 1. Xavier signed the draft on the front and returned it to Darla. Darla presented the draft again on May 3 and Xavier refused to pay. What does Darla do next? Against whom may Darla enforce any contract liability on the instrument? Does it matter whether Xavier is a bank?

d) Same facts as (c) above. Xavier is not a bank. Darla collects from Ari on Ari's drawer's contract. From whom may Ari recover?

F. Enforcement of the Obligation: Defenses, Claims in Recoupment, and Holder in Due Course

Reread U.C.C. § 3-308. That section sets forth the structure of litigation concerning contract liability on the instrument. As we have been learning, the plaintiff's case consists of proving that the instrument is a negotiable instrument, the defendant is responsible for the signature on the instrument, the plaintiff is a person entitled to enforce the contract liability on the instrument of that particular defendant, and the defendant's contract obligation on the instrument is due. All the material from Chapter 2 to this point in Chapter 3 demonstrate the elements of the plaintiff's case. Of course, the defendant may try to show that the plaintiff has not proven an element of its case. While in a litigation sense, that is a "defense," the defendant demonstrating that the plaintiff has not proven an element of the plaintiff's case is not a "defense" as the word is used in Article 3.

If the defendant cannot demonstrate that one or more of the elements of the plaintiff's case is lacking, the defendant then has to consider whether it has a defense to payment of the obligation on the instrument or a claim in recoupment that reduces the amount due on the instrument.

Read U.C.C. § 3-305(a). This section identifies various defenses based upon contract law and the availability of a claim in recoupment. A defense to payment means that the obligor on the instrument does not have to pay the instrument. A claim in recoupment is a type of "defense" that means the obligation on the instrument should be reduced by a counterclaim that the defendant may assert against the plaintiff. **Read comment 3 to U.C.C. § 3-305 for a discussion of claims in recoupment.** Claims in recoupment should not be confused with claims to an instrument under U.C.C. § 3-306. Claims to an instrument will be discussed in Chapter 4.

Identify various types of defenses that may be available to a defendant. All that you learned in your first year contracts course is applicable here. For example, assume that there is a mutual mistake that would justify not enforcing a contract under common law principles. That is an example of the type of defense referred to U.C.C. § 3-305(a)(2). Article 3 also provides defenses to a defendant. **Read comment 2 to U.C.C. § 3-305.** That comment lists various defenses to payment that are referred to by the statutory language of U.C.C. § 3-305(a)(2).

The plaintiff's response to an assertion of a defense to payment or a claim in recoupment is to argue that the defense or claim in recoupment is not assertable against the plaintiff because the plaintiff is a holder in due course or has the rights of a holder in due course that is not subject to that defense or claims in recoupment. The defenses listed in U.C.C. § 3-305(a)(1) are often referred to as the "real" defenses and the defenses set forth in subsection (a)(2) as the personal defenses. **Read comment 1 to U.C.C. § 3-305.**

Read U.C.C. § 3-305(b). Generally, a holder in due course is subject to the real defenses listed in U.C.C. § 3-305(a)(1) but not the personal defenses (subsection (a)(2)) or claims in recoupment (subsection (a)(3)). This general rule protecting a holder in due course is subject to an exception embodied in the phrase "against a person other than the holder." This phrase has been interpreted to mean that even if the plaintiff is a holder in due course, that plaintiff is subject to discharge of which it has notice, U.C.C. § 3-601, defenses arising contemporaneously or subsequent to the transfer of the instrument to the holder in due course, and defenses as a result of the holder in due course's own behavior. Of course, a holder in due course is also subject to any arguments that may serve to defeat one or more elements of its case, such as that the signature on the instrument is not authentic.

A holder in due course has such favored status (that is taking the instrument free from most defenses and claims in recoupment) because an ability to transfer instruments without the usual baggage connected to assignment of contract rights is thought necessary for commercial trade. Generally, an assignee of a contract is subject to all defenses that could be asserted by the obligor against the assignor (review the discussion in Chapter 2 on that point). The holder-in-due-course construct alters that common law principle.

So what does it take to be a holder in due course? **Read U.C.C. § 3-302.** In order to be a holder in due course, one must be a "holder." Everything that we have learned about negotiation of a negotiable instrument is relevant to that inquiry. Section 3-302 sets out many additional requirements that must be met in order for a person to qualify as a holder in due course. *All of the elements of the rule must be met.* In other words, if the person qualifies as a holder but does not take the instrument "for value," the person does not qualify as a holder in due course. If the person qualifies as a holder and takes the instrument for value but does not take the instrument "in good faith," the person is not a holder in due course. Some of the terms listed in U.C.C. § 3-302 are further explained in other sections. Read the following sections: value, **U.C.C. § 3-303**; notice, **U.C.C. § 1-202**; overdue, **U.C.C. § 3-304**; good faith, **U.C.C. § 3-103(a)(6) or 1-201(b)(20)**. Make a checklist of the elements of holder-in-due-course status, incorporating the meaning of the further definitions into your checklist.

At what point in time must the person asserting holder-in-due-course status meet all the requirements? Section 3-302 contains timing words by focusing in subsection (a)(1) on when the instrument was "issued or negotiated" to the holder and in subsection (a)(2) on when the holder "took" the instrument.

As you consider the following material, keep in mind these issues: (i) the requirements for becoming a holder in due course; (ii) defenses and claims in recoupment that may not be asserted against a holder in due course; and (iii) defenses that may be asserted against someone that does not have the status of a holder in due course.

MAINE FAMILY FEDERAL CREDIT UNION V. SUN LIFE ASSURANCE COMPANY OF CANADA
727 A.2d 335 (Me. 1999)

Saufley, J.

We are called upon here to address the concept of "holder in due course" as defined by recent amendments to the negotiable instruments provisions of the Maine Uniform Commercial Code. We conclude that, pursuant to those amendments, the Superior Court (Cumberland County, Calkins, J.) did not err when it entered a judgment based on the jury's finding that the Maine Family Federal Credit Union was not a holder in due course. Because we find, however, that Sun Life Assurance Company was not entitled to raise a third party's defense of fraud to its liability as drawer of the instruments, we vacate that portion of the judgment entered in favor of Sun Life and against the Credit Union.

I. Facts

Daniel, Joel, and Claire Guerrette are the adult children of Elden Guerrette, who died on September 24, 1995. Before his death, Elden had purchased a life insurance policy from Sun Life Assurance Company of Canada, through Sun Life's agent, Steven Hall, and had named his children as his beneficiaries. Upon his death, Sun Life issued three checks, each in the amount of $40,759.35, to each of Elden's children.[1] The checks were drawn on Sun Life's account at Chase Manhattan Bank in Syracuse, New York.[2] The checks were given to Hall for delivery to the Guerrettes.

The parties have stipulated that Hall and an associate, Paul Richard, then fraudulently induced the Guerrettes to indorse the checks in blank and to transfer them to Hall and Richard, purportedly to be invested in "HER, Inc.," a corporation

---

[1] "'Issue' means the first delivery of an instrument by the maker or drawer, whether to a holder or nonholder, for the purpose of giving rights on the instrument to any person." 11 M.R.S.A. § 3-1105(1) (1995).

[2] Accordingly, Sun Life was the drawer of the checks. "'Drawer' means a person who signs or is identified in a draft as a person ordering payment." 11 M.R.S.A. § 3-1103(1)(c) (1995). Chase Manhattan was the "drawee." "'Drawee' means a person ordered in a draft to make payment." 11 M.R.S.A. § 3-1103(1)(b) (1995). More specifically, Chase Manhattan was also the "payor bank." "'Payor bank' means a bank that is the drawee of a draft." 11 M.R.S.A. § 4-105(2) (1995).

formed by Hall and Richard.[3] Hall took the checks from the Guerrettes and turned them over to Richard, who deposited them in his account at the Credit Union on October 26, 1995.[4] The Credit Union immediately made the funds available to Richard.

The Guerrettes quickly regretted having negotiated their checks to Hall and Richard, and they contacted Sun Life the next day to request that Sun Life stop payment on the checks. Sun Life immediately ordered Chase Manhattan to stop payment on the checks.[5] Thus, when the checks were ultimately presented to Chase Manhattan for payment, Chase refused to pay the checks, and they were returned to the Credit Union.

The Credit Union received notice that the checks had been dishonored on November 3, 1995, the sixth business day following their deposit.[6] By that time, however, Richard had withdrawn from his account all of the funds represented by

---

[3] "'Indorsement' means a signature, other than that of a signer as maker, drawer or acceptor, that alone or accompanied by other words is made on an instrument for the purpose of: (a) Negotiating the instrument; (b) Restricting payment of the instrument; or (c) Incurring indorser's liability on the instrument." 11 M.R.S.A. § 3-1204(1) (1995).

[4] Maine Family Federal Credit Union is a "federally chartered credit union," regulated by the National Credit Union Administration. *See* 12 U.S.C.A. § 1752a (Law.Co-op.1996). It qualifies as an "insured credit union" under the Federal Credit Union Act, 12 U.S.C.A. §§ 1751-1795k (Law. Co-op.1996 & Supp.1998), and is therefore subject to the provisions of Regulation CC. 12 C.F.R. § 229 (1998).

By accepting the checks for deposit, Maine Family Federal Credit Union became the "depositary bank." Under Maine law, "'[d]epositary bank' means the first bank to take an item ... unless the item is presented for immediate payment over the counter." 11 M.R.S.A. § 4-105(1) (1995).

[5] "A customer ... may stop payment of any item drawn on the customer's account ... by an order to the bank describing the item or account with reasonable certainty received at a time and in a manner that affords the bank a reasonable opportunity to act on it before any action by the bank with respect to the item...." 11 M.R.S.A. § 4-403(1) (1995). Thus Sun Life, as the customer of Chase Manhattan Bank, had the right to order Chase Manhattan to stop payment on the three checks deposited by Paul Richard at the Maine Family Federal Credit Union.

[6] "Notice of dishonor may be given by any person and by any commercially reasonable means, including an oral, written or electronic communication, and is sufficient if it reasonably identifies the instrument and indicates that the instrument has been dishonored or has not been paid or accepted." 11 M.R.S.A. § 3-1503(2) (1995).

the three checks. The Credit Union was able to recover almost $80,000 from Richard, but there remained an unpaid balance of $42,366.56, the amount now in controversy.

The Credit Union filed a complaint against Sun Life alleging that Sun Life was liable as drawer of the instruments, and that Sun Life had been unjustly enriched at the Credit Union's expense. Although it could have done so, the Credit Union did not originally seek any recovery from the Guerrettes. Sun Life, however, filed a third-party complaint against Daniel Guerrette and Paul Richard, whose signatures appeared on the back of one of the checks.[7] The Credit Union then filed a cross-claim against third-party defendants Guerrette and Richard, alleging that they were liable as indorsers of the checks,[8] and Daniel Guerrette filed cross-claims against the Credit Union and against Sun Life. Finally, Sun Life eventually filed third-party complaints against Joel and Claire Guerrette.

The Credit Union moved for summary judgment. The Superior Court held, as a matter of law, that Daniel Guerrette had raised a "claim of a property or possessory right in the instrument or its proceeds," 11 M.R.S.A. § 3-1306 (1995), and therefore that Sun Life was entitled to assert that claim as a "defense" against the Credit Union. *See* 11 M.R.S.A. § 3-1305(3) (1995).[9] The court found, however, that a genuine issue of material fact remained as to whether the Credit Union had acted in "good faith" when it gave value for the checks--a fact relevant to determining whether the Credit Union was a holder in due course. *See* 11 M.R.S.A. § 3-1302(1)(b)(ii) (1995). Accordingly, the court denied the Credit Union's motion for summary judgment, and the matter proceeded to trial.

---

[7] For reasons that have remained unexplained, Daniel Guerrette and Paul Richard together filed a joint answer to the original third-party complaint. Paul Richard, of course, later stipulated that he had fraudulently induced Daniel Guerrette to transfer the check to him.

[8] Paul Richard ultimately consented to judgment being entered against him on the Credit Union's cross-claim.

[9] Section 3-1305(3) provides, in part:
> ... [I]n an action to enforce the obligation of a party to pay the instrument, the obligor may not assert against the person entitled to enforce the instrument a defense, claim in recoupment or claim to the instrument (section 3-1306) of another person, but the other person's claim to the instrument may be asserted by the obligor if the other person is joined in the action and personally asserts the claim against the person entitled to enforce the instrument.

11 M.R.S.A. § 3-1305(3).

At trial, the only issue presented to the jury was whether the Credit Union had acted in "good faith" when it gave value for the checks, thus entitling it to holder in due course status. (footnote omitted) At the close of evidence, the Credit Union made a motion for a judgment as a matter of law, which the Superior Court denied. The jury found that the Credit Union had not acted in good faith and therefore was not a holder in due course. Therefore, the Superior Court entered judgment in favor of Sun Life, Daniel, Joel, and Claire, and against the Credit Union. The court denied the Credit Union's renewed motion for judgment as a matter of law and motion to amend the judgment, and the Credit Union filed this appeal.

II. Obligations of the Parties

At the heart of the controversy in this case is the allocation of responsibility for the loss of the unpaid $42,366.56, given the fact that Paul Richard and Steven Hall, the real wrongdoers, appear to be unable to pay. Maine, like the other forty-nine states, has adopted the Uniform Commercial Code. Under the Maine U.C.C., Articles 3-A and 4 deal with "Negotiable Instruments" and "Bank Deposits and Collections." *See* 11 M.R.S.A. §§ 3-1101, 4-101 (1995). It is these statutes that govern the parties' dispute.

Pursuant to Article 4 of the Maine U.C.C., the Credit Union, as a depositary bank, is a "holder" of the instruments,[11] *see* 11 M.R.S.A. § 4-205(1) (1995),[12] making it a "person entitled to enforce" the instrument under Article 3-A. *See* 11 M.R.S.A. § 3-1301(1) (1995). Upon producing an instrument containing the valid

---

[11] An "instrument" refers to a "negotiable instrument." *See* 11 M.R.S.A. § 3-1104(2) (1995). A "negotiable instrument" is a signed writing evidencing an unconditional promise or order to pay a fixed sum of money on demand or at a definite time to order or to bearer. *See generally* 11 M.R.S.A. §§ 3-1104(1), 3-1103(1)(i), 3-1104 cmt. 1 (1995). A "draft" is a negotiable instrument that is an order. *See* 11 M.R.S.A. § 3-1104(5) (1995). The definition of a "check" includes "[a] draft, other than a documentary draft, payable on demand and drawn on a bank." *See* 11 M.R.S.A. § 3-1104(6)(a) (1995).

[12] 11 M.R.S.A. § 4-205(1) provides that a depositary bank becomes a holder of an item if the item was deposited by a customer who was also a holder. The Credit Union's customer, Paul Richard, became a holder of the checks when Daniel, Joel, and Claire indorsed them in blank and transferred them to Richard and Hall. *See* 11 M.R.S.A. § 3-1201(1) (1995) (" 'Negotiation' means a transfer of possession, whether voluntary or involuntary, of an instrument by a person other than the issuer to a person who thereby becomes its holder."); 11 M.R.S.A. § 3-1202(1)(b) (1995) ("Negotiation is effective even if obtained ... [b]y fraud.").

signature of a party liable on the instrument, a person entitled to enforce the instrument is entitled to payment, unless the party liable proves a defense or claim in recoupment, *see* 11 M.R.S.A. § 3-1308(2) (1995), or a possessory claim to the instrument itself. *See* 11 M.R.S.A. § 3-1306.

Because their signatures appear on the backs of the checks, Daniel, Joel, and Claire are "indorsers" of the checks. *See* 11 M.R.S.A. § 3-1204(1), (2) (1995). As indorsers, they are obligated to pay the amounts due on each dishonored instrument "[a]ccording to the terms of [each] instrument at the time it was indorsed." 11 M.R.S.A. § 3-1415(1)(a) (1995).[13] This obligation is owed "to a person entitled to enforce the instrument or to a subsequent indorser who paid the instrument under this section." *Id.*

As drawer of the checks, Sun Life is obligated to pay each dishonored instrument "[a]ccording to its terms at the time it was issued." 11 M.R.S.A. § 3-1414(2)(a) (1995). Again, this obligation is owed to a person entitled to enforce the instrument or to an indorser who paid the draft under section 3-1415. *See* 11 M.R.S.A. § 3-1414(2) (1995). Chase Manhattan, as drawee of these checks, was not obligated to accept them for payment, *see* 11 M.R.S.A. § 3-1408 (1995), and therefore has not been made a party to this action.

Unless the Credit Union is a holder in due course, its right to enforce the obligations of the drawer and indorsers of the instruments is subject to a variety of defenses, including all those defenses available "if the person entitled to enforce the instrument[s] were enforcing a right to payment under a simple contract." *See* 11 M.R.S.A. § 3-1305(1)(b) (1995). In addition, its right to enforce is subject to any claims in recoupment, *see* 11 M.R.S.A. § 3-1305(1)(c) (1995), or claims to the instruments themselves. *See* 11 M.R.S.A. § 3-1306. If, however, the Credit Union establishes that it is a "holder in due course," it is subject to only those few defenses listed in section 3-1305(1)(a). *See* 11 M.R.S.A. § 3-1305(2) (1995). None of those specific defenses is applicable here. Thus, the Credit Union argues that because it is entitled as a matter of law to holder in due course status, it is entitled to enforce the instruments against the Guerrettes and Sun Life.

---

[13] If, however, the instrument is accepted for payment, if the instrument is not presented for payment in a timely fashion, or if notice of dishonor is not given to an indorser in a timely fashion, her indorser's liability is discharged. *See* 11 M.R.S.A. § 3-1415(3)-(5) (1995).

III. Holder in Due Course
A. Burden of Proof and Standard of Review

A holder in due course is a holder who takes an instrument in good faith, for value, and without notice of any claims or defenses. *See* 11 M.R.S.A. § 3-1302(1) (1995). Once the persons who may be liable on the instruments have raised a recognized defense to that liability, the burden is on the holder to prove by a preponderance of the evidence that it is a holder in due course. *See New Bedford Inst. for Sav. v. Gildroy*, 36 Mass.App.Ct. 647, 634 N.E.2d 920, 925 (1994).[14] If it fails in that proof, the persons otherwise liable on the instruments may avoid liability if they prove a defense, claim in recoupment, or possessory claim to the instrument. *See* 11 M.R.S.A. §§ 3-1305(1)(b), 3-1308(2).

The issue of whether a party is a holder in due course is usually one of fact, although "where the facts are undisputed and conclusive, [a court] can determine ... holder in due course status as a matter of law." *See Triffin v. Dillabough*, 552 Pa. 550, 716 A.2d 605, 611 (1998). In this case, the Superior Court declined to decide the holder in due course issue as a matter of law, and submitted the question to the jury. The jury found that the Credit Union was not a holder in due course, implicitly because the Credit Union did not act in good faith.

The Credit Union argues that the court erred in failing to find, as a matter of law, that it was a holder in due course. "We review the denial of a motion for judgment as a matter of law 'to determine if any reasonable view of the evidence and those inferences that are justifiably drawn from that evidence supports the jury verdict.' " *Larochelle v. Cyr*, 707 A.2d 799, 1998 ME 52, ¶ 6, 707 A.2d 799 (*quoting Davis v. Currier*, 1997 ME 199, ¶ 3, 704 A.2d 1207). The question before us, therefore, is whether any reasonable view of the evidence, along with any justifiable inferences therefrom, can possibly support the jury's conclusion that the Credit Union did not act in good faith and therefore was not a holder in due course. Alternatively stated, the question is whether the evidence compelled a finding that the Credit Union was a holder in due course. If there is any rational basis for the

---

[14] The Credit Union argues that neither Sun Life nor Daniel Guerrette satisfied their burdens of pleading with respect to the issue of fraud. A party may satisfy his burden of pleading a specific affirmative defense if he puts the opposing parties on notice that the issue will be raised at trial. *See Bolduc v. Watson*, 639 A.2d 629, 630 (Me.1994); *Federal Deposit Ins. Corp. v. Notis*, 602 A.2d 1164, 1165 (Me.1992). Contrary to the Credit Union's argument, the pleadings were sufficient to alert the Credit Union that fraud would be raised as an issue to shield the defendants from liability. The Credit Union's argument is therefore without merit.

jury's verdict, we must affirm the judgment.

B. *Good Faith*

We therefore turn to the definition of "good faith" contained in Article 3-A of the Maine U.C.C.[15] In 1990, the National Conference of Commissioners on Uniform State Law recommended substantial changes in the U.C.C. The Maine Legislature responded to those recommendations in 1993 by repealing the entirety of Article 3 and enacting a new version entitled Article 3-A, which contains a new definition of "good faith." While the previous version of the good faith definition only required holder to prove that it acted with "honesty in fact," the new definition provides:

> "Good faith" means honesty in fact *and the observance of reasonable commercial standards of fair dealing.*

11 M.R.S.A. § 3-1103(1)(d) (1995) (emphasis added). Because the tests are presented in the conjunctive, a holder must now satisfy both a subjective and an objective test of "good faith."[16]

1. Honesty in Fact

Prior to the changes adopted by the Legislature in 1993, the holder in due course doctrine turned on a subjective standard of good faith and was often referred to as the "pure heart and empty head" standard. *See* M.B.W. Sinclair, *Codification of Negotiable Instruments Law: A Tale of Reiterated Anachronism*, 21 U. TOL. L.REV. 625, 654 (1990); *see also Seinfeld v. Commercial Bank & Trust Co.*, 405 So.2d 1039, 1042 (Fla.Dist.Ct.App.1981) (noting that the U.C.C. "seem[s] to

---

[15] We reject the Credit Union's argument that the good faith element of holder in due course status was not intended to encompass the giving of value for the check. Unless the depositary bank has given value, it cannot become a holder in due course, and its conduct is not scrutinized for compliance with section 3-1302. To determine whether a holder is a holder in due course, the factfinder must determine whether the holder acted with good faith when it took the checks and gave value for them.

[16] The U.C.C. Prefatory Note of National Conference of Commissioners on Uniform State Laws and the American Law Institute lists the new definition of "good faith" among the "benefits to users" of the revised Article 3. The Notes states that:

> The definition of good faith...is expanded to include observance of reasonable commercial standards of fair dealing. This objective standards for good faith applies to the performance of all duties and obligations established under Articles 3 and 4.

protect the objectively stupid so long as he is subjectively pure at heart"). That standard merely required a holder to take an instrument with "honesty in fact" to become a holder in due course.[17]

Courts interpreting this language have routinely declared banks to be holders in due course, notwithstanding the failures of these banks to investigate or hold otherwise negotiable instruments, when they took the instruments with no knowledge of any defects, defenses, or stop payment orders. *See, e.g., UAW-CIO Local # 31 Credit Union v. Royal Ins. Co.*, 594 S.W.2d 276, 279 (Mo.1980) (*en banc*); *Bank of New York v. Asati, Inc.*, 15 UCC Rep.Serv.2d (CBC) 521, 1991 WL 322989 (N.Y.Sup.Ct. July 8, 1991). This approach has been understood to promote the negotiability of instruments, particularly checks, in the stream of commerce. Rejecting a contrary approach, one court put it bluntly:

> The requirement urged by defendant would bring the banking system to a grinding halt. A stop payment order issued by the drawer to the drawee which is unknown to the paying-collecting bank cannot fasten upon the paying bank any legal disability; particularly it cannot reduce the status of the collecting bank to a mere assignee of the instrument or a holder of a non-negotiable instrument, or a mere holder of a negotiable instrument.
> *Mellon Bank, N.A. v. Donegal Mutual Ins. Co.*, 29 UCC Rep.Serv. (CBC) 912, 1980 WL 98414 (Pa. Ct. C.P. Alleghany County, Jan. 8, 1980).

Although courts were often urged to engraft an objective reasonableness standard onto the concept of "honesty in fact," most refused to do so.[18] Their refusals recognized that: "[T]he check is the major method for transfer of funds in commercial practice. The maker, payee, and indorsers of a check naturally expect it will be rapidly negotiated and collected.... The wheels of commerce would grind to a halt [if an objective standard were adopted]." *Bowling Green, Inc. v. State St. Bank & Trust*, 425 F.2d 81, 85 (1st Cir.1970).

---

[17] Because we are required to interpret the current definition of "good faith" for purposes of holder in due course status--a definition which is not without ambiguity--we look to the history of the definition for guidance. "When the language of a statute is ambiguous, we 'look beyond the words of the statute to its history, the policy behind it, and other extrinsic aids to determine legislative intent.'" *Arsenault v. Crossman*, 1997 Me. 92, ¶7, 696 A.2d 418 (1997)(*quoting State v. Fournier*, 617 A.2d 998, 1000 (Me. 1992)); *accord Salenius v. Salenius*, 654 A.2d 426, 429 (Me. 1995).

[18] *But see, e.g., Seinfeld*, 405 So.2d at 1042 n.4 (applying what many have viewed as an objective standard of good faith).

Moreover, under the purely subjective standard, a bank was not expected to require the presence of offsetting collected funds in the customers' account in order to give value on newly deposited checks: "A bank's permitting its customers to draw against uncollected funds does not negate its good faith." *Asati, Inc.*, 15 UCC Rep.Serv.2d at 521; *accord Vail Nat'l Bank v. J. Wheeler Constr. Corp.*, 669 P.2d 1038, 1039-40 (Colo.Ct.App.1983); *Flagship Bank of Orlando v. Central Florida Coach Lines, Inc.*, 33 UCC Rep.Serv. (CBC) 613, 1981 WL 138010 (Pa. Ct. C.P. Luzerne County, Oct. 13, 1981); *Mellon Bank*, 29 U.C.C. Rep.Serv. at 912; *Central Bank & Trust Co. v. First Northwest Bank*, 332 F.Supp. 1166, 1170 (E.D.Mo.1971), *aff'd*, 458 F.2d 511 (8th Cir.1972); *Citizens Nat'l Bank of Englewood v. Fort Lee Sav. & Loan Ass'n*, 89 N.J.Super. 43, 213 A.2d 315, 319 (Law Div.1965).

Application of the "honesty in fact" standard to the Credit Union's conduct here demonstrates these principles at work. It is undisputed that the Credit Union had no knowledge that Richard obtained the Sun Life checks by fraud. Nor was the Credit Union aware that a stop payment order had been placed on the Sun Life checks. The Credit Union expeditiously gave value on the checks, having no knowledge that they would be dishonored. In essence the Credit Union acted as banks have, for years, been allowed to act without risk to holder in due course status. The Credit Union acted with honesty in fact.

Thus, had the matter at bar been decided before the Legislature's addition of the objective component of "good faith," there can be little question that the Credit Union would have been determined to have been a holder in due course. Because it took the instruments without notice of any possible dishonor, defect, fraud, or illegality, it could have given value immediately and yet have been assured of holder in due course status. *See Mellon Bank*, 29 UCC Rep.Serv. at 912; *Industrial Nat'l Bank of Rhode Island v. Leo's Used Car Exchange, Inc.*, 362 Mass. 797, 291 N.E.2d 603, 606 (1973); *New Bedford Inst.*, 634 N.E.2d at 925; *Triffin*, 716 A.2d at 611. Today, however, something more than mere subjective good faith is required of a holder in due course.

2. Reasonable Commercial Standards of Fair Dealing

We turn then to the objective prong of the good faith analysis. The addition of the language requiring the holder to prove conduct meeting "reasonable commercial standards of fair dealing" signals a significant change in the definition of a holder in due course.[19] While there has been little time for the development of a body of law interpreting this new objective requirement, there can be no mistaking the fact that a holder may no longer act with a pure heart and an empty head and still obtain holder in due course status.[20] The pure heart of the holder must now be accompanied by reasoning that assures conduct comporting with reasonable commercial standards of fair dealing.

The addition of the objective element represents not so much a new concept in the doctrinal development of holder in due course status, but rather a return, in part, to an earlier approach to the doctrine. *See* JAMES J. WHITE & ROBERT S. SUMMERS, UNIFORM COMMERCIAL CODE § 14-6, at 62829 (3d ed.1988) (discussing the objective test of good faith in England, first applied by the King's Bench in *Gill v. Cubitt*, 3 B & C 466, 107 Eng.Rep. 806 (K.B.1824)). The concept of an objective component of good faith has been part of the discussion regarding the holder in due course doctrine since the first enactment of the U.C.C. *See id.* (noting that "[t]he good faith requirement has been the source of a continuing and ancient dispute"). The early drafters debated the need and wisdom of including such an objective component and ultimately determined *not* to include it in the definition of good faith because of its potential for freezing commercial practices. *See Sinclair, supra*, at 653-54 (noting, in particular, the objection by the banking industry to the addition of an objective good faith component). The "new" element of good faith requiring the holder to act according to reasonable commercial standards of fair dealing is actually a more narrow version of the "reasonable person" standard considered and rejected by the drafters o [sic] the 1962 Code.

The new objective standard, however, is not a model of drafting clarity. Although use of the word "reasonable" in the objective portion of the good faith test may evoke concepts of negligence, the drafters attempted to distinguish the concept of "fair" dealing from concepts of "careful" dealing:

---

[19] "The new definition of good faith *substantially affects*...the requirements for holder in due course status." HAWKLAND & LAWRENCE UCC SERIES § 3-103:05 (Rev Art 3)(emphasis added).

[20] The objective requirement, however, has generated a number of articles and commentaries on the reason, meaning, and anticipated interpretations of the changes. *See, e.g.*, Patricia L. Heatherman, *Comment, Good Faith in Revised Article 3 of the Uniform Commercial Code: Any Change? Should There Be?* 29 WILLAMETTE L. REV. 567 (1993); Kerry Lynn Macintosh, *Liberty, Trade, and the Uniform Commercial Code, When Should Default Rules be Based on Business Practices?* 38 WM. & MARY L. REV. 1465, 1466 (1997).

> Although fair dealing is a broad term that must be defined in context, it is clear that it is concerned with the fairness of conduct rather than the care with which an act is performed. Failure to exercise ordinary care in conducting a transaction is an entirely different concept than failure to deal fairly in conducting the transaction.

U.C.C. § 3-103 cmt. 4 (1991).

Unfortunately, the ease with which the distinction between "fair dealing" and "careful dealing" was set forth in the comments to the U.C.C. revisions belies the difficulty in applying these concepts to the facts of any particular case, or in conveying them to a jury. The difficulty is exacerbated by the lack of definition of the term "fair dealing" in the U.C.C.[21] The most obvious question arising from the use of the term "fair" is: fairness to whom? Transactions involving negotiable instruments have traditionally required the detailed level of control and definition of roles set out in the U.C.C. precisely because there are so many parties who may be involved in a single transaction. If a holder is required to act "fairly," regarding all parties, it must engage in an almost impossible balancing of rights and interests. Accordingly, the drafters limited the requirement of fair dealing to conduct that is reasonable in the commercial context of the transaction at issue. In other words, the holder must act in a way that is fair according to commercial standards that are themselves reasonable.

The factfinder must therefore determine, first, whether the conduct of the holder comported with industry or "commercial" standards applicable to the transaction and, second, whether those standards were reasonable standards intended to result in fair dealing. Each of those determinations must be made in the context of the specific transaction at hand. If the fact finder's conclusion on each point is "yes," the holder will be determined to have acted in good faith even if, in the individual transaction at issue, the result appears unreasonable. Thus a holder may be accorded holder in due course status where it acts pursuant to those reasonable commercial standards of fair dealing--even if it is negligent--but may lose that status, even where it complies with commercial standards, if those standards are not reasonably related to achieving fair dealing.

Therefore the jury's task here was to decide whether the Credit Union observed the banking industries' commercial standards relating to the giving of value on

---

[21] One commentator has suggested that fair dealing refers to "playing by the rules." *See* Heatherman, *supra*, at 585. Yet "the rules" ordinarily define the parameters of reasonable conduct, a concept which sounds much like a negligence analysis.

uncollected funds, and, if so, whether those standards are reasonably designed to result in fair dealing.

The evidence produced by the Credit Union in support of its position that it acted in accordance with objective good faith included the following: The Credit Union's internal policy was to make provisional credit available immediately upon the deposit of a check by one of its members. In certain circumstances--where the check was for a large amount and where it was drawn on an out-of-state bank--its policy allowed for a hold to be placed on the uncollected funds for up to nine days. The Credit Union's general written policy on this issue was reviewed annually--and had always been approved--by the National Credit Union Administration, the federal agency charged with the duty of regulating federal credit unions. *See* 12 U.S.C.A. § 1752a (Law.Co-op.1996). In addition, the policy complied with applicable banking laws, including Regulation CC. *See* 12 C.F.R. §§ 229.12(c), 229.13(b) (1998).

The Credit Union also presented evidence that neither Regulation CC nor the Credit Union's internal policy *required* it to hold the checks or to investigate the genesis of checks before extending provisional credit. It asserted that it acted exactly as its policy and the law allowed when it immediately extended provisional credit on these checks, despite the fact that they were drawn for relatively large amounts on an out-of-state bank.[22] Finally, the Credit Union presented expert testimony that most credit unions in Maine follow similar policies.

In urging the jury to find that the Credit Union had not acted in good faith, Sun Life and the Guerrettes argued that the Credit Union's conduct did not comport with reasonable commercial standards of fair dealing when it allowed its member access to provisional credit on checks totaling over $120,000 drawn on an out-of-state bank without either: (1) further investigation to assure that the deposited checks would be paid by the bank upon which they were drawn, or (2) holding the instruments to allow any irregularities to come to light.

The applicable federal regulations provide the outside limit on the Credit Union's ability to hold the checks. Although the limit on allowable holds established by law is evidence to be considered by the jury, it does not itself establish reasonable commercial standard of fair dealing. The fact finder must consider all of the facts relevant to the transaction. The amount of the checks and

---

[22] The Credit Union could also have withheld provisional credit under the law and its own internal policy if there were other reasons to doubt the validity of the checks. *See* 12 C.F.R. § 229.13(e) (1998).

the location of the payor bank, however, are relevant facts that a bank, observing reasonable commercial standards of fair dealing, takes into account when deciding whether to place such a hold on the account. The jury was entitled to consider that, under Regulation CC, when a check in an amount greater than $5,000 is deposited, or when a check is payable by a nonlocal bank, a credit union is permitted to withhold provisional credit for longer periods of time than it is allowed in other circumstances. *See* 12 C.F.R. § 229.13(b), (h) (1998). Therefore, the size of the check and the location of the payor bank are, under the objective standard of good faith, factors which a jury may also consider when deciding whether a depositary bank is a holder in due course.

The Credit Union's President admitted the risks inherent in the Credit Union's policy and admitted that it would not have been difficult to place a hold on these funds for the few days that it would normally take for the payor bank to pay the checks. He conceded that the amount of the checks were relatively large, that they were drawn on an out-of-state bank, and that these circumstances "could have" presented the Credit Union with cause to place a hold on the account. He also testified to his understanding that some commercial banks followed a policy of holding nonlocal checks for three business days before giving provisional credit.[23] Moreover, the Credit Union had no written policy explicitly guiding its staff regarding the placing of a hold on uncollected funds. Rather, the decision on whether to place a temporary hold on an account was left to the "comfort level" of the teller accepting the deposit. There was no dispute that the amount of the three checks far exceeded the $5,000 threshold for a discretionary hold established by the Credit Union's own policy.

On these facts the jury could rationally have concluded that the reasonable commercial standard of fair dealing would require the placing of a hold on the uncollected funds for a reasonable period of time and that, in giving value under these circumstances, the Credit Union did not act according to commercial standards that were reasonably structured to result in fair dealing.

We recognize that the Legislature's addition of an objective standard of conduct in this area of law may well have the effect of slowing the "wheels of commerce."[24]

---

[23] There was evidence that, on the second business day after he deposited the checks, Paul Richard notified the Credit Union that there may have been a problem with his deposit.

[24] The new definition of "good faith" has been forecasted by some to bring possible "undesirable changes" to the law of negotiable instruments. *See* Henry J. Bailey, *New 1990*
(continued...)

As one commentator noted:

> Historically, it was always argued that if negotiable instruments were to be usefully negotiable a subsequent holder should not have to investigate the transaction giving rise to the paper. The paramount necessity of negotiability has dominated thinking and legislation on negotiable instruments law. Drafts and promissory notes, it has been believed, must be able to change hands freely, without investigation beyond the face of the instrument, and with no greater requirement than the indorsement of the holder.

Sinclair, supra, at 630 (footnotes omitted). Notwithstanding society's oftcited need for certainty and speed in commercial transactions, however, the Legislature necessarily must have concluded that the addition of the objective requirement to the definition of "good faith" serves an important goal. The paramount necessity of unquestioned negotiability has given way, at least in part, to the desire for reasonable commercial fairness in negotiable transactions.

IV. Effect of Fraud Defense
A. The Guerrettes

Having failed to persuade the jury that it was a holder in due course, the Credit Union is subject to any defense of the Guerrettes or Sun Life "that would be available if the person entitled to enforce the instrument were enforcing a right to payment under a simple contract," 11 M.R.S.A. § 3-1305(1)(b), or any "claim of a property or possessory right in the instrument or its proceeds." 11 M.R.S.A. § 3-1306. Generally, fraud, such as that perpetrated by Paul Richard and Steven Hall, may be the basis for both a valid defense, *see Silber v. Muschel,* 190 A.D.2d 727, 593 N.Y.S.2d 306, 307 (1993), and a valid claim to the instrument itself. *See generally Bowling Green, Inc. v. State St. Bank & Trust Co.,* 307 F.Supp. 648, 651-52 (D.Mass.1969), *aff'd,* 425 F.2d 81 (1st Cir.1970).

Fraud is an affirmative defense to a contract. *See* M.R. Civ. P. 8(c). To prevail on their fraud defense, the Guerrettes were required to prove, by clear and convincing evidence, that a fraudulent or material misrepresentation induced them to transfer the proceeds of their father's life insurance policy, in the form of the Sun Life checks, to Steven Hall and Paul Richard. In addition, they were required to

---

[24] (...continued)
Uniform Commercial Code: Article 3, Negotiable Instruments, and Article 4, Bank Deposits and Collections, 29 WILLAMETTE L. REV. 409, 415 (1993).

prove they were justified in relying on the fraudulent misrepresentation. *See Kuperman v. Eiras*, 586 A.2d 1260, 1261 (Me.1991). The parties' stipulation that Hall and Richard fraudulently induced the Guerrettes to invest the checks in their company, HER, Inc., is sufficient to satisfy the Guerrettes' burden on this issue. The Guerrettes are not liable to the Credit Union for their indorsement of the Sun Life checks.

B. Sun Life

Sun Life, however, may not raise the fraud as a defense to its liability on the instrument. Section 3-1305(3) provides generally that:

> in an action to enforce the obligation of a party to pay [an] instrument, the obligor may not assert against the person entitled to enforce the instrument a defense, claim in recoupment or claim to the instrument (section 3-1306) of another person.

11 M.R.S.A. § 3-1305(3). Accordingly, a defense to liability on an instrument--such as fraud in the underlying transaction--raised by one party to an action may not be raised by another party to the action as its own defense to liability. Section 3-1305(3) provides, however, that "the other person's claim to the instrument may be asserted by the obligor if the other person is joined in the action and personally asserts the claim against the person entitled to enforce the instrument." *Id.* Therefore, only if the Guerrettes have made a claim to the instrument and are parties to the proceeding may Sun Life assert the fraud in defense of its own liability. *See* 11 M.R.S.A. 3-1305(3); *First Nat'l Bank of Nocona v. Duncan Sav. & Loan Ass'n*, 656 F.Supp. 358, 366 (W.D.Okla.1987), *aff'd*, 957 F.2d 775 (10th Cir.1992).

The Guerrettes, however, made no claim that they were entitled to possession of the instruments held by the Credit Union.[25] Instead, they merely argued that they were not liable as indorsers of the checks held by the Credit Union as a result of the fraud. The issue of fraud was therefore raised by the Guerrettes as a defense to their liability as indorsers of the instruments. *See Louis Falcigno Enters., Inc. v. Massachusetts Bank & Trust Co.*, 14 Mass.App.Ct. 92, 436 N.E.2d 993, 993-94 (1982). The Superior Court erred when it held that the issue of fraud had been raised as a "claim to the instruments."

Therefore, Sun Life may not raise the fraud against the Guerettes as a defense to its own liability. Because Sun Life raises no other relevant defenses, it is liable

---

[25] The Guerrettes were issued new checks for the same amounts by Sun Life after Sun Life stopped payment on the original instruments.

to the Credit Union as the drawer of the instruments, *see* 11 M.R.S.A. § 3-1414(2)(a), and we vacate that portion of the Superior Court's judgment finding that Sun Life was not liable to the Credit Union.

The entry is:

Judgment in favor of Daniel, Joel, and Claire Guerrette and against Maine Family Federal Credit Union affirmed. Judgment in favor of Sun Life Assurance Company of Canada and against Maine Family Federal Credit Union vacated and remanded for further proceedings consistent with the opinion herein.

Why was it important to determine whether the Credit Union in the *Maine* case was a holder in due course? For a different view of similar facts see *Mid Wisconsin Bank v. Forsgard Trading Inc.*, 668 N.W. 2d 830, 833 (Wis. Ct. App. 2003) (". . . it does not matter whether, as here, the account had been overdrawn previously. Mid Wisconsin's policy is to place holds on checks when it has reasonable doubt about the check based on the depositor's history. Here there was no reasonable doubt. Whenever Forsgard had been overdrawn previously, it always deposited funds to cover the overdraft when the bank alerted it to the problem. Mid Wisconsin had no reason to suspect there would be any problem if immediate credit was extended for this check. Consequently, we conclude that Mid Wisconsin observed reasonable commercial standards of fair dealing and therefore was a holder in due course.").

Problem 3-7

Notes

a) Denny issued a negotiable note to Electronics Inc. in payment for a big screen TV. Electronics Inc. promised to deliver the TV on Tuesday. Electronics Inc. fails to do so.

(i) Does Denny have a defense to payment of the note or a claim in recoupment?

(ii) Electronics Inc. negotiated the note to a holder in due course. May Denny assert a defense or claim in recoupment against the holder in due course?

b) Denny issued a negotiable note to Electronics Inc. in payment for a big screen TV. Electronics Inc. promised to deliver the TV on Tuesday. Electronics did so, but the TV did not have a good picture.   In the sale transaction between Electronics Inc. and Denny, Electronics had warranted that the TV would be merchantable.

   (i) Does Denny have a defense to payment of the note or a claim in recoupment?

   (ii) Electronics Inc. negotiated the note to a holder in due course. May Denny assert a defense or claim in recoupment against the holder in due course?

c) Ted is 14 years old but appears older. He contracted to buy a car from Acme Cars and signed a negotiable promissory note payable to the order of "Acme Cars" for $5,000, the purchase price of the car minus Ted's down payment.

   (i) Does Ted have a defense to payment of the note?

   (ii) Acme Cars negotiated the note to a holder in due course. Does Ted have a defense to payment that he may assert against the holder in due course?

d) Ted is 30 years old and a recent immigrant from Greece. He does not speak or read English. Ted decided to go into business for himself. He rented a store from Eddie, a landlord who is fluent in both Greek and English. Eddie put two documents in front of Ted, a lease and a negotiable promissory note. The lease obligated Ted to make reasonable rental payments for the store. The promissory note contained a promise to pay $10,000 on demand to the order of Eddie. Both documents were written in English. Ted signed both documents without reading them.

(i) Does Ted have a defense to payment of the note?

(ii) Eddie negotiated the note to a holder in due course. Does Ted have a defense to payment that he may assert against the holder in due course?

(iii) Assume Ted is fluent in English. The understanding between Ted and Eddie was that Eddie would not seek to collect on the note unless Ted defaulted on the lease. Eddie negotiated the note to a holder in due course. Does Ted have a defense to payment that he may assert against the holder in due course?

e) Barry issued a check to his landlord in payment of the rent for his apartment. The landlord agreed not to cash the rent check until the landlord had fixed the stove in Barry's apartment. The landlord did not fix the stove but deposited the check in his bank account. Barry stopped payment on the check so that the drawee bank dishonored the check.

(i) Does Barry have a defense to payment of the check?

(ii) The landlord in cashing the check negotiated it to his bank when he deposited the check to the landlord's bank account. When the drawee bank dishonored the check, the check was returned to the depositary bank. Assume the depositary bank is a holder in due course. Does Barry have a defense to payment that may be asserted against the holder in due course?

(iii) The depositary bank collected the amount of the dishonored check from the landlord. The landlord seeks to collect from Barry. Does Barry have a defense to payment against the landlord? Does it matter whether the landlord is a holder in due course when she took the check?

f) Craig issued a negotiable note to the order of First Bank in exchange for a loan. First Bank's president indorsed the note "First Bank" and transferred it to Second Bank in exchange for a promise to pay First Bank 80% of the face amount of the note. Second Bank then transferred the note to Third Bank in exchange for a cash payment of

Notes

85% of the face value of the note. Assume Third Bank is a holder in due course. Third Bank presented the note to Craig and he dishonored it. Third Bank sued First Bank on the note for indorser liability.

(i) Third Bank did not give notice of dishonor to First Bank as required by U.C.C. § 3-503. Does First Bank have a defense in the lawsuit by Third Bank?

(ii) Assume Third Bank gave timely notice of dishonor to First Bank and Second Bank had defaulted on its promise to pay First Bank. Does First Bank have a defense to payment it may assert against Third Bank?

Reread U.C.C. §§ 3-302, 3-303, 3-304, 1-202, and 3-103(a)(6). Remember that in order to be a holder in due course, *all* the elements of the rule stated in U.C.C. § 3-302 must be met.

Problem 3-8

Arnie issued a check to Barry in payment of wages of $100 payable to the order of "Barry" and signed by Arnie on the drawer's line. "Acme Inc." is imprinted on the upper left hand corner of the check. Barry indorsed the check "Barry" and gave the check to Carla in exchange for a lamp and some other items at a garage sale.

Notes

a) Assume that Barry gave the check to Carla in exchange for Carla's promise to deliver the items next week to Barry's house. Is Carla a holder in due course of the check?

b) Assume that Barry kept the check for 4 months because Barry misplaced the check. When Barry found the check, he then gave it to Carla as payment for the garage sale items. Is Carla a holder in due course of the check?

c) Assume that Barry is 10 years old and Arnie is Barry's parent. Barry gave the check to Carla in payment for the garage sale items after Barry indorsed the check "Barry" on the back. Is Carla a holder in due course of the check?

d) At the time Carla took the check from Barry, Carla knew that Acme Inc. was on the verge of bankruptcy because Acme Inc. had a reputation for selling shoddy merchandise. Is Carla a holder in due course of the check?

e) When Carla received the check from Barry, she noticed that the payee's name was smudged and part of the line for the payee's name looked like it had been erased. Is Carla a holder in due course of the check?

f)   Assume that Carla knew at the time she took the check from Barry that Arnie did not work for Acme Inc. Is Carla a holder in due course of the check?

g)   Assume that the lamp from the garage sale did not work. Carla had promised Barry that it worked. What is Barry's defense to payment on his indorser's contract on the check? Is Carla a holder in due course of the check? Does it make any difference when Carla found out that the lamp did not work, prior to or after taking the check from Barry? Even if Carla is a holder in due course, is she subject to Barry's defense to payment of his indorser's contract?

h)   Assume that Barry indorsed the check "Barry" and gave the check to Carla in payment of a longstanding debt that Barry owed Carla, not for items from the garage sale. Is Carla a holder in due course of the check?

i)   Assume that Barry indorsed the check in blank in anticipation of depositing the check in his bank account. Barry owed Carla money from a previous transaction and Carla had obtained a judgment on that debt. Carla seized the check through a lawful execution

Notes

procedure in order to collect on that judgment. Carla then bought the check at a properly conducted execution sale. Is Carla a holder in due course of the check?

j) While Barry has possession of the check and prior to any indorsement of the check, is Barry a holder in due course of the check?

Problem 3-9

Ted is 25 years old. He purchased a car from Acme Cars and signed a negotiable promissory note for $10,000 payable to bearer in equal monthly installments over the course of the next 5 years. Acme Cars sold the note and transferred possession of it to First Bank for $8,000.

Notes

a) First Bank knows that when Acme Cars sells cars to people that Acme Cars is not truthful in its representations about the cars' performance capabilities, but it has no specific knowledge that Acme Cars made any misrepresentations to Ted. Acme Cars represented that the car sold to Ted was in perfect operating condition. In fact, the car had a cracked block and needed major repairs. Acme Cars knew of the condition of the car when it sold the car to Ted. Does Ted have a defense or claim in recoupment to assert that is effective against First Bank?

b) Assume that the note Ted signed contained the following language: "Any Holder of this contract is subject to all claims and defenses which the debtor could assert against the seller of goods obtained with the proceeds hereof." This language is mandated in the FTC Holder in Due Course rules, 16 C.F.R. pt. 433. Is the note negotiable? Is First Bank a holder in due course of the note? Is First Bank subject to any defenses that Ted could have asserted against Acme Cars?

c) Assume that the note Ted signed should have had the language quoted in problem (b) above under the FTC Rule but does not. Ted has a claim in recoupment based upon a breach of warranty claim against Acme Cars. May Ted assert that claim in recoupment against First Bank?

d) Assume that Ted missed a payment on the installment note. After Ted missed the payment, First Bank negotiated the note to Second Bank for value. Is Second Bank a holder in due course?

A person entitled to enforce may have the rights of a holder in due course without being a holder in due course.* This generally occurs when the person in possession of the instrument takes the instrument from a holder in due course and shelters in that person's rights. **Read U.C.C. § 3-203.** What this means is that the rights of a holder in due course may be transferred to someone that is not a holder in due course. The transferee is able to assert whatever rights its transferor could assert. For example, assume that Darren issues a check to Able. Able indorses the check and negotiates it to Baker in a transaction in which Baker is a holder in due course. Baker then gives the check as a gift to Christopher. Christopher does not qualify as a holder in due course because he has not given value for the check. U.C.C. § 3-302. But, under U.C.C. § 3-203, Christopher could assert Baker's rights as a holder in due course as against Able on his indorser's contract and against Darren on his drawer's contract. A limitation on the ability to shelter in the transferor's rights is stated in U.C.C. § 3-203(b).

One more thing to realize about defenses and claims in recoupment. It is a cardinal rule of contract law that a person may only assert his or her own defenses to an obligation. That principle also applies to a negotiable instrument and is reflected in U.C.C. § 3-305(c). The court in *Maine* discussed this principle in the last segment of the case.

Problem 3-10

Jane bought a new computer from Jack and gave Jack a check made payable to the order of Jane for $1,500, signed by Sue and drawn on State Bank. Jane indorsed the check in blank. Sue had given the check to Jane in payment for a table. The new computer is defective and under Article 2 of the U.C.C., Jane properly rejected the computer and returned the computer

---

* Federal law may provide that the person seeking to enforce an instrument must be treated as if it were a holder in due course, even if that person would not qualify as a holder in due course under Article 3. An example of that principle is stated in 12 U.S.C. § 1823(e). Under this law and the doctrine from the case of *D'Oench, Duhme & Co. v. FDIC*, 315 U.S. 447 (1942), the FDIC is treated as a holder in due course of all instruments that it acquires when it acquires a failed bank, even if the FDIC would not be a holder in due course under the requirements of U.C.C. § 3-302. The status of the FDIC as a holder in due course under this doctrine was put in doubt by the Supreme Court's decision in *O'Melveny & Myers v. FDIC*, 512 U.S. 79 (1994) and *Atherton v. FDIC*, 519 U.S. 213 (1997). *See* Cherie Stephens Bock, Comment, *Alive, But Not Quite Kicking: Circuit Split Illustrates the Progressive Deterioration of the D'Oench, Duhme Doctrine*, 42 ST. LOUIS U. L.J. 945 (1998); Jason Kellog, Comment, *D'Oench Lives, But for How Long?: The Eleventh Circuit Breathes Life into an Ailing Banking Doctrine*, 30 FLA. ST. U. L. REV. 167 (2002).

to Jack. Jane told Sue of the problem with the computer and Sue stopped payment on the check.

Notes

a) When the check was presented to State Bank for payment, State Bank dishonored the check. Jack now has possession of the check. Is Jack a holder in due course of the check?

b) Same facts as (a) above. Jack wants to collect on the check from Sue. What is Sue's liability on the check? Does Sue have a defense to payment that she may assert against Jack? If Jack collects the amount of the check from Sue, may she enforce Jane's contract liability on the check?

c) Same facts as (a) above. Jack wants to collect on the check from Jane. What is Jane's liability on the check? Does Jane have a defense to payment that she may assert against Jack? If Jack collects the amount of the check from Jane, may she enforce Sue's contract liability on the check?

d) Assume that Jack negotiated the check to Bill who is a holder in due course. Bill presented the check to State Bank and State Bank dishonored the check. Bill wants to collect on the check from Jane. What is Jane's liability on the check? Does Jane have a defense to payment that she may assert against Bill? What if Bill is not a holder in due course?

e) Assume that Jack negotiated the check to Bill and Bill is not a holder in due course of the check. Bill presented the check to State Bank and State Bank dishonored the check. Bill has possession of the check. Jane did not return the computer to Jack but kept the computer and has a claim for damages against Jack for breach of a warranty. Her damages for breach of warranty are $2,000. What is Jane's liability on the check when Bill seeks to collect on her contract liability on the check?

f) Assume that Jack negotiated the check to Bill and Bill is a holder in due course of the check. Bill gave the check to Tom as a gift. Tom presented the check to State Bank and State Bank dishonored the check. Tom has possession of the check and seeks to collect the amount of the check from Jane. May Jane assert her breach of contract defense against Tom?

g) Assume that Jack negotiated the check to Bill and Bill is a holder in due course of the check. Bill then negotiated the check back to Jack in exchange for value. Jack presented the check to State Bank and State Bank dishonored the check. Jack has possession of the check. Jack seeks to collect the amount of the check from Jane. May Jane assert her breach of contract defense against Jack?

G. Discharge of the Obligation

1. Contract Obligation on the Instrument

Contract liability on an instrument may be discharged in various ways, including any manner sufficient to discharge a contract obligation under common law principles. **Read U.C.C. § 3-601(a).** An example of a discharge of liability under contract law principles would be a novation. In a novation, the parties agree to the issuance of a new note as a satisfaction of the liability under the original note. *See Cumberland Bank v. G & S Implement Co.*, 60 U.C.C. Rep. Serv. 2d 736 (Tenn. Ct. App. 2006). The most obvious manner in which an obligor may discharge its liability is by payment of the obligation stated on the instrument. **Read U.C.C. § 3-602.** Contract liability may also be discharged as stated in U.C.C. § 3-603 (tender of payment) and U.C.C. § 3-604 (cancellation).

Is a holder in due course subject to the obligor's argument that its contract obligation on the instrument has been discharged? **Read U.C.C. § 3-601(b).** If a person has notice of a discharge at the time it takes the instrument, does that prevent the person from being a holder in due course because it has notice of a defense to payment? **Read U.C.C. § 3-302(b).**

Consider the rules from U.C.C. §§ 3-601 through 3-604, 3-302, and 3-305 as you work through the following problems. In each instance, ask whether there is a discharge of the contract obligation and then ask whether that discharge may be asserted against the person seeking to enforce that contract obligation.

Problem 3-11

Notes

a) Allen drew a check on Bank and delivered the check to Clark, the payee. Clark indorsed the check in blank and delivered the check to David. David presented the check to Bank. Bank paid the amount of the check to David. Is Allen's drawer's liability discharged? Is Clark's indorser's liability discharged?

Notes

b) Allen issued a negotiable demand note payable to the order of Bank. Bank sold the note to Finance Co. which took possession of the note. Bank did not indorse the note. Finance Co. demanded payment from Allen. Allen paid Finance Co. the amount of the note. Is Allen's maker's liability discharged?

c) Allen issued a negotiable demand note payable to the order of Bank. While Bank had possession of the note, Allen paid the entire amount due on the note. After that payment, Bank indorsed the note and transferred possession of the note to Finance Co. Assume Finance Co. is a holder in due course. Finance Co. demanded that Allen pay. He refused. Is his defense of payment good as against Finance Co. when it sues him on the maker's contract?

d) Assume that in (c) above, Bank did not transfer the note to Finance Co. but presented the note to Allen and insisted that he pay again. Does Allen have a defense to payment that is good as against Bank?

e) Allen issued a negotiable installment note payable to the order of Bank. Bank indorsed the note in blank and transferred possession of the note to

Notes

Finance Co. Assume Finance Co. qualifies as a holder in due course. Allen did not know that Bank had transferred the note to Finance Co. Thereafter, Allen made a regular installment payment to Bank. If Finance Co. seeks to collect that installment payment from Allen, does Allen have a defense that he may assert against Finance Co.?

Problem 3-12

Notes

a) Acme Co. issued a check to Bruce in payment of wages. Bruce indorsed the check in blank and transferred the check to Charlie in exchange for a rare book. Charlie crossed out Bruce's indorsement and transferred the check to David as payment for a debt Charlie owed to David. The check was dishonored by the drawee. May David enforce any contract liability on the check against Bruce? Against Charlie? Against Acme?

b) Same facts as (a) above, except David intentionally burned up the check in the fireplace. Is anyone's contract liability on the check discharged? Is U.C.C. § 3-309 available to David to enforce liability on the check? Any change in your analysis if the check is burned up in an unfortunate house fire? What if David mistakenly gave

Notes

the check to Acme when David demanded payment even though Acme did not pay David?

c) Allen issued a negotiable demand note payable to the order of Bank. Bank sold the note to Finance Co. Bank indorsed the note in blank and delivered the note to Finance Co. Allen tendered full payment of the note to Finance Co. Finance Co. refused the tender of payment. Is Allen's maker's liability on the note discharged? Is Bank's indorser's liability on the note discharged?

2. Underlying Obligation

A negotiable instrument is usually issued or transferred in payment of an underlying obligation. That usual transaction raises several issues concerning the relationship between the underlying obligation and the contract obligation on the negotiable instrument. First, what is the effect of issuance or transfer of the negotiable instrument on the ability of the obligee to enforce the underlying obligation? Second, what is the effect of payment of the negotiable instrument on the underlying obligation? Third, what is the effect of dishonor of the negotiable instrument on the underlying obligation? Fourth, what is the effect on the underlying obligation of discharge of the obligation on the negotiable instrument (by a manner other than payment)?

The place to start in answering these questions is with U.C.C. § 3-310. **Read U.C.C. § 3-310.** The answer to the first question will differ depending on the type of instrument issued or transferred. Compare U.C.C. § 3-310 subsection (a) with subsection (b)(1) and (2). The issuance or transfer of the types of negotiable instruments specified in subsection (a) discharges the underlying obligation. In all other situations, the issuance or transfer of a negotiable instrument only suspends the underlying obligation.

If the underlying obligation is merely suspended, when does that suspension end? Subsection (b)(1) and (2) state that the underlying obligation is suspended until payment of the instrument or dishonor. If payment of the instrument results in a discharge of contract obligation on the instrument, the underlying obligation is also satisfied to the extent of the discharge.

In the event the instrument is dishonored, the suspension of the underlying obligation ends. **Read U.C.C. § 3-310(b)(3).** If the person entitled to enforce the instrument is the same person as the obligee on the underlying obligation, that person may enforce either the contract liability on the instrument or the underlying obligation.

What if the person who was the obligee on the underlying obligation is not the person entitled to enforce the instrument? For example, assume a purchase of goods from a retail store in exchange for a check. The store deposits the check into its bank account and when the check arrives at the drawee bank, the check is dishonored and returned to the depositary bank. The underlying obligation to pay for the goods is no longer suspended. The store is the obligee on the underlying obligation to pay for the goods but is not the person entitled to enforce the check (because it does not have possession of the check). The person entitled to enforce the check would be the depositary bank (because it has possession of the returned check). **Read U.C.C. § 3-310(b)(4) and comment 3 to that section.** If the depositary bank returns the check to the store, then the store has its choice to sue on either the underlying obligation to pay for the goods or to enforce the contract liability on the check as against the drawer.

Now consider the following situation. A negotiable note is issued in exchange for a loan of money. The payee indorses the note and transfers it to a transferee in order to pay an obligation that the payee owes the transferee. The transferee decides to forgive the payee its debt and rips up the note. What is the effect of that action on the maker's obligation on the note and the underlying obligation that maker owed payee? Under U.C.C. § 3-604, the maker's obligation and the indorser's obligation on the note would be discharged by cancellation. The maker's underlying obligation to the payee/indorser and the payee/indorser's underlying obligation to the transferee is also discharged. **Read U.C.C. § 3-310(b)(3) and comment 3.**

Problem 3-13

a) Pat is buying Frank's house. Pat procured a certified check drawn on her account with State Bank. Pat is the drawer of the check. Pat gave the check to Frank at the closing. Frank is the payee of the check. What is the effect of that transfer of the check on the underlying obligation of Pat to pay Frank for the house?

b) Pat is buying Frank's house. Pat gave Frank a negotiable promissory note payable to the order of Frank in payment for the house. What is the effect of that transfer of the note on Pat's obligation to pay Frank for the house?

c) Same facts as (b) above. Pat was unable to make the payments called for in the promissory note and defaulted. What are Frank's options to collect the money from Pat?

d) Same facts as (b) above. Assume that Frank sold the note after the closing to State Bank for 80% of the face value of the note. Frank indorsed the note in blank and delivered the note to State Bank. Pat defaulted on the payments required on the note. Who can sue Pat and what is the cause of action?

Problem 3-14

Notes

a) Arden drew a check on Bank, payable to the order of Crystal. Arden delivered the check to Crystal in payment of the price of some goods. Crystal took the check to Bank and obtained payment of the check. What is the effect of that payment on the underlying obligation of Arden to pay for the goods?

b) Arden issued a negotiable note payable to the order of Bank in return for a loan of funds. Bank sold the note to Crystal. Bank indorsed the note in blank and delivered the note to Crystal. Crystal presented the note to Arden and Arden paid the instrument. What is the effect of that payment on Arden's underlying obligation to Bank?

c) Arden issued a check payable to the order of Crystal, drawn on Bank. Arden issued that check as payment for some goods that Arden purchased from Crystal. Crystal indorsed the check in blank and delivered that check to Dry Cleaning Co. in payment of services that Dry Cleaning Co. rendered to Crystal. Dry Cleaning Co. presented the check to Bank and Bank paid the check. What is the effect of that payment on Arden's underlying

Notes

obligation to Crystal?   What is the
effect of that payment on Crystal's
underlying obligation to Dry Cleaning
Co.?

d)   Arden issued a negotiable note
payable to the order of Buford.
Buford indorsed the note and
transferred the note to Crystal in
payment of Buford's obligation to
Crystal to pay for goods.   Crystal
demanded payment from Arden and
Arden refused, dishonoring the note.
Crystal failed to send notice of
dishonor to Buford within 30 days of
the dishonor. Presentment and notice
of dishonor are not excused. What is
the effect of that failure on Buford's
underlying obligation to Crystal?
What should Crystal do?

3.   Accord and Satisfaction

Many people use the doctrine of accord and satisfaction as an informal method
of dispute resolution. When a debt is disputed, I may want to tender by check what
I think is owed on the debt and make clear to the payee that if the check is cashed,
the payee has agreed to the compromise of the obligation to that amount. Section
3-311 codifies an approach to accord and satisfaction that allows the payment of an
instrument to be satisfaction of the entire amount of the underlying obligation even
if the amount of the instrument is not the entire amount of the underlying obligation.
This is in effect an exception to the general rule that payment resulting in a
discharge of the contract obligation on the instrument is a discharge of the
underlying obligation only to the extent of the amount of the payment. *Compare*
U.C.C. § 3-310(b)(1) and (2).

Read U.C.C. § 3-311. The requirements of an accord and satisfaction when using a negotiable instrument are stated in U.C.C. § 3-311(a). The effect of the payment on the underlying obligation is stated in subsection (b). Subsection (c) is an exception to the rule stated in subsection (b). Subsection (d) is an exception to the rule of subsection (c). *See also* U.C.C. § 1-308.

Problem 3-15

Alvin bought goods on credit at Department Store, charging the amount to Alvin's account with Department Store. Department Store sent an invoice to Alvin, billing Alvin for the amount due for the goods.

Notes

a) Alvin decided that the goods were not worth the amount that he had been charged for those goods. Alvin sent a check payable to Department Store for less than the invoice amount with the notation written in capital letters "IN FULL PAYMENT." Department Store cashed the check. Has there been an accord and satisfaction?

b) Assume Alvin asserted that the goods were defective and Department Store was unwilling to take the goods back. After several weeks of arguing between Alvin and the credit department of Department Store about whether the goods were defective, Alvin sent the check to Department Store for less than the invoice amount with "IN FULL PAYMENT" written on the front of check. Department Store cashed the check. Has there been an accord and satisfaction?

Notes

c) Assume the same facts as (b), except
    Alvin sent the check to the head of
    Customer Service with a long letter
    explaining the purported defect and
    that the check was in full satisfaction
    of the amount of the debt. Department
    Store had included with its invoice a
    notice that all communications
    regarding disputes about the invoice
    should be sent to the Complaint
    Department. Department Store cashed
    the check. Has there been an accord
    and satisfaction? Would it matter if
    Department Store sent the amount of
    the check back to Alvin several weeks
    later?

4. Conclusion

As demonstrated in this section, discharge is a defense to payment that a
defendant may assert against a person seeking to enforce contract liability on an
instrument. Whether that defense succeeds depends on whether the plaintiff is a
holder in due course who took with notice of that defense. Add the various types
of discharges to your list of defenses to payment of the contract obligation.

Suit on the underlying obligation provides another avenue for payment in some
cases in addition to contract liability on an instrument. The doctrine of accord and
satisfaction is an exception to the rule in U.C.C. § 3-310 that payment of the
instrument satisfies the obligation only to the extent of the payment.

H. Suretyship Defenses

1. Defining a Secondary Obligor

A person entitled to enforce a contract obligation on the instrument may be
subject to the defenses to that obligation stated in U.C.C. § 3-605. These defenses
are available to someone who is a "secondary obligor." **Read the definition of
secondary obligor and principal obligor in U.C.C. § 3-103.** Notice that an

indorser, a drawer when the draft is accepted by a drawee that is not a bank, and an accommodation party are all "secondary obligors." We have already looked at the liability of an indorser and drawer as stated in U.C.C. § 3-415 and 3-414(d).

An accommodation party is a party to a negotiable instrument who is a surety for an accommodated party. A person may be a surety for an obligation represented by a negotiable instrument without signing the instrument but such a surety is not an accommodation party. **Read U.C.C. § 3-419.** As the comments to U.C.C. § 3-419 point out, an accommodation party is always a surety, but a surety is not always an accommodation party.* If a person signs an instrument for the purpose of incurring liability but not receiving the benefit of the value given for the instrument, that person is signing as an accommodation party. **Read U.C.C. § 3-205** on anomalous indorsement.

Signing for accommodation should be distinguished from signing as a party with joint and several liability. For example, assume that two people want to borrow money from a lender. The lender requires both people to sign the negotiable note as makers. These two people would be co-makers with joint and several liability on the instrument. **Read U.C.C. § 3-116.** Joint and several liability means that each person is obligated on the contract liability for the amount of the instrument to the person entitled to enforce but may be able to get contribution from their co-party. In the example given above, each party would be liable for the entire amount of the note to the holder of the note. If one party paid the entire amount of the note to a holder, that party would be able to get contribution from the other co-maker under non-U.C.C. principles. U.C.C. § 3-116(b). Those non-U.C.C. principles are based upon suretyship law. Assume that the principal amount of the note is $10,000 and two co-makers have agreed that each would be liable as between each other for half the amount. Co-maker 1 paid $8,000 to the person entitled to enforce. Co-maker 1 would have a right of recourse against Co-maker 2 for $3,000. Co-maker 1 is a secondary obligor as to Co-maker 2 to the extent of $3,000, the amount for which Co-maker 1 has a right of contribution against Co-maker 2.

In a suretyship relationship there are at least three parties: a principal obligor, a secondary obligor, and an obligee. The principal obligor is the person who is

---

* In 2002, several Article 3 provisions were amended to conform the rules in Article 3 concerning accommodation parties and suretyship to the common law rules of suretyship. One expression of the common law rules can be found in the RESTATEMENT (THIRD) OF SURETYSHIP AND GUARANTY (1996).

primarily liable for the obligation owed to the obligee. The secondary obligor is the surety for the performance of the principal obligor's obligation to the obligee.

Once you determine that there is a suretyship relationship between the persons who are signatories to the instrument, there are three major sub-issues to consider. First, when is the secondary obligor liable to the obligee for the obligation on the instrument? Second, what are the rights of the secondary obligor against the principal obligor? Third, what are the rights of one secondary obligor against another secondary obligor?

2. Secondary Obligor's Liability to the Obligee

Let us consider the first question. A secondary obligor signs the instrument in some capacity as we studied earlier. Thus a secondary obligor may sign as a maker, an indorser, a drawer, or an acceptor. Its contract liability to the obligee in the first instance will thus be determined by its status as a signor of the instrument. The secondary obligor has defenses to the obligation based upon its capacity on the instrument and the additional defenses that may accrue based upon being a secondary obligor. To illustrate, assume a maker issued a negotiable note payable on demand to the payee. The payee indorsed the instrument and negotiated it to a holder. The holder presented it to the maker and the maker dishonored the note. The holder sued the maker and the indorser on their respective contract liabilities. Assume the holder did not give timely notice of dishonor to the indorser and there was no excuse or waiver of the obligation to give notice of dishonor. The indorser may assert the lack of notice of dishonor as a defense to payment. That defense is assertable against the holder even if it is a holder in due course. Demonstrating timely notice of dishonor is part of the holder's prima facie case against the indorser. U.C.C. § 3-415. That defense of lack of notice of dishonor is based upon the contract liability of the indorser, not the fact that the indorser is a secondary obligor.

The indorser in the hypothetical above is a secondary obligor because it has a right of recourse, if it pays the instrument, as against the maker. **Review U.C.C. § 3-412.** The maker of the note is the principal obligor. Consider a defense based upon the status of the indorser as a secondary obligor. Assume that the holder releases the maker from its obligation on the instrument. If that release of the maker can be asserted by the maker as against the indorser, the holder has impaired the indorser's right of recourse as against the maker. **Read U.C.C. § 3-605(a)(1).** The second sentence of that section provides that the holder's release of the maker (principal obligor) discharges the maker from its liability to the indorser (secondary obligor). The holder may prevent that rule from taking effect if the holder preserves the indorser's (secondary obligor's) right of recourse against the maker (principal obligor) as part of the release of the maker from its liability to the holder.

Now read U.C.C. § 3-605(a)(2). The indorser may assert as a defense to the holder when the holder sues the indorser on its contract liability the fact that the holder released the maker from its obligation. This is a defense based upon the status of the indorser as a secondary obligor. The holder in its release of the maker may preserve its right to pursue the indorser. In that event, the rule of U.C.C. § 3-605(a)(3) is applicable.

Defenses to the contract obligation on the instrument based upon impairment of the right of recourse of the secondary obligor as against the principal obligor are often referred to as the suretyship defenses. The type of impairment of the right of recourse addressed in U.C.C. § 3-605(a) is a release of the principal obligor. Subsection (b) addresses impairment of the right of recourse based upon an extension of time for the principal obligor to pay the instrument. Subsection (c) addresses impairment of the right of recourse based upon modifications of the principal obligor's obligation other than a release or an extension of time. Subsection (d) addresses impairment of the right of recourse based upon impairing the the value of collateral securing the obligation to pay the instrument.

In some circumstances, the secondary obligor will not have the right to assert a suretyship defense even if it would be otherwise allowed under U.C.C. § 3-605(a) through (d). **Read U.C.C. § 3-605(f).** That subsection allows for waiver of the right to assert suretyship defenses. Waivers of suretyship defenses are commonly found in negotiable promissory notes. In addition, the person entitled to enforce the instrument must generally know that the person is a secondary obligor in order to be subject to a suretyship defense. **Read U.C.C. § 3-605(e).**

A secondary obligor that is an accommodation party has another type of defense to the contract obligation on the instrument, in addition to the defenses based upon the capacity in which it signed the instrument and the suretyship defenses discussed above. **Read U.C.C. § 3-305(d).** An accommodation party may assert against a person entitled to enforce the instrument the defenses or claims in recoupment that the principal obligor (the accommodated party) could assert against the person entitled to enforce. This is an exception to the rule stated in U.C.C. § 3-305(c) that a person may only assert its own defenses or claims in recoupment against the person entitled to enforce the instrument. This category of defenses is only available to an accommodation party.

As noted above, a secondary obligor who is an accommodation party on an instrument will be liable to the obligee for contract liability on the instrument based upon the capacity in which the accommodation party signed the instrument. **Read U.C.C. § 3-419(b).** Thus, a person could be an accommodation maker, accommodation drawer, accommodation indorser, or accommodation acceptor. Subsection (d) provides for a specific type of accommodation, "collection guaranteed," rather than payment guaranteed. Section 3-419(d) thus operates as a limited exception to the general rule of subsection (b). New subsection (e) (added by the 2002 amendments) addresses the usual situation where the accommodation party does not limit its liability on the instrument to "collection guaranteed." **Read U.C.C. § 3-419(d) and (e).**

3. Rights of the Secondary Obligor Against the Principal Obligor

Now let us consider the second question, the rights of a secondary obligor as against its principal obligor. Given that the idea of a secondary obligor is that it has a right of recourse against the principal obligor, it should not be surprising that the law of suretyship provides for remedies of the secondary obligor as against the principal obligor. If the secondary obligor is an indorser that is paid, the indorser has the ability to assert contract liability against the principal obligor as described in U.C.C. § 3-412 through § 3-415. If the secondary obligor is a drawer with liability that survives the drawee's acceptance of the draft, the drawer has a right of recourse as against the acceptor. U.C.C. § 3-413.

In addition, an accommodation party will have certain rights against an accommodated party. U.C.C. § 3-419(f) provides for the usual rights of a secondary obligor (accommodation party) against a principal obligor (accommodated party): reimbursement of what the secondary obligor has paid the obligee; subrogation to the obligee's rights against the principal obligor; and exoneration– the right to force the principal obligor to perform the obligation to the obligee. Presumably the indorser that has paid and the drawer that has a right of recourse against an acceptor of a draft may assert the common law rights of reimbursement, subrogation, and exoneration as well. Nothing in Article 3 precludes exercise of those common law rights. *See* U.C.C. § 1-103.

Section 3-605 addresses the rights of a secondary obligor as against the principal obligor in the event the person entitled to enforce alters the principal obligor's obligation to the holder or impairs the value of collateral securing the obligation. **Reread U.C.C. § 3-605(a)(1), (b)(1), and (c)(1).** Each of these subsections address the rights of the secondary obligor as against the principal obligor.

4. Rights of Secondary Obligors as Against Other Secondary Obligors

Now consider the third question: What are the rights of two or more secondary obligors as among themselves? Two or more secondary obligors who have signed an instrument may either be co-sureties or sub-sureties. If co-sureties, they have joint and several liability and have a right of contribution as against the other. **U.C.C. § 3-116**. If sub-sureties, they have no right of contribution, rather one surety will have the ability to recover the entire amount from another surety. An example of a sub-surety relationship is when there are a series of indorsements on the instrument. Later indorsers who have paid the instrument may recover from earlier indorsers. U.C.C. § 3-415. The later indorsers are sub-sureties in relationship to the earlier indorsers.

The following problems explore these issues in greater detail. In each problem, identify which parties to the instrument are principal obligors and which are the secondary obligors. After determining the party's status, determine what defenses it is able to assert against the person seeking to enforce the contract liability on the instrument. If someone who is a secondary obligor is potentially liable on their contract liability on the instrument, identify what rights they would have against the principal obligor and against other secondary obligors.

Problem 3-16

Notes

a)   Atlas issued a demand draft, payable to the order of Brutus, drawn on Cal. Brutus indorsed the draft in blank and delivered the draft to Del. Who is a secondary obligor? Who is a principal obligor? Is anyone an accommodation party?

b)   Atlas issued a demand draft, payable to the order of Brutus, drawn on Cal.

Brutus obtained Cal's signature on the draft. Cal is not a bank. Who is a secondary obligor? Who is the principal obligor? Is the secondary obligor an accommodation party?

c)   Atlas issued a demand draft, payable to the order of Brutus, drawn on Cal. Brutus would only take the draft if Atlas obtained the signature of Elise on the draft. Elise signed the draft on the back and then Brutus took the draft. Who is a secondary obligor? Who is the principal obligor? Is the secondary obligor an accommodation party?

d)   Atlas issued a demand draft, payable to the order of Brutus, drawn on Cal. Brutus indorsed the draft. Brutus offered to transfer the draft to Elise in satisfaction of a debt he owed her. Elise was unwilling to take the draft unless Del indorsed the draft. Brutus requested that Del indorse the draft and Del did so, signing his name on the back of the draft. Brutus then delivered the draft to Elise. Who is a secondary obligor? Is anyone an accommodation party? If someone is an accommodation party, in what capacity did they sign the instrument and who is the accommodated party?

e) Same facts as (d) above. Elise presented the draft to Cal who dishonored the draft. Elise sought payment from Atlas. Atlas and Elise agreed that if he paid her ½ the amount of the draft, Elise would delete Atlas' name from the draft. After Elise received payment from Atlas, Elise crossed out Atlas' name on the draft. Did Elise's action discharge Brutus or Del from their contract liability on the draft? Will Elise's actions prevent Brutus or Del from recovering from Atlas in the event one of them pays Elise?

f) Same facts as (d) above. Cal refused to pay the draft when Elise presented it. Assume Brutus paid the amount of the draft to Elise. Does Brutus have any rights against Del?

g) Same facts as (d) above. Cal refused to pay the draft when Elise presented it. Assume Del paid Elise the amount of the draft. Does Del have any rights against Brutus?

Problem 3-17

Atlas issued a negotiable note payable to the order of Bank in exchange for a loan of funds. Bank required Atlas to obtain a surety for the loan. Atlas convinced Cal to sign the note on the back. After both Atlas and Cal signed the note, Bank indorsed the note in blank and transferred possession of the note to Second Bank for value.

Notes

a)   Assume that the note is payable on May 3 and Second Bank gave Atlas until May 5 to pay the note. On May 4, Second Bank demanded Atlas pay the note. Atlas refused, citing the previous extension given. Second Bank gave timely notice of dishonor to Cal and demanded that Cal pay the note. Does Cal have any defense to payment? If Second Bank had given timely notice of dishonor to Bank and demanded payment from Bank would Bank have a defense to payment?

b)   Assume that the note is secured by a security interest in collateral provided by Atlas. Second Bank released the collateral from the security interest. Atlas subsequently dishonored the note. Second Bank gave timely notice of dishonor to both Bank and Cal. Second Bank then demanded that Cal pay the amount of the note. Does Cal have any defense to payment? If Second Bank had demanded payment from Bank, would Bank have a defense to payment?

c)   Assume that Second Bank presented the note to Atlas and Atlas paid the note. Atlas did not get the note back

Notes

from Second Bank. Second Bank then sold the note to Third Bank, transferring possession of the note to Third Bank. Third Bank demanded payment from Atlas who refused because he had previously paid. Third Bank gave timely notice of dishonor to Bank and Cal and then demanded payment from Bank and Cal. Do either of them have a defense to payment?

d) Assume that Atlas tendered payment of the note to Second Bank and Second Bank refused the money. Second Bank presented the note to Bank and Cal requesting payment. Do Bank and Cal have any defense to payment?

Problem 3-18

Atlas issued a negotiable note payable to the order of Bank in exchange for a loan of funds. Bank required Atlas to have a co-signor in order to obtain the loan. Cal signed the note when Atlas asked him to, on the front right under the signature line where Atlas signed the note. Bank indorsed the note in blank and transferred the note to Second Bank for value.

Notes

a) Second Bank demanded that Cal pay the amount of the note. Cal did so. What are Cal's rights after Cal paid the note? Could Cal have avoided paying the note? That is, did Cal have any defenses to payment?

b)   Assume the note was payable on May 3. The note was not paid when due. Six months later, Second Bank demanded that Atlas, Cal and Bank pay the note. Do they have any defenses to payment? Assume Second Bank recovers from Atlas, does Atlas have any right to recover from either Cal or Bank?

c)   Assume the note was payable on May 3. After the note was transferred to Second Bank, Atlas obtained a discharge in bankruptcy of all Atlas' obligations, including liability on the note. Second Bank demanded that Cal and Bank pay the note. Do Cal and Bank have any defenses to payment?

d)   Assume that Second Bank does not qualify as a holder in due course of the note. Atlas issued the note to Bank in exchange for goods that Bank sold Atlas. The goods were defective and breached a warranty that Bank gave regarding the quality of the goods. Atlas refused to pay the note when Second Bank presented it to Atlas. Second Bank sought payment from Bank and Cal. Do either of them have any defenses to payment?

e)   Same facts as (d) above. Assume Second Bank is a holder in due course of the note. How does that change the analysis?

Notes

f)   In any situation above where a discharge of contract liability occurred, what language in the instrument could have prevented that discharge?

Review

To put the material from this Chapter together, organize what you have learned according to the various causes of action discussed. For each cause of action, identify the elements of the plaintiff's case, the defenses of the defendant, the plaintiff's rebuttal, and the defense's rejoinder.

Problem 3-19

PROMISSORY NOTE

Dated May 1, 2006

For value received, the undersigned maker promises to pay to the order of First Bank, at its offices in San Francisco, California, the principal sum of $10,000 plus interest at the rate of 10% per annum, one year from the date stated hereon.

The maker of this note may prepay in whole or part any and all amounts due under this note at any time without penalty. Such prepayment in part does not relieve the maker from making payment on the due date stated above. Any payments on this note will be applied as follows: first, to payment of any fees, costs, or assessments due under the terms of this note and any document granting a security interest or mortgage to secure the maker's obligations under this note, second, to payment of any accrued unpaid interest and then to payment of the principal balance due hereunder.

This note is secured by a security interest in collateral as provided in the security agreement signed by the maker. In the event of default in the payment of principal or interest hereunder, the holder hereof may declare the entire unpaid balance due and payable and the maker will also be liable for all costs of collection, including reasonable attorneys' fees. Presentment for payment, demand, protest, and notice of dishonor are hereby expressly waived by the makers, and each endorser or guarantor hereof.

John Smith

John Smith issued this note to First Bank on May 1, 2006. First Bank required Mary Smith, John's wife, to sign the note on the back at the same time. Mary did not know why she signed the note or what John was going do with the proceeds from the loan. The First Bank officer told Mary her signature was required merely as a formality because John and Mary were married.

First Bank sold the note to Second Bank in exchange for $9,000 on May 10, 2006. First Bank signed the note on the back as follows: "Pay to the order of Second Bank, First Bank by Stan Frank, President, without recourse." First Bank delivered possession of the note to Second Bank on May 10, 2006.

On June 10, 2007, Second Bank sold the note to Third Bank for $8,000. Second Bank signed the note on the back as follows: "Second Bank" and delivered the note to Third Bank.

a)   Third Bank has sued John Smith, Mary Smith, First Bank, and Second Bank. Analyze Third Bank's arguments to impose liability on each party and each party's likely response to those arguments.

b)   Second Bank brings cross claims against John Smith, Mary Smith and First Bank. Analyze Second Bank's arguments to impose liability on each party and each party's likely response to those arguments.

c)   First Bank brings cross claims against John Smith and Mary Smith. Analyze First Bank's arguments to impose liability on each party and each party's likely response to those arguments.

d)   John and Mary Smith were divorced in July 2006. They bring cross claims against each other. Analyze the likely basis of those cross claims and possible defenses to those cross claims.

Notes

Notes

CHAPTER 4
NEGOTIABLE INSTRUMENTS AS PERSONAL PROPERTY

So far we have learned that negotiable instruments are a particular type of contract and that Article 3 provides rules for enforcing the various types of contract liability on the instrument. Negotiable instruments are also a type of personal property and have the characteristics of personal property. A negotiable instrument is treated as personal property because it represents a valuable right, the right to payment of the contract liability on the instrument. This is the "reified" obligation that we briefly discussed in Chapter 2. The obligation to pay is reified in the negotiable instrument so that the instrument itself symbolizes the obligation to pay. The negotiable instrument is an item of valuable personal property.

In this Chapter, we will explore this "property" aspect of negotiable instruments. Typical issues that concern property rights center around identifying the owner of the item, identifying who else other than an owner who may have a property-based claim to the item, the remedies of a person who has a property-based claim to the item, and the ability to transfer property rights related to that item. One concern in the ability to transfer property rights is the right and "title" that the transferee obtains when the property is transferred to the transferee. In other words, what "warranties" are made by the transferor to the transferee that protect and define the property rights that the transferee obtains?

A. Claims to the Instrument

1. How Claims to an Instrument Arise

Who is the owner of a negotiable instrument? We learned in Chapter 2 that we determine whether an instrument is negotiable depending, in part, on how it is payable at the time it "is issued or first comes into possession of a holder." U.C.C. § 3-104. Before an instrument is issued, U.C.C. § 3-105, who owns the instrument? Once an instrument is issued, who owns the instrument? Article 3 does not answer either question. Rather, Article 3 depends upon common law property principles to answer those questions. *See* U.C.C. § 1-103.

Article 3 does recognize that a person may have property claims to an instrument but does not specify how those property claims arise. **Read U.C.C. § 3-306.** Somewhat confusingly, Article 3 uses the term "claim" to refer to property-based rights in an instrument and the term "claims in recoupment" to refer to defenses to payment that may reduce the amount owed on an instrument. U.C.C. § 3-305(a)(3). As the comment to U.C.C. § 3-306 points out, these two ideas are not equivalent. They refer to two different concepts.

Ownership and possession rights in property are not necessarily held by the same person. For example, I may lend someone my car. I am still the owner, even if someone else possesses the car. The same thing is true for a negotiable instrument. The person who may be entitled to enforce the contract liability on an instrument (the possessor) is not necessarily the same person who is the owner of the instrument under property law principles. **Read comment 1 to U.C.C. § 3-203.** An example will illustrate this idea. Assume that Sam draws a check on State Bank payable to Greg. Greg indorses the check in blank and leaves the check on his desk. A burglar breaks into Greg's house and takes the check. The burglar would be a holder of the instrument and a person entitled to enforce Sam's drawer's contract liability under U.C.C. § 3-414. (If you do not understand why that statement is true, review the material from Chapter 3.) But the burglar is not the owner of the check. Greg is the owner of the check but not a holder because he is not in possession. (Greg may be entitled to enforce Sam's drawer's liability under U.C.C. § 3-309.) Greg will have a claim to the check based upon his property rights as an owner of the check.

What other types of property claims may arise in a negotiable instrument? Assume that a negotiable note is issued by a maker to two payees jointly. Under principles of property law, the two payees are tenants in common of the note. In essence, they are co-owners of the note. If one of the payees tried to assert that it was the sole owner of the note, the other payee would have a property claim to the note based upon its rights as a tenant in common under property principles.

Claims to a negotiable instrument could also arise if an instrument is given as payment in a transaction that is later rescinded under contract law. For example, assume that a negotiable promissory note is negotiated as payment for an item in a transaction where there is a misrepresentation sufficient to avoid the transaction for fraud under contract law principles. RESTATEMENT (SECOND) OF CONTRACTS § 164. If a transaction is avoided because of fraud, the usual remedy is to allow restitution of the benefit provided to each side. RESTATEMENT (SECOND) OF CONTRACTS § 376. In the example, the benefit provided to the party who committed the fraud is the negotiation of the negotiable promissory note. Under U.C.C. § 3-202, rescission of the negotiation of the negotiable promissory note is allowed if allowed under other law.

Another common situation in which claims to a negotiable instrument are asserted is when a secured party obtains a security interest in an instrument. Assume Alice is the payee of a negotiable promissory note with Quinn as the maker. This note is an asset of Alice. As we learned in the last Chapter, Quinn would owe his contract obligation on the note to Alice, the holder of the note. Now assume Alice borrowed money from First Bank. First Bank required Alice to secure repayment of the debt with an asset of Alice. Alice granted First Bank a security interest in the negotiable promissory note, an item of her personal property that has value (because of Quinn's maker's obligation to pay the note). First Bank's security interest is a type of property interest in the negotiable promissory note.[*]

These examples illustrate how claims to a negotiable instrument may arise based upon other law. Once you apply property law principles to determine that a claim to a negotiable instrument has arisen, the next issue is whether that claim can be asserted against the person in possession of the instrument.

2. Asserting Claims to an Instrument

If a party has a claim to the instrument, what action will they want to take to assert that claim? Return to the example of Greg and the burglar discussed above. Greg could take several different actions to recover on his ownership claim to the check. Of course, he could report the theft and seek to have the burglar prosecuted under criminal law. His possible civil remedies are governed by non-Article 3 property law. For instance, if Greg knew the identity of the burglar, he could sue the burglar to recover the check using the state law action of replevin. Replevin (sometimes called by different names, such as claim and delivery) is a state law process that seeks to recover possession of identified personal property. Alternatively, Greg could sue the burglar for conversion of the check, recovering damages for the amount of the loss. Conversion is the common law tort remedy for interference with property rights in personal property. It is often defined as the wrongful deprivation of another of the use and possession of personal property. BLACK'S LAW DICTIONARY (8th ed. 2004). **Read U.C.C. § 3-420(a) (first sentence).** Another option is for Greg to sue to enjoin enforcement of the check or

---

[*] Whether First Bank's security interest is perfected may be relevant to the priority of First Bank's security interest in the negotiable promissory note as against other parties who claim security interests or liens in the note, but perfection is not relevant to whether First Bank has a claim recognized under Article 3. As to how Bank would perfect its security interest in the negotiable promissory note, *see* U.C.C. §§ 9-310, 9-312(a), and 9-313(a).

to rescind the negotiation to the burglar for illegality. **Read U.C.C. § 3-202.** All of these possible remedies arise out of the law governing personal property, not out of Article 3. Article 3 merely does not *prevent* these remedies. U.C.C. § 3-202, comment 2.

Article 3 explicitly provides for only one type of property-based cause of action: conversion. **Read U.C.C. § 3-420.** The first sentence of subsection (a) brings into Article 3 the common law regarding the tort of conversion of personal property. The rest of subsection (a) then specifies an additional situation in which the instrument is considered converted. We will consider this provision in depth in Chapter 6 when we consider fraud and wrongdoing with respect to instruments. But for now, keep in mind this simple illustration of that second sentence of section 3-420(a). Assume that a negotiable note is issued payable to the order of Payee. Payee does not indorse the note. We learned in Chapter 3 that in order to make the next person a holder, Payee must indorse the note. U.C.C. § 3-301. Assume that Ted steals the note from Payee and forges Payee's indorsement. Ted is not a person entitled to enforce the note. Ted then sells the note and transfers possession of it to an unsuspecting Mary. Mary is not a person entitled to enforce because Payee has not indorsed the note. Ted's forgery of Payee's name is not Payee's indorsement. U.C.C. § 3-403. Ted has converted the note under the first sentence of section 3-420(a). Mary has converted the note under the second sentence of section 3-420(a).

Article 3 addresses conversion in another circumstance as well. **Read U.C.C. § 3-206(c).** In Chapter 3 we briefly addressed the concept of restrictive indorsements. A common type of restrictive indorsement is when a person deposits a check in a bank account and indorses the check "for deposit only." Once a check is indorsed in that manner, a non-bank purchaser of that check will have converted it unless the amount of the check is received by the indorser. A depositary bank that takes that check will have converted the check unless the proceeds are paid to the indorser or applied consistently with the indorsement.

Given that the person who has a property claim in the instrument may not be the same person as the person entitled to enforce, we must consider yet another issue. Is the person entitled to enforce the instrument subject to another person's property-based claim to the instrument? **Reread U.C.C. § 3-306.** Whether the person entitled to enforce the negotiable instrument is subject to the claim depends upon whether that person is a holder in due course. Return to the example with Greg and the burglar. Greg had indorsed the check in blank and then the burglar stole the check. Greg could successfully make a claim to the check while the check was in the burglar's hands because the burglar could not qualify as a holder in due course. U.C.C. § 3-302. Assume, however, that the burglar negotiated the check for value to Anne, who qualifies as a holder in due course. If Greg attempts to assert his ownership claim to the check against Anne, Anne will win. She is a holder in due course and takes the negotiable instrument free from claims to the instrument. U.C.C. § 3-306. What that means is in a lawsuit between Greg and Anne in which Greg is attempting to assert his property claim to the instrument, Anne would win the lawsuit and get to keep the check (and enforce it against Sam, the drawer, and Greg, the indorser). Anne has no liability to Greg for conversion.

This is a somewhat remarkable result. Typically, a person that takes an item of personal property from a thief generally acquires no greater property rights than what the thief had. That rule of derivative rights is codified in goods transactions in the first sentence of U.C.C. § 2-403. As we learned in Chapter 1, however, that rule does not apply in the context of currency. As the *Berry* case illustrated, a person that took currency in good faith and for value from a thief obtained good title to that currency even though the thief had no title to give. The commercial need for the free transferability of currency outweighed a fundamental property law principle. That same philosophy is behind the rule that protects a holder in due course from property-based claims to a negotiable instrument.

In order to qualify as a holder in due course, a person must not have notice of a claim to the instrument when they take the instrument. U.C.C. § 3-302(a)(2)(v). Whether someone has notice of a claim is the same as determining whether someone has notice of a defense. **Review U.C.C. § 1-202.** Notice of a claim that prevents a party from becoming a holder in due course may affect the ability of the holder to enforce the contract obligation on the negotiable instrument by making the holder subject to a defense to payment unrelated to the claim. Similarly, if a person is not a holder in due course because of notice of a defense, and it so happens that someone else has a claim, the holder is subject to that claim even if the holder did not have notice of that claim.

To illustrate how this works, assume that Martin signed a negotiable promissory note as maker and issued the note to a payee, Payton Parts, Inc., in exchange for a delivery of goods. Payton Parts indorsed the note in blank and transferred the note to State Bank. At the time of that transfer from Payton Parts to State Bank, State Bank had notice that the note was overdue so that State Bank did not qualify as a holder in due course, although it is a holder. When State Bank sues Martin to enforce the note, Martin contends that he has a claim to the note because he is entitled to rescind the transaction between him and Payton Parts because Payton

Parts defrauded him in the transaction. Because State Bank is not a holder in due course based upon its notice of the fact that the note was overdue, State Bank is subject to Martin's claim to the note based upon the alleged fraud of Payton Parts. Of course whether Martin will actually win on that ground depends upon whether there was sufficient fraud in the Payton Parts transaction with Martin to justify rescission for fraud. That question will be determined as a matter of contract law outside of Article 3. What U.C.C. § 3-306 means in this context is that State Bank would not be able to avoid a determination of the merits of that fraud dispute by asserting holder in due course status as to the note. Because State Bank is not a holder in due course, it is subject to all claims and defenses that Martin may assert regarding this note even though the basis of Martin's defense has nothing to do with why State Bank is not a holder in due course.

In the example above, the person is asserting his own claim to the instrument as a reason for not paying the obligation on the instrument. May the person who owes the contract obligation assert another person's claim to the instrument as a defense to payment of the contract obligation? Return to the example of Greg and the burglar given above. Assume that Greg has informed Sam, the drawer, that the check was stolen. Sam notifies the drawee not to pay the check when it is presented. The drawee dishonors the check and Anne, the person to whom the burglar transferred the check, sues to enforce Sam's drawer's obligation. Sam has no defense of his own to payment of his drawer's obligation, but wants to assert the fact that the check was stolen from Greg to avoid payment of the drawer's obligation.

Read U.C.C. § 3-305(c). What that section tells us is that Sam's ability to assert Greg's ownership claim to the check as a defense to Sam's drawer's obligation on the check depends upon two things. First, if Anne is not a holder in due course, Sam may assert the fact that it was stolen as a defense to his drawer's obligation. If Anne is a holder in due course, Sam will not be able to assert the fact that the instrument was stolen as a reason not to pay his drawer's obligation. Second, Sam may only assert Greg's ownership claim to the instrument as a defense if Sam joins Greg in the lawsuit that Anne has brought against Sam and Greg asserts his ownership claim in that lawsuit. We have encountered that last point before. Review the end of the *Maine* case in Chapter 3 where the court relied on that last point to reject the drawer's defense to payment of the obligation on the checks.

Now consider another type of defense to payment. We learned in Chapter 3 that one type of defense an obligor may raise to enforcement of the contract obligation on the instrument is that the obligor's obligation to pay has been discharged. If the obligor has notice that a person other than the person entitled to enforce has a claim to the instrument but the obligor pays the person entitled to enforce anyway, is the obligor discharged on its contract obligation? **Read U.C.C. § 3-602.** The general answer is yes, unless the special circumstance in U.C.C. § 3-602(e) exists.

Now try your hand at these problems which are designed to flesh out your understanding of the principles and sections discussed above.

Problem 4-1

Arnold issued a negotiable demand note payable to the order of Brad. Brad pledged the note to Bank to secure a loan that Bank gave to Brad. Brad indorsed the note in blank on the back. Bank took possession of the note. According to the terms of the security agreement between Bank and Brad, Bank may collect on the note only if Brad defaults in Brad's obligation to repay the loan to Bank.

Notes

a)   Who is entitled to enforce this note?

b)   Who has a claim to the note?

c)   Assume that Arnold issued the note in the principal amount of $10,000 to Brad in exchange for goods. The goods were defective and breached a warranty that Brad gave regarding the quality of the goods. The value of the breach of warranty claim was $7,000. Brad defaulted on his obligation to Bank. Brad owed Bank $6,000. Bank sought to enforce its security interest in the note by making a demand upon Arnold for payment. Does Arnold have any defenses to payment that he can assert against Bank? U.C.C. § 3-302(e).

d) Assume that Bank transferred the note to Second Bank. Second Bank paid Bank 80% of the face value of the note and did not know about the security arrangement with Brad. The transfer to Second Bank violated the terms of the security agreement between Bank and Brad. What can Brad do?

e) Same facts as (d) above, except Second Bank knew when it bought the instrument from Bank that Arnold bought shoddy goods from Brad in the transaction that resulted in Arnold issuing the note. Does that fact change Brad's rights?

Problem 4-2

Alice issued a check to Betty, drawn on State Bank. Betty indorsed the check in blank and then lost the check on the street. Chris found the check and presented the check over the counter to the teller at State Bank. The teller paid the check amount to Chris.

a) Is Alice's or Betty's contract liability on the check discharged?

b) Alice notified State Bank that the check was lost and gave State Bank a timely stop payment order. State Bank paid the check anyway. Is there a discharge of Alice's or Betty's contract liability?

c) Assume Alice notified State Bank that the check was stolen so that when the

Notes

check was presented for payment, State Bank did not pay the check but dishonored it. Chris seeks to collect from Alice for the amount of the check. May Alice raise the fact that Betty is the owner of the check as a defense to payment of the check?

d) Same facts as (c) above, does Betty have any rights that she can assert in this situation?

e) Assume that Chris did not present the check for payment to the drawee. Chris transferred the check for value to David, who qualifies as a holder in due course. Alice had stopped payment on the check when Betty told Alice the check was lost. David sued Alice and Betty on their contract liabilities on the instrument. What result?

f) Assume that Betty did not indorse the check before she lost it. Chris found the check, indorsed it with Betty's name and deposited the check to Chris's account at National Bank. The check was paid by the drawee bank, State Bank, when National Bank presented the check. Does Betty have any rights against Chris or National Bank?

g) Assume that Betty indorsed the check in blank and with the words "for deposit only." Then Betty lost the

Notes

check. Chris found the check and deposited it to Chris's account at National Bank. The check was paid by the drawee bank, State Bank, when National Bank presented the check. Does Betty have any rights as against Chris or National Bank?

A reoccurring fact situation regarding claims to the negotiable instrument involves defalcation of a fiduciary. Article 3 contains a special provision on when a taker of a negotiable instrument has notice of the claim of a represented person to the instrument based on the wrongdoing of a fiduciary. If a taker of a negotiable instrument has notice of the claim of a represented person to the instrument, the taker would not qualify as a holder in due course under U.C.C. § 3-302. **Read U.C.C. §§ 3-307 and 3-206(d)**.

Consider the following illustration. George is the treasurer of Inventions, Inc. He has encountered a problem with his personal finances due to gambling losses. He decides to embezzle funds from Inventions, Inc. to pay some of his gambling debts. One of George's responsibilities as treasurer is to take checks payable to Inventions, Inc., stamp them with the indorsement of Inventions, Inc., and deposit those checks to Inventions' deposit account at National Bank. George takes a check payable to Inventions, Inc., stamps it with the blank indorsement of Inventions, Inc., and deposits the check at an ATM to George's personal bank account at State Bank. The check is paid by the drawer's bank. Assume that the president of Inventions, Inc. finds out what George has done and makes a claim against State Bank to recover the funds that State Bank credited to George's account due to the check deposit.

The basis of Inventions' lawsuit against State Bank is conversion. U.C.C. § 3-420(a). George in effect stole the check which belonged to Inventions. Under the common law of conversion, a person need not know that the property was stolen to have liability. State Bank, in order to avoid liability for conversion, will want to argue that it was a holder in due course of the check so that it took the check free of Inventions' property-based conversion claim against it. U.C.C. § 3-306. Whether State Bank qualifies as a holder in due course will depend, in part, on whether it took the check with notice of Inventions' claim to the check. (State Bank will have had to give value and also take without notice of the facts listed in U.C.C.

§ 3-302. State Bank will have given value by giving credits to George's account that George can withdraw as of right. U.C.C. §§ 4-211, 4-210). Section 3-307 addresses the issue of whether State Bank had notice of Inventions' property claim to the check based upon George's actions in stealing the check.

In order to apply U.C.C. § 3-307 to this situation, several factual determinations must be made. First, George must be a "fiduciary" with respect to the check. Second, State Bank must have taken the instrument from George for payment, collection, or value. Third, State Bank must have knowledge that George is a fiduciary. Fourth, Inventions must make a claim to the check or its proceeds based upon George's breach of a fiduciary duty. These factual prerequisites are based upon U.C.C. § 3-307(a) and the first clause of subsection (b) (before the colon). If these four prerequisites are true, then the stage is set to apply the applicable subparagraphs (1) through (4) of subsection (b).

Subsection (b)(1) provides that if the taker of the instrument has notice of the breach of the fiduciary duty, the taker has notice of the claim of the represented person. That relates back to the requirements of a holder in due course. Notice of the claim of the represented person would preclude the taker from being a holder in due course, U.C.C. § 3-302, and make the taker vulnerable to the conversion cause of action, or other causes of action that are based upon the property rights of the represented person. U.C.C. § 3-306. (It will also make the taker vulnerable to any defenses to payment of the instrument that may be asserted by persons who have contract liability on the instrument. U.C.C. § 3-305.) Subsections (b)(2) through (b)(4) then describe different situations in which the taker is deemed to have notice of the breach of fiduciary duty.

Is George a fiduciary with respect to the check? Generally if an employee has responsibility with respect to instruments, such as indorsing them or writing them, most courts would find that person as a fiduciary with respect to the instrument. If an employee does not have job-related responsibilities with respect to that type of instrument, then a court may find that person is not a fiduciary with respect to the instrument.

Did State Bank take the check for collection, payment, or value? Yes. When George deposited the check into his deposit account at State Bank, State Bank is taking the instrument for collection. The collection process is started by that deposit and State Bank's processes will result in eventual presentment of that check for payment to the drawee bank.

Did State Bank have "knowledge" of the fact that George was a fiduciary? **Read the definition of knowledge in U.C.C. § 1-202.** What facts would give State

Bank actual knowledge that George was a fiduciary for Inventions, Inc.? State Bank must have "knowledge" not merely "notice" of that fact. Inventions could have a hard time demonstrating that State Bank had such knowledge from the mere deposit of the check payable to Inventions Inc. and indorsed in blank.

Is the basis of Inventions' cause of action against State Bank a claim to the check or proceeds based upon George's breach of fiduciary duty? Yes. Inventions is claiming conversion of the check and its proceeds. The basis of the conversion cause of action is George's action in stealing the check, i.e. converting it, a breach of his fiduciary duty (assuming George is a fiduciary).

Assuming that Inventions can surmount the hurdle of demonstrating State Bank's knowledge of George's fiduciary status, section 3-307(b)(2) would apply. The check was payable to the represented person, Inventions, Inc. and it was deposited to an account other than the account of the fiduciary as a fiduciary or an account of the represented person. George deposited the check to his personal account, not to an account he maintains as the fiduciary of Inventions. State Bank would have "notice" of the breach of fiduciary duty and thus notice of a claim. That notice of a claim prevents State Bank from being a holder in due course and thus subject to Inventions' conversion claim.

That result in this scenario hinges on one critical fact: Did State Bank have actual knowledge of George's fiduciary status? If the answer is yes, Inventions will be successful in its conversion action against State Bank. If the answer is no and State Bank otherwise qualifies as a holder in due course, Inventions will be unsuccessful in its conversion action against State Bank.

The other subparagraphs of U.C.C. § 3-307(b) focus on other situations in which a fiduciary might deal with instruments. Subsection (b)(3) addresses instruments payable to the fiduciary personally. Subsection (b)(4) addresses instruments issued by the fiduciary or represented person. Notice that subsection (b)(3) requires the taker to "know" of the breach of fiduciary duty. Why is the required standard in subsection (b)(3) ("know") different than the standard ("notice") in subsections (b)(2) and (b)(4)?

One more wrinkle. Suppose a negotiable note states it is payable to the order of Mary. Mary indorses that note "Pay to George, in trust for Inventions, Inc." George indorses the note in blank and sells it to First Bank. **Read U.C.C. § 3-206(d).** Has First Bank converted the note?

Now consider the following case.

MUTUAL SERVICE CASUALTY INSURANCE COMPANY
v. ELIZABETH STATE BANK
265 F. 3d 601 (7th Cir. 2001)

Ilana Diamond Rovner, Circuit Judge

In the course of his employment with Jo Daviess Services, Inc. ("Jo Daviess," or "the company"), Arlyn Hemmen managed to misappropriate more than $80,000 from the company's bank account at the Elizabeth State Bank ("ESB" or "the bank"). Mutual Service Casualty Company ("Mutual"), which insured Jo Daviess, compensated the company for its loss. Mutual then filed suit against ESB, contending that the bank had breached its contractual obligations to Jo Daviess by allowing Hemmen to abscond with its funds. The case proceeded to trial, and after both parties had presented their cases, Judge Reinhard entered judgment as a matter of law in favor of Mutual. ESB appeals, contending that Mutual was not entitled to judgment as a matter of law and that the prejudgment interest that the district court awarded to Mutual was inappropriate. We affirm the judgment in Mutual's favor but remand for recalculation of the award of prejudgment interest.

I.

During the period of time relevant to this case, Jo Daviess was a farm service cooperative located in the northwestern Illinois community of Elizabeth, a town of approximately 700 people. Among other things, Jo Daviess sold animal feed, seed, fertilizer, and fuel to its members.

Late in 1991, the company hired Hemmen to serve as its controller. Hemmen previously had worked at a number of banks. In his capacity as controller, Hemmen maintained the company's books and accounts, reviewed and reconciled its bank statements, prepared monthly operating statements and other financial reports, and supervised his co-workers in the absence of the office manager.

While Hemmen was employed with the company, Jo Daviess maintained two accounts with ESB: an operating account, into which the company deposited all of its revenue and out of which it paid for its day-to-day expenses and any products the company purchased, and a second account reserved for the company's payroll. ESB maintained another account, referred to as the treasury tax and loan ("TT & L") account, into which the bank's commercial customers deposited the federal income tax that they withheld from their employees' paychecks; funds from this account were forwarded to the federal government on a daily basis. As needed, Jo Daviess periodically transferred funds out of its operating account into either the payroll or the TT & L account.

Pursuant to the terms and conditions of the agreement governing the operating account at ESB, only authorized signers could withdraw or transfer funds from that account. Hemmen was never a signer on the operating account. He did have the authority to sign checks drawn on the payroll account (footnote omitted) – a power that company officials could not recall him ever having exercised– but witnesses from ESB as well as Jo Daviess agreed that Hemmen's status as a signer on one account did not authorize him to make withdrawals or transfers from another account.

Although Hemmen was not a signer on the operating account, he regularly prepared checks drawn on that account, both to pay Jo Daviess' suppliers and to transfer funds into one of the other accounts. These checks would be presented to the company's general manager for signature. On occasion, for purposes of transferring funds into the TT & L account, Hemmen would prepare a check payable to the order of ESB. Jo Daviess did not owe any money to the bank so the only legitimate reason for making a check payable to the bank would be to accomplish a transfer of funds from the operating account to the TT & L account.

The company kept a small amount of petty cash ($50 to $100) on hand in the office. This fund was primarily used to handle small, incidental expenses. Periodically a check would be drawn on the operating account to replenish that fund. Typically these checks were made out to "cash," "petty cash," or "Jo Daviess Service Company petty cash". On occasion, the check might be made payable to the bank, but if so, the check would bear a notation indicating that it was issued in order to "replenish petty cash." In practice, Jo Daviess allowed both Hemmen and office secretaries to cash these checks, although none was a signer on the operating account. Company officials never had any discussion with Hemmen regarding the limits of this authority. However, the amount of such checks never exceeded the total amount of the petty cash fund; they typically ranged from $25 to $50.

Beginning in January 1992, Hemmen began to embezzle money from Jo Daviess. Periodically, he would prepare a check on the company's operating account payable to the order of ESB, as if he were making a deposit into the TT & L account. He would then present the check to the general manager, who signed the check assuming that the proceeds were, indeed, destined for the TT & L account. So far as company officials were concerned, that was the only legitimate reason for preparing a check payable to the bank. In fact, however, Hemmen would divert the proceeds of the checks to his own use in one of several ways. On some occasions, Hemmen presented the check to an ESB teller and requested that a portion of the check be deposited into the TT & L account, with the balance to be disbursed to him either in cash or one or more cashier's checks payable to Hemmen's creditors. On other occasions, Hemmen would present the check and have the entirety of the proceeds issued to him, again either in the form of cash or a cashier's check. Bank personnel did not realize that Hemmen was diverting the proceeds to his own use; Hemmen would explain that the cash and cashier's checks were necessary in order to pay for supplies, parts or some other legitimate company expense. In case anyone at Jo Daviess should notice that not all of the check proceeds were being deposited into the TT & L account, Hemmen would make a false entry in Jo Daviess' internal records indicating that the cash or cashier's check issued to him was used to pay for something like postage, for example. "It was just a total fake, [a] total lie," Hemmen testified. Indeed, Jo Daviess paid its obligations with cash or cashier's checks only on rare occasions.

ESB was aware, of course that Hemmen was not an authorized signer on Jo Daviess' operating account, and Jo Daviess never indicated to the bank that Hemmen had authority to withdraw funds from that account. Nonetheless, the bank acceded to Hemmen's requests for cash and cashier's checks without first consulting with Jo Daviess to confirm his authority to receive the proceeds of these checks, and without even asking him to endorse the checks. In fact, it was the bank's custom during this period of time to honor such requests. So long as bank personnel knew the presenter, and so long as the check was signed by an authorized individual, the bank would disburse the proceeds of the check to the presenter notwithstanding the fact that the presenter himself was not an authorized signer. "We didn't question it if we knew them," explained one bank employee. And the bank's personnel knew Hemmen--shortly after Jo Daviess had hired Hemmen, a company secretary who once had worked at ESB took him down to the bank and introduced him to the bank's staff. In short, there was nothing that Jo Daviess did or said that induced the bank to comply with Hemmen's requests; the bank simply did so in compliance with its usual practice. On the other hand, Jo Daviess officials had never discussed with ESB whether Hemmen could legitimately receive the proceeds of any checks payable to the bank. "We weren't instructed whether he did or did not have authority to do that," said a bank official. "There were no instructions."[2]

---

[2] Bank teller Kathy McCall testified that when Hemmen first presented one of these checks to her and asked for a cashier's check in return, she sought approval from Marvin Wurster,

(continued...)

Banking experts who testified on behalf of Mutual and ESB disagreed as to whether it was proper for ESB to honor the checks that Hemmen presented. Mutual's expert, Charles Malony, a banking official from the Chicago area, opined that it is bad form for a bank to negotiate a check that is payable to the bank's own order and that is presented to the bank by someone who is not a signer on the account. The proper course of action for a bank to take in this situation, Malony believed, would be to send the presenter away or to contact an official of the drawer with signature authority in order to confirm the propriety of the transaction. If the presenter is given cash, he ought in the least be required to sign the back of the check. Moreover, the presenter's position with the drawer should have no bearing on his ability to receive the proceeds of such checks, Malony testified. Malony was willing to acknowledge, however, that in practice, a bank that knows its customer well is more likely to be liberal in its policies.

On the other hand, ESB's expert, Jeffrey Snyder, a banking official who had worked at a number of small-town banks, indicated that it is common for banks in small communities to rely on individuals who are not authorized signers for instructions as to the appropriate disposition of checks drawn to the bank's order. Snyder acknowledged that "the bank has a responsibility to post [a] transaction as the drawer expects[.]" But in practice, Snyder explained, the authorized signer typically is the owner of a business, who has better things to do with his or her time than to traipse down to the bank. Typically, a bookkeeper or another employee is sent instead of an authorized signer. In a larger metropolitan area, where a bank has no way of knowing each of the many persons who will transact business with it, bank employees will naturally be unwilling to accept instructions from

---

[2] (...continued)
the bank's vice-president, because the request struck her as unusual. According to McCall, Wurster approved the request, and from that point forward she and the other tellers allowed Hemmen to negotiate checks payable to the bank in this way, although they believed it was "a little different." (McCall would later go to work for a different bank in Elizabeth. At that bank, she said, an individual who presented a corporate check payable to the bank could not receive cash back if he was not an authorized signer, unless the transaction was authorized by the company.)

We note McCall's testimony but do not take it into consideration in assessing the propriety of the district court's decision to enter judgment as a matter of law in Mutual's favor. As noted above, we are obligated to construe the evidence in ESB's favor. Wurster himself could not recall having had such a conversation with McCall, and other bank personnel, who described McCall as a malcontent, doubted that the conversation had occurred.

non-authorized employees. But in a small community like Elizabeth, "we know all of these people," Snyder observed. "We probably know who their parents were."

> "And because we have that knowledge of our customers, it allows us to facilitate some of these transactions with the confidence that we're acting according to the instructions of the drawer. And we also know how these businesses--people run their businesses, and, you know, we have the confidence that if the business didn't intend to have that person tell us what to do with the item, they wouldn't have signed it and sent them down there with it."

Thus, so long as the bank is familiar with the presenter and knows that he is the drawer's employee, and in the absence of any suspicious circumstances, a small town bank in practice likely will honor the presenter's instructions--including an instruction to issue cash to the presenter himself. This amounts to a judgment call on the part of the bank employee to whom the item is presented, Snyder said, turning on such factors as one's familiarity with the presenter, the length of time he has been employed by the drawer, his position with the drawer, and the amount of money involved in the transaction.

Taking advantage of the small-town practice that Snyder described, Hemmen managed to embezzle approximately $83,000 from Jo Daviess over a three-year period. There was nothing irregular on the face of the checks themselves, and the monthly bank statements that the bank mailed to Jo Daviess revealed appropriate debits to the company's operating account. As far as Jo Daviess personnel knew, 100 percent of the proceeds of these checks were being transferred into the TT & L account. Company officials did no checking of their own to make sure that the proceeds of the checks were being handled as Hemmen had led them to believe; they trusted him. Because the bank never notified Jo Daviess that Hemmen was instead receiving cash and cashier's checks, and did not confirm his authority to do so, the company remained ignorant of Hemmen's embezzlement. Not until an outside audit was performed in February of 1995 did Jo Daviess discover what Hemmen had done. After coming across a check that had been recorded as a deposit to the TT & L account, auditors discovered that some cash had been returned to the presenter. The disbursement of cash struck the auditors as unusual, and they undertook a comprehensive review of all checks that culminated in the discovery of Hemmen's malfeasance.

Jo Daviess submitted a claim to its insurer, Mutual, which paid the company a total of $82,963. Mutual, as Jo Daviess' subrogee, in turn filed this action against the bank, seeking reimbursement on alternative theories of breach of contract (based on the deposit agreement) and negligence.

* * * *

[Mutual conceded its negligence claim was barred by the Illinois economic loss rule and that claim was dismissed-Ed.] The breach of contract claim proceeded to trial.

ESB attempted to pursue a number of defenses to the contract claim that the district court, in advance of trial, determined not to be viable as a matter of law. *First*, ESB wished to show that it had taken the checks underlying Mutual's claim as a holder in due course, and that as a result it took those checks free of all claims--including Mutual's claim for breach of contract. Judge Reinhard determined, however, that the bank could not qualify as a holder in due course because the checks were drawn to the order of the bank, and ESB had distributed the proceeds of the checks to a presenter who lacked authority to withdraw funds from the account. *Second*, ESB sought to prove that Hemmen was a fiduciary who was empowered to instruct the bank as to the disposition of proceeds of checks made payable to the bank, and that, consequently, under the Illinois Fiduciary Obligations Act, ESB was not liable for Hemmen's misdeeds unless it acted in bad faith. This defense was not viable, the district judge reasoned, because there was no evidence that would permit the jury to find Hemmen qualified as a fiduciary vis à vis checks drawn to the bank's order. Hemmen was not an authorized signer on the operating account, and thus had no authority to receive the proceeds of these checks. *Third*, under a theory of pure comparative negligence, ESB wished to show that Jo Daviess' own negligence in employing Hemmen, placing him in charge of the company's financial record-keeping, and in its handling of the checks that Hemmen made payable to the bank's order, was a substantial cause of the company's (and hence Mutual's) loss and therefore reduced ESB's liability. But Judge Reinhard concluded that a defense based on comparative negligence was not available to ESB given its written deposit agreement with Jo Daviess, which agreement did not authorize Hemmen to withdraw funds from the operating account. *Fourth*, ESB posited that as a compensated insurer, Mutual could not recover the monies it paid to Jo Daviess from a party like the bank, whose equities (in the bank's view) were equal or superior to those of Mutual. Judge Reinhard concluded that Illinois did not recognize this defense.

With these defenses eliminated, ESB resisted liability at trial on two principal theories. First, in the bank's view, the facts did not establish a breach of any contractual duty owed to Jo Daviess. ESB pointed out that nothing in the deposit agreement specifically addressed the bank's responsibility with respect to checks payable to itself. It further relied on the testimony of Snyder, as well as the testimony of its own officials, for the proposition that reasonable banking practice in small communities permits a bank to release funds to a known employee of the drawer even when that employee is not formally authorized to withdraw funds from an account. Second, ESB contended that Hemmen had either actual or implied authority to receive funds from Jo Daviess' operating account and that the bank had reasonably relied on that authority in disbursing the proceeds of the checks in question to him.

At the close of evidence, and before the case was submitted to the jury, Judge Reinhard concluded that Mutual was entitled to judgment as a matter of law. As a threshold matter, he determined that ESB had a duty, founded on the terms of the deposit agreement as well as the case law, not to disburse the proceeds of a check drawn to the bank's order to anyone other than an authorized signer. Thus, when Hemmen presented such a check to ESB, the bank ought either to have refused the check altogether, accepted it for deposit only, or held the check until such time as an authorized signer presented the check with instructions as to the appropriate disposition of the check proceeds. By electing instead to honor Hemmen's requests for cash and cashier's checks, ESB had breached that duty. Judge Reinhard rejected the notion that a bank's duty vis à vis checks payable to its own order might be different in a small town than it was elsewhere. The same rule must apply everywhere, he reasoned, lest the law of negotiable instruments be placed in jeopardy. Finally, he found that the facts precluded ESB's attempted resort to the theory that Hemmen had actual or implied authority to receive the proceeds of the checks in question. The testimony revealed that ESB made it a practice to release funds to the known employees of its commercial customers, the judge pointed out. Consequently, the bank could not show that it relied on any authority Hemmen might have possessed in releasing the check proceeds to him.

With the question of ESB's liability resolved, the parties quickly stipulated as to the amount of damages. Mutual had claimed total damages of $83,790.48, an amount slightly greater than the sum it paid to Jo Daviess. At trial, questions had arisen as to whether two of the checks that Hemmen had prepared and for which cash had been disbursed--one in the amount of $1,000 and the other for $89--might have been for legitimate company purposes. Mutual agreed to drop these checks from its claim and ESB stipulated that the balance of $82,701.48 represented the amount for which it was liable. The court entered judgment in that amount.

[Discussion of prejudgment interest issue omitted-Ed].

* * * *

II.

The bulk of ESB's arguments on appeal fall into two principal categories-- those directed at the validity and sufficiency of Mutual's claim for breach of contract and those focused on the defenses that the district court rejected. Within the first category, there are three contentions that ESB makes: (1) that the Uniform Commercial Code has displaced the common-law underpinnings of Mutual's claim; (2) that Mutual's claim for breach of contract is at bottom a negligence claim, and as such is barred by the Illinois Supreme Court's decision in *Moorman Mfg. Co. v. National Tank Co.*, 91 Ill.2d 69, 61 Ill.Dec. 746, 435 N.E.2d 443 (1982); and (3) that the evidence with respect to banking practice in small communities at the very least raised a question of fact as to whether ESB breached any duty to Jo Daviess by negotiating the checks drawn to its own order. As for the second category, ESB argues that Judge Reinhard erred in summarily rejecting three of its proffered defenses: (1) the holder-in-due-course defense; (2) its defense under the Illinois Fiduciary Obligations Act; and (3) the compensated surety defense. Finally, as we mentioned at the outset, ESB also contends that the award of prejudgment interest was inappropriate for a variety of reasons.

[The Court of Appeals stated that its review of entry of judgment as a matter of law was de novo and that in this diversity action, the law of the state of Illinois governed.–Ed.]

* * * *

A.

The commercial deposit agreement that governed Jo Daviess' operating account with the bank permitted only authorized signers to withdraw funds from that account. Hemmen, of course, was not an authorized signer; so had the bank, for example, negotiated checks on the operating account that Hemmen had signed, there would be no question that it would be liable for breach of the deposit agreement. (Citation omitted) But instead, Hemmen used a time-honored method of circumnavigating the signature requirement, by preparing checks payable to the bank and having them signed by an authorized company official, and then directing the bank to issue cash or cashier's checks to him in return.

Although the deposit agreement did not specify how the bank was to handle checks made payable to its own order, implicit in the duty of care that the bank owed to Jo Daviess by virtue of the deposit agreement, was an obligation to verify that Hemmen had the authority to receive the proceeds of such checks and that his instructions vis à vis those proceeds conformed to Jo Daviess' wishes. The rule is well- recognized:

> Where a check drawn to the order of a bank is presented to such bank, and the drawer owes no [debt] to the bank, the bank must see that the proceeds are not misapplied, and cannot without justification divert the proceeds to the use of one other than the drawer, and is authorized to pay the proceeds only to persons specified by the drawer. The bank takes a risk in treating the check as being payable to the bearer, and is placed on inquiry as to the authority of the drawer's agent to receive payment. The duty to inquire of the drawer is not satisfied by making inquiry of the bearer. If the bank assumes without investigation that the instructions of the presenter are those of the drawer, it takes a risk. Where the drawer's agent or one representing himself or herself to be such is not in fact authorized, the bank is liable to the drawer for paying the check to such person....

9 C.J.S. BANKS AND BANKING § 327, at 316-17 (1996) (footnotes omitted); *see also* Boyd J. Peterson, Annotation, *Liability of bank for diversion to benefit of presenter or third party of proceeds of check drawn to bank's order by drawer not indebted to bank*, 69 A.L.R.4th 778 (1989). This rule derives from the position of trust that the bank occupies with respect to funds that it has invited its customers to place in its custody.

> The public is invited to use [the bank's] conveniences as places of deposit; it holds itself out as trustworthy for such purposes; when it is named as the payee in a check by a party not indebted to it, it will be presumed that it accepts the same subject to the directions of the drawer and not to the directions of a stranger to the paper who happens to present it.

Douglass v. Wones, 120 Ill.App.3d 36, 76 Ill.Dec. 114, 458 N.E.2d 514, 522 (1983), quoting *Milano v. Sheridan Trust & Sav. Bank*, 242 Ill.App. 362, 368, 1926 WL 3944, at *3 (Ill.App.1926). Put another way, when a drawer owes nothing to a bank but writes a check payable to the bank's order, the drawer places that check in the bank's custody, with the expectation that the bank will negotiate the check according to the *drawer's* wishes; the bank may not, therefore, treat the check as bearer paper and blindly disburse the proceeds according to the instructions of any individual who happens to present the check to the bank. (Citation omitted). As *Wones* reflects, Illinois has long embraced this common-law rule. (Citations omitted). The Land of Lincoln is by no means an exception in that regard. "This general proposition enjoys the unwavering support of a vast body of judicial opinion originating both before and after the creation of the U.C.C." *Bullitt County Bank v. Publishers Printing Co.*, 684 S.W.2d 289, 292 (Ky.App.1984). (Citations omitted).

The evidence admits of no doubt that ESB breached its obligation to ensure that the proceeds of the checks payable to the bank's order were not misapplied. Never did the bank bother to inquire of a Jo Daviess official (someone other than Hemmen himself, of course) whether Hemmen's instructions as to the disposition of these checks were appropriate. Conversely, Jo Daviess never gave the bank any reason to believe that Hemmen was empowered to receive the proceeds of checks made payable to the bank. The bank, aware that Hemmen was the company's controller, simply assumed that he was acting within the scope of his authority. Yet, as the Illinois Supreme Court has observed in a similar context:

> Persons dealing with an assumed agent are bound, at their peril, to ascertain, not only the fact of the agency, but the extent of the agent's authority. They are put upon their guard by the very fact that they are dealing with an agent, and must, at their peril, see to it that the act done by him is within his power.

Paine, 174 N.E. at 370; *see also Bullitt*, 684 S.W.2d at 293. This the bank failed to do.

B.

The bank suggests that the common-law duty of care on which Mutual's claim is based has been superseded generally by the Uniform Commercial Code, but we find nothing in the UCC, as adopted by the Illinois legislature, that displaces the common-law rule. The Code itself provides for supplementation by common-law principles, "[u]nless displaced by the particular provisions of this Act." 810 ILL. COMP. STAT. 5/1-103. Although the scheme perpetrated by Hemmen is a common one, no provision of the Code delineates what a bank's rights and obligations are when a person presents a corporate check payable to the bank and instructs the bank to divert the proceeds of the check to his own benefit. *See Bullitt*, 684 S.W.2d at 291. As we noted earlier, the common-law rule governing this situation springs from the duty of care that the bank owes its depositors. The Code provisions governing the relationship between a bank and its customer recognize and embrace that duty. *See, e.g.*, 810 ILL. COMP. STAT. 5/4-103, 5/4-406; *see also* 810 ILL. COMP. STAT. 5/3-103(7) (defining "ordinary care"); *Bullitt*, 684 S.W.2d at 291-92; *Robertson's Crab House*, 389 A.2d at 392-93. Indeed, although the Code permits contracting parties to vary the effect of those provisions by agreement, it expressly disallows any term which purports to "disclaim a bank's responsibility for its lack of good faith or failure to exercise ordinary care or limit the measure of damages for the lack or failure." 810 ILL. COMP. STAT. 5/4-103(a); *see Robertson's Crab*

House, 389 A.2d at 392-93, *quoting Gillen v. Maryland Nat'l Bank*, 274 Md. 96, 333 A.2d 329, 333 (1975); *Inkrott*, 563 N.E.2d at 28. Accordingly, courts throughout the country have continued to apply the common-law rule on which Mutual's claim is founded notwithstanding the advent of the UCC. (Citations omitted). No court that we are aware of has found the rule to be inconsistent with any provision of the Code.

* * * *

[Discussion of the application of Illinois' economic loss rule is omitted.–Ed.]

D.

In an effort to fend off a finding that the bank had breached its contractual duty of care, ESB emphasized below that Elizabeth is a small town and posited that the duty of care on which Mutual's claim is founded must be defined with reference to small-town norms. Recall that Snyder, the bank's expert, testified that is a common practice for banks in small communities to honor a check drawn to the order of the bank when the presenter is known to the bank's staff. Informal practices like this one serve to facilitate the transaction of business by the bank's customers, he explained. Thus, in ESB's view, a small-town bank ought not be obliged to verify the presenter's authority to receive or disburse the proceeds of a check payable to the bank when bank personnel know the presenter, as they did in this case.

Judge Reinhard properly rejected the effort to modify or limit the bank's duty of care when he found, as a matter of law, that ESB had breached its contract with Jo Daviess. The bank cites no case which recognizes an exception to the common-law rule based on the size of the community, the idiosyncrasies of local banking practice, or the bank's familiarity with the presenter, and we have found none. Judge Reinhard reasoned that the rule must be uniform and he was right. The duty of care underlying the rule is one which inheres in every agreement between a bank and its depositor, and over the past century courts have given that rule a clear, simple, and consistent meaning with respect to checks payable to the order of the bank. Indeed, the UCC, to which the bank looks for a number of its appellate arguments, states that one of its purposes is "to make uniform the law among the various jurisdictions." 810 ILL. COMP. STAT. 5/1-102(c); *see also* Official UCC Comment regarding 1990 Revision of Article 3, 810 ILL. COMP. STAT. ANN., Act 5, Art. 3 (1993) (immediately preceding 5/3-101) ("The law for payments through checks and which governs other negotiable instruments ... should be uniform and up-to- date, either through state enactments or Federal preemption. Otherwise, checks as a viable payment system in international and national transactions will be severely hampered and the utility of other negotiable instruments impaired."). The obligation imposed by the common-law rule is not onerous. *See Sun 'n Sand, Inc. v. United California Bank, supra*, 148 Cal.Rptr. at 346, 582 P.2d 920. The very face of the check--payable, as it is, to a bank which is owed nothing by the drawer--alerts the bank to the need for caution. *Paine v. Sheridan Trust & Sav. Bank, supra*, 255 Ill.App. at 261, 1929 WL 3406, at *5. The rule simply requires the bank "not [to] ignore the danger signals inherent in such an attempted negotiation." *Sun 'n Sand*, 148 Cal.Rptr. at 346, 582 P.2d 920. We are given no reason to believe that a small-town bank will have a more difficult time than any other bank in verifying the presenter's authority to receive or disburse the proceeds of such a check--if anything, it ought to be easier for a bank in a small community to do so.

E.

Generally speaking, one who takes a negotiable instrument for value, in good faith, and without notice of any claim or defense to the instrument, acquires the rights of a holder in due course. *See* 810 ILL. COMP. STAT. 5/3-302. As such (with certain exceptions), he holds the instrument free of all claims either to the instrument or its proceeds. *See* 810 ILL. COMP. STAT. 5/3-302, 5/3-306; (citation omitted). In the court below, the bank wished to establish that when it negotiated the Jo Daviess checks that Hemmen presented, it became a holder in due course and was therefore shielded from Mutual's common-law claim. More particularly, it was the bank's theory that Hemmen had breached a fiduciary duty to Jo Daviess by diverting the proceeds of the checks to his own use. In the bank's view, Hemmen's status as a fiduciary brought UCC section 3-307 into play. The terms of that section would have protected the bank so long as it lacked knowledge of the facts constituting his breach of fiduciary duty. *See* 810 ILL. COMP. STAT. 5/3-307(b)(4). However, the district judge ruled in advance of trial that section 3-307 was inapplicable, because Hemmen did not have authority to receive the proceeds of checks payable to the bank under any circumstance, and so was not a fiduciary in that regard. Judge Reinhard also concluded that the holder-in-due-course defense is not available when a bank permits an individual like Hemmen to divert the proceeds of a check payable to the bank to the use of someone other than the drawer.

On appeal, the bank relies on the holder-in-due-course provisions of the Code to make two arguments. The bank suggests first that three provisions of the Code– sections 3-302, 3-306, and 3-307– comprehensively address the fraudulent-check scenario presented here and so foreclose Mutual's common-law claim.

Alternatively, the bank contends that these provisions supply it with a meritorious defense to the claim, and that Judge Reinhard erred when he excluded the holder-in-due-course concept from the case. Before we turn to these arguments, a brief overview of the provisions on which the bank relies is appropriate.

Each of the three Code provisions that the bank invokes relates either to the rights that a holder in due course enjoys or the conditions under which he qualifies as a holder in due course. Section 3-306 sets forth a basic rule addressing competing claims to a financial instrument or its proceeds:

> A person taking an instrument, other than a person having rights of a holder in due course, is subject to a claim of a property or possessory right in the instrument or its proceeds, including a claim to rescind a negotiation and to recover the instrument or its proceeds. A person having the rights of a holder in due course takes free of the claim to an instrument.

810 ILL. COMP. STAT. 5/3-306. Section 3-302(a) in turn spells out the criteria for identifying a holder in due course:

> ... "[H]older in due course" means the holder of an instrument if:
>
> (1) the instrument when issued or negotiated to the holder does not bear such apparent evidence of forgery or alteration or is not otherwise so irregular or incomplete as to call into question its authenticity, and
>
> (2) the holder took the instrument (i) for value, (ii) in good faith, ... [and]
>
> (v) without notice of any claim to the instrument described in Section 3-306
>
> ....

810 ILL. COMP. STAT. 5/3-302(a). Finally, section 3-307 deals with a subset of claims under section 3-306 involving a fiduciary who causes the proceeds of an instrument to be misapplied. *See* 810 ILL. COMP. STAT. 5/3-307, UCC Official Comment 2. Specifically, this provision spells out the various circumstances under which the holder of an instrument (including a bank) can be said to have taken the instrument with notice of the breach of fiduciary duty, such that the holder cannot assert the rights of a holder in due course. *See id.* As relevant here, the provision requires the holder to have knowledge of (1) the fiduciary status of the person from whom it took the instrument and (2) the facts indicating a breach of fiduciary duty. *See* 5/3- 307(b)(4) & UCC Official Comment 2.

As we have said, the bank's first contention is that these interacting provisions of the Code specifically address the scenario presented in this case, and in so doing displace the common-law claim that Mutual has asserted. This particular displacement argument is not one that the bank made below, however, and so we need not, and do not, undertake to resolve this argument on its merits. (Citation omitted). We do take the opportunity to make two observations in this regard. First, although the three provisions that the bank has cited describe in some detail the circumstances under which the holder takes an instrument free of claims, they are largely silent as to the types of claims that may be asserted when the holder-in-due-course criteria are not satisfied. Section 3-306, for example, indicates simply that a person who is not a holder in due course takes an instrument "subject to a claim of a property or possessory right in the instrument or its proceeds." 810 ILL. COMP. STAT. 5/3-306. The commentary to section 5/3-307 reveals that a claim founded on a breach of fiduciary duty would be one that could be asserted under section 3-306, *see* 810 ILL. COMP. STAT. 5/3-307, Official UCC Comment 2, but the Code otherwise offers little elucidation as to the scope of the claims that may be characterized as claims "of a property or possessory right in the instrument or its proceeds," and it does not undertake to identify the elements of such claims. Moreover, assuming that the facts in this case would permit Mutual to assert a claim under section 3-306, the bank has made no attempt to show how and why the common-law claim that Mutual has asserted might be inconsistent with relief under the Code. In short, the case for displacement is anything but obvious, as the courts' continued reliance on the common-law rule itself suggests.

As for the bank's alternative argument, we agree with Judge Reinhard that the nature of Mutual's claim renders the holder-in-due-course defense inapplicable as a matter of law. In order for the bank to qualify as a holder in due course, it must have negotiated the checks without notice of Jo Daviess' (and hence Mutual's) claim. The premise of the common-law claim, however, is that a bank *does* have notice of potential foul play when the employee of a drawer attempts to negotiate a check payable to the order of the bank, and the drawer owes no debt to the bank. *Paine*, 255 Ill.App. at 261, 1929 WL 3406, at *5. The check itself poses an unanswered question as to whom the bank is to pay. (Citations omitted). The bank knowingly risks liability, then, when it honors the instructions of the presenter without verifying that his instructions reflect the wishes of the drawer. Courts in Illinois and elsewhere have therefore rejected efforts to assert holder-in-due-course status as a defense to this type of claim. (Citations omitted).

The bank acknowledges that the cases are against it on this point but asserts they are out of date. A substantial re-write of Chapter Three took effect in 1992, and among the new provisions was section 3-307, on which the bank places such emphasis. The bank posits that Hemmen was a fiduciary, and therefore section 3-307, which spells out the level of notice required before a holder is subject to a claim for breach of fiduciary duty, controls the resolution of this case. But section

3-307 defines a "fiduciary" as "an agent, trustee, partner, corporate officer or director, or other representative owing a fiduciary duty *with respect to an instrument.*" 810 ILL. COMP. STAT. 5/3-307 (emphasis ours). It is undisputed in this case that Hemmen had no authority to direct the proceeds of checks drawn on Jo Daviess' operating account and payable to the bank's order anywhere but into either the payroll account or the TT & L account. The only Jo Daviess account on which Hemmen was an authorized signer was the payroll account, and witnesses testifying on behalf of both parties agreed that Hemmen's authority vis à vis the payroll account did not give him authority to disburse funds from any other account. Hemmen on occasion did negotiate checks on the operating account to replenish the company's petty cash fund, but these checks were always in small amounts ($25 to $50, typically), and the checks were either payable to "cash" or a variant thereof or they contained notations indicating that their purpose was to replenish the petty cash drawer. In sum, as Judge Reinhard recognized, Hemmen may have been a fiduciary for some purposes, but he did not qualify as a fiduciary with respect to checks drawn on the operating account and made payable to the bank's order. *See Empire Moving & Warehouse Corp. v. Hyde Park Bank & Trust Co.*, 43 Ill.App.3d 991, 2 Ill.Dec. 753, 357 N.E.2d 1196, 1202 (1976) (discussed *infra*) (applying Illinois Fiduciary Obligations Act); *cf. Alton Banking & Trust Co. v. Alton Building & Loan Ass'n,* 289 Ill.App. 177, 6 N.E.2d 921, 926 (1937) (building and loan association's practice of permitting secretary to have charge of its books, receive cash, and deposit funds into its bank account did not establish implied authority to borrow money on association's credit).

F.

The bank argues next that even if it was contractually obliged to see that the proceeds of checks payable to its own order were not misapplied, the Illinois Fiduciary Obligations Act, 760 ILL. COMP. STAT. 65/1, *et seq.* (the "FOA"), supplies it with a viable defense which, at a minimum, precluded the district court from granting judgment as a matter of law in favor of Mutual. As with its UCC defense, the bank's resort to the FOA rests on the premise that Hemmen was a fiduciary.

"The purpose of the [FOA] is to facilitate banking and financial transactions and place on the principal the burden of employing honest fiduciaries." *County of Macon v. Edgcomb*, 274 Ill.App.3d 432, 211 Ill.Dec. 136, 654 N.E.2d 598, 601 (1995), *citing Johnson v. Citizens Nat'l Bank of Decatur*, 30 Ill.App.3d 1066, 334 N.E.2d 295, 300 (1975). Section 1 of the FOA defines "fiduciary" to include a "partner, agent, officer of corporation, public or private, ... or any other person acting in a fiduciary capacity for any person, trust or estate." 760 ILL. COMP. STAT. 65/1. The statute then goes on to provide, in relevant part:

> A person who in good faith pays or transfers to a fiduciary any money or other property which the fiduciary as such is authorized to receive, is not responsible for the proper application thereof by the fiduciary....

760 ILL. COMP. STAT. 65/2. Broadly speaking, a person will be deemed to have acted in "good faith" for purposes of this provision even if his actions are negligent, so long as he acts honestly and is unaware that the fiduciary is breaching the duty he owes to his principal. *See* 760 ILL. COMP. STAT. 65/1(2); *Edgcomb*, 211 Ill.Dec. 136, 654 N.E.2d at 601; *Johnson*, 334 N.E.2d at 299-300. In appropriate circumstances, then, the FOA will supersede the common-law rule and relieve the bank of the duty to see that the proceeds of a check are properly applied, even if the check at issue is one payable to the bank itself. *St. Stephen's Evangelical Lutheran Church v. Seaway Nat'l Bank*, 38 Ill.App.3d 1021, 350 N.E.2d 128, 132 (1976); *Johnson*, 334 N.E.2d at 298.

In *St. Stephen's*, for example, Ferguson, the treasurer of his church, wrote multiple checks on the church's account payable to the bank's order, the bank issued the proceeds to him, and Ferguson then used the funds for his own benefit. The church sued the bank for negligence and conversion and prevailed at trial. The appellate court reversed, however, concluding that because Ferguson qualified as a fiduciary who was authorized to receive and disburse church funds, the FOA absolved the bank of liability for releasing money to him. Naturally, as treasurer, Ferguson maintained the church's financial books and records, including its checking account. More importantly, the church had executed a bank resolution that not only authorized Ferguson to sign checks on the bank's behalf, but also authorized him, and only him, to supply the bank with directions as to disbursement of church funds. The resolution also expressly authorized the bank to honor checks drawn to Ferguson's order, without further inquiry concerning his authority or the designated use of the check proceeds. 350 N.E.2d at 129. This made application of the FOA straightforward:

> Section 2 of the Act provides the bank with additional protection if Ferguson was authorized to receive the funds the bank paid him. The [church] argues that because the checks were payable to the bank and not to Ferguson or to cash, Ferguson was not entitled to receive their proceeds. However, Ferguson's authority to receive funds out of the church's account is supplied by the bank resolution which designates him as the only signator on the account and permits him to draw checks, drafts and orders to his

individual order without need for further inquiry by the bank or question as to the use of the proceeds of such withdrawals. The broad power to withdraw funds which the church granted to Ferguson as well as his right under the resolution to give the bank orders or directions ... was the authority for Ferguson to receive the proceeds of checks he drew payable to the bank. When Ferguson presented the checks signed by him the logical response for the bank was to inquire of the depositor what disposition it wished made of them.... As the only person named by the church to make withdrawals from the account or give directions to the bank, Ferguson was the proper person for the bank to look to for instructions. Thus, the payment by the bank was to a fiduciary authorized to receive funds from the account, and Section 2 of the Act protects the bank against Ferguson's misapplication of the proceeds of the checks....

350 N.E.2d at 130 (citation omitted).

The bank suggests that this case is no different than *St. Stephen's*. In its view, the undisputed facts establish that Hemmen was Jo Daviess' agent, thus rendering him a fiduciary for purposes of the FOA. The bank points out that Hemmen handled the bookkeeping for the company, made deposits, had signature authority over the payroll account, had authority to cash checks drawn on the operating account in amounts of up to $100 to replenish the petty cash fund, and, most importantly, had actual authority to tell the bank how to distribute the proceeds of checks made payable to the bank. Hemmen regularly exercised the latter authority when he presented checks, drawn on the operating account and payable to the bank's order, and directed that the proceeds be deposited into the TT & L account, for example.

However, it is the agent's specific authority to receive the proceeds of checks drawn to the bank's order which is crucial to the bank's ability to invoke the FOA. The very language of the statute highlights this point. Section 1 defines the term "fiduciary" as, inter alia, an "agent ... or any other person *acting in a fiduciary capacity* for any person...." 760 ILL. COMP. STAT. 65/1 (emphasis ours). The reference to the capacity in which the agent is acting suggests that his status as a fiduciary depends upon the particular activity in which he is engaged. (Citations omitted). Moreover, section 2 grants a person protection when he distributes to a fiduciary in good faith "any money or other property *which the fiduciary as such is authorized to receive*." 760 ILL. COMP. STAT. 65/2 (emphasis ours). This language reiterates the need to focus on the agent's authority with respect to the particular transaction at issue. In other words, as Judge Reinhard recognized, the fact that Hemmen may have been a fiduciary for some purposes did not render him a fiduciary for all purposes. Section 2 will not absolve the bank of liability for the presenter's misapplication of the check proceeds unless the evidence reveals that he was authorized to receive those proceeds. In *St. Stephen's*, the treasurer was so authorized. The same was true in *Johnson*, where an individual who was authorized to draft checks in his employer's name made a series of them payable to the bank's order and deposited the proceeds into his personal checking account. (Citation omitted). By contrast, in *Empire Moving & Warehouse Corp. v. Hyde Park Bank & Trust Co., supra*, the errant bookkeeper who took a series of checks issued to his employer, endorsed them over to a bank with a rubber stamp, obtained cash in exchange, and then absconded with the proceeds, was not an authorized signer on his employer's bank account. He did have the authority to make deposits into the account; moreover, company employees would often endorse their paychecks over to the company, and the bookkeeper's routine and accepted practice was to endorse them with the same rubber stamp that he eventually put to his own use, present them to the bank, and receive cash in return. In the court's view, however, the bookkeeper's authority in these respects was not sufficient to render him a fiduciary and therefore to relieve the bank of responsibility for cashing the checks that he had made payable to the bank:

> The record shows that he was employed as a bookkeeper and that his authority extended only to depositing checks payable to plaintiff in plaintiff's bank account. He had no authority to cash checks payable to plaintiff or to receive cash proceeds of such checks.... Any negotiation of checks payable to plaintiff would necessarily be governed by the corporate resolution lodged with [the bank]. To exonerate [the bank] here it would be obliged to prove that [the bookkeeper] came into possession of the proceeds of the checks as a fiduciary and that he had authority to endorse the checks....

2 Ill.Dec. 753, 357 N.E.2d at 1202.

Here, no evidence demonstrates that Hemmen was ever given broad authority to receive cash on checks drawn to the bank's order, or to divert funds from the operating account to anywhere but the payroll or TT & L accounts, and it is Hemmen's lack of authority in this regard that precludes the bank's resort to Section 2. The fact that Hemmen could order funds moved from the operating account to one of the company's other accounts is of no moment; what is key is his authority to have funds from the operating account issued to himself. The simple fact is that Hemmen was never an authorized signer on the operating account. That he had signature authority on Jo Daviess' payroll account may have rendered him a fiduciary as to that account, but no other. The witnesses were in agreement on that point. The sole manifestation of Hemmen's authority to receive money from the operating account was his occasional negotiation of checks made out to petty cash, which were invariably for $100 or less. We see nothing in the informal practice of cashing checks to replenish the petty cash fund that would have signaled to the bank that Hemmen had the equivalent of signature authority on the operating account. The checks at issue here were payable to the bank's order--a fact which, as we have discussed, put the bank on notice of the need to inquire into the presenter's authority--and in contrast to the checks for petty cash, they contained no indication that their purpose was to replenish the petty cash fund. Also unlike the petty cash transactions (the largest of which involved a check for $87.02), these checks typically involved substantial sums of money. The first of the checks at issue in this case, for example, was for the sum of $2,997. The entire amount of that check was disbursed to Hemmen in the form of two cashier's checks payable to his creditors. In short, whatever limited authority Hemmen may have enjoyed with respect to petty cash withdrawals did not give him authority to receive or disburse the proceeds of any and all checks payable to the bank's order. The bank thus took a risk in negotiating the checks for which it may now be held to account. As Judge Reinhard recognized, the fact that Hemmen may have been a fiduciary for some purposes did not render him a fiduciary for all purposes. Because he had no signature authority on the operating account, he cannot be treated as a fiduciary with respect to checks made payable to the bank's order. * * * *

[Discussion of the compensated surety defense and of liability for prejudgment interest is omitted.–Ed.]

III.

For the foregoing reasons, we AFFIRM the district court's decision to grant judgment as a matter of law in favor of Mutual on its contract claim against ESB. We VACATE the judgment and REMAND the case to the district court for the limited purpose of recalculating the award of prejudgment interest to commence on the date or dates that Mutual made payment to its insured. Mutual shall recover its costs of appeal. We commend Judge Reinhard for his able handling of this case.

Now consider the application of property-based claims to instruments, the ability to bring a conversion cause of action, and the provision on notice of breach of fiduciary obligations, to analyze the following problem.

Problem 4-3

Ernie is the trustee for a trust of a minor child, Bruce. On occasion, Ernie has to deposit checks to the trust bank account maintained at State Bank. Ernie is listed as the trustee on the account and the account is designated as a trust account for benefit of Bruce. Ernie also maintains Ernie's personal bank account at State Bank.

Notes

a) Ernie took a check made payable to Bruce, indorsed the check on the back as follows: "Bruce, by Ernie, trustee." Ernie deposited the check to his personal bank account. State Bank gave Ernie credit in Ernie's account for the amount of the check. Ernie withdrew the funds and disappeared. The new trustee, Marilyn, asserted a right to return of the check or the proceeds from State Bank. Is State Bank a holder in due course of that check?

b) Ernie wrote a check on the trust account, payable to Ernie, signed as follows: "Bruce by Ernie, trustee." Ernie indorsed the check in blank and without recourse, deposited the check to his personal bank account, and withdrew the credited funds from the account. The new trustee, Marilyn, asserted a right to return of the check or the proceeds from State Bank. Is State Bank a holder in due course of that check?

c) Ernie wrote a check on the trust account payable to Tailor, signed as follows: "Bruce by Ernie, trustee." Ernie gave the check to Tailor to pay for some suits that Ernie purchased for himself. State Bank dishonored the check when it was presented because the new trustee, Marilyn, stopped payment on the check. Tailor sued Bruce on the drawer's contract. Marilyn asserted that Bruce does not have to pay the check. Is she correct? Is Tailor a holder in due course?

d) Leon wrote a check drawn on Leon's account payable to Ted. Ted indorsed the check as follows: "Pay to Ernie in trust for Bruce, Ted." Ernie indorsed the check, deposited the check into his personal bank account, withdrew the funds, and disappeared. The new trustee, Marilyn, asserted a claim to the check or the proceeds. Is State Bank a holder in due course of that check? *See* U.C.C. § 3-206(d).

c) Assume that Bruce is not a minor. Bruce drew a check on the trust account payable to State Bank because Ernie told Bruce that Ernie was going to purchase a certificate of deposit from State Bank. Ernie took the check to State Bank and cashed the check. Ernie took the cash and disappeared. The new trustee, Marilyn asserted a right to the proceeds of the check from State Bank. Is State Bank a holder in due course of the check?

B. Warranty Liability

As we have already learned in Chapter 3, the right to payment reified in the negotiable instrument may be transferred to another person through transfer of the instrument. Because the negotiable instrument is an item of personal property, the usual rules that govern transfers of personal property also govern instruments. The usual rule for transfer of personal property is that the transferee takes all the rights that the transferor has, and no more. We have already encountered this idea of derivative rights when we examined U.C.C. § 3-203. The concept of derivative rights is part of the law of personal property.

Just as a person who transfers personal property may make a warranty of the state of the title and the quality of the property transferred, *see* U.C.C. §§ 2-312 through 2-315, a person who transfers a negotiable instrument makes a warranty about the state of the title and the quality of that instrument. Article 3 provides for two different types of warranties: transfer warranties and presentment warranties. Warranty liability arising out of the transfer or presentment on an instrument is a separate obligation unconnected to contract liability on an instrument. A person need not sign an instrument to incur the warranty liability.

Read U.C.C. § 3-416. Transfer warranties are made upon a transfer of the instrument. **Review U.C.C. § 3-203.** Notice that to make a transfer warranty, the transfer has to be for consideration. Review U.C.C. § 3-303. For the transfer to "run with the negotiable instrument" to subsequent transferees beyond the first transferee, the transferor must indorse the instrument.

The transfer warranties are stated in subsection(a). These warranties are made without regard to the state of the transferor's knowledge regarding the instrument. For example, the transferor warrants that it is a person entitled to enforce the instrument even if the transferor has no knowledge or notice that the transferor has failed to achieve that status. Consider the following scenario. A payee of a check transfers the check for consideration to transferee. The payee is unaware that the drawer's signature is forged. The payee has breached the warranty stated in subsection (a)(2) even though it had no notice or knowledge that the drawer's signature was forged.

Subsection (b) addresses damages for breach of warranty and subsection (d) addresses accrual of a cause of action for breach of warranty. Note that the statute of limitations for breach of warranty claims is provided in U.C.C. § 3-118(g). Subsection (c) provides that notice of a breach of warranty claim must be given to the warrantor within a certain time period or the liability is discharged. Subsection

(c) also addresses in abbreviated form the ability of a transferor to disclaim warranty liability. **See comment 5 to U.C.C. § 3-416.** The transferor may not disclaim transfer warranties if the instrument is a check. The disclaimer of contract liability by using the phrase "without recourse," is not a sufficient disclaimer of warranty liability. U.C.C. § 3-416, comment 3. Transfer warranties will also be considered when we discuss the bank collection process in Chapter 5. *See* U.C.C. § 4-207.

Presentment warranties are made to the person paying the instrument or accepting a draft. **Read U.C.C. § 3-417.** Subsection (a) addresses presentment warranties made to a drawee regarding an unaccepted draft. Review the meaning of "acceptance" in U.C.C. § 3-409(a). Subsection (d) addresses presentment warranties made in presentations made to persons obligated to pay the instrument. The only persons obligated to pay an instrument (that is, have contract liability on an instrument) are a drawee of an accepted draft, drawer, maker, or indorser. Presentment of an instrument is *NOT* transfer of an instrument. **Review U.C.C. § 3-501 on presentment and U.C.C. § 3-203 on transfer.** Thus presentment warranties are *NOT* made to transferees. Transfer warranties are *NOT* made to drawees, drawers, makers, and indorsers when the instrument is presented to them for payment.

Presentment warranties are only made when the person to whom presentment is made actually pays the instrument, or in the case of a drawee to whom presentment is made for acceptance, when the drawee actually accepts the draft. The person presenting the negotiable instrument and prior transferors of the instrument make the presentment warranties. The drawee of a draft that pays or accepts the draft is the beneficiary of the warranties stated in U.C.C. § 3-417(a). All other persons to whom presentment is made and who pay their contract obligation on the instrument get the warranty stated in subsection (d)(1). Notice that the warranties in subsection (a) are more extensive than the simple warranty in subsection (d).

Subsections (b) and (c) further address the rights of a drawee to whom a presentment warranty is made including certain defenses that the warrantor may assert to the breach of warranty claim and the amount the drawee may recover on the breach of warranty claim. Subsection (d) addresses the rights of a payor of a dishonored draft or other instrument. Subsection (e) and (f) address notice of the breach of warranty claim and accrual of the cause of action. Just as with transfer warranties, presentment warranties may be disclaimed by specific language to that effect except as limited by subsection (e). Presentment warranties will also be discussed when we encounter the bank collection process in Chapter 5. *See* U.C.C. § 4-208.

As you work your way through the following problems on warranty liability, keep in mind the following issues:

▸ Who has made the warranty?

▸ Was the warranty adequately disclaimed?

▸ To whom was the warranty made?

▸ What warranty was made?

▸ What warranty was breached?

▸ Who breached the warranty?

▸ What must the person to whom the warranty was made do to preserve a cause of action for breach of warranty?

Problem 4-4

Bill Smith wrote a check payable to John Doe drawn on First Bank. John signed his name on the back and lost the check. Sue picked up the check, went to Check Cashing, Inc. and received cash for the check. Check Cashing presented the check to First Bank for payment.

Notes

a) Assume that First Bank did not pay the check because Bill Smith stopped payment when John Doe told Bill that the check was lost. Who has contract liability on the check? To whom is any contract liability owed? Do the persons who may owe contract liability on the check have any defenses to payment?

b) Same facts as (a) above. Who made transfer warranties and to whom were the warranties made? If any transfer warranties were made, were any of the transfer warranties breached?

c) Same facts as (a) above. Did anyone make any presentment warranties and, if so, were they breached?

Notes

d) Same facts as (a) above. What is a cause of action that John has against Sue?

e) Assume that First Bank paid the check when Check Cashing presented the check to First Bank because Bill did not stop payment. Does that fact change your analysis of the transfer and presentment warranties?

f) Assume that instead of John Doe losing the check, he gave it to Sue in exchange for a table. He forgot to indorse the check, so Sue wrote "John Doe" on the back of the check. Sue gave the check to Check Cashing and received cash for the check. First Bank paid the check when it was presented. Who has made transfer and presentment warranties, to whom were they made, and were any warranties breached?

Problem 4-5

Jane Doe issued a demand negotiable note for $500 payable to the order of Acme Co. in payment of a debt to Acme Co. Acme Co. sold the note to First Bank for $400, indorsing the note on the back as follows: "Pay to the order of First Bank, Acme Co. by Ed Acme, Treasurer, without recourse." Lou Grimes, the vice president of First Bank skillfully raised the amount of the note to $800, and sold the note to Second Bank for $700, pocketing $200, and turning $500 over to First Bank. Lou indorsed the note as follows, "First Bank." Second Bank presented the note to Jane Doe.

Notes

a) Has anyone made or breached any transfer warranties to anyone else?

Notes

b) Has anyone made or breached any presentment warranties to anyone else?

c) What procedural requirements must be met in order to bring a lawsuit for breach of transfer or presentment warranties? What is the amount of the recovery?

We will return to presentment and transfer warranties when we learn about fraud, forgery, and alteration of instruments.

Review

Add to your list from Chapter 3 the causes of action we have studied in this Chapter. Again, make sure you have the elements of the plaintiff's case as well as the defenses that would be asserted to various causes of action.

Problem 4-6

Connie Rutledge is the chief financial officer of Dodge Trucks and Auto Resellers, Inc. Connie is authorized to write checks on behalf of Dodge. Connie wrote three checks drawn on Dodge's checking account at State Bank. Each check was imprinted with Dodge's name and address. Connie signed each check on the drawer's line as follows: "Connie Rutledge, CFO."

Check No. 9000 was payable to the order of Connie Rutledge for $5,000. Connie took the check to National Bank and deposited it to a checking account she holds jointly with her husband, Sean.

Check No. 9001 was payable to the order of Sean Rutledge for $6,000. Sean Rutledge is Connie's spouse. Sean indorsed the check in blank and deposited it to their joint checking account at National Bank.

Check No. 9002 was payable to the order of First Bank for $9,000. Connie owed First Bank $3,000 on a personal loan. Connie took the check to First Bank and paid off the loan and received $6,000 back from First Bank.

Connie was not owed any funds by Dodge. Dodge's president found out what Connie had done and after firing Connie, sued National Bank and First Bank to recover the funds. Evaluate Dodge's causes of action against each defendant.

In the event that National Bank or First Bank are liable to Dodge, would each bank have a cause of action under Article 3 to recover from Connie or Sean?

Notes

CHAPTER 5
COLLECTION THROUGH THE BANKING SYSTEM

A. Overview

We have studied enforcement of contract liability on negotiable instruments, claims to negotiable instruments, and warranty liability based on transfer and presentment of negotiable instruments. Modern banking practice relies upon these principles to collect on negotiable instruments (primarily checks) in the event that something goes wrong in the collection process. Article 3 thus provides a good foundation for studying collection of items through the banking system.

Article 4 governs the collection of items through the banking system. *See* U.C.C. § 4-102. As we learned in Chapter 3, checks are negotiable instruments. If they qualify as "items" under Article 4, Article 4 will govern the process for collection of that check. To the extent that a conflict exists between an Article 3 rule and an Article 4 rule, Article 4 governs. **U.C.C. § 4-102. Read the definition of "item" in U.C.C. § 4-104.** Consider the following situations. Do these transactions involve "items" as defined in Article 4?[*]

1. At the grocery store, the merchant takes a check from the customer and runs it through the cash register to capture the data on the bottom of the check (the MICR line). The merchant then keys in the amount of the purchase and hands the check back to the customer. The electronic information is transmitted via a secure network to the customer's bank and the customer's account is debited.

2. At the grocery store, the merchant takes the customer's debit card and runs it through the card reader. The customer types in her PIN to authorize the debit from her bank account for the amount of her purchases. The information from the card and the PIN are transmitted via a secure network to the customer's bank and the customer's account is debited.

---

[*] See Stephanie Heller, *An Endangered Species: The Increasing Irrelevance of Article 4 of the UCC in an Electronics-Based Payments System* (forthcoming 40 LOY. L.A. L. REV., Issue 1, 2007).

3. At the grocery store, the merchant takes the customer's credit card and runs it through the card reader. The customer signs a paper credit slip which contains the amount of her purchase. The information from the credit slip is transmitted to the merchant's bank and then to the card issuer. The card issuer then bills the customer on her monthly credit card statement for the amount of the purchase.

4. At the grocery store, the merchant takes the customer's check which the customer has completed for the amount of the purchase and signed. The merchant transmits the check to its bank for deposit. The check is electronically imaged at the merchant's bank and the information from the check is transmitted electronically to the customer's bank. The paper check is destroyed. The customer's bank account is debited based on the electronic transmission of information from the merchant bank.

5. Same as scenario 4 above, except that the check travels by courier from the merchant's bank to the customer's bank. The customer's account is debited based on the presentation of the paper check.

Most of the items collected through the banking system are checks, U.C.C. § 4-101, comment 2, but notes or other promises or orders may be routed through the system.*

In addition to the rules we have studied from Article 3 and the rules from Article 4 that we will address in this Chapter, we will study federal rules adopted pursuant to the authority of the federal government to regulate banking institutions. Regulation CC and Regulation J were promulgated by the Federal Reserve Board as part of its authority to regulate the banking system and pursuant to the Board's authority under the Expedited Funds Availability Act (codified at 12 U.S.C. §§ 4001–10) and the Check Clearing for the 21st Century Act, otherwise known as

---

* As reported by the Federal Reserve, 36.7 billion checks were paid in the United States in 2003, representing $39.3 trillion in value. This is significant decline from the number of checks paid in 2000 (41.9 billion). The report, *2004 Federal Reserve Payments Study (December 2004)*, is available at http://www.federalreserve.gov/paymentsys.htm. Electronic payments now outpace checks as a medium of payment. *See* Geoffrey R. Gerdes et al., *Trends in the Use of Payment Instruments in the United States*, FEDERAL RESERVE BULLETIN 180 (Spring 2005).

"Check 21" (codified at 12 U.S.C. §§ 5001–18). Regulation CC, 12 C.F.R. part 229, and Regulation J, 12 C.F.R. part 210, supplement the rules in Articles 3 and 4, preempting those state law rules only when there is a conflict between the state law rule and the regulation. U.C.C. § 4-103, comment 3.

The Federal Reserve also promulgates operating circulars that may vary the effect of Article 4 provisions. **U.C.C. § 4-103(b) and comment 3.** Operating circulars are periodically revised as processes evolve. Operating Circular 3 governs collection of "cash" items through the Federal Reserve system.* Checks are generally processed as cash items. The Federal Reserve plays a major role in the check processing system by offering check collection services,** in addition to its role as a regulator.

In addition to the Federal Reserve system, private organizations called clearinghouses, consisting of a group of banks or other institutions, have been formed to facilitate collection of items. These organizations promulgate rules governing the clearing of items through the clearinghouse. The first and perhaps best known clearinghouse is The Clearing House (formerly the New York Clearinghouse Association).*** Clearinghouse rules may vary the effect of Article 4 rules as provided in U.C.C. § 4-103. Clearinghouses may also use the Federal Reserve system to process items that need to move outside the clearinghouse.

Another method for processing items is for the banks to exchange items directly pursuant to direct agreements with each other. This is usually referred to as a correspondent banking relationship. Correspondent banks may enter into agreements that vary the effect of the provisions of Article 4. The effect of the provisions of Article 4 may also be varied by agreements between the bank and its customer. **Read U.C.C. § 4-103.**

Because of all of these different sources of rules, in analyzing any question that involves collecting an item through the banking system, you need to be familiar with the rules from Article 3, Article 4, Regulation CC, Regulation J, operating

---

* Operating circulars are available at http://www.frbservices.org.

** In 2005, the average daily volume of checks processed through the Federal Reserve system was 49 million and the average daily value of those checks was 57 billion dollars. Reports of the volume and dollar amount of checks processed through the Federal Reserve are available at http:// www.federalreserve.gov/paymentsystems/checkservices/default.htm.

*** The Clearing House clears 40 million checks worth 1.6 trillion dollars in value per day. *See* http://www.theclearinghouse.org/press_releases/svpco_2006/002684.php.

circulars, the clearinghouse rules, the agreements between banks, and the agreements between banks and their customers.

As we study the banking system's collection process, it is helpful to keep in mind a simple example. Assume that you have a checking account at State Bank. You have a sufficient balance in that account to cover the price of a car you wish to purchase. You write a check drawn on the account, payable to the car seller. The car seller deposits the check in the seller's account at a bank. The seller's bank gives the seller a credit in the seller's account in the amount of the check deposited. The seller's bank then transfers the check to a clearinghouse which credits the account of the seller's bank with the clearinghouse. The clearinghouse transfers the check to your bank and debits your bank's account with the clearinghouse. Your bank then debits your checking account and returns the check to you in your bank statement for the month. This system can be represented graphically as follows:

Car Buyer	Check for car purchase ▸				**Car Seller**
▲ Check to Buyer in bank statement					Deposit check ▼
State Bank	◂Check transferred	**Clearing House**	◂Check transferred	**Seller's Bank**	
Debit to Buyer's account at State Bank.	Debit to State Bank's account at Clearinghouse		Credit to Seller's Bank's account at Clearinghouse	Credit to Seller's account at Seller's Bank	

The bank collection system illustrated above can be divided into four stages.

The first stage is forward collection. The forward collection stage consists of the process of routing the instrument from the first bank in the process to the bank that pays the instrument. In the example above, the forward collection stage is when the seller's bank routes the check through the clearinghouse which then routes the check to the buyer's bank.

The next stage is the payment stage. In this stage, the payor bank decides whether to pay or return the item. In the example above, the buyer's bank, State Bank, has to decide whether to pay the check or return the check to the seller's bank. If the item is returned, the third stage comes into play.

The item return and chargeback stage (the third stage) consists of the process of routing the instrument back to the person who initiated the bank collection process and charging back the various credits given for the instrument during the forward collection process. Thus, in the hypothetical, if the check is returned, the buyer's bank will refuse to pay the check, which refusal is exhibited by returning the check either through the clearinghouse or directly to the seller's bank. The seller's bank will charge back the check to the seller's account by reversing the credit previously given to the seller

The final stage is making funds available to the person who initiated the item collection process. In the hypothetical, seller's bank, upon taking the item for deposit, has to make the funds the check represented available to the seller by a certain point in time, even though it may not yet know whether the buyer's bank will pay or return the item.

This settlement process has several types of risk imbedded within it. First there is the credit risk. In the hypothetical above, the seller is taking a credit risk as the check may be dishonored by the buyer's bank, State Bank. The seller's bank is taking a credit risk by making funds available to the seller without knowing whether the check will be honored by State Bank. The clearinghouse is taking a credit risk if the credit it gives the seller's bank is not covered by available funds from the State Bank's account at the clearinghouse. Finally, State Bank is taking a credit risk if the buyer's account does not have enough available credits to cover the amount of the check that is debited from the buyer's account (commonly known as an overdraft).

Another type of risk is the risk of fraud. In the hypothetical above, when the seller takes the check from the buyer, the seller has no way of knowing that the buyer actually has an account at State Bank. This is different than the credit risk. The buyer may have made up "fake" checks drawn on a non-existent account at a non-existent bank. On the other hand, the account and bank could be legitimate, but the buyer may not be the person authorized to write checks on the account. These are risks associated with a scheme to defraud participants in the transaction.

Finally, there is a risk that one of the intermediaries in this transaction may fail. A typical example of that type of risk is if one of the banks or the clearinghouse fails due to insolvency while the check collection is in process. This intermediary insolvency is rare given that in the usual check collection scenario, the check is being processed through regulated entities such as banks. One situation where there is a greater risk of intermediary failure is if the check processing is carried out by an entity that is not regulated, such as a check processing service.

In addition to the risks identified above, this process of physically transporting checks from the first bank (the depositary bank) to State Bank (also known as the payor bank or drawee) is expensive. Checks are transported across the country by various types of courier services. To ameliorate the risks identified above, the banks have every incentive in the forward collection process to get the check from the depositary bank to the payor/drawee bank as fast as possible. Of course, the faster the service, the more expense that is usually incurred. Balancing risk of harm against the expense of taking care against that risk should be a familiar balance to you from your study of legal principles in a variety of areas.

To reduce the expense and increase the speed of the forward collection process, the check clearance process is undergoing technological change that results in truncation of the check collection process. The truncation may happen at any point in the collection process, from the depositary bank (sometimes at the payee's business), to the payor/drawee bank. The depositary bank may use electronic transmission of the information from the check to the payor/drawee bank and thus obtain a credit transfer from the payor/drawee bank, without having to transport the check. Large institutional payees (think utility companies, for example) may capture the electronic information and transmit this information to the depositary bank, which then transmits the information to the payor/drawee bank.

Many check clearance services, including the Clearing House and the Federal Reserve offer "electronic check presentment," the capture of electronic information from the check. The electronic representation of the information from the check may be completed by capturing the MICR line information and the amount of the check, or it could be a full electronic imaging of the check. The essence of this methodology is that the payor/drawee bank has agreed to accept electronic check presentment instead of presentment of the physical check. *See* U.C.C. § 4-110. In our example above, this type of electronic conversion may happen at the seller's place, the seller's bank, or the clearinghouse.

Another method of shortening the check collection process is for the depositary bank or the clearinghouse to use the MICR line information to initiate a different type of payment mechanism called an ACH (Automated Clearing House) transaction. An ACH transaction is run through a private network managed by NACHA (National Automated Clearing House Association). An ACH transaction is an electronic funds transfer and not governed by Article 4 (there is no "item"). In an ACH transaction, information is transmitted through the private network so that the payor/drawee bank receives an instruction to debit the drawer's account for the amount of the check. We will study electronic funds transfer in Chapter 8.

Finally the payor/drawee bank may decide not to store and transfer the presented checks to the drawer in the monthly bank statement. The payor/drawee bank will generally image the checks it has received and transmit the images to the drawer. This results in cost savings for the payor/drawee bank.

Using electronics to increase the speed and reduce the expense of the check collection process creates issues regarding whether the legal infrastructure is sufficient to allocate the risks inherent in this process with the required degree of efficiency and certainty. Keep these issues in mind as we study the rules from U.C.C. Article 4 and the applicable federal regulations.

One of the goals of Article 4, as originally developed, was to create certainty concerning allocation of the various types of risk inherent in the collection process. In each stage of the check collection process, legal rules provide that certain actions must be taken, in a certain amount of time, and pursuant to a certain standard of care. In addition, the consequences of failing to comply with those rules is specified. As we consider the legal rules, ask yourself whether Article 4 is still fulfilling this purpose of certainty of risk allocation.

In addition to the bank collection system, Article 4 contains rules governing the depositary bank's and payor bank's relationships with its customers. These rules, like the other rules in Article 4, may be varied by agreement. U.C.C. § 4-103. Thus, a lawyer is never "safe" in answering a question about the customer's or a bank's rights and obligations solely by consulting Article 4. Careful review of the agreement between the customer and the bank, as well as all of the other sources referred to above, is always required.

In order to make the collection system easier to understand, we will first study the Article 4 rules on the payor/drawee bank-customer relationship. We will then study the collection process, starting with forward collection. We will consider the payor/drawee bank's decision to pay or dishonor the check. We then turn to the check return process if the payor/drawee bank dishonors the check. We then return to the depositary bank and customer relationship by looking at funds availability rules. We will generally start with the rules in Article 4 and then examine the applicable federal regulations to determine how those federal rules supplement or override the Article 4 rules.

As you study this complex system, consider the effect of U.C.C. § 4-103. Why would the parties involved in this process want to vary the effect of the rules in Article 4? What is encompassed within a bank's obligation of "good faith" and "reasonable care" in this process which cannot be disclaimed but may be defined as long as that definition is not "manifestly unreasonable"?

Article 4 has its own nomenclature. **Review the definitions in U.C.C. §§ 4-104 and 4-105** before you start the next section so that you have a working idea of the labels used for the various players in Article 4.

B. Payor/Drawee Bank and Customer Relationship

1. Properly Payable

The payor bank and the drawer of a check (the customer of the payor bank) have a relationship founded on contract and supplemented with the rules from Article 4. When opening a checking account, the bank usually has the customer sign a signature card wherein the customer agrees to the terms of the agreement. When an item, usually a check, is presented to the drawee bank, the bank has to decide whether to pay or return the item. The bank has to evaluate whether the item is properly payable from the customer's account. If the bank pays an item that is not properly payable, then the bank may not charge the customer's account. **Read U.C.C. § 4-401**.

An item is properly payable if "it is authorized by the customer and is in accordance with any agreement between the customer and bank." U.C.C. § 4-401(a). What does "authorized by the customer" mean? Does payment by a payor bank to a "person entitled to enforce" the check comply with the "properly payable" rule? *Compare* U.C.C. § 3-602. What if the drawer's signature is unauthorized or forged? What about an item that contains a forged necessary indorsement so that payment is made to a person not entitled to enforce? What about paying a check that creates an overdraft in the bank account? *See* U.C.C. § 4-401(b). What about paying a check that is post-dated? See U.C.C. §§ 3-113, 4-401(c). What about a check presented to the payor bank long after its date? U.C.C. § 4-404; *IBP, Inc. v. Mercantile Bank of Topeka*, 6 F. Supp. 2d 1258 (D. Kan. 1998). What about a check that is altered (such as by changing the payee name or by changing the amount)?

What actions does the payor bank have to take to determine if the item is properly payable? Does the payor bank have to look at the check, compare it to the signature on file, or check with the drawer? *See* U.C.C. § 4-104(c) and § 3-103(a)(9) (definition of "ordinary care"). Does the customer have any obligation to discover and notify the bank that an item was not properly payable? *See* U.C.C. § 4-406. What other issues do you see that may affect whether the check is properly payable?

What is the effect of paying a check that is properly payable? Does that discharge contract liability on the check? U.C.C. § 3-602. Does that discharge the underlying obligation for which the check was issued or transferred? U.C.C. § 3-310.

Problem 5-1

Craig issued a check for $50 payable to the order of Ann, drawn on Craig's checking account at State Bank. Ann gave the check to Shelly. Shelly took the check to State Bank and presented the check for payment.

Notes

a) Assume that State Bank gave Shelly $50 when she presented the check. Is the check properly payable from Craig's account?

b) Assume that prior to Ann giving the check to Shelly, Ann indorsed the check as follows: "Ann, without recourse." Is the check properly payable from Craig's account? Would it make any difference if Shelly then lost the check and David picked it up and presented it to State Bank?

c) Assume that prior to Ann giving the check to Shelly, Ann indorsed the check as follows: "Pay to Shelly, Ann." Is the check properly payable from Craig's account?

d) Assume that Ann indorsed the check in blank when she gave the check to Shelly. When Shelly presented the check to State Bank, Craig's account had only a $10 balance. State Bank paid the check anyway. Was the check properly payable? What can State Bank do now?

e)   Assume that when Craig issued the check on July 1, he dated the check July 5. Ann indorsed the check in blank and gave the check to Shelly. Shelly presented the check to State Bank on July 3. State Bank paid the check amount to Shelly. Was the check properly payable from the account? What should Craig have done to prevent payment prior to July 5?

f)   Assume that Craig issued the check on May 1. Ann indorsed the check in blank and gave the check to Shelly. Shelly presented the check to State Bank on January 15 of the next year. Is the check properly payable?

g)   Assume that Craig issued the check, drawn on a joint account with his wife, Cindy. They are currently separated, but not divorced. Ann indorsed the check in blank and gave the check to Shelly. Shelly presented the check to the bank. Even though there was not sufficient funds in the account to pay the check, the bank paid the check amount to Shelly. Can the bank collect the amount of the overdraft from Cindy?

Notes

h)   Same scenario as (b) above. Did the payment of the check result in a discharge of the contract obligations on the check? U.C.C. § 3-602. Did the payment result in a discharge of the underlying obligation that Craig owed to Ann or that Ann owed to Shelly? U.C.C. § 3-310.

The bank-customer agreement may specify the items that are properly payable from the account. *See Spear Ins. Co., Ltd. v. Bank of America, N.A.*, 40 U.C.C. Rep. Serv. 2d 807 (N.D. Ill. 2000) (Corporate customer authorized bank to pay checks bearing facsimile signatures that matched the signatures of certain identified persons at the corporation. When officer fired from corporation, corporation failed to change authority. Counterfeit checks with officer's facsimile signature properly payable by virtue of bank-customer agreement.). If you were drafting the payor bank-customer agreement, what would you want to say about which items are properly payable from the customer's account? Does U.C.C. § 4-103 limit the extent to which the effect of the rule in U.C.C. § 4-401 can be altered?

2.   Paying an Item that is Not Properly Payable

If the payor bank pays an item that is not properly payable, because the payor bank cannot charge the customer's account, the payor bank will try to recover the amount of money paid on the instrument from someone else. If a payor bank pays the item but cannot charge its customer's account, in essence, the payor bank has paid the item with its own funds, not the customer's funds. Thus the payor bank will attempt to recover the amount of the payment from someone in the collection chain prior to the payor bank, such as the entity that presented the item to the payor bank or a previous person in the collection chain.

One way the payor bank will try to recover is to use presentment warranties. **Read U.C.C. § 4-208. Compare U.C.C. § 3-417.** We have already looked at these warranties in Chapter 4. These warranties are made to a payor bank that has paid or accepted the item. Review U.C.C. § 3-409 on the meaning of acceptance. Obviously "paid" in this section cannot mean the same thing as "paid" in U.C.C. §

3-602 as payment in that section means payment only to a person entitled to enforce. If payment had the same meaning in both sections, the warranty of subsection (a)(1) would rarely be breached.

Based on the presentment warranty, does the payor bank take the risk that the draft has been altered, has a forged or unauthorized indorsement, or has a forged or unauthorized drawer's signature? What does the payor bank have to do to pay in "good faith"?

A payor bank may also argue that it is entitled to restitution from the person to whom payment was made. **Read U.C.C. § 3-418.** To illustrate this section, assume that the payor bank made payment on a check on which the drawer's signature was forged. The drawer is successful in arguing that the check is not properly payable from the drawer's account because it was not "authorized" by the drawer (due to the forgery). Under U.C.C. § 4-208, the payor bank may recover from the person making presentment, or a prior transferor, if that person had knowledge that the drawer's signature was unauthorized. If the presenter or prior transferor did not have knowledge that the drawer's signature was unauthorized, the payor bank will attempt to use the restitution cause of action. Under U.C.C. § 3-418(a), paying an item based upon a forged drawer's signature is a situation where restitution is appropriate. The difficulty with the restitution cause of action is that normally the person making presentment (the person to whom payment was made) generally is able to take advantage of the defense in U.C.C. § 3-418(c).

Another method of recovery is for the payor bank to subrogate to someone else's rights on the instrument. **Read U.C.C. § 4-407.** Consider the case of the forged drawer's signature. The drawer is not liable on the instrument (as we learned in Chapter 3) because the drawer did not sign the instrument. The payor bank's subrogation rights do not help the payor bank as against the drawer because the drawer is not liable on the instrument. We will come back to the payor bank's subrogation rights after we consider stop payment orders.

Problem 5-2

Notes

a) Craig issued a check for $50 payable to the order of Ann, drawn on Craig's checking account at State Bank. Ann did not indorse the check. She lost it and Pete picked up the check. Pete signed Ann's name on the back of the check. State Bank paid Pete $50 when he presented the check at the teller's window. Craig objected to the payment as Ann had told Craig she lost the check. What are State Bank's obligations and options as to Craig, Ann, and Pete?

b) Craig issued a check for $50 payable to the order of Ann, drawn on Craig's checking account at State Bank. Ann indorsed the check in blank and lost it. Pete picked up the check, and altered the amount to $500. State Bank paid Pete $500 when he presented the check at the teller's window. Craig objected to the payment. What are State Bank's obligations and options as to Craig, Ann, and Pete?

c) Darren stole Craig's checkbook and wrote a check for $1,000 payable to the order of "cash" drawn on Craig's account at State Bank and signed "Craig" on the drawer's line on the bottom right hand corner. Darren deposited the check in his bank account at National Bank. National Bank presented the check to State Bank. State Bank paid the check. Craig objected to the payment. What are State Bank's obligations and options as to Darren, Craig, and National Bank?

3. Wrongful Dishonor

If the bank returns (i.e. dishonors, U.C.C. § 3-502) an item that is properly payable from the account, it has wrongfully dishonored the item. **Read U.C.C. § 4-402.** Wrongful dishonor is a cause of action that the customer of the account has as against the payor bank that is holding the customer's account. The payee of the item does not have a cause of action for wrongful dishonor as against the payor bank. The payor bank (the drawee) is not obligated to the payee (or other person entitled to enforce) unless the payor bank has incurred acceptor's liability on the item. **Review U.C.C. §§ 3-408, 3-409, 3-413.**

Consider the following excerpt from *Maryott v. First National Bank of Eden*, 624 N.W. 2d 96 (S.D. 2001) on damages for wrongful dishonor. In that case the payor bank had dishonored several checks issued by a cattle dealer, Maryott, because it was concerned that several checks made payable to the cattle dealer had been dishonored. The bank, without consulting Maryott, decided to dishonor the checks drawn by Maryott, thinking that something "suspicious" was taking place. The bank froze Maryott's account and refused to honor another outstanding check, even though the account had sufficient funds. A payee of one of the dishonored checks made a claim against Maryott's bond, which eventually resulted in Maryott going out of business. The jury awarded "$600,000 in damages for lost income, lost value of [the dealer's] business and emotional distress." On emotional distress damages, this is what the South Dakota Supreme Court held:

> Bank argues that the evidence fails to establish the necessary elements for recovery of damages for emotional distress. Bank notes that damages for emotional distress are recoverable in South Dakota only when the elements of either intentional or negligent infliction of emotional distress are proven. *See Stene v. State Farm Mut. Auto.Ins. Co.*, 1998 SD 95, ¶ 29, 583 N.W.2d 399, 404. According to Bank, Maryott has failed to establish the elements of either cause of action. Maryott argues that his emotional damages are recoverable under SDCL 57A-4-402, which provides that a bank is liable for "actual damages proved and may include ... other consequential damages." Maryott argues that damages for emotional distress are part of his consequential damages, and he is therefore not required to establish the elements of intentional or negligent infliction of emotional distress. In the alternative, Maryott claims he has nevertheless met those requirements.
>
> Our initial inquiry must be whether SDCL 57A-4-402 has created a

new breed of emotional damages or whether those damages are commensurate with theories of recovery already recognized under South Dakota law. This inquiry requires statutory interpretation, which is reviewed de novo as a question of law. *Steinberg v. S.D. Dept. of Military*, 2000 SD 36, ¶ 6, 607 N.W.2d 596, 599. The text of SDCL 57A-4-402 provides no assistance on this issue. Nor does the official comment to the U.C.C. offer guidance as to the requirements to establish emotional damages. *See* Uniform Commercial Code (U.L.A.) § 4-402.

In support of his claim, Maryott directs us to *Twin City Bank v. Isaacs*, 283 Ark. 127, 672 S.W.2d 651 (1984). That case involved a wrongful dishonor under U.C.C. § 4-402. The plaintiffs sued their bank and the jury awarded them damages for mental anguish. On appeal, the Supreme Court of Arkansas stated, "[i]n general, the type of mental anguish suffered under § 4- 402 does not need to rise to the higher standard of injury for intentional infliction of emotional distress." *Id.* at 654.

However, a number of courts have not interpreted § 4-402 so broadly. In *Farmers & Merchants State Bank of Krum v. Ferguson*, 617 S.W.2d 918 (Tex.1981), a bank froze its customer's checking account, without informing the customer, causing several checks to be wrongfully dishonored. The court stated that, in accordance with Texas law, "[d]amages for mental anguish [under § 4-402] cannot be recovered absent a showing of an intentional tort, gross negligence, willful and wanton disregard, or accompanying physical injury." *Id.* at 921. Likewise, the court in *First Nat'l Bank of New Castle v. Acra*, 462 N.E.2d 1345 (Ind.App.1984) examined a claim of emotional damages for wrongful dishonor in light of its state law requirements for intentional or negligent infliction of emotional distress. The *Acra* court noted that Indiana allowed recovery of damages for emotional distress only when intentionally inflicted or accompanied by a physical injury. *Id.* at 1350. In addition, the California courts require a plaintiff to prove either physical impact and resulting injury or intentional wrongdoing by the defendant before damages for emotional distress can be recovered under § 4-402. *Lee v. Bank of America*, 218 Cal.App.3d 914, 267 Cal.Rptr. 387, 390 (1990). Furthermore, the New Jersey Supreme Court applies a more stringent test, requiring proof of intentional infliction of emotional distress before emotional damages are recoverable under § 4-402. *Buckley v. Trenton Sav. Fund Soc.*, 111 N.J. 355, 544 A.2d 857, 864 (N.J.1988).

Like those jurisdictions just discussed, South Dakota allows recovery of emotional damages only when intentionally inflicted or accompanied by actual physical injury. *Stene,* 1998 SD 95, ¶ 29, 583 N.W.2d at 404. The U.C.C. provides that our common-law is effective in commercial transactions unless specifically displaced by a particular Code section. SDCL 57A-1- 103. Because § 4-402 does not define the consequential damages that may be recovered and does not clearly indicate an independent right of recovery of emotional damages, we must interpret that section in light of our precedent which requires a plaintiff to prove either intentional or negligent infliction of emotional distress to recover emotional damages. In *Wright v. Coca Cola Bottling Co.,* 414 N.W.2d 608, 610 (S.D.1987), we noted that:

> three principal concerns continue to foster judicial caution and doctrinal limitations on recovery for emotional distress: (1) the problem of permitting legal redress for harm that is often temporary and relatively trivial; (2) the danger that claims of mental harm will be falsified or imagined; and (3) the perceived unfairness of imposing heavy and disproportionate financial burdens upon a defendant, whose conduct was only negligent....

These concerns are equally applicable today. The best way to balance these concerns while still providing adequate relief for injured plaintiffs is to require plaintiffs to meet the standards already established in this state for the recovery of emotional damages. The simple statement that consequential damages are recoverable under § 4-402 will not convince us otherwise. Therefore, while emotional damages may be recoverable under § 4-402, they are not recoverable unless the plaintiff can establish the requirements of either intentional or negligent infliction of emotional distress.

We must now determine if the evidence introduced by Maryott is legally sufficient to satisfy the requirements of either of those causes of action. When reviewing the sufficiency of the evidence, we accept all evidence favorable to the verdict, and reasonable inferences therefrom, without weighing credibility or resolving conflicts. *State v. Buchholz,* 1999 SD 110, ¶ 33, 598 N.W.2d 899, 905. We will affirm the verdict if there is evidence, which if believed by the fact finder, could support the jury's verdict. *Id.*

To recover for intentional infliction of emotional distress, Maryott must show:

1) an act by defendant amounting to extreme and outrageous conduct;

2) intent on the part of the defendant to cause plaintiff severe emotional distress;

3) the defendant's conduct was the cause in-fact of plaintiff's distress;

4) the plaintiff suffered an extreme disabling emotional response to defendant's conduct.

Stene, 1998 SD 95, ¶ 31, 583 N.W.2d at 404. For conduct to be deemed "outrageous," "it must be so extreme in degree as to go beyond all possible bounds of decency, and to be regarded as atrocious, and utterly intolerable in a civilized community." *Id.* ¶ 32, 583 N.W.2d at 404. While Bank's actions were illegal and irresponsible, they do not rise to the level of outrageous conduct. Nor was any evidence introduced that Bank acted with the requisite intent. Indeed, Maryott did not even argue in his brief that he met the requirements of intentional infliction of emotional distress. Therefore, the issue is waived. *Spenner v. City of Sioux Falls*, 1998 SD 56, ¶ 30, 580 N.W.2d 606, 613.

We have repeatedly held that negligent infliction of emotional distress requires "manifestation of physical symptoms." (Citations omitted). Maryott argues that his clinical depression and the symptoms thereof that resulted from Bank's wrongful dishonor are sufficient to establish "manifestation of physical symptoms." The physical symptoms of his depression included shame, interruption of sleep, and humiliation. We discussed a similar claim in *Drier,* where the trial court refused to instruct the jury that physical injury included a diagnosed severe mental illness. We affirmed the trial court's decision, stating "Driers' proposed instruction is not consistent with South Dakota law because it expands the definition of 'physical injury'...." *Drier,* 1998 SD 1, ¶ 13, 574 N.W.2d at 600.

Likewise, Maryott's claim that clinical depression satisfies the requirement of physical symptoms is inconsistent with our established law. Nor can shame and humiliation be classified as physical symptoms. Finally, interruption of sleep on its own cannot be considered a physical symptom that would allow for recovery of emotional damages. (footnote omitted) Because Maryott has failed to establish the elements of either intentional or negligent infliction of emotional distress, his claim for emotional damages under § 4-402 must fail as a matter of law.

The South Dakota Supreme Court then went on to evaluate the verdict to determine if it was excessive and to determine whether Maryott's request for punitive damages should have been submitted to the jury. The Court stated:

> After the jury's verdict, Bank moved for a new trial pursuant to SDCL 15-6-59(a)(5), claiming the damages were awarded "under the influence of passion or prejudice." Bank now appeals the denial of that motion. A motion for a new trial based upon an excessive damages award
>
>> is addressed to the sound discretion of the trial court and a denial of the motion will not be reversed absent an abuse of that discretion.... If the jury's verdict can be explained with reference to the evidence rather than by juror passion, prejudice or mistake of law, the verdict should be affirmed.

Berry v. Risdall, 1998 SD 18, ¶ 9, 576 N.W.2d 1, 4. In addition, "it must be remembered that the amount of damages to be awarded 'is peculiarly a question for the jury.' " *Id.* ¶ 10. Finally, "[t]he trial court is best able to judge whether the damages awarded by a jury are the product of passion or prejudice." *Id.*

The jury awarded Maryott $250,000 damages for lost income and $200,000 for the lost value of his business. After reviewing the record, we cannot conclude that the jury's verdict could only have been reached through passion or prejudice. Maryott's expert, Don Scholten, first estimated Maryott's lost income based on the average number of cattle sold in the previous four years; 42,334. As a conservative figure, he used 40,000 head per year, with average weight of 700 pounds, earning $.50 per hundred weight. At that rate, Maryott could expect an annual income of $140,000 per year. At the time of trial, three and a half years had elapsed since the wrongful dishonor, so the annual revenues multiplied by 3.5 years amount to $490,000. Scholten also calculated Maryott's damages assuming that Maryott would switch to a consignment based business. This type of business model would produce fewer sales because, according to Maryott's testimony, not as many producers want to use that system. Scholten used Maryott's estimate that sales would be reduced by one-half. Using the same weight and commission assumptions, Maryott's income would be reduced to $70,000 per year, which multiplied by 3.5 years amounts to $245,000. Based on these calculations there is sufficient evidence by which the jury's verdict can be explained.

Nevertheless, Bank contends that Scholten failed to take into account various factors including the failure to include 1995 sales, Maryott's health problems, the fact that he spent winters in Arizona, and the possibility that Maryott could continue to work in some other capacity in the cattle industry. Each of these concerns was raised by Bank during cross-examination, and was taken into account by the jury. Scholten testified that the 1995 sales were not included in the average number of cattle sold because Maryott was working in a salaried position with Central at that time and was not actively brokering cattle through his business. Each of Bank's claims essentially go to the weight that should be given to Scholten's testimony. The jury determined Scholten's estimates were credible. When reviewing a jury verdict, we are "not free to reweigh the evidence or gauge the credibility of the witnesses." *Id.* ¶ 10. The trial court did not abuse its discretion in denying Bank's motion for a new trial as to damages for lost income.

The jury also awarded Maryott $200,000 for the lost value of his business. Bank challenges this award, claiming that Maryott's business had value only because of Maryott's ability to buy and sell cattle and the contacts he had developed in the industry. This argument relies heavily on Bank's previous assertion that the loss of Maryott's bond did not proximately cause any damages. As we have determined that claim to be without merit, this argument also fails. Bank's actions caused the forfeiture of Maryott's bond, which effectively put him out of business. On October 27, 1995, after inspecting the property, Bank valued Maryott's business at $300,000. Hofer later estimated the value to be only $100,000. There was also testimony from Brett Bunger that in early 1996, he entertained an offer to buy Maryott's business for $324,000. The jury's verdict comports to the evidence on valuation and was not the result of passion or prejudice. The trial court did not abuse its discretion in denying Bank's motion for new trial on lost value of Maryott's business. (footnote omitted).

* * * *

Our initial inquiry must be whether punitive damages are recoverable under SDCL 57A-4-402. That section is silent on the issue, but as discussed above, allows for recovery of consequential damages. Whether punitive damages are included under § 4-402 is therefore determined by non-U.C.C. state law. *See* SDCL 57A-1-103; 57A-1-106; *Uniform Commercial Code, supra,* § 4-402, cmt 1. A majority of states that have examined this issue allow punitive damages under § 4-402, but only when a bank's conduct has been malicious, intentional, or fraudulent. (Citations omitted).

In South Dakota, punitive damages are permitted in actions other than breach of contract, when a defendant acts with oppression, fraud or malice. SDCL 21-3-2. The breach of a statute, such as SDCL 57A-4-402, is an action "not arising from contract." *Groseth Int'l, Inc. v. Tenneco Inc.*, 440 N.W.2d 276, 279 (S.D.1989). In light of our statutory authority, we agree that punitive damages are recoverable under § 4-402, but only when there is oppressive, fraudulent or malicious conduct by the bank. Because we have determined that punitive damages are recoverable, we must resolve whether the trial court should have submitted the issue to the jury under SDCL 21-1-4.1.

Under SDCL 21-1-4.1, the trial court must find by "clear and convincing evidence, that there is a reasonable basis to believe that there has been willful, wanton or malicious conduct on the part of the party claimed against." The trial court found that Maryott had failed to satisfy that burden. Before we will reverse the trial court's finding to the contrary, Maryott must show the trial court was clearly erroneous. *Berry,* 1998 SD 18, ¶ 34, 576 N.W.2d at 9. Under this standard, we will reverse only if after reviewing all the evidence, "we are left with a definite and firm conviction that a mistake has been made." *City of Deadwood v. Summit, Inc.*, 2000 SD 29, ¶ 9, 607 N.W.2d 22, 25.

We have previously examined the issue of punitive damages in the banking context. In *Vreugdenhil v. First Bank of South Dakota*, 467 N.W.2d 756 (S.D.1991), the bank's president requested the sheriff break down the door of Vreugdenhil's business so the bank could take possession of its collateral. These actions were a clear violation of Vreugdenhil's constitutional due process rights and we reversed the trial court's decision denying a claim for punitive damages. *Id.* at 760. The bank in *Brandriet v. Norwest Bank*, 499 N.W.2d 613 (S.D.1993), fraudulently misrepresented that Brandriet's loan had been denied, when the application had in fact never been processed. This Court affirmed the trial court's decision allowing a claim for punitive damages. *Id.* at 618. In addition, punitive damages were allowed against a bank when its employee embezzled a customer's funds. *Olson v. Tri-County State Bank*, 456 N.W.2d 132, 135 (S.D.1990). However, we refused to allow punitive damages where there was no evidence that the bank acted with bad faith, ill will or malice toward its customer. *Yankton Prod. Credit Ass'n v. Jensen*, 416 N.W.2d 860, 863 (S.D.1987).

Maryott argues Bank acted with malice when it violated the midnight deadline rule and because of "irregularities" in Maryott's checking account. According to Maryott, these actions show that Bank acted with reckless disregard of his rights. *See Isaac v. State Farm Mut. Auto. Ins. Co.*, 522 N.W.2d 752, 761 (S.D.1994). The violation of a statute, on its own, is insufficient to support punitive damages; there must also be oppression, fraud, or malice. *Groseth,* 440 N.W.2d at 279 (citing SDCL 21-3-2). There is no evidence that Bank acted with oppression, fraud, or malice when it violated the midnight deadline rule. On the contrary, it consulted an attorney as well as officials with the Federal Reserve before dishonoring the checks. These parties did not admonish Bank's proposed actions as being oppressive or fraudulent.

The "irregularities" involve an alleged discrepancy between Maryott's monthly statement and Bank's daily activity report. While Bank noted the credits and debits associated with the dishonored checks on its daily activity report, there was no corresponding credits or debits shown on Maryott's monthly statement. According to Maryott, this creates "the logical inference" that Bank was covering itself and acting with presumed malice. However, that inference is not supported by the testimony at trial. Mehlhaff testified that when items are returned, the transaction is removed from the customer's account. Although Bank's internal records would record the appropriate credits and debits, those transactions would not be shown on the customer's monthly statement, because for purposes of account records, the transaction never occurred. There is no reason to believe Bank was acting with malice simply because it did not record a credit and debit for each returned check on Maryott's monthly statement.

Bank suspected Maryott was involved in or the victim of fraudulent activity when it dishonored the checks. Although later events did not support Bank's beliefs, its conduct did not rise to the level of willful, wanton or malicious conduct. In light of our precedent, Maryott has failed to show that the trial court was clearly erroneous in not submitting the issue of punitive damages to the jury.

One judge dissented on the question of emotional distress damages:

The citizens of South Dakota, represented by this Marshall County jury, found that the bank's wrongful dishonor was the cause of Maryott's mental anguish. The majority opinion jumps in the jury box and reverses the jury's award of $150,000 for Maryott's emotional damage which was clearly precipitated by the bank's wrongful conduct. In so holding, the majority opinion sidesteps the legislative pronouncement that when a bank chooses to wrongfully dishonor a properly payable item it is liable for any "actual damages." As the jury's determination is supported by law and fact, it should stand and not be overturned on a whim.

SDCL 57A-4-402 provides in part:

A payor bank is liable to its customers for damages proximately caused by the wrongful dishonor of an item. Liability is limited to *actual damages proved* and may include damages for an arrest or prosecution of the customer or other consequential damages. *Whether any consequential damages are proximately caused by the wrongful dishonor is a question of fact to be determined in each case.*

(Emphasis added). This determination is supposed to be made by a jury on proper instructions, not by the Supreme Court.

The instructions to this jury properly stated that the Bank was liable for the foreseeable consequences proximately caused by its conduct. The jury was instructed that emotional distress "means mental suffering, mental distress or mental anguish. It includes all highly unpleasant mental reactions, such as fright, nervousness, horror, grief, shame, anxiety, humiliation, embarrassment, mortification, anger, worry and stress, as well as physical pain." Additionally, "the measure of damages is the amount which will compensate the party aggrieved for all detriment proximately caused thereby." The jury properly found that Maryott suffered emotional damages as a result of the Bank's wrongful conduct.

First National Bank of Eden and the majority opinion urge the view that emotional damages are never available unless the torts of negligent infliction of emotional distress or intentional infliction of emotional distress are independently asserted. Though this view is not without support in other forums, I concur with the commentators and courts that maintain that recovery for "actual damages proved" encompasses the mental suffering caused by a wrongful dishonor. The majority opinion's requirement for an independent tort theory of emotional distress to safeguard against baseless claims is an outdated approach supported only by jury distrust. I submit the juries of this state are capable of discerning when actual damages include mental anguish, as they did here.

In *Twin City Bank v. Isaacs*, 283 Ark. 127, 672 S.W.2d 651 (1984), the Supreme Court of Arkansas recognized that "the type of mental anguish suffered under § 4-402 does not need to rise to the higher standard of injury for intentional infliction of emotional distress." *Id.* at 654. It further compared these intangible injuries to those types of damages recognized in defamation actions. *Id.* In addressing this issue, we are faced with the economic reality that "embarrassment and humiliation" suffered from the bank's wrongful acts are very real, though sometimes intangible harms. *See id.* The damage to Maryott's reputation and the ensuing effect on his credit, a lifeline in his type of business, created very real and incredible damage. The jury recognized it based on proper instructions and so should we.

Leading commentators on the UCC have addressed the issue. "Might one argue that 'actual damages' excludes recovery for mental distress? We think not." White & Summers, HANDBOOK OF THE LAW UNDER THE UNIFORM COMMERCIAL CODE § 17-4 p. 675 (2d Ed 1980). Explaining further, White & Summers note: "It is inconsistent to allow recovery for embarrassment and mental distress deriving from arrest and prosecution and to deny similar recovery in other cases. Moreover, cases under the predecessor to 4-402, the American Banking Association Statute, held that 'actual damages' includes damages for mental distress." *Id.*

This rationale, coupled with the evidence adduced by Maryott and the jury's findings on proper instructions, demonstrate that the award was proper. Inability on the part of some members of this appellate court to appreciate or recognize these damages is no reason to vacate them. Therefore, I respectfully dissent.

Problem 5-3

Craig issued a check for $50 payable to the order of Ann, drawn on Craig's checking account at State Bank. Ann gave the check to Shelly. Shelly took the check to State Bank and presented it for payment.

Notes

a) Assume that prior to Ann giving the check to Shelly, Ann indorsed the check as follows: "Ann." State Bank did not pay the check when Shelly presented it to State Bank even though there were sufficient funds available in Craig's account. Is this a wrongful dishonor? If so, what is Craig's remedy? Does Shelly have any remedies?

b) Same facts as (a) above, except the reason State Bank did not pay the check was because Craig did not have sufficient credit in his account to cover the $50 check. Does that change your analysis?

c) Assume that when Craig issued the check on July 1, he dated the check July 5. Ann indorsed the check in blank and gave it to Shelly. Shelly presented the check to State Bank on July 3. State Bank did not pay the check but dishonored it. Is that a wrongful dishonor?

d) Assume that Craig issued the check on May 1. Ann indorsed the check in blank and gave the check to Shelly. Shelly presented the check to State Bank on January 15 of the next year. State Bank did not pay the check. Has it wrongfully dishonored the check? U.C.C. § 4-404.

e) Assume that Ann indorsed the check in blank prior to giving it to Shelly. Shelly deposited the check in her account at National Bank. National Bank presented the check the next morning to State Bank. State Bank's employee checked the account at 12 noon and determined that Craig's account had insufficient funds to pay the check. The employee put the check aside and made a notation that the account should be checked later that day to determine whether the check should be dishonored. The employee went home sick and no one else checked the account balance. The check was dishonored. If the account had been checked later that day, enough funds would have been present to pay the check. Does Craig have a cause of action against State Bank? Does National Bank or Shelly have a cause of action against State Bank?

A payor bank receives many items in a given day to be charged against a particular account. Sometimes payment of one item will deplete the account to such a degree that other items, if paid, would create an overdraft. In that situation, the payees on items that are dishonored because of the drawer's insufficient funds may claim that the bank should have paid their items first. Alternatively, the customer of the account may argue that items that were returned were wrongfully dishonored if the customer contends the dishonored items should have been paid first. **Read U.C.C. §§ 4-303, 3-408**.

Problem 5-4

On March 20, drawee bank received the following three items for payment at the

Notes

following times: 10 a.m., check for $200; 11 a.m., check for $500; 12 noon, check for $100. The balance in the account at the beginning of the day was $800. No additional deposits were made that day. The bank has a valid setoff claim against the debtor based on an overdue promissory note for $400. The bank officer decided to set off the bank debt of $400, pay the $100 check and the $200 check and dishonor the $500 check. Does the payee of the $500 check have a cause of action against the bank? Does the drawer have a cause of action against the bank?

4. Stop Payment Orders

Sometimes a customer will have a reason to stop payment on an item that the customer has already issued. **Read U.C.C. § 4-403**. There are two basic questions answered in the text of that section. The first question is who is entitled to issue a stop order to the payor bank. The second question is how is an effective and timely stop order given. To determine if the stop order is timely, one must also consult **U.C.C. § 4-303**. If an effective stop order is given in a timely manner, is the item still properly payable from the account? What is the payor bank's liability to the drawer for paying over an effective and timely stop order?

If the payor bank pays over a valid stop payment order, does that mean that the payor bank may not charge the drawer's account? **Reread U.C.C. § 4-407.** Consider the following scenarios.

Drawer issues a check to Payee. Drawer discovers that it was a mistake to issue the check to Payee because Drawer does not owe Payee any obligation. Drawer gives Payor Bank a timely and effective stop order that the check should not be paid. Meanwhile, Payee indorses the check and deposits it at Depositary Bank. Depositary Bank presents the check to Payor Bank. In spite of the stop payment order, Payor Bank pays the item. Drawer objects and insists that Payor Bank recredit its account. Using U.C.C. § 4-407(a), Payor Bank asserts subrogation to Depositary Bank's rights as against Drawer. If Depositary Bank qualifies as a holder in due course of the item, Drawer's defense, that it does not owe any obligation to Payee and issuance of the check was a mistake, is a defense that is precluded as against Depositary Bank. U.C.C. § 3-305. Drawer would have to pay the amount of the item to Depositary Bank. Payor Bank subrogates to the rights of Depositary Bank as a holder in due course and thus will successfully defend the action to recredit Drawer's account.

But assume that Payor Bank recredits Drawer's account and does not assert subrogation to the rights of Depositary Bank as against Drawer. Payor Bank will seek to recover the funds from Payee by subrogating to the rights of Drawer as against Payee. (U.C.C. § 4-407(c)). Drawer did not owe any obligation to Payee and should have a restitution right as against Payee.

Now assume that the issuance of the check to Payee was not a mistake as Drawer does owe an obligation to Payee. Drawer issues an effective and timely stop order to Payor Bank to stop payment on the check because Drawer has a dispute with Payee on an unrelated obligation. Payor Bank pays the check over the stop order. Payor Bank could assert subrogation rights to the rights of Payee on the check and thus resist Drawer's action to recredit Drawer's account. This is not as good as subrogating to the rights of a holder in due course of the item, such as Depositary Bank in the first scenario, because Payor Bank would be subject to any counterclaims that Drawer could assert against Payee on Drawer's contract liability on the instrument.

One more thing about the payor bank's right of subrogation. Notice that in order for this subrogation section to work, we have to pretend that the check was dishonored, not paid. That is because the drawer's obligation on the check only arises upon dishonor. U.C.C. § 3-414. Because the check is paid, it has not been dishonored. So in order for the payee, holder, or holder in due course to have any rights as against a drawer on the check, we have to pretend that the check has been dishonored.

The payor bank's right of subrogation is in addition to whatever rights it may have based upon breach of presentment warranties, U.C.C. § 4-208, or based upon restitution under U.C.C. § 3-418. In the scenarios above, the presentment warranties would not be helpful to the payor bank because none of them were breached. The right of restitution may be helpful as long as the person to whom the payment was made does not have the defense in U.C.C. § 3-418(c).

Problem 5-5

Acme Company purchased new equipment from Supplier Company. Acme's treasurer and president both must sign any checks drawn on Acme's account. Acme issued a check to Supplier Company, drawn on Acme's checking account at State Bank, properly signed, in full payment for the equipment. When Acme received the equipment, Acme claimed the equipment was defective. Acme's president called State Bank and instructed the bank not to pay the check.

Notes

a) Is that an effective stop order? May the bank charge Acme's account a fee for the stop order?

b) Would the stop order have been effective if the vice president, instead of the president, called the bank?

c) How long is the stop order effective?

d) The drawee bank received the check at 10 a.m. on Friday. The next banking day was the following Monday. The oral stop order was given at 12 noon on that following Monday. Was the stop order given in time to allow the bank to stop payment on the check? U.C.C. § 4-303.

e) Same facts as (d) above. Assume the drawee bank had established a cutoff hour of 10 a.m. for receipt of stop payment orders. Was the stop order given in time to allow the bank to stop payment on the check?

f) Assume the drawee bank received the stop order in time to allow it to act on the order. The regular clerk who usually dealt with stop orders was not at work that day. The temporary clerk put the stop order in the wrong file. The drawee bank paid the check. What are the drawer's rights against the drawee bank? Can the drawee bank defend on the basis that the drawer will have to pay the payee anyway, therefore the drawer is not damaged? U.C.C. § 4-407.

g) Do any of your answers change if the equipment is not defective?

5. Customer Death or Incompetence

Are items still properly payable if the customer dies or is incompetent? **Read U.C.C. § 4-405.**

Problem 5-6

Joe Drawer died on March 10. The administrator of his estate notified the bank on March 12 that Joe had died but to continue paying checks written before March 10. The bank continued to pay checks. On March 15, a man named Ed told the bank officer that he was Joe's long lost nephew and that the bank should stop paying checks. The bank officer had never seen this person before. The bank officer calls you. What is your advice? Should the bank continue paying checks?

C. The Collection Process: Overview

Recall that collecting an item through the banking system is the process of giving the item to the first bank in the collection chain (a collecting bank and maybe a depositary bank) and transferring the item to successive entities (other collecting banks which are intermediary banks, or clearinghouses, or the Federal Reserve) until the item is presented to the bank on which the item is drawn (the payor bank). The bank on which the item is drawn decides whether to pay or return the item.

Generally, if a payor bank fails to return the item, the payor bank will have paid the item. **U.C.C. § 4-215.** This payor bank process is generally referred to as "final payment or return." Only a payor bank makes "final payment" of an item. As we have already learned, if the item is properly payable from the account of the payor bank's customer (generally the drawer of the item), the payor bank will be entitled to charge the customer's account the amount of the item. **U.C.C. § 4-401.** At a certain point in time, the depositary bank will make funds available to its customer based on the presumed payment of an item that has not been returned. **Reg. CC, 12 C.F.R. part 229.**

If the payor bank does not want to pay the item, the payor bank needs to make timely return of the item either to the entity that presented the item to the payor bank or directly to the first bank in the collection chain. **U.C.C. § 4-301.** If the item is returned to an intermediary bank, a clearinghouse, or a Federal Reserve Bank, those entities will then return the item either to the entity that transferred the item to them or directly to the first bank in the collection chain. Eventually the returned item ends up back at the first bank that took the item for collection. That first bank will then seek to recover from its customer who deposited the item in the customer's bank account at that bank. **U.C.C. § 4-214.** Assuming the item is a check, which is a negotiable instrument, the first bank may also seek to recover on the parties' contract liability on the instrument as the check has been dishonored when the payor bank timely returned the check. If transfer warranties have been breached, the first bank may seek to assert a breach of warranty claim. **U.C.C. § 3-416 and § 4-207**.

This collection system can be segmented into the following four stages: forward collection (moving the item from the first bank in the chain to the payor bank), payment (payor bank either paying or returning the item), return (moving the item from the payor bank to the first bank in the collection chain), and funds availability (the first bank making funds available to its customer based on collection of the item).

D. Collecting Bank: Forward Collection

The forward collection process is the banking system's method of taking an item from a person and sending it through a series of banks until the item arrives at the payor bank's location.

Read U.C.C. § 4-201. The presumption is that the banks in the collection process are acting as agents of the owner of the item. The bank that receives the item from the owner for deposit in the owner's bank account gives provisional credit to the owner's account for that item. Thus, when I deposit a check in my checking account and that check is drawn on another bank, my bank (the depositary and collecting bank), gives my account provisional credit for that check. I am still the owner of the item and my bank is acting as my agent in forwarding the item for collection.

My bank will then forward the check to either the payor bank or an intermediary that will forward the check on to either the payor bank or other intermediary until the check arrives at the payor bank. Because of the credit, fraud, and insolvency risks identified earlier in this Chapter, the banks have every incentive to move the check as fast as possible from the bank of first deposit to the payor bank.

Each bank that receives the check will settle for the check to the entity that transferred check to it. To illustrate this settlement process, assume that the depositary bank, First Bank, transferred the check to collecting bank, Second Bank. Second Bank will transfer value to First Bank in exchange for the check. That settlement may be by crediting an account of First Bank held by Second Bank or by First Bank debiting an account of the Second Bank held by First Bank. Second Bank may also give a settlement to First Bank by giving First Bank a cashier's or teller's check. *See* **U.C.C. § 4-213.**

Once the check is presented to the payor bank, the payor bank will give the presenter a provisional credit for the check as well. **Read U.C.C. § 4-301(a).** These provisional credits are called provisional settlements. If the check is not finally paid by the payor bank, the provisional settlements that have been made in the forward collection process are revoked. **Read U.C.C. § 4-214.**

Regulation CC makes only one change to the forward collection process. **Reg. CC, 12 C.F.R. § 229.36(d).** Regulation CC provides that provisional settlements made in the forward collection process are final when made in order to speed up the check return process. Final settlement under Reg. CC does not limit the ability of the collecting bank to revoke the provisional settlement, U.C.C. § 4-214, and does not constitute final payment of the item by a payor bank under U.C.C. § 4-215.

Reg. CC Commentary to § 229.36(d).

Even though it is in the best interest of the banks to forward the check quickly to the payor bank, Article 4 sets out provisions that prescribe the obligations of the collecting bank. A collecting bank must send the item for collection by a reasonably prompt method. **Read U.C.C. § 4-204.** In addition, a collecting bank must send the item within a certain time frame and must act with a certain standard of care. **Read U.C.C. § 4-202.** To determine whether the collecting bank has acted in time and with the proper level of care, you must take into account several additional sections: **U.C.C. § 4-108** (time of receipt of items); **§ 4-107** (whether a branch of a bank is considered a separate bank for purposes of computing time deadlines); **§ 4-109** (excuses for delay); **§ 4-103** (the bank's ability to define ordinary care and the obligation of good faith); **§ 4-104(c) and § 3-103(a)** (definition of ordinary care). **Read these sections.** Persons that are harmed by the failure of a collecting bank to forward the item in accordance with the duties stated in U.C.C. § 4-202 and § 4-204 have causes of action for damages caused by those failures. **Reread U.C.C. § 4-103.**

In the collection process, each bank is responsible for its own actions, **U.C.C. § 4-202(c)**, and must follow instructions from its transferor, **U.C.C. § 4-203**. Once the item is in the collection chain, notations must be made on the item to allow for demonstrating the banks that have handled the item. **U.C.C. § 4-206.**

Transfers of the item in the forward collection change result in, the customer and the collecting banks making transfer warranties. **Read U.C.C. § 4-207.** Compare that section with **U.C.C. § 3-416**. Do you see any differences? The warranty liability of a transferor such as a collecting bank is in addition to the collecting bank's obligations under U.C.C. §§ 4-202, 4-204.

When a customer deposits a check with a depositary bank, the depositary bank will generally become a holder of the check under the rules we have studied on Article 3. *See also* U.C.C. § 4-205. Thus, if the check is dishonored and returned to the depositary bank, the depositary bank will have rights as a holder to enforce the contract liability of drawers and indorsers on the check. We will consider this when we discuss the check return process.

When a check is taken for collection, the first bank in the collection chain usually encodes the check. Encoding is a process of putting the MICR information on the bottom of the check. This information consists of the amount of the check, the payor bank's numerical designation, and the drawer's account number. *See* W. David East, *Check Encoding Warranties Under Revised Uniform Commercial Code Article 4 and Regulation CC*, 51 U. MIAMI L. REV. 97 (1996). Usually, the payor bank's designation and the drawer's account number are already encoded when the checks are printed. Thus when the item is transferred to the depositary bank, the only the amount is typically encoded. **Read U.C.C. § 4-209 and Reg. CC, 12 C.F.R. § 229.34(c)(3).** These sections provide for warranties concerning the accuracy of the encoding. Who makes the encoding warranty? To whom is the encoding warranty made? What are the damages for breach of the warranty?

We have already considered the use of electronics in the collection process. Article 4 allows for electronic presentment agreements. **Read U.C.C. §§ 4-110, 4-209.** The difficulty is that the efficacy of this provision on electronic presentment is that it rests on "agreement." U.C.C. § 1-201 (definition of agreement). In a multi-party environment dealing with millions of instruments, it is extremely difficult to obtain agreements with all of the involved entities. Federal Reserve Operating Circular 3 allows for electronic images of checks to be sent through the federal reserve system and also allows for electronic presentment through submission of the MICR line information. This circular thus takes advantage of the provision for electronic presentment agreements in Article 4.

If a check is sent through the Federal Reserve system Regulation J, 12 C.F.R. part 210, is applicable (in addition to Article 4, Regulation CC, and the operating circulars). **Read Reg. J, 12 C.F.R. §§ 210.3, 210.4, 210.5, 210.6, 210.7.** What are the obligations of a bank that sends the item to the Federal Reserve Bank? What are the obligations of the Federal Reserve Bank? What are the obligations of a bank that receives an item from the Federal Reserve Bank?

Problem 5-7

To organize this material, set forth a checklist of all of the obligations of a collecting bank in handling a check in the forward collection process. Your checklist should differentiate between when a Federal Reserve Bank is involved in the forward collection process and when a Federal Reserve Bank is not an intermediary in the forward collection process. For each obligation, identify the content of the obligation, who is a potential plaintiff, the applicable damages measure, and any procedural steps that must be taken in order to bring the lawsuit.

Notes

Notes

Problem 5-8

Paul Payee took a check payable to him to his bank at First National Bank, indorsed the check in blank, and deposited it in his checking account at First National Bank. First National Bank transferred the check to Second National Bank. Second National Bank transferred the check to the drawee, Third National Bank.

Notes

a) Payee deposited the check at 4 p.m. on Monday at First National Bank. First National Bank forwarded the check to Second National Bank on Wednesday at 9 a.m. using a private courier service. Did First National Bank act properly?

b) Assume Second National Bank received the check from First National Bank at 10 a.m. Tuesday. How long does Second National Bank have to send the check on to Third National Bank?

c) Would your answer to (a) above change if First National Bank had a 2 p.m. cutoff hour for receipt of checks?

d) Would your answer to (a) above change if First National Bank had a computer failure on the banking day that it received the check?

e) Assume that First National Bank sent the check to the main office of First National Bank located in a town 20 miles away. The First National Bank in which the check was deposited is only one branch of First National Bank. How long does the main office have to send the check on to another bank?

f) If First National Bank has a banking relationship with Third National Bank, is sending the item to Second National Bank an unreasonable action? If it is, what is First National Bank's liability and to whom is First National Bank liable?

g) Payee deposited the check at 4 p.m. on Monday at First National Bank. First National Bank forwarded the check to Second National Bank on Tuesday at 9 a.m. by placing the check in the first class mail, properly stamped and addressed to the payments processing center of Second National Bank. Did First National Bank act properly?

h) Payee deposited the check at 4 p.m. on Monday at First National Bank. First National Bank forwarded the check to Second National Bank on Tuesday at 9 a.m. by private courier service. Assume that Paul Payee forgot to indorse the check. No one inspected the check. Has First National met its standard of care? Is First National Bank a holder of the item? U.C.C. § 4-205.

i) Payee deposited the check at 4 p.m. on Monday at First National Bank. Assume that Paul Payee indorsed the check: "For deposit only, Paul Payee." What effect does that indorsement have on the forward collection process? U.C.C. § 3-206(c), (e).

j) Payee deposited the check at 4 p.m. on Monday at First National Bank. First National Bank forwarded the check to the Federal Reserve Bank in its district at 9 a.m. Tuesday by private courier service. What obligations does First National Bank have? What obligations does the Federal Reserve Bank have?

k) The amount of the check was $100. First National Bank encoded $1,000 on the MICR line of the check. When First National Bank forwarded the check to Second National Bank, Second National Bank credited First National Bank for $1,000. When

Notes

Second National Bank presented the check to Third National Bank, Third National Bank credited Second National Bank with $1,000 and debited the drawer's account for $1,000. For what amount is that check properly payable? Who bears the liability for that mistake and who can recover for that mistake?

l) When the check was eventually presented to Third National Bank, Third National Bank dishonored the check because the drawer had stopped payment on the check. The check is returned to First National Bank. What are First National Bank's rights as against Payee? Would it matter if Payee had indorsed the check in blank and "without recourse"?

E. Payor Bank: Settlement and Final Payment

When the item is presented to the payor bank, the bank must decide whether to pay or dishonor the item. There are two main methods of presentment contemplated by Article 4. The first method is presentment "over the counter." The paradigm example is when a payee of a check takes the check to drawee bank (the payor bank) and presents the check to the teller "over the counter." If the teller pays the amount of the check to the presenter, the payor bank has made "final payment." **Read U.C.C. § 4-215(a).**

The second method of presentment is the more usual case. The check is forwarded to the payor bank by an intermediary bank, a Federal Reserve Bank, or a clearinghouse. When the payor bank receives the check, it makes a provisional settlement for the check. In order to preserve a right to revoke that provisional settlement, the payor bank must make the provisional settlement by midnight of the banking day it received the check. **Read U.C.C. § 4-301(a).** The timely made provisional settlement is not "final payment" because the payor bank has preserved its right to revoke the settlement. U.C.C. § 4-215(a). In order to revoke the settlement, the payor bank must not make final payment and must return the item before its midnight deadline. U.C.C. § 4-301(a). As we have already learned, the midnight deadline is midnight of the banking day following the banking day of receipt. U.C.C. § 4-104(a)(10).

If the payor bank timely returns the item after the timely provisional settlement, the item has been dishonored. **Read U.C.C. § 3-502(b)(1).** A return is effectuated as provided in U.C.C. § 4-301, which requires that the item be "sent" by the midnight deadline. If the payor bank makes the provisional settlement but does not return the item by its midnight deadline, then it has made final payment for the item. **U.C.C. § 4-215.**

Has the payor bank made final payment if it fails to make the provisional settlement by midnight of the banking day of receipt? No, final payment has not been made. But if the payor bank fails to make the provisional settlement by midnight of the banking day of receipt, it is accountable for the item. Under U.C.C. § 3-502, when the payor bank is "accountable" for the item, the item has been dishonored. **Read U.C.C. § 4-302 and comment 4 to U.C.C. § 3-502.**

Other sections that must be consulted to determine whether the payor bank has acted within the required time frame are **U.C.C. §§ 4-107, 4-108, and 4-109.** While other banks in the collection process make provisional settlements for items, it is only the payor bank that makes "final payment." Final payment is a watershed event. After final payment, the item has been paid and can no longer be dishonored. Final payment also firms up the provisional credits granted by the collecting banks and makes those credits final settlements. U.C.C. § 4-215(c). Upon final settlement, a collecting bank is liable to its customer for the amount of the item. U.C.C. § 4-215(d).

Final payment is not the same thing as whether the item is properly payable from the drawer's account. A payor bank (the drawee) may make final payment of the item but not have a right to charge the customer's account under U.C.C. § 4-401. Whether the payor bank has made final payment on the item is a different question than whether the drawer's contract liability on the item is discharged under U.C.C. § 3-602 and whether the underlying obligation for which the item was issued or transferred is discharged under U.C.C. § 3-310.

If there is nothing wrong with the instrument (no forgeries, no alterations, no unauthorized signatures), a payor bank will make final payment on the item. The item will be properly payable from the drawer's account. The payor bank will have paid a person entitled to enforce the item and thus discharged the drawer's and indorser's contract liability on the instrument. That payment will discharge the underlying obligation for which the instrument was issued or transferred. It is when there is something wrong with the instrument that the analysis gets interesting. In Chapter 6, we will consider how these issues play out when there is fraud and wrongdoing.

The time frames set out for the payor bank in U.C.C. § 4-301 are not generally subject to alteration by agreement between the bank and its customer. That is because the primary effect of these deadlines is not on the payor bank's customer, but rather those parties upstream in the collection process. Final payment happens because the payor bank fails to return the item after giving the provisional settlement. It is very difficult for the depositary bank to know whether the item has been finally paid because there is no positive action by the payor bank that gets communicated to the depositary bank. The clear deadlines set by U.C.C. § 4-301 thus provide a certainty to the process that would be lacking if the deadlines could be altered by agreement.

Having said that, however, Regulation CC allows extension of the payor bank's midnight deadline if the payor bank complies with **12 C.F.R. § 229.30(c).** Read that section. *See Oak Brook Bank v. Northern Trust Co.*, 256 F. 3d 638 (7th Cir. 2001) (court used Reg. CC to extend the midnight deadline). The theory of Regulation CC is to create a structure that gets returned checks back to the depositary bank as fast as possible. Remember that for a payor bank to "return" an item and thus not make final payment requires the payor bank to "send" the item. "Send" does not mean the same thing as "receipt." **Review the definitions in U.C.C. § 1-201 and § 1-202.** The extension of the midnight deadline allowed by Regulation CC is keyed to the receiving bank's receipt of the item in the time it would have normally received the item if the payor bank had complied with the midnight deadline.

If a check is presented to the payor bank by a Federal Reserve Bank, **Reg. J, 12 C.F.R. § 210.9 and § 210.12** must be consulted for the effect on the payor bank's obligations regarding settlement and final payment. Generally a payor bank must immediately settle with the presenting Federal Reserve Bank in available funds to the Federal Reserve in the payor bank's district. This is in effect the "provisional" settlement referred to in U.C.C § 4-301. The payor bank's immediate settlement does not prevent the payor bank from returning the item by its midnight deadline as outlined above. A payor bank may return an item to a Federal Reserve Bank even if the Federal Reserve Bank was not the presenting bank.

When a payor bank returns an item, it makes warranties about that item. Those warranties are not imposed by Article 4 but by Regulation CC, 12 C.F.R. § 229.34, and Regulation J, 12 C.F.R. § 210.12. We will discuss these warranties in the next section when we consider the return process.

If the payor bank is unable to charge the drawer's account or the drawer does not have available funds but the payor bank has made final payment, the payor bank may seek to recover from others that came before it in the forward collection chain. The usual theories are breach of presentment warranty, **U.C.C. § 4-208**, or fraud, **U.C.C. § 4-302(b)**, or the common law or statutory right of restitution allowed for payments by mistake. **U.C.C. § 3-418.** The payor bank may also try to subrogate to someone's rights on the item or in the underlying transaction. **U.C.C. § 4-407.**

As we will see, the payor bank will have great difficulty in succeeding on these theories in two primary circumstances where the payor bank has made final payment. First, when the drawer's signature is forged, the payor bank is generally not able to charge the drawer's account as the item is not properly payable. Second, the payor bank often seeks to recover from other parties when the drawer's account has insufficient funds and the drawer is unable to pay the overdraft. In these circumstances the payor bank will usually not have a viable cause of action for breach of presentment warranty, usually cannot prove the type of fraud referred to in U.C.C. § 4-302(b), and has no viable defendant for the restitution cause of action under U.C.C. § 3-418 (because of the defense in subsection (c)).

Payor banks have thus asserted other causes of action such as negligence or violation of the obligation of good faith in order to try to pass liability to those entities in the collection chain that handled the item prior to presentment. Courts have not been sympathetic to those arguments. *See Frost National Bank v. Midwest Autohous, Inc.*, 241 F. 3d 862 (7th Cir. 2001) (no good faith obligation of depositary bank to let payor bank know there is a possible check kite[*] taking place).

---

[*] As explained by the judge in *First National Bank in Harvey v. Colonial Bank*, 898 F. Supp. 1220 (N.D. Ill. 1995):

> Check kiting is a form of bank fraud. The kiter opens accounts at two (or more) banks, writes checks on insufficient funds on one account, then covers the overdraft by depositing a check drawn on insufficient funds from the other account.
>
> To illustrate the operation, suppose that the defrauder opens two accounts with a deposit of $500 each at the First National Bank and a distant Second National Bank. (A really successful defrauder will have numerous accounts in fictitious names at banks in widely separated states.)

(continued...)

Problem 5-9

Notes

a) Paul Payee took a check payable to him and drawn on State Bank to the teller window at State Bank. Payee indorsed the check at the teller window and requested the teller pay him the amount of the check. The teller did so. Has State Bank made a

---

* (...continued)

> The defrauder then issues for goods or cash checks totaling $3000 against the First National Bank. But before they clear and overdraw the account, he covers the overdrafts with a check for $4,000 drawn on the Second National Bank. The Second National account will be overdrawn when the $4,000 check is presented; before that happens, however, the defrauder covers it with a check on the First National Bank. The process is repeated innumerable times until there is a constant float of worthless checks between the accounts and the defrauder has bilked the banks of a substantial sum of money.

John D. O'Malley, *"Common Check Frauds and the Uniform Commercial Code,"* 23 RUTGERS L.REV. 189, 194 n. 35 (1968-69). By timing the scheme correctly and repeating it over a period of time, the kiter can use the funds essentially as an interest-free loan. *Williams v. United States*, 458 U.S. 279, 281 n. 1, 102 S.Ct. 3088, 3090 n. 1, 73 L.Ed.2d 767 (1982) (*quoting* Brief for the United States).

* * * *

A kite crashes when one of the banks dishonors checks drawn on it and returns them to the other banks involved in the kite. Clark, *supra*. Usually, such a dishonor occurs when one bank suspects a kite. *Id.* However, an individual bank may have trouble detecting a check kiting scheme. "Until one has devoted a substantial amount of time examining not only one's own account, but accounts at other banks, it may be impossible to know whether the customer is engaged in a legitimate movement of funds or illegitimate kiting." JAMES J. WHITE & ROBERT S. SUMMERS, UNIFORM COMMERCIAL CODE § 17-1 (3d ed. 1988 & Supp.1994). But each bank is usually able to monitor only its own account, and "[t]here is no certain test that distinguishes one who writes many checks on low balances from a check kiter." White & Summers, *supra*, § 17-2. Even if a bank suspects a kite, it might decide not to take any action for a number of reasons. First, it may be liable to its customer for wrongfully dishonoring checks. § 4-202. Second, if it reports that a kite is operating and turns out to be wrong, it could find itself defending a defamation suit. White & Summers, *supra*, § 17-1 (Supp.1994). Finally, if it errs in returning checks or reporting a kite, it may risk angering a large customer. *Id.*

provisional settlement? Has State Bank made final payment?

b) Paul Payee is in possession of a check made payable to him, and drawn on State Bank. Paul indorsed the check in blank, and deposited it in his checking account at First Bank. First Bank sent the check to State Bank for payment. State Bank received the item on Monday at 4 p.m and did not give a provisional settlement for the check to First Bank. On Wednesday at 2 p.m., State Bank returned the check to First Bank because the drawer's account had insufficient funds to cover the amount of the check. Has State Bank made final payment?

c) Same facts as (b) above. When State Bank received the check on Monday, State Bank gave a provisional settlement to First Bank. State Bank had a cutoff time of 3 p.m. for receipt of checks for payment. Has State Bank made final payment?

d) Paul Payee is in possession of a check made payable to him, drawn on State Bank. Paul indorsed the check in blank, and deposited it in his checking account at First Bank. First Bank sent

Notes

the check to State Bank for payment. State Bank received the item on Monday at 4 p.m. and gave a provisional settlement for the check to First Bank. On Wednesday at 1 p.m., State Bank returned the check to First Bank because the drawer's account had insufficient funds to cover the amount of the check. First Bank received the check on Wednesday at 2 p.m. Has State Bank made final payment?

e) Paul Payee is in possession of a check made payable to him, drawn on State Bank. Paul indorsed the check in blank, and deposited it in his checking account at First Bank. First Bank sent the check to Federal Reserve Bank on Monday at 2 p.m. Federal Reserve Bank sent the check to State Bank on Monday at 10 p.m. State Bank received the item on Monday at 11 p.m. On Tuesday at 11 p.m., State Bank returned the check to the Federal Reserve Bank, which received it at 1 p.m. Has State Bank made final payment?

f) Paul Payee is in possession of a check made payable to him, drawn on State Bank. Paul indorsed the check in blank, and deposited it in his checking account at First Bank. First Bank mistakenly encoded the check for $1000 when the amount of the check

Notes

was $100. State Bank did not return the item. What amount is properly payable from the drawer's account? What is State Bank's cause of action?

g) Paul Payee is in possession of a check made payable to him, drawn on State Bank, signed by Fred as drawer. Paul indorsed the check in blank, and deposited it in his checking account at First Bank. State Bank did not return the item. Florence, the customer on the account at State Bank on which the check was drawn, objected to the debit of her account, contending the drawer's signature was forged. State Bank recredited her account and sought to recover from First Bank. Will State Bank succeed?

F. Item Return and Chargeback

If the payor bank decides to return an item, the item must be returned to the first bank in the collection chain. Prior to the passage of the Expedited Funds Availability Act (EFAA), and Regulation CC, the item would be passed back along the chain with the provisional credits granted in the forward collection process being revoked as the item traveled to the first bank in the collection chain. This revocation of the provisional credit is called a chargeback. Because the first bank in the chain would not know for some time whether final payment had occurred, the bank would put a "hold" on the funds and not let the person who had submitted the item for collection have access to the funds, until the first bank was quite sure that enough time had passed to ensure that the check would not be returned. Congress passed the EFAA in an effort to limit the time that banks could place a hold on funds. In order for banks to avoid losing money by giving credit that could be withdrawn from the bank even if the check was returned, the check return process had to be faster.

The EFFA and Regulation CC, promulgated pursuant to the Federal Reserve Board's authority under the Act, have quite a few provisions on the check return process. We have already looked at one change that was required in order to make the check return process faster. In order to return checks faster, the check could not necessarily take the same path back to the initial bank as it took to get to the payor bank. Thus, the intermediary banks would not know whether the provisional credit had become final. That is why Reg. CC makes all provisional settlements final in the forward collection process. Reg. CC, 12 C.F.R. § 229.36(d). These materials will refer you to the provisions in Regulation CC.*

First, consider the Article 4 rules on check return. We already know that the payor bank starts the check return process by sending the check to someone that preceded it in the collection chain. **U.C.C. § 4-301**. Article 4 allows for return of an image of the item if the parties have agreed to that method of return or notice of return if the item is unavailable for return. The payor bank also revokes the provisional credit that the payor bank had given the entity that presented the item to the bank. **U.C.C. § 4-301(a)**. A timely check return is a dishonor of the check. **U.C.C. §§ 4-301(c), 3-502**.

What are the duties of the collecting banks in the return process? A collecting bank must exercise "ordinary care" in handling the item that has been returned. As we learned in the forward collection process, a collecting bank has exercised ordinary care if it takes the required action by its midnight deadline. **Review U.C.C. § 4-202**. When a collecting bank receives a returned item, it revokes any provisional settlement given for the item. U.C.C. § 4-214.

What are the rights of a collecting bank when it receives a returned item? Remember, the payor bank has revoked the provisional settlement it gave for the item when the payor bank received it. The collecting bank will be seeking to recover that amount from someone else. The collecting bank can charge back against its customer's account or obtain a refund from the customer. **Read U.C.C. § 4-214**. A collecting bank will also usually be a person entitled to enforce the item (assuming the item is a check or other negotiable instrument). Thus, it may enforce

---

* A good lawyer, however, will also check the EFAA's provisions. The Federal Reserve Board only has authority to promulgate regulations that are consistent with the requirements of the EFAA. If a part of Regulation CC is not consistent with those requirements, that part would not be valid.

the contract obligations on the instrument using the principles from Article 3 that we learned in Chapter 3. Remember that in order to enforce the contract obligation of an indorser on a dishonored item, the indorser must be given timely notice of dishonor. **Review U.C.C. § 3-415 and 3-504.** A collecting bank may also have a viable cause of action for breach of transfer warranties under U.C.C. § 3-416 or § 4-207. If there is a problem with the encoding on the check, the collecting bank may have a viable cause of action for breach of the encoding warranty under U.C.C. § 4-209.

The point of these "pass the loss" provisions in Article 4 is to move the loss to the person who introduced the item into the bank collection system, if at all possible.

Regulation CC provides additional rules governing the check return process. The Regulation CC provisions do *not* displace the Article 4 rules given above. Rather, Regulation CC imposes additional obligations on the banks in the check return process.

Remember, the goal of Regulation CC is to get the check back to the depositary bank as quickly as possible. Regulation CC facilitates this faster return by imposing an obligation of expeditious return on the payor bank (paying bank in Reg. CC terminology), **12 C.F.R. § 229.30**, and on collecting banks (returning banks in Reg. CC terminology), **12 C.F.R. § 229.31**. If the amount of the check returned is large, then the payor bank has an additional notice obligation as described in **12 C.F.R. § 229.33**. Do the expeditious return and large check return notice constitute adequate notice of dishonor for purposes of U.C.C. § 3-504 if given to an indorser of the item? The depositary bank has the obligations stated in **12 C.F.R. § 229.32**.

Read each of those sections and the related commentary. In each section, the primary concerns are the time in which the bank has to act and the requirement of settlement for the returned item. Regarding settlement for the check, see **12 C.F.R. § 229.36(f)**. Now read **12 C.F.R. § 229.38 and the related commentary.** That section imposes liability for failure to exercise ordinary care or good faith in complying with the obligations imposed in Regulation CC. Thus, the liability of the banks for failure to comply with these additional requirements of expeditious return and the large check return notice is not absolute.

In the return process, the payor and returning banks make warranties specified in **12 C.F.R. § 229.34**. These warranties are an additional source of liability. They do not substitute for the obligation to make an expeditious return or for the payor bank to give the large check return notice.

Problem 5-10

Make a checklist of the obligations that Regulation CC imposes on the payor bank and on the collecting banks. Specify the content of the obligation owed and who would be seeking to recover on those obligations.

Notes

Regulation CC applies no matter which banks are involved in the check return process. Regulation J applies when checks are returned through the Federal Reserve Banks. When a Federal Reserve Bank is involved, there are two basic avenues of inquiry. First, what is the obligation of the bank that returns an item to the Federal Reserve Bank? Second, what is the obligation of the Federal Reserve Bank when it receives a returned item? With those two questions in mind, **read Reg. J, 12 C.F.R. §§ 210.12, 210.13, 210.14**.

Problem 5-11

On Friday, a check for $3,000 was presented for payment to First National Bank, the drawee. The check was drawn on an account with insufficient funds to pay the check. First National decided to return the check. The depositary bank was Dunning National Bank.

Notes

a) What should First National Bank do to comply with Article 4 and Regulation CC? What do you need to know about the location of each bank in order to fully answer this question?

b) Assume that First National Bank made a provisional settlement for the check but missed its midnight deadline. First National Bank still wants to return the check. Can it do so and avoid liability for the item under U.C.C. § 4-215?

c) Assume that First National Bank returned the check before its midnight deadline to the Federal Reserve Bank in its area. Has First National Bank made an expeditious return? What is First National Bank's liability to the Federal Reserve Bank? What is the Federal Reserve Bank's obligation?

Notes

d) First National Bank timely returned the check to Second National Bank. What is Second National Bank's obligation?

e) First National Bank returned the check to Second National Bank by its midnight deadline under U.C.C. § 4-301, but failed to meet the deadline for an expeditious return under Reg. CC. Who can recover against First National Bank and for what can they recover?

f) Assume First National Bank failed to make an expeditious return due to a computer failure. Is that an acceptable excuse for failing to meet the deadlines?

g) When Dunning National Bank receives the timely returned check, what are its rights and duties as to the bank returning the check to Dunning and as to Dunning's customer?

h) Assume that First National Bank's customer contends that the check was not authorized as the customer did not sign the check and thus First National Bank cannot charge the customer's account as the item is not properly payable under U.C.C. § 4-401. First

National Bank does not return the check by its midnight deadline but returned the check when its customer told the bank the item was unauthorized. Will First National Bank be successful in passing the liability upstream to a previous bank or the payee of the item?

i)   First National properly returned the check by its midnight deadline and made an expeditious return directly to Dunning National Bank. May Dunning National Bank seek to collect from the drawer on its contract liability on the instrument? Assume the drawer has a defense to contract liability based upon failure of consideration in the transaction for which the check was issued. Can Dunning National Bank qualify as a holder in due course? Review the relevant parts of Chapter 3 and *see* U.C.C. § 4-205, § 4-210, § 4-211.

G. Funds Availability

When a provisional settlement becomes final, a collecting bank is liable to its customer. U.C.C. § 4-215(d). Liability of the collecting bank to the customer, however, does not mean that the funds are actually available to the customer. Article 4 says very little about the timeline for making funds available to a bank's customer. **U.C.C. § 4-215(e) and (f).**

Regulation CC contains extensive provisions on funds availability. The relationship between Regulation CC and Article 4 on funds availability is stated in **Reg. CC, 12 C.F.R. § 229.20.** The reason the Expedited Funds Availability Act was passed and Regulation CC was promulgated was to decrease the amount of time it took for depositary banks to make funds deposited available to its customers. Regulation CC sets forth time deadlines by which the depositary bank must make funds deposited available for withdrawal to its customers.

The question of funds availability has brought us full circle back to the bank-customer relationship. Instead of looking at the drawer-drawee relationship, we are now examining the depositor-depositary bank relationship. The obligation to make the funds available to the depositor has nothing to do with whether final payment has been made by the payor bank. It also has nothing to do with whether the depositary bank (a collecting bank) can exercise rights of chargeback against its customer. U.C.C. § 4-214. Indeed, often the depositary bank will be required to make the funds available to the customer before the payor bank makes final payment and before the depositary bank's right of chargeback terminates. The obligation of the depositary bank to make the funds available to its customer also has nothing to do with whether either the payor bank or any collecting bank has met the requirements for an expeditious return, or whether the payor bank has given the required large check return notice under Regulation CC. The obligation of the depositary bank to make the funds available to its customer also has nothing to do with whether timely notice of dishonor has been given to any indorser. In other words, the funds availability obligation of the depositary bank is a separate obligation.

Having said that, consider how the funds availability question might relate to the question of whether there is a wrongful dishonor of an item drawn on the account. Assume that Customer has a checking account at Bank. Customer deposited a check for $1,000. Assume under the applicable funds availability rule, Bank must make the funds fully available to the customer on Wednesday. On Wednesday, the account balance is $1,200 (counting the value from the $1,000 check). The next day, Thursday, a check for $800 drawn on the account with Customer as the drawer is presented to Bank. If Bank pays the check the account balance will be $400. However, Bank is concerned about whether the $1,000 check deposited earlier will actually clear. Thus Bank dishonors the $800 check at a time when the funds availability rules would lead to a determination that Customer had sufficient available funds on deposit so that the $800 check was properly payable. Bank may be liable for wrongful dishonor of the $800 check and may be liable for failure to follow the funds availability rules in Regulation CC.

Now read Reg. CC, 12 C.F.R. §§ 229.10, 229.12 and all applicable definitions. These two sections set up the time periods for making funds available.

As we explore the rules on funds availability, a helpful exercise is to make a chart based on when funds from certain types of deposits must be available if none of the exceptions apply. The time line starts to run from the day of deposit. So first determine what day the item is considered deposited. **Reg. CC, 12 C.F.R. § 229.19(a)**. Then determine what type of item has been deposited. Is the deposit cash or a check? If a check, is it a local check or a nonlocal check? Is it a government check? Is it a cashier's check? Then determine in what type of facility the item has been deposited. Is it over the counter at the depositary bank, at an ATM on the bank premises, at an ATM in a shopping mall, at a night deposit box, or by mail? With that information in mind, find the appropriate availability schedule in either **Reg. CC, 12 C.F.R. § 229.10 or § 229.12**. Then consider whether all or only part of the funds that item represents must be made available, at what time of day the funds must be made available, and whether "availability" means for all purposes. **Reg. CC, 12 C.F.R. § 229.19(b), § 229.2(d), § 229.12(d)**.

After considering all of those factors, your chart may begin to look something like this if you start counting from the banking day (defined in **Reg. CC, 12 C.F.R. § 229.2**) of deposit:

next business day	second business day	third business day	fourth business day	fifth business day	sixth business day
cash "in person" deposit 229.10(a)	*cash* not "in person" deposit 229.10(a)				
	local check 229.12(b)(1) at least $400 for cash withdrawal 229.12(d) unless deposited at non proprietary ATM 229.12(f).	over $ 400 from a local check 229.12(d)		local check deposited at non proprietary ATM 229.12(f)	

Continue filling in the chart using the information in Regulation CC. Regulation CC also requires the depositary bank to disclose its funds availability policy to its customers. **Reg. CC, 12 C.F.R. § 229.15 through § 229.18**. Ask your bank for its funds availability policy and compare it to the requirements of Regulation CC.

Regulation CC contains exceptions for situations in which the bank need not meet the otherwise applicable deadlines. **Reg. CC, 12 C.F.R. § 229.13**. Once you determine the usual schedule for making available the funds from the particular deposit you should then determine whether any exceptions apply that would allow the bank to extend the time period for availability. If one of the exceptions apply, when must the bank make the funds available? **Reg. CC, 12 C.F.R. § 229.13(h)**.

If the bank fails to follow the funds availability rules, **Reg. CC, 12 C.F.R. § 229.21** governs the bank's liability for failure to comply with the funds availability rules.

Problem 5-12

Ace Hardware has an account at First National Bank, located in Minneapolis. Ace receives checks in payment of goods sold at its retail store. Ace deposits checks every day at First National Bank at two different times, 12 noon and 6 p.m. On Thursday it deposited the following items at 12 noon:

- a check for $1,000 payable to Ace drawn on State Bank, California, located in San Francisco;
- a check for $2,000 payable to Ace drawn on Second National Bank, St. Paul;
- a cashier's check for $500 payable to Ace;
- a check for $3,000 payable to Ace drawn on a branch bank of First National located in Shoreview, a Minneapolis suburb.

All deposits were made in person to an employee of the bank located in Minneapolis.

Notes

a) When must First National make the funds from those checks available for withdrawal?

b) First National stated in its agreement with Ace that none of the amounts deposited are available for cash withdrawal for 10 business days after deposit. Is that an acceptable restriction? When is Ace allowed to make cash withdrawals of these amounts?

c) Would your answer change if the checks were deposited to an ATM?

d) Would your answer change if the checks were deposited at 6 p.m. and the bank had a cutoff hour of 4 p.m.?

e) Does making these funds available to Ace prevent First National Bank from charging back against Ace's account in the event a check is timely returned by the payor bank?

f) If First National Bank does not make the funds available in the time period required by Regulation CC, what is Ace's recourse?

g) Would it matter if Ace's account at First National had been opened only 20 days ago?

h) Would it matter if Ace's account had been overdrawn 6 separate times for a period of 2 banking days each time in the previous 6 months?

i) What can First National do to take advantage of an extension of time?

H. Check 21 and Substitute Checks

The federal Check Clearing for the 21st Century Act ("Check 21") (codified at 12 U.S.C. §§ 5001–18) became effective October 28, 2004. The Federal Reserve Board has promulgated amendments to Regulation CC and Regulation J to implement Check 21.

Check 21 is very simple in concept. Under the current check processing system, banks and others have been hampered in their ability to truncate checks at the depositary bank and collect the checks through electronic presentment. This is because in order to do so, each bank or collection facility in the middle, as well as the drawee bank, must have agreed to accept the information electronically. U.C.C. § 4-110. The inability to obtain agreements by all parties in the collection chain presents an obstacle to using electronic means for check presentment, resulting in costly transportation and processing of the paper item.

Rather than attack the problem directly by requiring all banks to allow electronic presentment of checks, Check 21 authorizes a new species of negotiable instrument called the "substitute check." **Reg. CC 12 C.F.R. § 229.2.** A substitute check is **NOT** an electronic representation of the original check, rather it is a paper copy of the original check that complies with the four stated requirements for a "substitute check." That substitute check is deemed to be the legal equivalent of the original check if it meets the requirements for being a substitute check, contains a required legend, and a bank has made the warranty provided in Check 21. The legend must state "This is a legal copy of your check. You can use it the same way you would use the original check." **Reg. CC, 12 C.F.R. § 229.51(a).** Thus a bank could create a paper object that is a substitute check with legal equivalence, a substitute check without legal equivalence, or an object that does not qualify as a substitute check.

How this "substitute check" scheme will allow for electronic processing of data from checks is best illustrated by an example. Assume Bank A, a depositary bank located in New York, receives a check for deposit to a customer's account. The check is drawn on Bank Z, located in California. Bank Z does not allow for electronic presentment of checks. Bank A may still truncate the deposited check by converting the information from the check to electronic data, and send that data for collection through the banking system with entities that have agreements with Bank A to process the data. When the data reaches the entity immediately prior in the collection chain to Bank Z, that entity may convert the data to a paper "substitute check" with legal equivalence and present it to Bank Z. Bank Z must treat that "substitute check" as the legal equivalent of the original check and pay or dishonor it accordingly.

This example is very simple in that it contemplates one "substitute check with legal equivalence" being created. There is no limit, however, on the number of "substitute checks with legal equivalence" that may be created in the collection chain. For example, Bank A may truncate the original check to electronic data and transfer that data to Bank B. Bank B may create a "substitute check" and send that item to a check collection service that truncates the "substitute check" into electronic data for transfer to Bank C. Bank C may then create a "substitute check" to present the item to Bank Z for payment. Each "substitute check" that meets the requirements for legal equivalence is deemed to be the legal equivalent of the original check. This scheme violates one of the primary hallmarks of the concept of negotiable instruments, that is, that the obligation to pay is reified into **one** piece of paper so that the person obligated to pay will know that it is paying the right person upon presentment of that one piece of paper.

Obviously, one of the risks of the substitute check with legal equivalence scheme is that the customer who issued the original check must be vigilant to avoid paying more than once. The banking industry will have to develop operational controls to avoid the risk that multiple items created out of the original item will find their way to presentment for payment from the customer's account. This problem is addressed in Check 21 by creating a warranty that any bank that transfers, presents, or returns a substitute check and receives consideration for that check warrants that no depositary bank, drawee, drawer, or indorser will have to pay twice because of the substitute check. **Reg. CC, 12 C.F.R. § 229.52(a).** Non-banks do not make this warranty even when they are the entities that create a substitute check. Banks dealing with non-banks in the collection process must use contractual agreements to pass on losses caused by the non-bank's actions in creating or dealing with substitute checks.

Notice that the warranty is made only when a substitute check is created. What about the entity that truncates the original check and forwards on only electronic data (such as MICR line information and an electronic image of the check)? Check 21 does **NOT** provide any rights as against the truncating entity. Neither does Article 4 as all of Article 4 is geared to providing rights as to "items" transferred through the banking system. Electronic data is not an item. U.C.C. § 4-104(a)(9). Now look at Regulation J, 12 C.F.R. § 210.5 and § 210.6 The Federal Reserve Banks are receiving and giving transfer warranties as to electronic data.

Another risk is that the bank dealing with what it thinks to be a substitute check as the legal equivalent of the original check, is in fact wrong. For example, a drawee bank that treats the item as a substitute check with legal equivalence and thus properly payable from the customer's account may find out later that the substitute check did not meet the requirements for legal equivalence or was not in fact a substitute check. Any bank that transfers, presents, or returns a substitute check for consideration warrants that the substitute check is in fact a substitute check that meets the requirements for legal equivalence. **Reg. CC 12 C.F.R. § 229.52.** That warranty is not given, however, if the paper document does not meet the requirements for a substitute check (or a paper or electronic representation of a substitute check) in the first instance. So if a paper document is not a substitute check, Check 21 imposes no liability on a bank that handles that item. Which of the three categories of possible paper documents (substitute checks with legal equivalence, substitute checks without legal equivalence, and paper objects that are not substitute checks) qualify as "items" under Article 4? **Before you answer, read the definition of "check" in Reg. CC, 12 C.F.R. § 229.2 and the staff commentary to that definition.** Check 21 contains a general liability provision that persons injured by the breach of warranty may recover the amount of the loss up to the amount of the substitute check plus interest and expenses, including attorney's fees. **Reg. CC, 12 C.F.R. § 229.56.**

In addition to the recovery for breach of warranty, the indemnity provision operates to pass losses caused by receiving a substitute check instead of the original check back to the bank that created the substitute check. **Read 12 C.F.R. § 229.53.** The amount recoverable through the indemnity depends upon whether there is a breach of one or both of the above warranties that caused a loss. If there is a breach of the warranties provided in Reg. CC, 12 C.F.R. § 229.52, the indemnity amount is any loss, including attorney's fees, caused by the breach of warranty. Presumably this could include consequential damages suffered by a customer whose account was debited more than once due to the substitute check creation. If there is no breach of warranty, the indemnity amount is limited to the amount of the loss but no more than the amount of the substitute check plus interest and expenses including attorney's fees. The ability to recover under the indemnity provisions is subject to a comparative negligence analysis that may reduce the amount recoverable. An indemnifying bank may reduce its liability by producing the original check or a sufficient copy of the check necessary to determine the validity of the claim of loss.

The other major pieces of Check 21 are the expedited recredit process for consumers in Reg. CC, 12 C.F.R. § 229.54 and the expedited recredit process for banks in Reg. CC, 12 C.F.R. § 229.55. Notably non-consumer bank customers have **NO** recredit rights at all. The recredit right is somewhat limited as it is predicated on the assumption that the issue will require production of the original check in order to determine whether the substitute check was properly charged to the consumer's account or whether the consumer has a warranty claim with respect to the substitute check. Production of the original check will be somewhat irrelevant if the issue is that multiple substitute checks or the original and a substitute check have both been charged to the customer's account. Production of the original check will likely be most helpful with regard to issues such as forgery, alteration, MICR encoding errors and the like where information on the original check needs to be examined.

  To analyze the following problems, ask yourself these questions. First, was a substitute check created? Second, if so, did that substitute check qualify for legal equivalence? Third, what was the problem with the paper document that was created? Fourth, how is the risk of that problem occurring allocated as between the banks and as between the bank and its customer?

Problem 5-13

Notes

Bank A in California received a check for $1,500 from its customer for deposit in her checking account. The check was drawn on Bank C located in Iowa. Bank A forwarded the check to the Check Clearing Association. Check Clearing Association took possession of the check and converted the check to electronic data and forwarded that electronic data to Bank B in Nebraska. From that data, Bank B created a paper copy of the check inscribed with the legend "This is a legal copy of your check. You can use it the same way you would use the original check." The paper copy met all of the requirements for a substitute check under Check 21 except that the MICR line on the paper copy stated the amount was $15,000. The paper copy was presented to Bank C and the drawer's account was debited $15,000. The drawer's account then had insufficient funds to pay other checks drawn on the account, resulting in checks totaling approximately $4,000 being returned for insufficient funds.   What are drawer's rights under the U.C.C. and Reg. CC?

Problem 5-14

Bank A in California received a check for $1,500 from its customer for deposit in her checking account. The check was drawn on Bank C located in Iowa.   Bank A forwarded the check to the Check Clearing Association. Check Clearing Association took possession of the check and converted the check to electronic data and forwarded that electronic data to Bank B in Nebraska. From that data, Bank B created a paper copy of the check, which was a valid substitute check and met the requirements for legal equivalence under Check 21. Bank B forwarded the substitute check to Bank C for payment. Bank C honored the check. Through a processing error, Check Clearing Association forwarded the original check directly to Bank C and Bank C honored the check.   What are the drawer's rights under the U.C.C. and Reg. CC?

Review

To bring the concepts of this Chapter together, organize the obligations of each bank in the collection chain. What are the obligations of a depositary bank, a collecting bank other than a depositary bank, and a payor bank? Separate out these obligations according to the phases of the collection process: forward collection, payment by a payor bank and obligations of a payor bank to its customer, check return and chargeback, and funds availability. Add in the obligations created by Check 21. In setting out those obligations, identify the content of the obligation, to whom the obligation is owed, and the liability for failure to fulfill the obligation.

Use your outline you have created and your knowledge of the various causes of action studied in Chapters 3 and 4 to analyze the following problem.

Problem 5-15

Sue issued a check for $5,000 drawn on her account at Second Bank payable to Value Hardware in payment for a lawn tractor. Value Hardware indorsed the check "Value Hardware, by James, without recourse, for deposit only" and deposited the check in its account at First National on Monday.

Monday evening, First National sent the check to the Federal Reserve Bank for the region. Tuesday morning, the Federal Reserve Bank sent the check to Second Bank. Second Bank received the check, and checked Sue's account. The clerk found that Sue's account did not have a sufficient balance to pay the check. The clerk placed the check in the pile of checks to return. Later that day, Sue deposited a cashier's check for $10,000 providing enough credit in her account to pay all checks including the $5,000 check to Value Hardware. When another clerk took the pile of checks to return to the Federal Reserve Bank on Tuesday evening, the $5,000 check dropped out of the pouch and underneath the table at Second Bank.

During the evening shift on Wednesday, a clerk at Second Bank noticed the $5,000 check and placed the check in the pile to return to the Federal Reserve Bank. The courier left Second Bank with the pouch of returned checks at 11:50 p.m. Wednesday and arrived at the Federal Reserve Bank at 12:30 a.m. Thursday morning. The Federal Reserve returned the $5,000 check to First National on Thursday at 10:00 a.m.

On the previous day, Wednesday, Value Hardware decided to close its account at First National. The clerk at First National had certified a check that Value Hardware drew on its account in order for Value Hardware to take the funds to another bank. This check was payable to the order of Value Hardware. Value Hardware's account is now closed with a zero balance. When the check Sue wrote is returned to First National, it calls you to advise it of its rights.

Notes

Notes

CHAPTER 6
FORGERY AND FRAUD IN THE USE
OF NEGOTIABLE INSTRUMENTS

A. Introduction

In the last several chapters, you have worked through three of the four concerns common to payment systems. Chapters 3 and 4 explored the issues relating to incurring, satisfying, and enforcing the obligation to pay that the negotiable instrument represents, including the various defenses to the obligation to pay. Chapter 5 addressed collection through the banking system of the value that a negotiable instrument represents. The fourth concern, allocation of the risks of errors and wrongdoing, is the subject of this Chapter.

In order to learn how the risk of error and wrongdoing is allocated you must integrate your knowledge of negotiable instruments law. In other words, everything that we have studied in Chapters 2 through 5 will be relevant to the material in this Chapter. If you are uncertain about the material we have covered so far, **stop, go back, and review the previous material until you understand it**. This Chapter will build upon that knowledge to create a schematic of who will ultimately bear the loss for the types of wrongdoing we will discuss in this Chapter.

When there is wrongdoing with respect to a negotiable instrument, the person who has suffered a loss as a result of the wrongdoing usually attempts to recover that loss from someone else. To recover the loss from someone else, the person usually sues as many people as possible. Those people, in turn, will assert defenses to the cause of action as well as attempt to sue other people to whom they can pass on the loss. This loss-passing approach to allocation of the risks of wrongdoing resembles the game of "hot potato" you may have played as a child. No one wants to hold the loss (the "hot potato") and thus when the loss is passed to a person, that person attempts to pass the loss on to someone else. The one left holding the "hot potato" bears the ultimate loss on the instrument.

Your goal, therefore, is to determine who can sue the possible defendants and the various causes of action against each defendant. The plaintiff (the person initially suffering the loss) must be able to articulate a cause of action that imposes liability on a defendant. Review your lists of causes of action you have developed so far. Remember, these causes of action are plaintiff and defendant specific. For instance, only the person entitled to enforce or a subsequent indorser that has paid the instrument has a cause of action against an indorser for the indorser's contract liability on a negotiable instrument. As another example, only a drawee that has paid an unaccepted draft has a cause of action for breach of presentment warranty under U.C.C. § 3-417(a) or § 4-208(a). Only a person who has transferred that draft that was then paid by the drawee is a potential defendant on that presentment warranty claim. *For each cause of action you have identified so far, identify who is the correct plaintiff on that cause of action and who are the potential defendants in that cause of action.*

Now determine whether the defendant has any defenses it can assert to the cause of action that will excuse or limit the defendant's liability. When a defendant is sued based on one of those causes of action that may impose liability on the defendant for the loss, the defendant has several avenues of defense. The defendant may be able to defeat one of the elements of the plaintiff's prima facia case. For example, one of the elements of contract liability is that a person signed the instrument. A defendant may be able to show that it did not sign the instrument or should not be responsible for the signature. In that case, the plaintiff's cause of action based on contract liability on the instrument will be defeated. Even if the plaintiff proves its case in chief, the defendant may have defenses to the plaintiff's cause of action that arise under Articles 3 and 4 or other law. ***Stop.*** *For each cause of action you have identified, list all possible defenses that could be asserted by a defendant to each of the plaintiff's causes of action.*

If the defendant is liable to the plaintiff for the loss, then you must determine who that defendant will sue, for what cause of action and that next defendant's defenses. Continue attempting to pass the liability until someone is holding the loss and unable to assert a cause of action against anyone else. Unlike "hot potato" where the passer has to pick his or her next victim, plaintiffs playing the game of "passing the loss" usually try to sue as many people as possible at the same time, hoping to be able to pass the loss to at least one of the defendants.

Notice that the discussion above has been keyed to a plaintiff's claim as against a particular defendant on a particular cause of action. The typical plaintiff is the person where the loss initially came to rest. The plaintiff should analyze all causes of action against all defendants who may have liability concerning the particular instrument in issue. In playing the "pass the loss" game, savvy plaintiffs will not only sue multiple defendants, they will also assert multiple causes of action against each defendant. Such a strategy helps to increase the plaintiff's likelihood of success in passing the loss. What this means for your analysis is that you must analyze separately each of the plaintiff's causes of action against each defendant and the relevant defenses of each defendant against each cause of action.

The following materials are organized around what went wrong. Find the person who has suffered a loss. Analyze what causes of action they would be able to bring against each potential defendant. For each cause of action against each defendant, identify the potential difficulties with the plaintiff's cause of action and the potential defenses the defendant may raise. Then determine whether the plaintiff has any arguments for defeating the defendant's arguments. The key to analyzing these problems is to remain organized, focused, and methodical.

So what types of wrongdoing occur with respect to negotiable instruments? The usual possibilities are unauthorized signatures, incomplete or altered instruments, and lost or stolen instruments. Many of these types of problems may occur in combination as well. A person may steal an instrument, place an unauthorized signature on the instrument and alter the instrument. The rest of the Chapter will address these various types of wrongdoing.

B. Unauthorized Signatures

Unauthorized signatures come in two basic varieties, (i) drawer's or maker's signatures or (ii) indorser's signatures. **Review U.C.C. § 3-401 through § 3-403** on authorized and unauthorized signatures. The consequences are different depending on what type of signature is unauthorized.

1. Unauthorized Maker's Signature

First consider an unauthorized maker's signature. If a negotiable note is not paid when due **(review U.C.C. § 3-501 and § 3-502)**, the person entitled to enforce the note **(review U.C.C. § 3-301)** will attempt to enforce the maker's contract liability on the note **(review U.C.C. § 3-412)**. Thus the plaintiff is the person entitled to enforce. The defendant is the maker.

In order to contest the plaintiff's case of contract liability against the maker based upon an unauthorized maker's signature, the maker needs to specifically place the authority to make the signature in issue **(review U.C.C. § 3-308)**. If placed in issue, the plaintiff (the person entitled to enforce) will have the burden of proving the maker's signature was authorized. The argument that the maker did not authorize the signature is assertable even against a plaintiff that is a holder in due course as the authorized signature of the maker is part of the prima facia case of the person entitled to enforce. If the plaintiff proves the maker's signature authorized and that the plaintiff is a person entitled to enforce, the maker will have the burden to prove that it has another defense to enforcement of its contract liability on the instrument (review U.C.C. § 3-305). At that point, the plaintiff its holder in due course status to try and successfully argue it is not subject to that other defense (review U.C.C. § 3-302).

The person holding the note may have other causes of action other than enforcement of the contract liability on the instrument. For instance, if the note was transferred from the initial payee to subsequent transferees of the note, the person holding the note may assert that those previous transferors breached transfer warranties, notably the warranty that all signatures are authentic and authorized (review U.C.C. § 3-416 and § 4-207). The correct defendant in the transfer warranty cause of action is not the maker, rather it will be any person that transferred the note after the maker issued the note. The correct plaintiff in the transfer warranty cause of action is not necessarily a person entitled to enforce, rather it is any transferee to whom the transfer warranties were made as stated in the relevant transfer warranty sections.

In addition, the person entitled to enforce the note may have a cause of action based upon an underlying obligation in the transaction in which it took the note (review U.C.C. § 3-310).

Now consider this additional wrinkle. Assume the maker's signature is unauthorized and the maker puts the matter into issue when it is sued on its maker's contract liability on the instrument. The plaintiff (person entitled to enforce) may assert that the maker is precluded from asserting the signature is forged. **Read U.C.C. § 3-406.** This section operates like a statutory form of estoppel against assertion of a defense.[*] If the plaintiff (person entitled to enforce) proves that the negligence of the maker substantially contributed to the making of the forged maker's signature, the maker may try to prove that the plaintiff was also negligent and that negligence substantially contributed to the loss. If so, the liability for the loss is apportioned based upon the relative degree of negligence of the plaintiff and the maker. If the maker's negligence substantially contributed to the forged signature, and the plaintiff is not negligent, the maker is precluded from asserting the forgery. This in effect means that the maker is estopped from asserting the forgery and thus the maker would be liable on the note to the plaintiff (person entitled to enforce).

Notice that U.C.C. § 3-406 refers to "forged" signatures, not "unauthorized"

---

[*] Common law principles such as waiver and estoppel may also come into play to prevent the plaintiff from passing the loss to the defendant. **U.C.C. § 1-103.**

signatures. Although all forged signatures are unauthorized, not all unauthorized signatures are forgeries. **See comment 2 to that section.**

2. Unauthorized Drawer's Signature

Consider now the forged drawer's signature on a draft. It is critical to the loss allocation scheme to determine if the drawee paid the draft or dishonored it.

If the draft is dishonored, the person who is holding the loss may sue the drawer on its drawer's contract on the instrument. **Review U.C.C. § 3-414.** The same analysis as briefly explained above concerning a maker's liability will occur. The drawer must place the authority or authenticity of the drawer's signature in issue and the person entitled to enforce (the plaintiff) must prove that the drawer's signature is authorized or authentic. If the drawer's signature is so proved and the plaintiff also proves it is entitled to enforce, the drawer may raise other defenses to its contract liability on the instrument. The drawer's defenses may be defeated if the plaintiff (person entitled to enforce) is a holder in due course. Again, the plaintiff may assert the preclusion of U.C.C. § 3-406 if the drawer's negligence substantially contributed to the making of a forged drawer's signature. If the plaintiff was also negligent, then the loss is allocated based on the comparative degree of negligence. *See Mercantile Bank of Arkansas v. Vowell*, 117 S.W.3d 603 (Ark. Ct. App. 2003); *Clean World Engineering, Ltd. v. MidAmerica Bank, FSB*, 793 N.E. 2d 110 (Ill. Ct. App. 2003).

The typical plaintiff suing the drawer based on the drawer's contract liability in the dishonored check case is the depositary bank who has some difficulty in collecting from its customer (the payee or a subsequent taker from the payee) **(review U.C.C. § 4-214)** usually because the customer's account has insufficient funds. The depositary bank may also try to collect from an indorser of the draft based upon the indorser's contract liability on the instrument **(review U.C.C. § 3-415)**. To collect from indorsers, the depositary bank will have to give timely notice of dishonor **(review U.C.C. § 3-503 and § 3-504)**. Because the issue of whether the drawer's signature is authorized is of no consequence to the indorser's contract liability on the instrument, the indorser will have to find a different type of defense to assert against the depositary bank. A depositary bank may qualify as a holder in due course which might preclude many of the indorser's typical defenses. **Review U.C.C. § 3-302 and § 3-305.**

The depositary bank may also seek to collect for breach of a transfer warranty from previous transferors of the check **(review U.C.C. § 3-416 and § 4-207)**.

Notice that transferors that make the transfer warranties to subsequent transferees warrant that all signatures are authentic and authorized. If the drawer's signature is forged or unauthorized, that warranty will have been breached and the previous transferor will be liable regardless of the transferor's lack of knowledge of any problem with the drawer's signature.

If the check is an unaccepted draft, the person entitled to enforce the instrument may also have a cause of action on the underlying obligation **(review U.C.C. § 3-310)**.

If the draft is dishonored with an unauthorized drawer's signature, the effect of the U.C.C. provisions on transfer warranty and on contract liability on the draft is to place liability on the first person that took the item from the wrongdoer, the person who forged the drawer's signature. This assumes the wrongdoer is nowhere to be found or has no assets to compensate the loss holding party. The wrongdoer, is of course, liable for the drawer's contract liability on the draft. **U.C.C. § 3-403**.

Consider this wrinkle on the liability allocation when a draft with an unauthorized drawer's signature is dishonored. Assume that when the check was presented to the drawee bank (payor bank in Article 4 terminology), the drawee bank failed to make a provisional settlement and so is accountable for the item **(review U.C.C. § 4-301 and § 4-302)**. The check is considered dishonored **(review U.C.C. § 3-502)**. The person entitled to enforce may enforce the drawer's liability on the check. Of course the purported drawer will raise the unauthorized signature issues as described above. A transferee may also assert the transfer warranty provisions as described above.

What this scenario adds is the right to enforce the payor bank's liability under U.C.C. § 4-302 in addition to the drawer's liability under U.C.C. § 3-414, and the transfer warranty rights under either U.C.C. § 3-416 or § 4-207. Logically, however, that person should get only one satisfaction of the amount of the instrument.

In the lawsuit asserting payor bank accountability under U.C.C. § 4-302, the payor bank may assert as a defense to that acccountability that there was a breach of a presentment warranty or fraud by the person seeking to hold the payor bank accountable. **Review U.C.C. § 4-302(b) and § 4-208.** For an unauthorized drawer's signature, however, notice that the presentment warranties are not very robust defenses for the payor bank.

If the payor bank is accountable under U.C.C. § 4-302, the payor bank would seek to subrogate to the rights of a holder in due course against the wrongdoer as the drawer. **Review U.C.C. §§ 3-403, 3-414, 4-407.**

Try your understanding of these provisions in analyzing the following problem.

Problem 6-1

Sam has a checking account at State Bank. One night, Sam lost his checkbook. Harry picked up the checkbook, took a check, wrote the check payable to cash for $100, and forged Sam's name as drawer. Harry sold the check to Bill for $50. Bill took the check to Check Cashing Inc. who paid Bill $90 for the check. Check Cashing Inc. sent the check to State Bank for payment.

Notes

a) State Bank made a provisional settlement for the check and then returned the check by its midnight deadline to Check Cashing Inc. State Bank returned the check because Sam had stopped payment on all checks in his lost checkbook. Check Cashing Inc. has the check. Analyze all of Check Cashing's causes of action and all defenses that would be asserted to each cause of action against:

Bill;

Harry;

Sam; and

State Bank.

b) Same facts as (a) above. Assume that Check Cashing recovered the amount of the check from Bill. Analyze all of Bill's causes of action against:

Harry;

Sam; and

State Bank.

Notes

c) Same facts as (a) above. Assume that in the lawsuit between Check Cashing and Sam that Check Cashing can prove that Sam was negligent in losing his checkbook and that negligence contributed to Harry's signing of Sam's name. How does that finding affect the outcome of the lawsuit Check Cashing Inc. v. Sam? U.C.C. § 3-406. Would those findings have any effect on Bill's liability to Check Cashing?

d) Same facts as (a) above except that State Bank failed to make a provisional settlement for the check but returned the check anyway after its midnight deadline. Who will bear the ultimate liability for this check?

Now consider the situation where the drawee bank has made final payment of the check with the forged drawer's signature. Assume that the drawee bank made a provisional settlement for the check but failed to return the item by its midnight deadline **(review U.C.C. § 4-215)** so that the check was finally paid. The check is not dishonored so the drawer's contract liability on the check does not arise. U.C.C. § 3-414. The drawee bank will charge the drawer's account for the check.

The drawer will be the one holding the loss and argue that the drawee bank should recredit the account as the check was not properly payable **(review U.C.C. § 4-401)**. The payor bank will attempt to assert that the item was properly payable because either the drawer's signature was authorized **(review U.C.C. § 3-401 through 3-403)** or that the drawer is precluded from asserting the unauthorized signature. The payor bank has two alternatives for arguing that preclusion. We have already discussed under U.C.C. § 3-406. The other preclusion is based on the "bank statement" rule. **Read U.C.C. § 4-406.** Notice that this provision has an absolute bar against the customer asserting the forgery of its signature as stated in subsection (f). Courts have consistently upheld shortening this time period through provisions in the bank-customer agreement. *See Stowell v. Cloquet Co-op Credit Union*, 557 N.W.2d 567 (Minn. 1997) (agreement limiting time period to 20 days upheld); *National Title Insurance Corp. v. First Union National Bank*, 559 S.E.2d 668 (Va. 2002); *American Airlines Employees Federal Credit Union v. Martin*, 29 S.W.3d 86 (Tex. 2000). Notice that for the payor bank to take advantage of the bank statement rule preclusion in U.C.C. § 4-406, the bank need only "send or make available" a statement. Remember, sent does not equal received. U.C.C. § 1-201 (definition of send); U.C.C. § 1-202 (receive). *See Union Planters Bank, Nat. Ass'n v. Rogers*, 912 So. 2d 116 (Miss. 2005); *Spacemakers of America, Inc. v. SunTrust Bank*, 609 S.E. 2d 683 (Ga. Ct. App. 2005).

One of the ways payor banks attempt to shift losses on drafts that are paid but have a forged drawer's signature is through the use of positive pay agreements. A positive pay agreement is an agreement between the bank and its customer that the customer will send a list of authorized checks and the bank will only pay checks that are on that list. If a check is not on the list, the bank reports the check presented for payment as an exception. The customer then instructs the bank whether to pay that check. If the bank follows the positive pay process and pays a check according to the process, the agreement usually provides that the bank is not liable for the payment even if other law would put that liability on the bank. Stephanie Heller and Paul S. Turner, Subcommittee on Payments, U.C.C. Committee Business Law Section, American Bar Association, *Deterring Check Fraud: The Model Positive Pay Services Agreement and Commentary*, 54 BUS. LAW. 637, 644 (1999).

If the payor bank is unsuccessful in the dispute with its customer regarding whether the check was properly payable, then the payor bank is the entity left holding the loss. The payor bank will attempt to pass the loss on to parties that handled the check prior to the payor bank paying the check. The payor bank has three main avenues of attack: subrogation to someone else's rights **(review U.C.C. § 4-407)**; breach of presentment warranties **(review U.C.C. § 3-417 and § 4-208)** and restitution **(review U.C.C. § 3-418)**.

If the payor bank is successful in passing the loss upstream to a previous entity, that entity will often use transfer warranty liability **(review U.C.C. § 3-416 and § 4-207)** to pass the liability to the first taker from the thief. In a forged drawer's signature case where the check is not timely dishonored, however, the person left holding the loss is most often the payor bank as the likelihood of success using its three avenues of attack to pass the loss upstream is usually very small.

Assume that the drawer is unsuccessful in the dispute regarding whether the item is properly payable from the account because of the allegedly unauthorized drawer's signature. Now the drawer is left holding the loss because the payor bank has charged the drawer's account the amount of the check. The drawer will attempt to pass that loss to someone else. The usual causes of action that the drawer uses when the drawer's signature is forged but the drawer is precluded from asserting the forgery as against the payor bank using the properly payable rule are conversion **(review U.C.C. § 3-420)** and common law negligence. These two cause of action are typically against the depositary bank which took the check for deposit, or the payee of the check who took the check from the thief who forged the drawer's signature.

The depositary bank or payee typically respond to the conversion cause of action with two arguments. First, U.C.C. § 3-420 precludes a drawer of a check from suing for conversion. *Compare Heche v. Chase Manhattan Bank*, 45 U.C.C. Rep. Serv. 2d 549 (Conn. Super. Ct. 2001) (cause of action for conversion by drawer against depositary bank allowed) *with Amzee Corp. v. Comerica Bank-Midwest*, 48 U.C.C. Rep. Serv. 2d 833 (Ohio Ct. App. 2002) (cause of action by drawer against payee of check not allowed); *Mid-Continent Specialists, Inc. v. Capital Homes*, 106 P.3d 483 (Kan. 2005) (same); *Condor v. Union Planters Bank, N.A.*, 384 F.3d 397 (7th Cir. 2004) (same). Second, even if there is an action for conversion by the drawer, the depositary bank is a holder in due course and not subject to the conversion cause of action. *See United Catholic Parish Schools of Beaver Dam Educational Association v. Card Services Center*, 636 N.W.2d 206 (Wis. Ct. App. 2001) *rev. denied,* 643 N.W.2d 93 (Wis. 2002).

The depositary bank or payee typically respond to the common law negligence cause of action with the assertion that the U.C.C. loss allocation scheme preempts the cause of action for negligence. *Compare White Sands Forest Products, Inc. v. First National Bank of Alamogordo*, 50 P.3d 202 (N.M. Ct. App. 2002) (negligence cause of action not allowed) *and Halifax Corp. v. Wachovia Bank*, 604 S.E.2d 403 (Va. 2004) (same) *with Mutual Service Casualty Insurance Company v. Elizabeth State Bank*, 265 F.3d 601 (7th Cir. 2001) (negligence cause of action allowed when check payable to depositary bank and no debt is owed by the drawer to the depositary bank) *and Cassello v. Allegiant Bank*, 288 F.3d 339 (8th Cir. 2002) (negligence cause of action against depositary bank allowed).

At stake in this debate about the conversion and/or negligence cause of action is whether the payor bank and drawer should be able to pass the risk of the forgery of the drawer's signature to the depositary bank or payee, who is often the first taker of the check from the thief. What policies do you think should inform that debate? Do you think the reason for finding that the drawer does not have a cause of action for conversion makes sense? **Read comment 1 to U.C.C. § 3-420.** Shouldn't the drawer be able to sue to rescind the issuance of the check with its forged signature? *See* U.C.C. § 3-202. Should that depend on whether the drawer is thought to have a property interest in the instrument? **Read U.C.C. § 3-417(a)(4), 4-208(a)(4).** *See also* U.C.C. § 3-416(a)(6), 4-207(a)(6). These provisions were added by the 2002 amendments to Articles 3 and 4. **Now read Reg. CC, 12 C.F.R. § 229.34(d) and the definition of remotely created check in 12 C.F.R. § 229.2.** How do these provisions change the risk allocation for this type of drawer signature forgery?

This analysis may be further complicated if the collecting or returning banks failed to comply with their obligations under Article 4, Regulation CC or Regulation J in the forward collection process or the check return process.

Problem 6-2

Sam has a checking account at State Bank. One night, Sam lost his checkbook. Harry picked up the checkbook, took a check, wrote the check payable to cash for $100, and forged Sam's name as drawer. Harry sold the check to Bill for $50. Bill took the check to Check Cashing Inc. who paid Bill $90 for the check. Check Cashing Inc. sent the check to State Bank for payment.

Notes

a)　State Bank made a provisional settlement for the check and did not return the check. When Sam received his statement from the bank, he noticed the check that Harry wrote. The signature that Harry wrote looks nothing like Sam's signature. Sam called State Bank and told the clerk that he did not write the check. Must State Bank recredit Sam's account?

b) Same facts as (a) above. If State Bank recredits Sam's account, may State Bank recover the amount of the check from anyone else?

c) Same facts as (a) above. Assume that Sam did not call and tell the bank about the check until 3 months after Sam received the bank statement. What if Harry had written 4 checks and Sam had waited the three months to tell the bank? Any change in the analysis?

d) State Bank made a provisional settlement for the check and did not return the check. State Bank sent a bank statement to Sam. In that statement are several checks that Harry has written, forging Sam's signature as drawer. Sam looked at his statement several months later. He put off calling the bank about the forged checks. Thirteen months after Sam received his bank statement with the forged checks, he called State Bank. Because State Bank valued Sam's business, it recredited his account. May State Bank recover from anyone else?

e) Based on U.C.C. § 4-406, what would you advise State Bank to provide in its bank-customer agreement?

f) Sam received a phone call from a telemarketer who convinced Sam to give the telemarketer Sam's bank account information. Sam eventually declined to purchase any product. Much to Sam's surprise, when he received his bank statement, there was a check written by the telemarketer for $1,000 drawn on Sam's account. The drawer's line contained the notation "authorization on file with payee." Sam called State Bank, the drawee, to complain. How will this be resolved? Who will ultimately bear the liability?

3. Unauthorized Indorsements

Now consider the case of an unauthorized indorsement. Assume that a negotiable note is issued by the maker payable to the order of the payee. The note is stolen from the payee and the payee's indorsement is forged. The forger sells the note to an unsuspecting buyer for value. The buyer will attempt to enforce the maker's contract liability on the note **(review U.C.C. § 3-412)**. Remember that the maker's obligation is owed to a person entitled to enforce. The buyer is not a person entitled to enforce **(review U.C.C. § 3-301, § 3-204, § 3-205)** because the necessary indorsement of the payee has been forged. If the maker is successful in asserting the forged necessary indorsement, the buyer will not be able to enforce the maker's contract liability on the instrument. The buyer's response will be to assert that the maker is precluded from asserting the forged indorsement under **U.C.C. § 3-406**, if the maker's negligence substantially contributed to the making of the forgery. In this scenario, that is hard to prove as the forgery was of the payee's indorsement after the maker issued the note to the payee.

The buyer has two other preclusion sections it may attempt to use against the maker. Remember, the basis of the maker's non-liability to the buyer is that the buyer is not a person entitled to enforce due to the payee's forged necessary indorsement. If the maker is precluded from asserting that forgery, then the buyer would be treated as if it was entitled to enforce. **Read U.C.C. § 3-404 and § 3-405.**

On these facts, section 3-404 does not look promising. That section is designed to preclude the issuer of the instrument from arguing that the person in possession of the instrument is not a person entitled to enforce because of the forgery of a necessary indorsement. This instrument was not issued to an imposter (U.C.C. § 3-404(a)) nor to a person who is fictitious or who was not intended to have an interest in the instrument (U.C.C. § 3-404(b)). If this section applied to preclude the maker from asserting the forged payee's indorsement, the comparative negligence analysis we first encountered in U.C.C. § 3-406 is also used here. U.C.C. § 3-404(d).

Also on these facts, U.C.C. § 3-405 does not look very promising. For U.C.C. § 3-405 to apply in this hypothetical, the thief would have to be an employee of the payee of the note, the employee would have to have responsibility with respect to this note,[*] and the employee would have had to make a fraudulent indorsement on the note. **Read the definitions of these terms found in U.C.C. § 3-405(a).** If all of those are true, then the indorsement is "effective as the indorsement of the named payee." This provision too is subject to the comparative negligence analysis we first encountered in U.C.C. § 3-406.[**] U.C.C. § 3-405(b).

If the maker is precluded from asserting the forgery of the payee's indorsement, the buyer will indeed be a person entitled to enforce and may collect on the maker's contract liability on the instrument (as tempered by the comparative negligence analysis). If the maker is not precluded from asserting the forgery, then the buyer will not be able to successfully assert the maker's contract liability.

The buyer may also seek to recover from the payee on the indorser's contract of the payee **(review U.C.C. § 3-403 and § 3-415)**. However, because the payee's signature was forged, the only way the buyer could collect from the payee is if the payee was precluded from asserting the forgery. Again, U.C.C. § 3-406 may come in handy. If the payee's negligence substantially contributed to the forgery, the payee will be precluded from asserting its signature is forged and the buyer will be able to assert the indorser's contract liability against the payee.

---

[*] *See Schrier Bros. v. Golub*, 123 Fed. Appx. 484 (3d Cir. 2005) on the meaning of responsibility with respect to an instrument.

[**] *See Auto-Owners Ins. Co. v. Bank One*, 852 N.E.2d 604 (Ind. Ct. App. 2006) (evaluating ordinary care by the depository bank under U.C.C. § 3-405).

But what if the payee is not negligent under U.C.C. § 3-406? Do either U.C.C. § 3-404 or § 3-405 apply to preclude the payee from contesting the forgery in the event the payee is sued on its indorsement contract? If the sections apply, both sections make the indorsement effective as the indorsement of the payee. What does "effective" mean?

Return to the original scenario of a forged payee's indorsement after the instrument is first issued to the payee and before the fraudfeasor sells the item to the buyer. Consider the payee's other options. The payee would have a claim to the instrument **(review U.C.C. § 3-306)** which it could assert against the buyer as the buyer cannot be a holder in due course because the buyer is not a holder. The payee would also have a claim for conversion against the buyer and the forger **(review U.C.C. § 3-420)**. The preclusions we have looked at come into play here too. Assume that the payee sues the buyer for conversion. The buyer resists the conversion cause of action by arguing that the payee is precluded from asserting the forgery under U.C.C. § 3-405 because the thief (the payee's employee) had responsibility with respect to the instrument. If the preclusion is successful, the payee will lose its conversion cause of action against the buyer because the payee will not be able to successfully assert that the buyer is not a holder and thus could not be a holder in due course. If the payee can prove that the buyer was also negligent and that negligence substantially contributed to the loss, the loss will be allocated between the payee and the buyer using the comparative negligence analysis. *See Rodrique v. Olin Employee's Credit Union*, 406 F.3d 434 (7th Cir. 2005).

If the buyer is unable to recover against the maker or payee, the buyer will be stuck with the loss unless the buyer is able to recover from the forger based upon breach of a transfer warranty **(review U.C.C. § 3-416)**. Notice how this scheme moves the loss to the first taker from the thief in the case of a forged necessary indorsement.

Now assume the forged indorsement is on a check. Just as with forged drawer's signatures, it is critical to determine whether the check is dishonored or paid in order to sort through the rights of the parties. It is also critical to determine if the forged indorsement is a "necessary" indorsement. A "necessary" indorsement is an indorsement that is needed in order to make the next transferee a holder.

As with a forged drawer's or maker's signature, the best place to start is with the person on whom the loss initially rests. Evaluate all of the causes of action the person initially bearing the loss would have against anyone who has handled the instrument. If the initial person bearing the loss is successful in passing the loss to another person, then evaluate that second person's causes of action against anyone else who has handled the instrument. Continue the process until there is no longer any place to pass the loss.

Try your understanding of these various provisions on the following problems.

Problem 6-3

Sam has a checking account at State Bank. Sam wrote a check for $100 payable to Jane. Jane lost the check. Harry found the check, forged Jane's signature and sold the check to Check Cashing Inc. for $90. Check Cashing Inc. sent the check to State Bank.

Notes

a) Sam stopped payment on the check when Jane told him the check was lost. State Bank returned the check to Check Cashing Inc., meeting all of the Article 4 and Regulation CC deadlines. Check Cashing Inc. called you for advice. Evaluate Check Cashing's causes of action against:
Jane;
Harry;
Sam;
and State Bank.

b) State Bank made a timely provisional settlement for the item and did not return the check. Sam called State Bank the next day and told State Bank not to pay the check. Advise State Bank whether it can recover the amount of the check from Sam, Jane, Harry, or Check Cashing. Would it matter if Sam waited three months to call State Bank? *Compare* U.C.C. § 4-406, § 4-111, and § 3-118.

Notes

c) Assume that Jane indorsed the check in blank before she lost it. Harry picked up the check and took it to Check Cashing Inc. Check Cashing made Harry indorse the check. Harry indorsed the check "Bill Smith." Sam stopped payment on the check in a timely manner. State Bank returned the check in a timely manner to Check Cashing, complying with all Article 4 and Regulation CC deadlines. Advise Check Cashing of all of its options against State Bank, Jane, Harry, Sam and Bill Smith.

d) Assume that Jane indorsed the check in blank before she lost it. Harry picked up the check and took it to Check Cashing Inc. Check Cashing made Harry indorse the check. Harry indorsed the check "Bill Smith." Sam stopped payment on the check in a timely manner. Although State Bank made a timely provisional settlement for the item, it did not return the check to Check Cashing until after State Bank's midnight deadline. What are Check Cashing's options against State Bank, Jane, Harry, Sam and Bill Smith?

e) Assume that Jane had indorsed the check "For deposit only, Jane" prior to losing the check. Harry picked up the check and took it to Check Cashing

Inc. Check Cashing made Harry indorse the check. Harry indorsed the check "Bill Smith." Sam stopped payment on the check in a timely manner. State Bank made a timely provisional settlement for the check but did not return the check to Check Cashing until after State Bank's midnight deadline. What are Check Cashing's options against State Bank, Jane, Harry, Sam and Bill Smith? U.C.C. § 3-206(c) and (e).

f) Assume that Jane had indorsed the check "For deposit only, Jane" prior to losing the check. Harry picked up the check and took it to Check Cashing Inc. Check Cashing made Harry indorse the check. Harry indorsed the check "Bill Smith." Sam stopped payment on the check in a timely manner. State Bank returned the check to Check Cashing in a timely manner, complying with all Article 4 and Regulation CC deadlines. What are Check Cashing's options against State Bank, Jane, Harry, Sam and Bill Smith? U.C.C. § 3-206(c) and (e).

g) Assume the same facts as (b) above. What are Jane's rights against State Bank, Check Cashing, Sam and Harry?

Problem 6-4

Sam has a checking account at State Bank. He sent a check for $400 payable to the order of Paul Payee drawn on that account. When Payee received the check, he put it on his desk. That night, Payee's office was robbed and the check was stolen. The burglar forged Payee's indorsement, and sold the check to Check Cashing Inc. for $380. Check Cashing Inc. deposited the check in its account at First National Bank. First National Bank sent the check the next day to State Bank.

Notes

a)   State Bank did not return the check and debited Sam's account. Who should bear the liability for this loss assuming that the burglar is nowhere to be found? Explain fully.

b)   State Bank returned the check in a timely manner to First National Bank, complying with all deadlines in Article 4 and Regulation CC. Who should bear the liability for this loss assuming that the burglar is nowhere to be found? Explain fully.

Ingenuity and gullibility are two human traits that contribute to fraud in the use of negotiable instruments. For an in-depth discussion of various types of fraudulent schemes, *see* Daniel E. Murray, *Check Scams—The Facts Remain the Same, Only the Law Changes*, 49 U. MIAMI L. REV. 607 (1995). The table of contents to the article provides a shorthand representative list of fraudulent conduct such as:

Authorized Signing Employees Who Steal;

Consigning Employees—One of Whom Is a Crook;

Crooked Nonsigning Employees Who Supply the Names of the Fictitious Payees;

Employee Who Decides to Steal After She Signs as Drawer or After She Supplies the Payees' Names;

Crooked Employees Who Prepare Fictitious Payee Checks and Then Increase the Amounts Payable After the Checks Are Signed;

Genuine Invoice Payee Checks—When Is a Real Payee Fictitious and When Is a Fictitious Payee Genuine?;

Crooked Employee of or Attorney for Payee Supplies Payee's Name to Drawer;

Crooked Employee of Drawer Forges Both the Drawer's Name and the Payee's Name—The 'Double Forgery' Caper;

Crooked Employee of Drawer Forges Payee's Name with a Restrictive Indorsement;

Crook Impersonates the Payee; Crook Expressly or Impliedly Represents that He Is an Agent for Another.

We have briefly considered U.C.C. § 3-404 concerning making a forged indorsement effective. This section operates in three different fact situations. Subsection (a) addresses the situation where the issuer is fooled into issuing an instrument to someone that is an imposter or impersonating someone else. Subsection (b) addresses the situation where the issuer issues an instrument to someone who is not intended to have any interest in the instrument. That subsection also addresses the situation where the issuer issues the instrument to a fictitious person. In these situations, the issuer wants to argue that it should not be liable on the instrument to a person entitled to enforce because of the indorsement of the payee that is forged. One of the effects of the operation of U.C.C. § 3-404 is to make the forged indorsement effective and the person in possession of the instrument a holder in order to enforce the issuer's contract obligation on the instrument. Thus the issuer's risk of being taken advantage of in the circumstances addressed in this section rests on the issuer.

This rule also has an effect on the question of whether the item is properly payable from the drawer's account. Consider the case in which the drawer issues a check to an imposter, who indorses the check in the name of the payee (the impersonated person). The check is presented to the drawee bank and paid. The drawer alleges that the check was not properly payable as the right person did not indorse the item. Generally the check would not be properly payable if there is a forged necessary indorsement. Because U.C.C. § 3-404(a) makes the indorsement effective in favor of a person that has paid the instrument, the drawee will be able to successfully argue that the check is in fact properly payable from the drawer's account.

The effect of the preclusion in U.C.C. § 3-404 is stated in that section. It makes any person in possession a holder and it protects good faith transferees who take it for value and good faith payors. If the indorsement is deemed effective and the taker or payor has failed to exercise ordinary care and that failure substantially contributed to the loss, the loss is allocated between the parties based upon comparative negligence. Making the forged indorsement effective, however, does not mean that the transfer warranty that all signatures are authentic and authorized has not been breached. U.C.C. §§ 3-416, 4-207.

Consider the following case on the application of the imposter provision.

KING V. WHITE
962 P.2d 475 (Kan. 1998)

Larson, Justice

In this case we must decide who suffers the loss after an attorney improperly obtained settlement drafts from two insurance companies, forged his client's endorsement on the checks, deposited the checks in his trust account, and then converted the funds. The question arises in the context of a suit for conversion by the client, Jerry C. King, against his Kansas attorney, John L. White, the insurance companies Auto-Owners Insurance Company (Auto-Owners) and American Family Mutual Insurance (American Family), and the depository bank, Commerce Bank, N.A. (Commerce).

The trial court granted summary judgment in favor of King against all defendants but ultimately held that the loss falls upon Commerce, although granting judgment against White, who is currently incarcerated. The trial court further determined that King was only entitled to recover a two-thirds interest in the drafts due to his contingency fee agreement with White.

The appeals and cross-appeals raise numerous issues, most of which pertain to interpretations of Article 3 of the Uniform Commercial Code (UCC): (1) Does the imposter defense of K.S.A. 84-3-404(a) protect a depository bank that paid the instruments in good faith? (2) If the imposter defense is applicable, does it also protect a drawee of an instrument who pays in good faith? (3) Does King's ratification of the settlement agreements also ratify White's actions in endorsing and depositing the instruments representing the settlement proceeds? (4) May the true payee of a draft sue the drawee for paying on a forged endorsement when the payee has also sued the collecting bank? (5) Does Article 3 of the UCC permit conversion liability for nonbank drawees? (6) May King recover for conversion of a draft payable to the estate of King's wife? (7) Is King required to bear the loss occasioned by the wrongful conduct of his agent? (8) Is an attorney entitled to a contingency fee after entering into an unauthorized settlement agreement and fraudulently endorsing and converting the settlement proceeds?

Factual statement

Jerry C. King and his wife, Judith, were involved in an automobile accident in January 1994. King sustained personal injuries in the accident, but his wife was killed. King employed White to represent him in his claims for personal injuries and wrongful death.

Although King and White did not enter a written agreement regarding White's representation, the essential terms of the representation are not disputed. White was to pursue King's claims or causes of action with respect to possible recovery against the State of Alabama, the driver of the other vehicle, and the owner of the vehicle. In exchange, White was to receive one-third of the amounts recovered.

White negotiated a policy-limits settlement of $25,000 for King's wrongful death claims and $3,500 for his personal injury claims with Auto-Owners, the insurance carrier of the driver of the other vehicle involved in the accident. White also negotiated a settlement with American Family for the full amount of underinsured motorist benefits available under King's policy. White represented to both insurance companies that he was authorized to act on King's behalf, although King had not authorized settlement with either party and was unaware that settlements had been reached.

Auto-Owners drew a draft payable through Michigan National Bank (MNB) in the amount of $28,500, copayable to King, individually and as surviving spouse of Judith, and to White. American Family drew a draft payable through United Missouri Bank, Northwest (UMB) in the amount of $25,000, copayable to White and the Estate of Judy King.

White received the drafts, endorsed his name, forged King's signature on the drafts without King's knowledge or consent, and deposited the drafts into his trust account at Commerce. Commerce granted provisional credit to White's trust account and presented them to the "payable through" banks for final payment. Auto-Owners and American Family authorized payment of the drafts. White later withdrew the proceeds of the drafts from his Commerce trust account and converted them to his own use. White did disburse $2,257.84 to King for his share of the $3,500 personal injury settlement after deducting his contingency fee and expenses, but King remained unaware of the remaining settlement amounts.

After King discovered these events, he filed suit alleging counts of fraud against

White and conversion against White, Commerce as depository bank, MNB and UMB as drawee banks, and American Family and Auto-Owners as drawers or nonbank drawees. White confessed judgment, and judgment was entered against him. The remaining defendants filed cross-claims and motions to dismiss, and Commerce, the insurance companies, and King all moved for summary judgment. King dismissed his claims against MNB and UMB after it was established they were collecting banks rather than drawee banks.

In ruling on the motions for summary judgment, the trial court found Commerce was the depository bank for both drafts pursuant to K.S.A. 84-4-105(2); MNB and UMB were intermediary or collecting banks pursuant to K.S.A. 84-4-105(4) and (5) and K.S.A. 84-4-106(a)(1); Auto-Owners and American Family were makers/drawers pursuant to K.S.A. 84-3-103(3) and (5) and also drawees pursuant to K.S.A. 84-3-103(2) and K.S.A. 84-4-104(a)(8).

The trial court ruled that K.S.A. 84-3-404, pertaining to impostors, did not govern the liabilities of the case because White did not act as an imposter within the meaning of the statute. The court held Commerce liable to King pursuant to K.S.A. 84-3-420(a) as a depository or payor bank which took an instrument bearing a forged endorsement. The court also held the insurance companies liable to the payee due to their status as drawees pursuant to K.S.A. 84-3-420(a). The court found MNB and UMB not liable through their status as collecting banks.

The court determined that the extent of King's interest in the forged instruments was the amount of the drafts less White's attorney fees. The court also found that although King's action for conversion of the drafts may constitute ratification of the settlement agreements, it did not constitute ratification of White's separate wrongful act of forging King's endorsement and converting the draft amounts. The court further rejected a claim that King must bear the loss occasioned by the wrongful conduct of his agent and a claim that King released one of the insurance companies. The court concluded King was not required to elect his remedy and was not barred from pursuing actions against the remaining defendants after suing White and the collecting banks.

The court found that Commerce, Auto-Owners, and American Family were entitled to indemnity from White and that the insurance companies were entitled to indemnity from Commerce pursuant to K.S.A. 84-3-417, the presentment warranty statute. The court also found that Commerce and the insurance companies were jointly and severally liable to King on the drafts pursuant to K.S.A. 84-3-116(a), and each is entitled to contribution pursuant to 84-3-116(b). The court granted judgment of $33,333.33 against Commerce and $16,666.66 against both

Auto-Owners and American Family.

Commerce and Auto-Owners appeal, and American Family cross-appeals. King also cross-appeals the determination that White was entitled to one-third of the proceeds from the settlement checks. We have jurisdiction under K.S.A. 60-2102(a)(4) of a case transferred to this court pursuant to K.S.A. 20-3018(c).

* * * *

The issues in this case involve interpretations of Article 3 of the Kansas UCC and other questions of law over which we have unlimited review. *See Marais des Cygnes Valley Teachers' Ass'n. v. U.S.D. No. 456*, 264 Kan. 247, 249, 954 P.2d 1096 (1998).

In Estate of Soupene v. Lignitz, 265 Kan. 217, 220, 960 P.2d 205 (1998), we said:

> " 'We initially note our fundamental rule of construction that it is the intent of the legislature, where it can be ascertained, which governs the construction of a statute. *See City of Wichita v. 200 South Broadway*, 253 Kan. 434, 436, 855 P.2d 956 (1993). The legislature is presumed to have expressed its intent through the language of the statutory scheme it enacted. We will not read into legislation provisions which do not there exist. *See Joe Self Chevrolet, Inc. v. Board of Sedgwick County Comm'rs*, 247 Kan. 625, 633, 802 P.2d 1231 (1990).' *Marais des Cygnes Valley Teachers' Ass'n. v. U.S.D. No. 456*, 264 Kan. 247, 954 P.2d 1096 (1998).
>
> "Although appellate courts will not speculate as to the legislative intent of a plain and unambiguous statute, *State v. Lawson*, 261 Kan. 964, 966, 933 P.2d 684 (1997), where the construction of a statute on its face is uncertain, the court may examine the historical background of the enactment, the circumstances attending its passage, the purpose to be accomplished, and the effect the statute may have under various suggested interpretations. *Brown v. U.S.D. No. 333*, 261 Kan. 134, 142, 928 P.2d 57 (1996).
>
> " 'Ordinarily, there is a presumption that a change in the language of a statute results from the legislative purpose to change its effect, but this presumption may be strong or weak according to the circumstances, and may be wanting altogether in a particular case.' *Board of Education of U.S.D. 512 v. Vic Regnier Builders, Inc.*, 231 Kan. 731, 736, 648 P.2d 1143 (1982). However, we have also stated: 'Ordinarily, courts presume that, by changing the language of a statute, the legislature intends either to clarify its meaning or to change its effect.' * * * **Watkins v. Hartsock*, 245 Kan.

756, 759, 783 P.2d 1293 (1989) (*citing* U.S.D. 512, 231 Kan. 731, 648 P.2d 1143)."

Imposter defense

Commerce first argues the endorsement of White is that of an imposter posing as King's agent and is therefore effective as King's endorsement to Commerce as a payor who paid in good faith. Commerce relies upon the amended version of K.S.A. 84-3-404[(a0] to support its position,

* * *

The Kansas Comment to this statute reads:

"This section codifies the 'imposter' and 'fictitious payee' rules, throwing the loss for forged endorsements on the issuer who was duped into issuing an instrument to the wrong person. These rules are a codification of variations of the general negligence provisions of 84-3-406.... If the section is successfully invoked, the loss arising from a forged indorsement is shifted away from later 'holders' and on to the issuer. Note that the 'imposter' rule has been expanded to cover situations where a misrepresentation of agency is involved and the instrument is made payable to the real principal. The 'fictitious payee' rule has been broadened to include indorsements which are substantially similar.

"Subsection (a). The rule stated in this subsection validates the endorsement where the issuer intended the instrument to go to that impostor him or herself, or as agent of the named payee, or a confederate. The key words in the statute are 'to issue the instrument to the impostor, or to a person acting in concert with the impostor.' The controlling factor is whether the issuer intended the person receiving the instrument to receive it. The subsection can only be invoked by a good faith payor or transferee for value."

Prior to the enactment of the revised Article 3 in 1991, the impostor defense was codified at K.S.A. 84-3-405(1)(a) (Ensley 1983), which provided:

"(1) An indorsement by any person in the name of a named payee is effective if

(a) an impostor by the use of the mails or otherwise has induced the maker or drawer to issue the instrument to him or his confederate in the name of the payee."

The Official UCC Comment to this section states:

" 'Impostor' refers to impersonation, and does not extend to a false representation that the party is the authorized agent of the payee. The maker or drawer who takes the precaution of making the instrument payable to the principal is entitled to have his indorsement."

The imposter defense as it existed prior to the 1991 revision has been discussed in numerous cases and treatises; the revised version, however, which added impersonations of agents, has hardly been addressed by any authority. Clark & Clark, THE LAW OF BANK DEPOSITS, COLLECTIONS AND CREDIT CARDS (1995 and 1998 Supp.), which extensively discusses cases under the old impostor defense provision of § 3-405, has little to say about the effect of the revision. It does seem clear from cases both before and after the revision that someone must still impersonate someone else in order for the imposter defense to apply. There must be an impersonation of an actual agent; a misrepresentation of agency authority is generally not sufficient to invoke the defense.

One of the few cases to discuss the revised impostor defense and to reach this result is *Title Ins. Co. v. Comerica Bank*, 27 Cal.App.4th 800, 32 Cal.Rptr.2d 735 (1994). The case involved a son who obtained a loan by falsely representing to a lender that he was his mother's agent by forging a power of attorney. The lender issued a check payable to the mother, and the son forged her endorsement. The California Court of Appeal ruled that even if the case were decided under the revised UCC impostor provision, the defense would not apply because the son never impersonated his mother. The court held that the comment to § 3-404(a) "makes it clear that impersonation is still required to invoke the impostor rule, whether the perpetrator of the deception pretends to be the principal or the agent. Misrepresentation of the perpetrator's agency status does not suffice." 27 Cal.App.4th at 807, 32 Cal.Rptr.2d 735 (*citing Intelogic v. Merchants Nat. Bank*, 626 N.E.2d 839, 845 [Ind.App. 1993]).

Another recent case which discusses the revised impostor defense, *Lewis v. Telephone Employees Credit Union*, 87 F.3d 1537, 1550 (9th Cir.1996), agreed with Title Insurance and stated:

> "Where a person merely represents that he or she is an agent of an actual existing principal and the check is issued in the name of that principal, it is the bank that bears the loss because it was in the better position to detect a fraudulent indorsement--the bank paid to someone other than an existing principal while the drawer was only tricked about the true powers of the agent."

One case decided under the prior impostor defense provision involved facts very similar to those before us in the present case. In *Clients' Sec. Fund v. Allstate*

Ins., 219 N.J.Super. 325, 530 A.2d 357 (1987), the New Jersey Superior Court held that the impostor rule did not apply to an attorney who forged the signatures of clients on settlement drafts. The court ruled:

> "The term 'impostor' refers to 'impersonation' and does not extend to a false representation that the party is the authorized agent of the principal. Uniform Commercial Code Comment § 2.... 'Impersonation' is the act of pretending or representing oneself to be another. BLACK'S LAW DICTIONARY, (5 ed. 1979) at 679. Such impersonation is of an identity, either real or fictitious, with which the drawer believes he is dealing. [Citation omitted.]
>
> ....
>
> "We are satisfied that on the facts before us, the 'impostor rule' is inapplicable. Allstate did not deal with Yucht as an 'impersonator'. Yucht never pretended to be someone other than himself. He always represented that he was the attorney for the claimants: he never claimed to be the clients themselves. It was Allstate's intent to deal with both Yucht and his respective clients and it so issued the settlement drafts. It was Yucht's misrepresentation of fact that his clients had agreed to settle, rather than imposturing, that '... induced the maker ... to issue the instrument[s] to him....' [Citation omitted.] Yucht strengthened this misrepresentation by presenting forged releases to Allstate. There was no intent on Allstate's part that Yucht should supply the indorsements of his clients. The forged indorsements were therefore not rendered 'effective', and thus the loss was not shifted to Allstate as the drawer of the settlement drafts."

219 N.J.Super. at 331-33, 530 A.2d 357.

This same reasoning is likewise applicable to the present case, despite the revised version of the impostor defense. Here, although White's misrepresentation of his authority to settle the claims on behalf of King may have induced the insurance companies to issue the drafts, the drafts were not issued to an impostor. The insurance companies made the drafts payable to both White and King and intended King himself, not anyone pretending to be King, to receive the proceeds. The insurance companies did not intend for White to forge King's endorsements, and the forged endorsements may not be deemed effective.

The trial court correctly concluded that the impostor defense of K.S.A. 84-3-404(a) has no application to the facts of this case and Commerce may not invoke its provisions to avoid liability. As the impostor defense is not applicable to this case, we need not discuss the claim made by the insurance companies that the impostor defense should also apply to them as drawees.

Ratification

Commerce argues that because King ratified the settlements with the insurance companies, he has also ratified White's forged endorsements on the drafts. Commerce cites a string of cases for the proposition that a principal's election to ratify an unauthorized act requires ratification of the whole act, as a principal may not accept the benefits of the act and reject its burdens. *See, e.g., Adrian v. Elmer*, 178 Kan. 242, 284 P.2d 599 (1955); *Watson v. Woodruff*, 154 Kan. 61, 114 P.2d 864 (1941). King argues White's unauthorized settlements of two separate claims are separate and distinct from and unrelated to White's subsequent forgery and conversion. We agree with the trial court's conclusion that King's ratification of the unauthorized settlement of the claims does not constitute ratification of White's separate wrongful act of forging King's signatures to the drafts.

White's acts of settling King's claims with the insurance companies were separate and apart from his additional acts of forging King's endorsements on the settlement drafts. This is not a situation where only one act confers both benefits and liabilities. Such might be the case if King wanted to both accept the benefits of the settlements by obtaining the settlement amounts, but reject the burdens, such as the release of all further claims against the insurance companies pertaining to the accident.

Here, however, there are two very distinct acts: obtaining an unauthorized settlement and forging an endorsement. There is no reason why King should not be permitted to ratify one but not the other, especially when we have long held that granting authority to an attorney to handle a lawsuit does not generally confer authority to endorse an instrument on behalf of the client. *See Pearcy v. First National Bank*, 167 Kan. 696, 700, 208 P.2d 217 (1949). The trial court correctly determined that Commerce's position on this issue has no merit. The settlement and the conversion are two separate and distinct transactions.

Conversion suits against both collecting bank and drawees

Both Auto-Owners and American Family assert that King has no cause of action against them as drawees on the instruments paid on the forged endorsements because King sued their respective collecting banks, MNB and UMB, as well as Commerce. They essentially rely upon a 1973 California case, *Cooper v. Union Bank*, 9 Cal.3d 371, 107 Cal.Rptr. 1, 507 P.2d 609 (1973), and a pre-UCC Kansas case, *Mackey-Woodard, Inc. v. Citizens State Bank*, 197 Kan. 536, 419 P.2d 847

(1966), to contend that a payee cannot sue both a collecting bank and the drawee for conversion.

These cited authorities provide little support for the insurance companies' position, which also runs counter to the express provisions of K.S.A. 84-3-420 regarding conversion. Further, this argument, which would be an important defense in an action for conversion, has not been mentioned in any recent cases or in the legal commentaries. *See, e.g.,* Clark, ¶ 12.03.

In addition, we point out that *Mackey-Woodard* merely holds that a plaintiff must elect his or her remedies and can either pursue a tort action for conversion or a contract action to recover proceeds. If a plaintiff chooses the latter, the plaintiff loses the right to recover against the drawer and drawee because he or she has thereby ratified the payment to the collecting bank. The case does not hold, however, that if the plaintiff chooses to pursue a conversion action, he or she is deemed to have ratified the payment of the proceeds and cannot sue the drawee.

The insurance companies appear to suggest their argument has more merit when collecting banks are sued in addition to the depository bank and drawee. Insofar as their argument is premised on this distinction, it lacks any merit under the facts of this case. UMB and MNB were never sued in their capacity as collecting banks and were dismissed from the suit when it was determined they were not the drawees of the drafts, but merely payable through banks.

We hold that a suit for conversion against the collecting bank does not prohibit a claim also being made against the drawees.

Conversion liability of nonbank drawees

Auto-Owners next makes the argument that the revised version of the UCC eliminates the conversion liability of a nonbank drawee. The prior provision on conversion liability, K.S.A. 84-3-419(1) (Ensley 1983), stated that an instrument was converted if it was paid on a forged endorsement. K.S.A. 84- 3-420(a) now provides that a conversion occurs when "a bank makes or obtains payment with respect to the instrument for a person not entitled to enforce the instrument or receive payment."

Auto-Owners cites no authority in support of its interpretation of the effect of the revision. Nothing in the comments to the section remotely implies that the intended effect was to remove conversion liability from non-drawee banks, nor do the authorities discussing the new revision comment upon this possibility. Furthermore, Auto-Owners claims that all cases holding nonbank drawees liable relied upon the old provision. However, the 1998 supplement to Clark's treatise does again specifically discuss the issue of when an insurance company plays a dual role as both drawer and drawee and cites two recent cases where insurance company drawees were held liable for conversion, although both relied upon UCC 3-419(1)(c). *See Mandelbaum v. P & D Printing*, 279 N.J.Super. 427, 652 A.2d 1266 (1995); *Glazer v. First American Nat. Bank*, 930 S.W.2d 546 (Tenn.1996). Clark did not discuss how the revision could have changed the result in such cases.

We do not believe the Kansas Legislature, by enacting the revised code, intended to change established law permitting a conversion action by an intended payee against a nonbank drawee who paid on a draft with a forged endorsement. K.S.A. 84-3-420(a) does not discuss who is liable for the conversion, but merely defines what a conversion is. Further, the Official UCC Comment 2 to 84-3-420 discusses how the former 84-3-419 was amended "because it is not clear why the former law distinguished between the liability of the drawee and that of other converters." This implies that all drawees should be treated as converters in a forged endorsement case such as this, and nothing in this comment indicates that nonbank drawees should be considered a special case apart from other converters.

We refuse to adopt the defense suggested by Auto-Owners and rule that the revised Article 3 does not prohibit actions for conversion against nonbank drawees.

* * * * *

Does the distinction between impersonating someone and misrepresenting the extent of one's agency authority make sense? As a matter of policy regarding allocation of loss from wrongdoing, why should a misrepresentation of agency authority be treated differently? Test your understanding of the application of U.C.C. § 3-404 with the following problem.

Problem 6-5

Bob Smith told Jill that he was the attorney for Best Insurance Company and that her premium was overdue. Jill wrote a check on her account at State Bank payable to Best Insurance Company and gave the check to Bob Smith. Bob Smith is really Bob Smith but he is not an attorney for Best Insurance Company because that Company does not really exist. Bob Smith indorsed the check "Best Insurance Company." Bob Smith deposited the check in his account at First National. Jill's bank, State Bank, received the check, made a timely provisional settlement for the check, and did not return it. Bob Smith withdrew all of the credit from his account at First National, including the credit for Jill's check.

Notes

a)   What are Jill's options? What are State Bank's options when Jill calls to tell the bank that she has been fooled? What are First National's options if State Bank attempts to recover against First National?

b)   Assume that State Bank made a timely provisional settlement for the item and returned the check by its midnight deadline to First National because Jill had issued a timely stop payment order.   What are First National's options? What are Jill's options?

c)   Assume that Best Insurance Company exists, but Bob Smith is not an attorney for the company. Answer question (a) above.

d)   Assume that Best Insurance Company exists, Bob Smith is an attorney for the Company,   but   the   person   who contacted Jill is Peter Doe who said he was Bob Smith. Jill sent the check to Peter, who indorsed the check, "Best Insurance Company" and deposited the check in Peter's checking account at First National. First National sent the check to State Bank. State Bank received the check and did not return the check.   What are Jill's options? What are State Bank's options when Jill calls to tell the bank that she has

Notes

been fooled? If State Bank attempts to
recover from First National, what are
First National's options?

Reread U.C.C. § 3-405. This section addresses issues arising from forged
indorsements by employees. As with U.C.C. § 3-404, this section makes forged
indorsements effective in certain situations. The theory of this section is that an
employer should bear the risk of the fraudulent activities of its employees to whom
the employer has entrusted responsibility to deal with instruments. Read the
definitions in subsection (a). Notice that the definition of "employee" includes
independent contractors, the term "fraudulent indorsement" covers two situations
where employees tend to forge indorsements, and "responsibility" is a defined term.

As with the other preclusion sections we have studied, if the section applies to
make the indorsement effective, the person who needs that indorsement in order to
be considered a person entitled to enforce will be able to sue to enforce contract
liability on the instrument. If the instrument is a check issued by the employer, the
employer will not be successful in arguing that the item is not properly payable
from the account due to the forged indorsement. The effect of making the
indorsement effective under this section is also to protect good faith transferees who
take the instrument for value and good faith payors. It does not make the forged
indorsement authorized and authentic for purposes of transfer warranty liability.
U.C.C. §§ 3-416, 4-207. Would it make a warrantor "entitled to enforce" for
purposes of warranty liability?

Consider this situation as well. What if the employer issues a check to a real
payee. An employee with responsibility with respect to the check forges the
payee's name and deposits the check in employee's account at the depositary bank.
Before the check reaches the drawee bank, the employer stops payment on the check
so that it is dishonored. The employer stopped payment because it discovered the
employee's scheme. The check is returned to the depositary bank. Predictably, the
employee has withdrawn all funds from its account and disappeared. The
depositary bank is left holding the loss. No one would quarrel with the result that
the employer should bear the risk of the bad employee and the depositary bank
should be able to have the indorsement deemed effective under this section so that
the depositary bank can sue the employer on its drawer's liability on the check. But
what of the payee? Is the payee, who had nothing to do with this scheme and has

not received payment of the obligation that the employer owes to it, be subject to indorser's liability on the instrument? Should the words in U.C.C. § 3-405(b) that the "indorsement is effective as the indorsement of the person to whom the instrument is payable" be applied to allow the depositary bank sue the payee on the indorsement contract? Does that make any sense? For a discussion of the operation of this section see, Donald J. Rapson, *Loss Allocation in Forgery and Fraud Cases: Significant Changes Under Revised Articles 3 and 4*, 42 ALA. L. REV. 435 (1991).

If the section applies to make the indorsement effective, the comparative negligence analysis provided for in subsection (b) may result in some loss being allocated to the entity that took or paid the instrument.

Problem 6-6

Jill is an employee who works for Acme Company. On occasion, she submits invoices to the company treasurer for payment. Jill does not otherwise handle any money or checks for the company. She submitted an invoice showing that Acme Company owed $200 to Supply Co. Supply Co. exists but Acme does not really owe it any money. Acme issued a check payable to Supply Co. signed by the appropriate people at Acme, drawn on Acme's account at State Bank. Jill obtained the check and indorsed the check "Supply Co." She then deposited the check in her bank account at First National. First National sent the check in a timely manner to State Bank.

Notes

a) State Bank made a timely provisional settlement for the check and did not return the check. Acme found out that the check should not have been issued and called State Bank to complain. What are State Bank's options? What are Acme's options? If State Bank attempts to recover from First National, what are First National's options?

b) Answer (a) above, assuming that State Bank returned the check in a timely manner to First National, complying with all Article 4 and Regulation CC deadlines.

Notes

c) Assume that Acme really owed Supply Co. the money. Does that change your analysis of (a) and (b) above? How about if Supply Co. did not exist?

d) Assume that Jill supplied an accurate invoice resulting in a check made payable to Supply Co. When the bookkeeper had his back turned, Jill took the check payable to Supply Co. She later indorsed the check "Supply Co." She deposited the check in her bank account at First National. First National sent the check in a timely manner to State Bank. Answer questions (a) and (b) above. What if Jill did not prepare the invoice that resulted in the check being made out to Supply Co.?

C. Incomplete Instruments and Alterations

So far we have focused on forged signatures and the allocation of the risk of those forgeries. Now we turn to alterations of instruments. Alterations typically are of the amount of the instrument or of the payee's name.

Read U.C.C. § 3-115 and § 3-407. The first step in the analysis is to determine whether the item has been altered. Notice that an incomplete item that is completed without authority of the signer is treated as an alteration. The second step is to consider the effect of the alteration. What is the liability of various signers on their contract liability on the instrument when the item has been altered? **Review U.C.C. § 3-412 through § 3-415.**

If a holder has notice that an item is altered, can it be a holder in due course? **Review U.C.C. § 3-302.**

What is the warranty liability of transferors when an item has been altered? **Review U.C.C. § 3-416, § 3-417, § 4-207, § 4-208; Reg. J, 12 C.F.R. § 210.5, §**

210.6, and Reg. CC, 12 C.F.R. § 229.34.

Is an item that has been altered properly payable? **Review U.C.C. § 4-401.** Can a person be precluded from asserting an alteration? **Review U.C.C. § 3-406 and § 4-406.** Notice that U.C.C. § 3-404 and § 3-405 do not apply to the alteration situation. Those sections only apply to forged indorsements.

Problem 6-7

Jane Doe wrote a check for $200 payable to Acme Co. drawn on First National Bank. Bob Zoe, president of Acme Co. indorsed the check as follows: "Acme Co. by Bob Zoe, President." Bob Zoe has the authority to indorse checks for Acme Co. Bob then skillfully raised the amount of the check to $800 and used the check to buy a new fishing rod at Pro Sports Shop. Pro Sports Shop deposited the check in its account at Second National Bank, indorsing the check as follows: "For deposit only, Pro Sports Shop, without recourse." Second National Bank sent the check to the Federal Reserve Bank. The Federal Reserve Bank then sent the check to First National Bank.

Notes

a) First National Bank made a provisional settlement for the check, debited Jane's account for $800, and did not return the check. Jane objected when she received her bank statement from First National Bank that the check had been altered. Who will ultimately bear the loss for this alteration? Explain fully.

b) Same facts as (a) above. Instead of Jane Doe issuing the check for an amount, she gave the check to Bob Zoe, payable to Acme Co., requesting that Bob fill in the correct amount of $200. Bob filled in $800 instead of $200. Does that change your analysis of who will ultimately bear the loss for this problem?

c) Assume that Jane timely stopped payment on the check because the goods she purchased from Acme were defective. First National timely returned the check to the Federal Reserve Bank, complying with all deadlines in Article 4 and Regulation CC. Each bank in the return process fully complied with Regulation CC and Article 4 deadlines for return. Second National Bank has debited Pro Sports' bank account for $800 when the item was returned to Second National. Who will ultimately bear the loss for this alteration? Explain fully.

d) Instead of Jane giving Bob a check, she gave Bob a note that stated, "I promise to pay to Acme Co. $200 on June 5." Jane signed the note. Bob filled in "to the order of" in front of Acme's name. Bob indorsed the note "Acme Co. by Bob Zoe, President" and then sold the note to First National Bank for $180. First National presented the note to Jane demanding payment of $200. Jane refused to pay because the product she bought from Acme Co. was defective. Is First National subject to that defense?

D. Lost or Stolen Instruments

Read U.C.C. § 3-309. Review U.C.C. § 3-301. If a person can satisfy the requirements of U.C.C. § 3-309, that person may be a person entitled to enforce the instrument. U.C.C. § 3-309 is usually used in determining the appropriate person to enforce a party's contract liability on the instrument.

Read U.C.C. § 3-312 which provides a special rule for lost or stolen cashier's, teller's, or certified checks. **Review U.C.C. § 3-104 regarding the definition of a cashier's check and a teller's check and § 3-409 for a certified check**. A bank incurs contract liability on an instrument that is a cashier's check **(review U.C.C. § 3-412)**, a teller's check **(review U.C.C. § 3-414)**, or a certified check **(review U.C.C. § 3-409, § 3-413 and § 3-414)**.

Some courts have mistakenly held that a bank cannot stop payment or refuse to pay these types of checks. *See Flatiron Linen, Inc. v. First American State Bank*, 23 P. 3d 1209 (Colo. 2001). However, that is not a correct analysis of the Article 3 provisions that govern those types of checks. A bank that refuses to honor a cashier's check, teller's check, or a certified check has contract liability on that check and is able to assert defenses to its contract liability on the check **(review U.C.C. § 3-305)**. If the holder of the check is a holder in due course **(review U.C.C. § 3-302)**, the bank's defenses may be barred unless they are the types of defenses to which a holder in due course is subject. *See Gentner and Company Inc. v. Wells Fargo Bank*, 90 Cal. Rptr. 2d 904 (Cal. Ct. App. 1999).

In some circumstances, a remitter of a cashier's or teller's check **(review U.C.C. § 3-103)** or a drawer of a certified check, may want to stop payment on the check. Th remitter of a check and the drawer of a certified check do not have authority to stop payment. The remitter is not the issuer of the cashier's or teller's check. The drawer of a draft accepted by the bank is discharged from its contract liability. **Read U.C.C. § 3-411**. In other circumstances, a remitter may want to enforce the cashier's or teller's check. The comments to U.C.C. § 3-301 were amended in 2002 to provide that a remitter who has not yet transferred or negotiated the instrument may be a person entitled to enforce the instrument. Is this comment enough to make a remitter a "claimant" under U.C.C. § 3-312? *Compare In re Cohen*, 300 F.3d 1097 (9th Cir. 2002) (remitter was not a person entitled to enforce a cashier's check and thus had no interest in the check for purposes of determining the initial transferee under 11 U.S.C. § 550).

With these principles in mind, consider the following problem.

Problem 6-8

Notes

Craig bought a house. In preparation for the closing the next day, he requested that

First National Bank certify a check drawn on Craig's account at the bank. Craig wrote out a check for $4,000 payable to the order of Scott and Marion Sellers. The teller at First National Bank checked Craig's account balance. Craig had $10,000 in available funds. The teller certified the check by writing on the face of the check: "Certified by First National Bank on June 2, 1996 for $4,000." Later that day, Craig was in a car accident. When he awoke in the hospital, the check was gone, along with his wallet and credit cards. What are Craig's options with regard to the certified check and the house closing? What are the Sellers' options with regard to the certified check and the house closing?

Review

These problems are designed to get you to think about how the process of loss allocation works in these typical scenarios. It is usually helpful when organizing your thoughts in these fact patterns to draw a timeline based upon the route the instrument took. That will help you visualize the relationships between the various actors and help you think through which causes of action should be asserted against which actors in the problem, what defenses could be asserted, and what the responses are to the defenses. Keep going up and down the chain of actors until you find someone who cannot pass the loss any further.

Problem 6-9

Acme Corp., located in San Francisco, California, needed money to finance the manufacture of carburetors for automobiles. Acme's Board of Directors authorized John Smith, Acme's president, to obtain a loan of $10,000. Smith obtained a loan for that purpose from First Bank. Smith signed a negotiable note for $10,000 payable to the order of First Bank or holder, on demand. Smith's signature at the bottom right hand corner of the note was as follows: "Acme Corp., John Smith." Smith also signed a separate document promising to pay the debt if Acme did not pay the debt when due. First Bank sold the note to Second Bank for $9,000 on May 10. Second Bank is located in Chicago, Illinois. First Bank stamped the note on the back as follows: "Pay to Second Bank, /s/ First Bank."

Later that month, Second Bank's president left the note out on his desk. That night, when the janitor, Shifty, was cleaning, he took the note. Second Bank did not notify either First Bank or Acme that the note had been stolen. Shifty signed Second Bank's name under First Bank's name on the back of the note and took the note to Acme at its California office. Shifty stated that he was Second Bank's president and asked Acme to pay the note. Smith looked at the Second Bank identification card for Second Bank's president, also stolen from the president's desk. Smith called Second Bank and left a message for a bank officer to call him back. No one from Second Bank returned the phone call. At 5 p.m. that day, after failing to hear from Second Bank, Smith paid the note with Acme's funds and received the note from Shifty.

Later that month, Second Bank demanded that Acme and Smith pay the note. Both refused. Second Bank sued Acme, Smith, First Bank, and Shifty. Shifty is in jail for theft of the note. Analyze all parties' claims to the note, liabilities on and off the note, and any defenses that each party would have to the various claims and liabilities.

To get started, consider the following questions. Start with Second Bank. It is the entity that is currently holding the loss. Acme has the note. In order for Second Bank to enforce the note, it has to get the note back. How will it do so? Once you figure that out, then analyze whether Second Bank may enforce the note and against whom it could do so. Determine whether those defendants have any defenses.

If Second Bank is able to recover against any defendant, consider whether that defendant is able to pass the loss any further. For example, if Second Bank is able to recover from Acme, Acme will in effect have paid twice, once to Shifty and once to Second Bank. What will Acme do to try and recover? Who are potential defendants that Acme could sue?

Notes

Problem 6-10

Ed is Sue's gardener. His responsibilities include purchasing gardening supplies using Sue's checks. One day, while working at Sue's house, Ed took a check from Sue's checkbook that she left lying on the table. Sue maintains her checking account at Second Bank. Later that day, Ed wrote a check for $2,000 payable to Ed's father, John, writing Sue's name in as drawer. Ed then wrote John's name on the back, without recourse.

Ed took the check to Value Hardware, using the check to buy an expensive riding lawn mower. Value Hardware has dealt with Ed on numerous occasions and had previously taken checks payable to Ed signed by Sue to pay for various gardening supplies.

Value Hardware deposited the check to its account at First Bank at 5 p.m. Monday. First Bank sent the check across town to Second Bank that night. Second Bank received the check at 1 a.m. Tuesday and made a provisional settlement for the check. During business hours on Tuesday, Second Bank decided not to pay the check because Sue's account had only a $1,000 collected balance. Second Bank's clerk stamped the check NSF and placed the check in the pile of checks to return. A different clerk, sorting the checks so as to return them directly to the various depositary banks, dropped the check on the floor and did not notice that it had dropped. On Thursday, at approximately 11 a.m., a third clerk found the check and placed it in the pile to be returned to First Bank. First Bank received the returned check on Thursday at 4 p.m. First Bank debited Value's account $2,000 plus a returned check fee. Value Hardware's account was now overdrawn by $1,000 because it had written checks on the account in reliance on the available funds from the check that Ed gave Value Hardware.

Explain fully all parties' rights and liabilities.

Notes

Problem 6-11

Acme Corp. is in the business of buying various electronic goods and then selling those goods to retailers around the country. Acme Corp. maintains a bank account at Dulles National Bank.

On February 10, Dale Acme signed a check for $20,000 payable to Power Tools Co. for some equipment for Acme Corp.'s office. The check was drawn on Acme Corp.'s account at Dulles National Bank and Acme Corp.'s name and address were imprinted at the top of the check. The check was signed in the lower right hand corner "Dale Acme." Dale is authorized to sign checks on behalf of Acme Corp. Dale sent the check by mail to Power Tools Co. Power Tools' treasurer took the check and stamped it on the back "Power Tools Co." using a rubber stamp.

The treasurer then took the check and deposited it in the treasurer's personal bank account at First Bank at 12 noon on Monday, February 11. First Bank forwarded the check to Second Bank at 1 a.m. Tuesday, February 12. Second Bank forwarded the check to Dulles National Bank at 1 a.m. Wednesday, February 13. Dulles National Bank received the check at 4 a.m. Wednesday, February 13, and immediately made a provisional settlement for the check. Dulles National Bank then determined that enough money was in the account and debited Acme Corp.'s account.

By telephone on February 13, Dale Acme instructed Dulles National Bank not to pay the check to Power Tools Co. as Dale thought the equipment was defective. On Thursday, February 14, Dulles National Bank recredited Acme Corp.'s account and sent the check directly to First Bank. First Bank received the check on Friday, February 15. First Bank could not charge back against the treasurer's account because the treasurer had withdrawn all funds from the account and closed the account.

Explain fully all of the parties' rights and liabilities.

Notes

Problem 6-12

Sue Bookkeeper, an Acme Inc. employee, had, as part of her regular duties as a bookkeeper, the obligation to make up a list of creditors needing payment. Acme's treasurer then would review the list and approve payments. Bookkeeper would write the checks drawn on Second National Bank and sign on the drawer's line as follows: "/s/ Acme Inc. by Sue Bookkeeper, bookkeeper."

Bookkeeper was depressed by the failure of spring to arrive and decided to go on vacation to the Bahamas. She was short of cash to finance the trip. Bookkeeper put a $3000 debt to Bob's Widgets on the list of creditors. Acme in fact owed Bob's Widgets $3000. Acme's treasurer approved the list and Bookkeeper wrote a check payable to the order of Bob's Widgets signing the check in the usual manner. Bookkeeper then took the check and signed the back as follows: "/s/ Bob's Widgets, without recourse."

Bookkeeper took the check to her bookie, Shifty. Shifty told Bookkeeper that he would accept the check in payment of Bookkeeper's $1,000 gambling debt and would give her $1,900 in cash for the check. Bookkeeper agreed and left for the Bahamas. Shifty then skillfully raised the amount of the check to $4000 and deposited the check at his bank, First National. First National credited Shifty's account with $4,000 and let Shifty withdraw $3,000. First National sent the check to Second National. Second National debited Acme's account for $4,000.

Three weeks later, Second National sent to Acme the bank statement and checks, including the Bob's Widgets check. By that time, Bookkeeper was back from vacation and examined the statement, removing the check to Bob's Widgets. Through the procedure described above, Bookkeeper had the treasurer approve another check to Bob's Widgets for $3,000 and sent that check to Bob's Widgets.

Acme's treasurer discovered all of the above facts when the books were audited approximately eight months after Acme received the bank statement. By that time Bookkeeper had quit her job and moved to the Bahamas permanently.

Analyze all parties' rights and liabilities.

Notes

CHAPTER 7
LETTERS OF CREDIT

A. Overview

So far we have studied three different payment systems: currency, credit cards, and negotiable instruments. Most people use one or more of these payment systems at some point. We now turn to a payment system with which many people are unfamiliar: letters of credit. This payment system is similar to others we have studied in that it addresses the four main concerns of all payment systems: (i) the mechanics of value transfer; (ii) incurring and satisfying the obligation to pay; (iii) enforcing the obligation to pay; and (iv) allocating the risk of errors and wrongdoing.

The law that governs letter of credit transactions is part statutory, part agreement, and part common law principles. The domestic statutory regime is contained in U.C.C. Article 5. Article 5 was revised in 1995 and all states have adopted it.

Instead of Article 5, parties may agree to use the Uniform Customs and Practices for Documentary Credits (UCP), issued by the International Chamber of Commerce (ICC). In December 2006, the ICC issued a new version of the UCP, No. 600, which replaces No. 500. The ICC also previously issued the International Standby Practices called ISP98. Finally, the United Nations has adopted a convention on Independent Guarantees and Stand-by Letters of Credit (1996).

Because Article 5 is an incomplete statement of letter of credit rules that may apply to any particular letter of credit, any advice about a letter of credit transaction must take into account the sources cited above as well as any other agreement of the parties that is given effect by virtue of U.C.C. § 5-103(c). One of the motivations for promulgating Revised Article 5 was to adapt the article to international and current practice. This Chapter is designed to explore the Article 5 rules while keeping in mind that if the parties have agreed to incorporate UCP500, UCP600, or ISP98, or if the transaction falls within the UN convention, the rules of Article 5 may be altered. **Read U.C.C. § 5-101 and § 5-103.**

B. Mechanics of Value Transfer

A letter of credit is an undertaking by an issuer to a beneficiary to honor a documentary presentation by delivering an item for value. The usual issuers of letters of credit are banks. Examples of various letters of credit can be found in John F. Dolan, COMMERCIAL LAW: ESSENTIAL TERMS AND TRANSACTIONS (2d ed. 1997). You may want to look ahead at the *Intraworld Industries* case, reproduced later in this Chapter. The letter of credit involved in that case is reproduced in footnote 7.

To illustrate this payment mechanism, imagine the following scenario. You are a seller of goods. You want to sell to a particular buyer located some distance away. You are not willing to trust that a check or other draft the buyer negotiates to you will be honored when presented for payment. You do not want to extend credit to the buyer, so you do not want to take a note in payment for the goods. You do not want to ship the goods to the buyer unless you are sure that you have the money in hand for those goods. An electronic funds transfer is not feasible because you cannot be sure that the money will be available to you by the time you have to ship the goods to the buyer. (We will learn about electronic funds transfers in Chapter 8.) The buyer does not want to release the money until he or she knows that the goods have been shipped from the seller's business. Obtaining a commercial letter of credit will allow this transaction to go forward and solve the problem of the parties' distrust of each other.

The seller and the buyer will negotiate what documents need to be presented to the bank in order for the bank to honor the letter of credit. Typically, the documents are shipping documents stating that the goods have been placed in the carrier's hands (such as a bill of lading), invoices listing the type and amount of goods shipped, a draft drawn on the issuing bank, and an insurance certificate noting that insurance has been purchased for the buyer's benefit in the event the goods are lost or damaged in shipment. The buyer (the applicant) will request its bank to issue a letter of credit for the benefit of the seller (the beneficiary).

The bank (the issuer) will issue a document that will state the amount of the credit, the date issued, and the terms for honoring the credit. The terms of the letter of credit generally consist in large part of an exact listing of the documents that must be presented in order for the issuer to honor the credit. Other terms, such as when the letter of credit expires and where the presentation of documents must take place, will also be given. All of the requirements for honoring the letter of credit must be stated in the credit itself.

Once the letter of credit is drafted, the bank issues the letter by sending it to the beneficiary: in this example, the seller. The letter of credit is the bank's engagement to pay according to the terms of the credit. The seller will ship the goods, gather the documents that the letter of credit requires, and present those documents along with the letter of credit to the bank for payment. The bank will examine the documents to determine if the documents and the presentation comply with the terms of the letter of credit. If the documents comply with the letter of credit, the bank will pay the amount of the credit to the seller. The bank will give to the buyer the documents that the seller presented to the bank. The buyer will use the shipping documents to retrieve the goods from the carrier. The seller has been paid and the buyer has the goods.

This transaction may be illustrated graphically as follows:

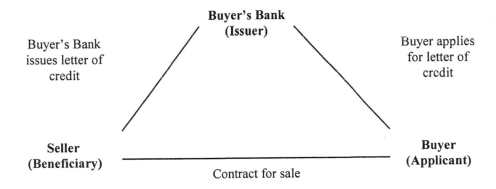

One can see that in this transaction, there are three relationships: the contract between the buyer and seller; the buyer's application to the issuing bank to issue the letter of credit, and the bank's issuance of the letter of credit to the beneficiary. **Read the definitions of "issuer," "applicant," and "beneficiary" in U.C.C. § 5-102.**

Another type of letter of credit is called a standby letter of credit. These credits are issued in transactions for the purpose of guaranteeing payment of an obligation which is really supposed to be paid another way. To illustrate the way a standby letter of credit works, assume a construction company borrows money from a lender to finance construction of a building for a person that will own the building. Under the construction contract between the building owner and the construction company, the building owner is not required to pay unless everything is finished in a satisfactory manner. The lender, however, may not want to rely solely on the building's owner for the funds that will enable the construction company to repay the loan. The lender might require the construction company to procure a standby letter of credit, to be issued for its benefit in the event the construction company does not pay the loan. This letter of credit is thus a "standby" form of payment to be used only if another payment mechanism fails. The standby letter of credit in this situation can be illustrated by the following diagram:

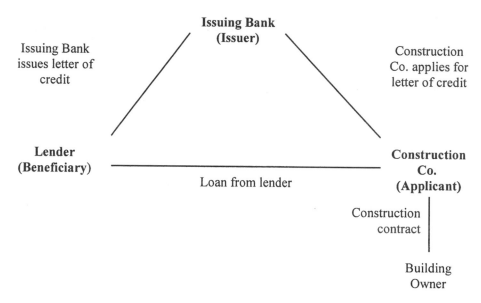

Even though the underlying transaction is different and different documents are required in a standby letter of credit, the parties' rights and obligations are the same in both commercial and standby letters of credit. Article 5 does not distinguish between commercial and standby letters of credit in defining the rights and obligations of the parties in the letter of credit transaction.

In some letter of credit transactions, the issuer will request that another bank take on the obligations of the letter of credit (confirm the credit) or advise the beneficiary that the letter of credit was issued. **Read the definitions of "confirmer," "nominated person," and "advisor" in U.C.C. § 5-102.** Return to the example of the commercial letter of credit given above. The issuing bank may contact a bank in the seller's geographical region with whom it has a relationship to have that second bank confirm the credit. This second bank is known as a confirming bank. The confirming bank will examine the letter of credit and the documents. If the documents and presentation comply with the terms of the letter of credit, the confirming bank will pay the beneficiary the amount of the credit. The confirming bank will then send the documents to the issuing bank. The issuing bank will give the documents to the buyer. The confirming bank will expect that the issuing bank reimburse it for its payment to the seller. **Read U.C.C. § 5-107.** How does an advising bank's obligations differ from a confirming bank's obligations?

A letter of credit is different than any other type of obligation. It is not a negotiable instrument. (If you are not sure why that statement is true, review the requirements of a negotiable instrument in Chapter 2.) **Read the definition of "letter of credit" in U.C.C. § 5-102 and the formal requirements for a letter of credit in U.C.C. § 5-104.** Notice that the letter of credit must meet very few formal requirements, unlike a negotiable instrument.

A letter of credit is also not a guarantee obligation, even though it might on the surface operate like a guarantee, as in the case of a standby letter of credit. The reason for the distinction from other forms of obligation such as a guarantee is the "independence principle." **Read U.C.C. § 5-103(d) and comment 1.**

What the independence principle means in our seller of goods example is that even if the goods the seller ships to the buyer do not conform to the contract for sale with the buyer, the seller who presents the correct documents in the correct form to the bank for payment on the letter of credit is entitled to payment on the letter of credit. The buyer is taking the risk that the money will be paid to the seller even if the goods are not conforming goods. The issuing bank has no obligation to determine whether the seller has properly performed its duties under the contract with the buyer.

Similarly, in our standby letter of credit example, if the lender makes a conforming documentary presentation to the issuer, the lender is entitled to payment on the letter of credit regardless of the status of the loan between the lender and the construction company and regardless of the parties' performance of the construction contract with the building owner.

The letter of credit is also not a contract between the issuing bank and the applicant. **Read U.C.C. § 5-105.** As stated in the definition of letter of credit in U.C.C. § 5-102, a letter of credit is an undertaking by the issuing bank to honor a conforming documentary presentation. The issuing bank owes its obligation to the beneficiary of the letter of credit.

C. Incurring, Satisfying, and Enforcing the Obligation to Pay

As we have already learned, a letter of credit is issued by a bank and is an undertaking by the bank to honor a conforming documentary presentation. The letter of credit must be in an authenticated record. U.C.C. § 5-102, 5-104. Now consider the following questions:
- When is an issuing bank obligated on a letter of credit?
- When does a letter of credit expire?

▸　Once the issuing bank is obligated on a letter of credit, can the issuing bank cancel or revoke the letter of credit?

▸　Once the issuing bank is obligated on a letter of credit, can the letter of credit be amended?

To answer these questions, **read U.C.C. § 5-106.**

Once a letter of credit is effective, the issuer is obligated to honor the letter of credit if there is a documentary presentation that strictly complies with the terms and conditions of the letter of credit. **Read U.C.C. § 5-108(a).** Consider the following discussions of this standard of "strict compliance."

JOSEPH D. GUSTAVUS
LETTER OF CREDIT COMPLIANCE
UNDER REVISED UCC ARTICLE 5 AND UCP 500
114 BANKING L. J. 55, 55-60 (1997)[*]
* * * * *

Subsection 5-108(a) requires that documents submitted for presentation appear strictly to comply with the terms of the Credit. Strict compliance does not mean slavish conformity to the terms of the Credit, rather it is construed in the context of standard practice. By adopting standard practice as a way of measuring strict compliance, UCC Article 5 endorses the conclusion of the court in *New Braunfels National Bank v. Ordiorne* [780 S.W.2d 313 (Tex. Ct. App. 1989)].

The strict compliance rule rests on the judgment that issuers should not be forced into the position of determining whether a documentary discrepancy is significant. As the *New Braunfels* court explained, the rule assumes that issuers are not in a position to know whether discrepancies matter to the commercial parties. Nothing in that assumption requires courts to absolve the issuer from knowing the significance of discrepancies for their own business. Under the strict compliance rule, an issuer is not responsible for knowing whether an air-bill, rather than an ocean-bill, covering computer components is a significant defect. However, the strict compliance rule does hold the issuer responsible for knowing whether the abbreviation of the word "number" to "No." in the legend on a draft is a significant defect. Issuers have no knowledge about the transportation limitations on computer components, but they do know what type of legend inscription is consistent with a properly completed draft. Thus, the strict compliance rule is for the protection of the issuer from having to know the commercial impact of a discrepancy in the

---

[*] Footnotes omitted. Reprinted by permission.

documents.

A survey of cases illustrates application of the commercial-banking distinction of discrepancies under strict compliance. The *New Braunfels* court held that a beneficiary could collect when a draft requested payment on "Letter of Credit No. 86-122-5" and the Credit specified "Letter of Credit No. 86-122-S," as the "S" indicated standby. In *Beyene v. Irving Trust Co.* [762 F.2d 4 (2nd Cir. 1985)] the court held that the misspelling on a bill of lading, the buyer's name, Muhammad Soran, as "Sofan" was a material discrepancy justifying dishonor. In *Voest-Alpine International Corp. v. Chase Manhattan Bank* [707 F.2d 680 (2nd Cir. 1983)] the court held that a "glaring discrepancy" was evident when certificates presented showed goods loaded between February 2 and 6 when the letter required proof of shipment by January 31. The court in *Tosco Corp. v. FDIC* [723 F.2d 1242 (6th Cir. 1983)] held that a draft containing "l" instead of "L" in "letter," "No." instead of "Number," and the addition of the city and state of the drawee did not warrant dishonor even under the strictest rule. The court in *Flagship Cruises, Ltd. v. New England Merchants National Bank* [569 F.2d 699 (1st Cir. 1978)] held that "No. 18506" sufficed instead of "Drawn under [issuer's initials] Credit No. 18506." The court in *Courtaulds North America, Inc. v. North Carolina National Bank* [528 F.2d 802 (4th Cir. 1975)] held that a commercial invoice showing "Imported Acrylic Yarn" instead of "100% Acrylic Yarn" warranted dishonor.

An issuer is not responsible for observance or knowledge of the usage of a particular trade other than the standard practice referred to in subsection 5-108(e). Thus, based upon the reasoning in *New Braunfels* the issuer is expected to know usage commonly encountered in the course of document examination. For example, an issuer should know the common usage with respect to documents in the maritime shipping trade but not be expected to understand synonyms used in a particular trade for product descriptions appearing in a Credit or an invoice.

Thus, a document examiner is required to know the significance of banking discrepancies, not commercial discrepancies. The document examiner is held to know usages commonly encountered in the course of document examination.

* * * * *

By requiring that a "presentation" appear strictly to comply, subsection 5-108(a) requires not only that the documents themselves appear on their face strictly to comply, but also that the other terms of the Credit, such as those dealing with the time and place of presentation are strictly complied with. It appears that the "strict compliance" standard, as construed by UCC Article 5, is no longer limited to the documents presented.

It is important not to apply this expansive view of strict compliance as allowing non-documentary conditions. If a Credit contains non-documentary conditions, under subsection 5-108(g), an issuer is required to disregard the non-documentary conditions and treat them as if they were not stated. However, subsection 5-108(g) would not permit a beneficiary or issuer to disregard terms in a Credit such as place, time, and mode or presentation.

Typically, a Credit will provide that presentation is timely if made to the issuer of [sic] confirmer prior to the expiration of the Credit.

The section does not preclude the issuer from contacting the applicant during its examination. Inland banks that issue irrevocable Credits have few, if any, international correspondents. These banks view themselves as ministerial document checkers, meticulously verifying documentary compliance for their applicant. They make it a practice to consult their customers about the acceptability of doubtful documents prior to, or in connection with, the decision to honor the Credit. Large banks with a significant international practice regard the inland banks' "consultation" as an abdication of the issuing banks' duty to the beneficiary banks to exercise independent and strictly documentary judgment on whether the documents comply. Yet, a beneficiary to a Credit may be successful in asserting that the practice of contacting the applicant for document review is evidence of a local or regional practice, and hence, standard practice. The court may interpret this standard practice as imputing the applicant's opinion on the presentation to the bank. A failure of a bank to contact the applicant for document review may cause a bank to prematurely and wrongfully dishonor under subsection 5-108(a). Thus, issuers must be cognizant of all aspects of local or regional standard practice for determining compliance of a presentation.

By applying standard practice to the presentation as a whole, strict compliance embodies considerations other than just facial examination of the documents.

VOEST-ALPINE TRADING USA CORP. V. BANK OF CHINA
167 F. Supp. 2d 940, 946-47 (S. D. Tex. 2000)
affirmed 288 F.3d 262 (5th Cir. 2002)

* * * * *

The Court notes the wide range of interpretations on what standard banks should employ in examining letter of credit document presentations for compliance. Even where courts claim to uphold strict compliance, the standard is hardly uniform. The first and most restrictive approach is to require that the presentation documents be a mirror image of the requirements. *See Banco General Runinahui, S.A. v. Citibank Int'l*, 97 F.3d 480, 483 (11th Cir.1996) ("This Court has recognized and applied the 'strict compliance' standard to requests for payment under commercial letters of credit ... '[T]he fact that a defect is a mere technicality' does not matter.' ") (*quoting Kerr-McGee Chem. Corp. v. FDIC*, 872 F.2d 971, 973 (11th Cir.1989)); *Alaska Textile Co. v. Chase Manhattan Bank*, 982 F.2d 813, 816 (2d Cir.1992) (Noting that documents that are nearly the same as those required by the letter of credit are unacceptable for presentation in a letter of credit transaction).

Second, there are also cases claiming to follow the strict compliance standard but support rejection only where the discrepancies are such that would create risks for the issuer if the bank were to accept the presentation documents. *See Flagship Cruises Ltd., v. New England Merchants Nat'l Bank of Boston*, 569 F.2d 699, 705 (1st Cir.1978) ("We do not see these rulings as retreats from rigorous insistence on compliance with letter of credit requirements. They merely recognize that variance between documents specified and documents submitted is not fatal if there is no possibility that the documents could mislead the paying bank to its detriment"); *Crist v. J. Henry Schroder Bank & Trust Co.*, 693 F.Supp. 1429, 1433 (S.D.N.Y.1988) (where a party who has succeeded by operation of law to the rights of the beneficiary of a letter of credit, refusal was improper, even though the terms of the credit provided for payment only to the beneficiary); *Bank of Cochin, Ltd. v. Manufacturers Hanover Trust Co.*, 612 F.Supp. 1533, 1541 (S.D.N.Y.1985) (even under the strict compliance standard, a variance is permitted between the documents specified in a letter of credit and the documents presented thereunder where "there is no possibility that the documents could mislead the paying bank to its detriment"); *Vest*, 996 S.W.2d at 14 (noting that strict compliance does not demand "oppressive perfectionism").

A third standard, without much support in case law, is to analyze the documents for risk to the applicant. *See* INT'L CHAMBER OF COMMERCE, COMM'N ON BANKING TECHNIQUE AND PRACTICE, PUBLICATION NO. 511, UCP 500 & 400 COMPARED 39 (Charles del Busto ed.1994) (discussion of a standard that would permit "deviations that do not cause ostensible harm" to the applicant); *see also Breathless Assoc. v. First Savings & Loan Assoc.*, 654 F.Supp. 832, 836 (N.D.Tex.1986) (noting, under the strict compliance standard, "[a] discrepancy ... should not warrant dishonor unless it reflects an increased likelihood of defective performance or fraud on the part of the beneficiary").

The mirror image approach is problematic because it absolves the bank reviewing the documents of any responsibility to use common sense to determine if the documents, on their face, are related to the transaction or even to review an entire document in the context of the others presented to the bank. On the other hand, the second and third approaches employ a determination-of- harm standard that is too unwieldy. Such an analysis would improperly require the bank to evaluate risks that it might suffer or that might be suffered by the applicant and could undermine the independence of the three contracts that underlie the letter of credit payment scheme by forcing the bank to look beyond the face of the presentation documents.

The Court finds that a moderate, more appropriate standard lies within the UCP 500 itself and the opinions issued by the International Chamber of Commerce ("ICC") Banking Commission. One of the Banking Commission opinions defined the term "consistency" between the letter of credit and the documents presented to the issuing bank as used in Article 13(a) of the UCP to mean that "the whole of the documents must obviously relate to the same transaction, that is to say, that each should bear a relation (link) with the others on its face ..." INT'L CHAMBER OF COMMERCE, BANKING COMM'N, PUBLICATION NO. 371, DECISIONS (1975-1979) OF THE ICC BANKING COMMISSION R. 12 (1980). The Banking Commission rejected the notion that "all of the documents should be *exactly* consistent in their wording." *Id.* (emphasis in original).

A common sense, case-by-case approach would permit minor deviations of a typographical nature because such a letter-for-letter correspondence between the letter of credit and the presentation documents is virtually impossible. *See* INT'L CHAMBER OF COMMERCE, COMM'N ON BANKING TECHNIQUE AND PRACTICE, PUBLICATION NO. 511, UCP 500 & 400 COMPARED 39 (Charles del Busto ed.1994)(noting the difficulty in attaining mirror-image compliance). While the end result of such an analysis may bear a strong resemblance to the relaxed strict compliance standard, the actual calculus used by the issuing bank is not the risk it or the applicant faces but rather, whether the documents bear a rational link to one another. In this way, the issuing bank is required to examine a particular document in light of all documents presented and use common sense but is not required to evaluate risks or go beyond the face of the documents.

* * * * *

When the letter of credit is presented, the issuer has to make a decision about whether to honor or dishonor the letter of credit based upon this strict compliance standard. The issuer has a limited period of time in which to make this decision. If the issuer is not going to honor the letter of credit, it must give notice and disclose the discrepancies that it intends to rely on to justify its refusal to honor the letter of credit. **Read U.C.C. § 5-108.**

If the issuer rightfully honors the letter of credit, the issuer is entitled to reimbursement from the applicant, U.C.C. § 5-108(i), and is subrogated to the rights of the applicant and the beneficiary. **U.C.C. § 5-117.** Because of the relationship between rightful honor and reimbursement from the applicant, the issuer may ask that the applicant waive discrepancies between the presented documents and the terms of the letter of credit. The applicant is not usually under any obligation to do so, but often will waive discrepancies.

If the issuer wrongfully honors the letter of credit, the issuer is liable under **U.C.C. § 5-111** and does not obtain the rights under U.C.C. § 5-108(i). If the issuer wrongfully dishonors the letter of credit, it will be liable under **U.C.C. § 5-111.**

As protection for the issuer and the applicant in this process, the beneficiary makes warranties to the issuer and the applicant upon the issuer's honor of the letter of credit. **U.C.C. § 5-110.**

Sometimes the beneficiary of a letter of credit will want to give the right to draw on the letter of credit to someone else, or will assign the right to receive proceeds of the letter of credit. **Read U.C.C. §§ 5-112, 5-114.** There is a key difference between making someone a transferee beneficiary of a letter of credit and assigning the right to receive the proceeds of the letter of credit. That key difference is the right to draw on the letter of credit, that is, make the demand to the issuer to honor the letter of credit. Only a transferee beneficiary has the right to draw on the letter of credit. An assignee of the right to receive the proceeds does not have the right to make the documentary presentation to the issuer and demand the issuer pay on a complying presentation. In order to be a transferee beneficiary, the issuer has to agree to the transfer of the beneficiary's rights to the transferee.

Problem 7-1

Acme Computer Company ordered computer chips from Computer Parts, Inc. As a condition of the sale, Computer Parts required that Acme have a letter of credit for $100,000 issued in Computer Parts' favor. Acme asked its bank, National Bank, to issue a letter of credit to Computer Parts. National Bank sent a fax to Second Bank, located in Computer Parts' community stating that National Bank would pay $100,000 to Computer Parts when Computer Parts presented a sight draft, a clean on board bill of lading showing shipment to Acme Computer, a commercial invoice, and a certificate of insurance for the benefit of Acme.

a) Is the fax that National Bank sent to Second Bank a letter of credit as defined in Article 5?

b) Second Bank sent a notice to Computer Parts that it had received notice of a letter of credit in Computer Parts' favor.   Label the parties to this transaction using the Article 5 terms.

c) Second Bank sent a notice to Computer Parts that it will honor National Bank's letter of credit. Label the parties to this transaction using the Article 5 terms.

d) What is the difference between Second Bank's liability in (b) and (c) above? U.C.C. § 5-107.

e) Can Acme change its mind about the transaction and cancel the letter of credit after National Bank has sent the notice to Second Bank?

f) Assume Acme and Computer Parts renegotiated the sale transaction so that Computer Parts will be selling Acme only $50,000 worth of goods. How can Acme amend the letter of credit that National Bank has issued?

Notes

g)   Will the letter of credit expire?

h)   Second Bank sent a notice to Computer Parts that National Bank issued a letter of credit in Computer Parts' favor and that Second Bank would honor that letter of credit. Computer Parts presented the required documents to Second Bank. Advise Second Bank.

i)   Same facts as (h). If Second Bank pays the letter of credit amount to Computer Parts, what are the parties' rights and obligations?

j)   Same facts as (h). Computer Parts wants to sell its right under the letter of credit in order to have the cash sooner. How could it do that?

D.   Allocation of the Risk of Errors and Wrongdoing

Fraud or allegations of fraud in the underlying transaction for which the letter of credit is issued is a troublesome and reoccurring issue in letter of credit law. Allegations of fraud to stop payment on the letter of credit is an important exception to both the strict compliance standard and the independence principle. **Read U.C.C. § 5-108(d) and § 5-109.** If the applicant for a letter of credit does not want the issuer to pay the letter of credit after issuance, the applicant may assert that the beneficiary is engaged in some type of fraud. Section 5-109 governs the rights and obligations of the parties in that context. Consider how the issue of fraud would complicate the issuer's decision to honor or dishonor the presentation on a letter of credit.

The following case is cited with approval in the comment to that section and is construing former section 5-114, the section that dealt with fraud in the transaction prior to the revision of Article 5.

INTRAWORLD INDUSTRIES, INC. V. GIRARD TRUST BANK
336 A.2d 316 (Penn. 1975)

Roberts, Justice

This appeal requires us to review the trial court's denial of a preliminary injunction to restrain honor of a draft under an international letter of credit. A precise statement of the facts, which are complex, is necessary for a proper understanding.

On February 11, 1972, a lease was executed by Intraworld Industries, Inc., a corporation[1] headquartered in Wilkes-Barre, Pennsylvania, and Paulette Cymbalista, a citizen of Switzerland and resident of Italy. Cymbalista agreed to lease to Intraworld the Hotel Carlton, a luxury hotel located in St. Moritz, Switzerland, for a term of 15 years at an annual rental of 800,000 Swiss francs, payable in semi-annual installments.[2] The lease provided that Intraworld was required to prepay the rent for the initial 18-month period. Intraworld was also obligated to procure, within the first 100 days of the term, a performance bond in the amount of $500,000.00 'to insure to lessor the payment of the rent.'[3]

Intraworld entered into possession of the hotel on May 1, 1972. Shortly thereafter, Intraworld assigned its interest in the lease to its subsidiary, Vacanze In Paradiso Hotels, S.A., a Swiss corporation.[4]

---

[1] Intraworld is incorporated in either Pennsylvania or Delaware; the record is unclear on this point.

[2] The lease contained a formula for the adjustment of the annual rental with respect to changes in the value of the Swiss franc. At the time of the execution of the lease, the annual rental was approximately equivalent to $200,000.00.

[3] The record does not establish whether Intraworld performed its obligation to procure a performance bond. The lease also provided: 'This agreement shall be governed by the Swiss law. The competent forum shall be in Saint Moritz Court.'

[4] For convenience we will refer to the lessee as Intraworld.

At a later time,[5] Intraworld and Cymbalista executed an addendum to the lease (to which the parties have referred by its German title 'Nachtrag'). The Nachtrag cancelled Intraworld's obligation to procure a performance bond and substituted a duty a provide letters of credit issued by 'the Girard Trust Company of Philadelphia' in order to guarantee rental payments one year in advance. Two letters of credit were specifically required, each in the amount of $100,000.00, maturing in November, 1973, and May, 1974, to secure the rent due at those times. After each rental payment, Intraworld was to provide a new letter of credit 'in order that the lessor remains secured one years (sic) rent in advance.' The Nachtrag also provided:

> 'In the event the lessee should not fulfill its obligation to pay, so that the letter of credit must be used, . . . then the lessor can terminate the lease immediately without further notice. In this case, the lessor retains the rent paid or guaranteed for the following year as a stipulated penalty for non-performance of the contract from the lessee, in doing so the lessor retains the right to make a claim for additional damages not covered by the stipulated penalty.'

On September 1, 1972, Intraworld and the Girard Trust Bank, Philadelphia, entered into an agreement to provide the letters of credit required by the Nachtrag. Girard agreed to

> 'issue a letter of credit . . . in the amount of $100,000 under which the Lessor may draw a sight draft on (Girard) for payment of the sum due under said lease (a) on November 10, 1973 and (b) May 10, 1974. Under the terms of such letter of credit, payments will be made if the Lessor presents a draft as provided in such letter of credit. Each such letter of credit will expire . . . on the twentieth day after the payment under said lease is due.' [6]

In accordance with the agreement, Girard issued two irrevocable letters of credit on September 5, 1972. Each authorized Cymbalista to draw a draft on Girard

---

[5] The record does not establish the exact date.

[6] The agreement also provided: 'This agreement shall be construed in accordance with the law of the State of Pennsylvania and the Acts of Congress of the United States affecting transactions under the provisions hereof.'

in the amount of $100,000.00 if Intraworld failed to pay the rent when due.[7]

In the summer of 1973, the relationship between Cymbalista and Intraworld began to go awry. Norbert Cymbalista, Paulette's husband, visited the hotel in August and, after discussions with the manager, became very concerned over the hotel's financial condition. He discovered that there were unpaid bills in excess of $100,000, that all telephone and Telex communications had been cut off for nonpayment of bills, and that the filing of mechanics liens against the hotel was imminent. After a trans-Atlantic telephone call, the Cymbalistas traveled to the United States within several days of Norbert's discoveries to attempt to resolve the hotel's difficulties with Intraworld. However, as Norbert testified,

'I tried to reach (the president of Intraworld) innumerable times by telephone and each time his secretary answered that he would call me

---

[7] 'IRREVOCABLE LETTER OF CREDIT NO. 35798
Date: September 5, 1972
'Amount: $100,000.00
'Beneficiary: Paulette Cymbalista
C/o Carlton Hotel
St. Moritz, Switzerland
'For account of: Intraworld Industries, Inc.
116 South Main Street
Wilkes Barre, PA 18701
'Madam:
    'You are hereby authorized to draw on us at sight the sum of One Hundred Thousand and 00/100 Dollars United States Currency ($100,000.00) due on November 10, 1973 under a lease, a copy of which is attached to both Beneficiary's copy and Bank's copy of this letter of credit as Exhibit 1, available by your draft for said amount, accompanied by:
    '1. Simple receipt for amount drawn.
    '2. A signed statement of the drawer of the draft to the effect that the drawer is the lessor under said lease and that the lessee thereunder has not paid the installment of rent due under said lease on November 10, 1973 within 10 days after said installment was due and payable.
    'This credit expires on November 30, 1973.
    'Drafts under this credit must contain the clause 'drawn under Credit No. 35798 of Girard Trust Bank, dated September 5, 1972.'
    'Girard Trust Bank hereby agrees with the drawers, endorsers and bona fide owners of the bills drawn strictly in compliance with the terms of this credit that the same will be duly honored upon presentation.
    'Except so far as otherwise expressly stated, this credit is subject to the uniform customs and practices for documentary credits (1962 revision), International Chamber of Commerce Brochure No. 222.'
Credit No. 35799 was identical to 35798, except that it applied to the rent due on May 10, 1974, and expired on May 30, 1974.

back and he never did. I stayed a whole month in the United States trying continually to reach him and it was never possible.'

On August 20, 1973, apparently while the Cymbalistas were in the United States, their Swiss counsel sent a letter to Intraworld reciting the unpaid bills, erosion of the Carlton's reputation, and internal corporate difficulties (apparently of Intraworld's Swiss subsidiary). It concluded:

'Based upon (Swiss law) and in reference to the provisions of the Lease Contract, we herewith extend to you a final time limit up to September 15, 1973 in order to:

(a) to pay all due debts,

(b) to supply the necessary means to safeguard proper management of the business,

(c) to complete the Board of Directors according to the law.

Within this time limit you must prove to the Hotel Owners that the aforementioned measures have been effectuated. Should you (fail to?) comply with this demand within the time-limit, the Lease Contract will be regarded as void.'

Intraworld's Swiss counsel replied to the August 20 letter (but this reply is not in the record). Finding this reply unsatisfactory, Cymbalista's Swiss counsel answered on September 18, 1973:

'As (Intraworld) did not comply with our demand within this time-limit, we regard the leasing contract as terminated effective from 15 September 1973 . . .. From now on, the proprietor will have direct and sole control over the hotel real estate respective to the hotel management.'[8]

Further correspondence was exchanged by Swiss counsel, including, apparently, a demand on November 3 for the rent due in November. On November 7, 1973, Intraworld's Swiss counsel wrote to Cymbalista's counsel:

'You state on behalf of the lessor that (Intraworld) has the obligation to pay . . . rent by November 1. My client (Intraworld), who is presently in close contact with their American Bank (Girard), however, have (sic) informed me that the payment of the rent can be made up to November 10 . . . My client informed me further that accordingly these payments shall be legally undertaken by the 'Girard Trust Bank' . . . (M)y client cannot

---

[8] Both letters were originally written in German. The translations which we have quoted were introduced by Intraworld in the trial court without objection by any party.

agree with your position according to which the lease contract can be considered as terminated either because of (Swiss law) or because of the terms of the lease agreement . . ..'

That letter was followed on November 9, 1973, by another from Intraworld's counsel to Cymbalista's counsel in which he stated:

'If the transfer of the rent from the United States should not be made in timely fashion, your client (Cymbalista) is at liberty to obtain payment by way of the guarantee contracts (*i.e.*, letters of credit). In any event, there exist the two guarantee contracts, valid until November 30, 1973 and May 30, 1974, respectively, in order to preserve the rights of your client.'[9]

The rent due on November 10, 1973, was not paid by Intraworld. Accordingly, on November 21, 1973, Cymbalista's American counsel presented to Girard a draft drawn on Girard for $100,000.00 under Credit No. 35798. The draft was accompanied, all parties agree, by documentation that conformed to the terms of the credit. In his letter to Girard, Cymbalista's counsel stated:

'Your attention is directed to correspondence dated November 7 and November 9, 1973, copies of which are attached, in which Swiss counsel representing the Lessee invites the Lessor to draw upon the Letters of Credit; our client, as Lessor, takes the position that the lease . . . has terminated for various reasons, including the failure timely to pay the amount due pursuant to the 'Nachtrag'...'

Girard informed Intraworld on November 21 that it intended to honor the draft. Intraworld immediately filed an action in equity in the Court of Common Pleas of Philadelphia seeking injunctive relief prohibiting Girard from honoring the draft. Cymbalista filed a petition to intervene, which was granted by the trial court.

---

[9] Intraworld's Swiss counsel's letters were also in German. The record is confusing on the issue of translation. Apparently, Cymbalista offered two translations of each letter as exhibits in the trial court; exhibits 1(T) 3(T) are translations of the November 7 letter, 2(T) and 4(T) of the November 9 letter. One set of translations was prepared by Girard, although it is unclear which one is Girard's. The other set seems to have been prepared by an associate of Cymbalista's American counsel. The confusion was compounded when an officer of Girard was cross-examined by Cymbalista's counsel. The witness was requested to read exhibit 4(T) into the record. What he actually read, as stenographically recorded in the notes of testimony, corresponds to the document in the record labeled 2(T). At the close of the trial, Intraworld's counsel objected to the admission of 2(T). However, Intraworld's counsel failed to object when the officer of Girard read 2(T) into the notes of testimony. In any event, we find the differences between the translations to be immaterial. The translations we have quoted are exhibits 1(T) and 2(T).

The November action was terminated on December 6, 1973, by agreement of all parties. Pursuant to the agreement, Girard placed $100,000.00 in escrow with a Swiss bank, with entitlement to that fund to be determined by the courts of Switzerland.

The situation remained unchanged for about six months. The rent due on May 10, 1974, was not paid. On May 21, 1974, Cymbalista's American counsel presented to Girard a draft for $100,000.00 under Credit No. 35799, accompanied by conforming documentation. Girard immediately advised Intraworld that it intended to honor the draft.

On May 24, Intraworld filed this equity action in the Court of Common Pleas of Philadelphia. It sought preliminary and permanent injunctions restraining Girard from honoring Cymbalista's draft under the letter of credit. The court issued a preliminary restraining order and set a date for a hearing. Cymbalista again petitioned for leave to intervene, which the court granted on May 29.

After the filing of additional pleadings, including preliminary objections and an amended complaint, a hearing was held and testimony taken on May 30 and 31, 1974. On July 11, the trial court issued a memorandum and decree in which it denied a preliminary injunction. Intraworld has appealed to this Court.[10] We affirm.

At the outset we note the limited scope of our review:

> 'In *Pa. P.U.C. v. Alleg. Co. Port Auth.*, 433 Pa. 495, 499, 252 A.2d 367 (1969), we stated that: 'It has long been the rule in this Court that on an appeal from a decree, whether granting or denying a preliminary injunction, we will not inquire into the merits of the controversy, but will, instead, examine the record only to determine if there were any apparently reasonable grounds for the actions of the court below. (Citing cases.) Moreover, we will not 'pass upon the reasons for or against such action unless it is plain that no such grounds existed or that the rules of law relied on are palpably wrong or clearly not applicable . . ..'''

Credit Alliance Corp. v. Philadelphia Minit-Man Car Wash Corp., 450 Pa. 367, 370--71, 301 A.2d 816, 818 (1973) (citations omitted).

* * * * *

Letters of credit have long served as a financial device in international sales of

---

[10] Appellate Court Jurisdiction Act of 1970, Act of July 31, 1970, P.L. 673, art. II, § 202(4), 17 P.S. § 211.202(4) (Supp.1974); *see* 17 P.S. § 211.501(a) and Act of June 12, 1879, P.L. 177, § 1, 12 P.S. § 1102 (1953); *cf.* 17 P.S. § 211.509(g)(22).

goods.[11] The primary purpose of a letter of credit is to provide assurance to the seller of good, (*i.e.*, the 'beneficiary,' *see* 12A P.S. § 5-103(1)(d)) of prompt payment upon presentation of documents. A seller who would otherwise have only the solvency and good faith of his buyer as assurance of payment may, with a letter of credit, rely on the full responsibility of a bank. Promptness is assured by the engagement of the bank to honor drafts upon the presentation of documents.

The great utility of letters of credit flows from the independence of the issuer-bank's engagement from the underlying contract between beneficiary and customer. Long-standing case law has established that, unless otherwise agreed, the issuer deals only in documents. If the documents presented conform to the requirements of the credit, the issuer may and must honor demands for payment, regardless of whether the goods conform to the underlying contract between beneficiary and customer. Absent its agreement to the contrary, the issuer is, under the general rule, not required or even permitted to go behind the documents to determine if the beneficiary has performed in conformity with the underlying contract. (Citations omitted).

This principle of the issuer's right and obligation to honor upon presentation of conforming documents has been codified in 12A P.S. § 5-114:

'(1) An issuer must honor a draft or demand for payment which complies with the terms of the relevant credit regardless of whether the goods or documents conform to the underlying contract for sale or other contract between the customer and the beneficiary. . . .

'(2) Unless otherwise agreed when documents appear on their face to comply with the terms of a credit but a required document . . . is forged of fraudulent or there is fraud in the transaction

'(b) in all other cases as against its customer, an issuer acting in good faith may honor the draft or demand for payment despite notification from the customer of fraud, forgery or other defect not apparent on the face of the documents but a court of appropriate jurisdiction may enjoin such honor.'

Intraworld seeks to enjoin honor under 12A P.S. § 5-114(2)(b) on the basis that there is 'fraud . . . not apparent on the face of the documents.' It points to what

---

[11] For an illustration of the operation of a letter of credit in an international sales transaction, *see* J. White & R. Summers, HANDBOOK OF THE LAW UNDER THE UNIFORM COMMERCIAL CODE § 18-1 (1972); *and see Kingdom of Sweden v. New York Trust Co.*, 197 Misc. 431, 441, 96 N.Y.S.2d 779, 788 (Sup.Ct.1949).

it believes are two respects in which Cymbalista's demand for payment and supporting documentation are false and fraudulent, although conceding that the documents on their face conform to the credit. First, it contends that Cymablista's statement (as required by the credit) that 'lessee . . . has not paid the installment of rent due under said lease on May 10, 1974,' is false and fraudulent because, after Cymbalista purported to terminate the lease in September, 1973, Intraworld was not obligated to pay rent and because the statement failed to disclose the termination of the lease. Second, it argues that the demand is fraudulent because Cymbalista is not seeking rent at all (as, Intraworld contends, she represents in the documents) but rather the 'stipulated penalty' pursuant to the Nachtrag.

In light of the basic rule of the independence of the issuer's engagement and the importance of this rule to the effectuation of the purposes of the letter of credit, we think that the circumstances which will justify an injunction against honor must be narrowly limited to situations of fraud in which the wrongdoing of the beneficiary has so vitiated the entire transaction that the legitimate purposes of the independence of the issuer's obligation would no longer be served. A court of equity has the limited duty of

> 'guaranteeing that (the beneficiary) not by allowed to take unconscientious advantage of the situation and run off with plaintiff's money on a *pro forma* declaration which has *absolutely no basis in fact.*' *Dynamics Corp. of America v. Citizens and Southern National Bank*, 356 F.Supp. 991, 999 (N.D.Ga.1973) (emphasis supplied).

The leading case on the question of what conduct will justify an injunction against honor is *Sztejn v. J. Henry Schroder Banking Corp.*, 177 Misc. 719, 31 N.Y.S.2d 631 (Sup.Ct.1941). In that case as here, the customer sought an injunction against the issuer of a letter of credit restraining honor of a draft drawn by the beneficiary. The customer had contracted to purchase a quantity of bristles from the beneficiary and arranged to have the issuer issue a letter of credit in favor of the beneficiary. The credit required that the draft be accompanied by an invoice and bill of lading.

The beneficiary placed fifty cases of merchandise on a steamship and obtained a bill of lading describing the material as bristles. The beneficiary then drew a draft and presented it, along with the required documents, through a collecting bank. The customer's complaint alleged that the material shipped was not bristles as described in the documents, but rather 'cowhair, other worthless material and rubbish (shipped) with intent to simulate genuine merchandise and defraud the plaintiff . . . .'

The collecting bank moved to dismiss the complaint for failure to state a cause of action. The court, assuming the pleaded facts to be true, denied the motion. The court recognized that the issuer's obligation was independent from the underlying contract between customer and beneficiary. That independence is predicated, however, on the genuineness of the documents. The court noted:

> 'This is not a controversy between the buyer and seller concerning a mere breach of warranty regarding the quality of the merchandise; on the present motion, it must be assumed that the seller has intentionally failed to ship any goods ordered by the buyer.'

177 Misc. at 721, 31 N.Y.S.2d at 634. When the beneficiary has intentionally shipped no goods at all, the court held, the documentation was not genuine and therefore the predicate of the independence of the issuer's engagement was removed.

We conclude that, if the documents presented by Cymbalista are genuine in the sense of having some basis in fact, an injunction must be refused. An injunction is proper only if Cymbalista, comparable to the beneficiary in Sztejn, has no bona fide claim to payment under the lease. *Dynamics Corp. of America v. Citizens and Southern National Bank*, 356 F.Supp. 991, 999 (N.D.Ga.1973). Of course, neither the trial court nor this Court may attempt to determine Cymbalista's actual entitlement to payment under the lease. Such is not the proper standard for the grant or denial of an injunction against honor. Moreover, questions of rights and obligations under the lease are required by the lease to be determined under Swiss law in the courts of Switzerland. *See Dynamics Corp. of America v. Citizens and Southern National Bank, supra*.

On this record, we are unable to conclude that Intraworld established that Cymbalista has no bona fide claim to payment or that the documents presented to Girard have absolutely no basis in fact. Intraworld's argument rests on the basic premise that the lease was terminated in September, 1973. From this premise Intraworld asserts the falsity of Cymbalista's representations that she is the lessor and that the rent was due and unpaid. However, Intraworld did not attempt to prove to the trial court that, under Swiss law, Cymbalista's attempted termination was effective. In fact, Intraworld's Swiss counsel informed Cymbalista's counsel on November 7, 1973, that Intraworld 'cannot agree with your position according to which the lease contract can be considered as terminated . . ..' Counsel added that Cymbalista was 'at liberty to obtain payment by way of' the letters of credit. Thus, Intraworld failed to prove that, under Swiss law, Cymbalista had no bona fide claim to rent under the lease despite Intraworld's repudiation of termination.

Intraworld's argument that Cymbalista fraudulently concealed the purported termination from Girard is unpersuasive. When presenting the draft and documents to Girard in November, 1973, Cymbalista's American counsel candidly admitted that 'our client, as Lessor, takes the position that the lease has terminated . . . for various reasons . . ..' In addition, Girard was a party to the first equity action and its counsel joined the agreement which terminated that action. Cymbalista could reasonably have assumed in May, 1974, that Girard was fully aware of the positions of both Intraworld and Cymbalista.

Intraworld's further contention that Cymbalista's demand was fraudulent in that she was not seeking 'rent' at all but the 'stipulated penalty' pursuant to the Nachtrag is more substantial but, under scrutiny, also fails. It argues that payment under the credit was permitted only for 'rent,' and that Cymbalista (as she concedes) was in fact seeking the 'stipulated penalty,' which is not 'rent.' Intraworld concludes that Cymbalista was fraudulently attempting to draw under the credit for satisfaction of an obligation not secured by the credit. There are two flaws in this argument.

First, we are not persuaded that the credit was issued for payment of 'rent,' narrowly defined, only. The letter of credit (*see* note 7 *supra*) authorized Cymbalista to draw 'the sum . . . due . . . under (the) lease,' without specifying that the 'sum due' contemplated was only 'rent.' The letter required that a draft must be accompanied by Cymbalista's statement that 'the lessee . . . has not paid the installment of rent due under said lease.' This is not equivalent to a limitation on availability of the credit only for nonpayment of rent; in fact, such non-payment of rent is precisely the condition which triggers Cymbalista's entitlement to the 'stipulated penalty.' In short, Intraworld has failed to persuade us that the letter of credit was not available to Cymbalista for satisfaction of the 'stipulated penalty.'

Second and more important, the Nachtrag does not, in our view, create the sharp distinction between 'rent' and 'stipulated penalty' that Intraworld hypothesizes. It provides that '(i)n the event the lessee should not fulfill its obligation to pay, so that the letter of credit must be used,' then the lessor was entitled to terminate the lease and 'retain the *rent* paid or *guaranteed* (by the letters of credit) for the following year as a stipulated penalty for non-performance of the contract . . ..' (Emphasis supplied.) Because Intraworld did fail to pay the rent due on November 10, 1973, and May 10, 1974, Cymbalista could reasonably and in good faith have concluded that she had the right to draw on the credit for the 'rent . . . guaranteed for the following year.'

Whether Intraworld was in fact obligated to pay the rent nonpayment of which triggered Cymbalista's right to retain the 'rent guaranteed' by the credit or whether Cymbalista is not entitled to the 'stipulated penalty' for some other reason are questions to be decided under Swiss law in the courts of Switzerland. We hold only that Intraworld failed to establish that Cymbalista lacked a bona fide claim to the 'rent . . . guaranteed . . . as a stipulated penalty' or that her demand under the credit lacked some basis in fact. Therefore, her documented demand was not shown to be fraudulent because she was seeking satisfaction of the 'stipulated penalty.'

In summary, we are unable to conclude on this record that Intraworld succeeded in proving that Cymbalista had no bona fide claim for payment under the lease and that her documented demand had absolutely no basis in fact. Accordingly, it is clear that there is an apparently reasonable ground for refusing an injunction.

In addition, Intraworld alleged in its complaint and contends in this Court that Girard's decision to honor Cymbalista's draft was not formed in good faith.[12] Intraworld asserts that Girard's bad faith constituted an additional ground justifying an injunction. It is clear that an issuer of a letter of credit must act in good faith, *see* 12A P.S. §§ 5-114(2)(b), 5-109(1). However, we are not persuaded that issuer bad faith is a circumstance justifying an injunction against honor; in most if not all instances of issuer bad faith, it would seem that a customer would have an adequate remedy at law in a claim against the issuer or a defense against the issuer's claim for reimbursement. In any event, in this case Intraworld has failed to prove the existence of bad faith on the part of Girard. It has proved no more than that Girard failed to resolve the dispute over the rights and obligations of the parties to the lease in Intraworld's favor. This Girard was not obligated to do. Its obligations included a careful scrutiny of the documents, but once it determined that the documents conformed to the requirements of the credit, it bore no responsibility for the performance of the lease obligations or the genuineness of the documents. 12A P.S. § 5-109(1)(a) & (2). It would, we think, place an issuer in an intolerable position if the law compelled it to serve at its peril as an arbitrator of contract disputes between customer and beneficiary.

'The question between the customer and the bank which issues the letter of credit is whether the documents presented with the draft fulfill the specific requirements, and if they do . . ., the bank has the right to pay the draft no matter what may be the defects in the goods which have been shipped. The bank is not obliged to assume the burdens of a controversy

---

[12] *See* 12A P.S. § 1-201(19); *cf.* 12A P.S. § 2-103(1)(b).

between the beneficiary and customer and incur the responsibility of establishing as an excuse for not paying a draft that the customer's version is the correct one.'

Laudisi v. American Exchange National Bank, 239 N.Y. 234, 243, 146 N.E. 347, 350 (1924); (citations omitted).

* * * * *

MID-AMERICA TIRE, INC. V. PTZ TRADING LTD.
768 N.E.2d 619 (Ohio 2002)

Alice Robie Resnick, J.

I. FACTS
A. Overview

These appeals arise out of an action brought in the Clermont County Court of Common Pleas to enjoin payment under a letter of credit ("LC") on the basis of fraud in the underlying transaction. The underlying transaction involved extensive overseas negotiations toward an agreement to import blemished Michelin tires for sale in the United States. A blemished or "blem" tire is one that is cosmetically but not operationally affected by a surface imperfection.

The gravamen of the fraud claim is that the overseas seller's agents made certain false promises and representations concerning the sale of more lucrative summer tires in order to induce the American buyers to purchase and open an LC securing the purchase of less lucrative mud and snow tires, many of which could not legally be imported or sold in the United States. The buyers claim that they discovered the fraud after the LC was issued and instructed the seller not to ship the tires, but the seller went ahead with shipment anyway and presented its invoice and shipping documents for payment under the supporting LC. The buyers then instituted this action pursuant to R.C. 1305.08(B), [U.C.C. 5-109-ed.] alleging that honoring the LC in this case would facilitate and consummate the seller's fraud.

B. Parties and Participants

Given the multilateral nature of the negotiations and arrangements in this case, it is beneficial to provide a working list of the various parties and key participants and their relationships to one another and the transactions at hand.

The American parties and participants are as follows:

(1) Plaintiff-appellant and cross-appellee, Mid-America Tire, Inc. ("Mid-America"), is an Ohio corporation doing business as a tire wholesaler. Mid-America provided the financing for the purchase of the tires in this case and was the named applicant by whose order and for whose account the LC was issued.

(2) Arthur Hine is the president of Mid-America and signatory to the LC application.

(3) Plaintiff-appellant and cross-appellee, Jenco Marketing, Inc. ("Jenco"), is a Tennessee corporation doing business as a tire wholesaler. Jenco formed a joint venture with Mid-America to purchase the tires at issue.

(4) Fred Alvin "F.A." Jenkins is the owner of Jenco and also acted as Mid-America's agent in the underlying negotiations.

(5) Paul Chappell is an independent tire broker who resides in Irvine, California. Chappell works as an independent contractor for Tire Network, Inc., a company owned by his wife, and acted throughout most of the negotiations as an agent for Jenco.

(6) First National Bank of Chicago ("First National"), on behalf of NBD Bank Michigan, is the issuer of the LC in this case. First National was a defendant below, but is not a party to this appeal.

The European parties and participants are as follows:

(1) Defendant-appellee and cross-appellant, PTZ Trading Ltd. ("PTZ"), is an offshore import and export company established in Guernsey, Channel Islands. PTZ is the seller in the underlying transaction and the beneficiary under the LC.

(2) Gary Corby is an independent tire broker operating as Corby International, a trading name of Corby Tyres (Wholesale) Ltd., in Wales, United Kingdom. Corby was the initiator of the underlying negotiations. The trial court's findings with regard to Corby's status as PTZ's agent form the subject of PTZ's cross-appeal.

(3) John Evans is the owner of Transcontinental Tyre Company located in Wolverhampton, England, and PTZ's admitted agent in the underlying negotiations.

(4) Aloysius Sievers is a German tire broker to whom PTZ owed money from a previous transaction unconnected to this case. Sievers, also an admitted agent for PTZ, procured and shipped the subject tires on behalf of PTZ, and signed and presented the draft for payment under the LC.

(5) Patrick Doumerc is the son of the proprietor of Doumerc SA, a French company that is authorized to sell Michelin overstock or surplus tires worldwide. Doumerc is the person from whom Sievers procured the mud and snow tires for sale to Jenco and Mid-America.

(6) Barclays Bank PLC in St. Peter Port, Guernsey, is the bank to which

Sievers presented the invoice and shipping documents for payment under the supporting LC. Barclays Bank was a defendant below, but is not a party to this appeal.

C. Events Leading to the Issuance of the LC

In October 1998, Corby approached Evans about obtaining large quantities of Michelin winter tires. Evans contacted Sievers, to whom PTZ owed money. Evans knew that Sievers had a relationship with a sole distributor of Michelin surplus tires out of France. Eventually, an arrangement was worked out under which Sievers would buy the tires from Doumerc's warehouse in France and Evans would sell them on behalf of PTZ through Corby to an American purchaser.

Meanwhile, Corby contacted Chappell in California and asked whether he was interested in importing Michelin tires on the gray market for sale in the United States. "Gray imports" are tires that are imported without the knowledge or approval of a manufacturer into a market that the manufacturer serves, at a greatly reduced price. Corby told Chappell that he had a large client who negotiated an arrangement directly with Michelin to handle all of its overstock blem tires from France and who could offer 50,000 to 70,000 Michelin tires per quarter at 40 to 60 percent below the United States market price on an exclusive and ongoing basis. Chappell contacted Jenkins in Tennessee, who called Hine in Ohio, and it was arranged that Jenco and Mid- America would pursue the deal through Chappell.

On October 28, 1998, Corby faxed Chappell a list of Michelin mud and snow tires that were immediately available for shipment and Chappell forwarded the list to Jenkins. The list was arranged in columns for quantity, size, pattern, and other designations applicable to the European market with which Chappell and Jenkins were unfamiliar. In particular, many of the tires on the list bore the designation "DA/2C." Chappell and Jenkins understood that DA meant "defective appearance," a European marking for a blem, but they were not familiar with the "/2C" portion of the designation. When they asked for clarification, Corby told Chappell that "DA/2C" means the same thing as "DA," but since all of the listed tires are not warehoused at a single location, "/2C" is used merely to indicate that those blemished tires are located in a different warehouse.

Chappell also asked Corby whether he could procure and offer summer or "highway" tires, along with the winter tires. Chappell, Jenkins, and Hine had no interest in purchasing strictly snow tires, as it was already too late in the season to market them profitably. However, they would have an interest in buying both winter and highway tires and marketing them together as a package deal.

Corby told Chappell that 50,000 to 70,000 highway tires would be made available on a quarterly basis at 40 to 60 percent below the United States market price. However, when Chappell received another list of available tires from Corby on November 11, 1998, he complained to Corby that this list contained no summer tires and nowhere near 50,000 units. Corby responded that Michelin was anxious to get rid of these tires first, as the market for snow tires in Europe was coming to a close, that a list of summer highway tires would be made available over the next few weeks, and that Chappell and appellants would not have an opportunity to procure the highway tires unless they first agreed to purchase the snow tires. Corby explained that Michelin does not list available summer tires in the mid-month of a quarter. Instead, it waits for these tires to accumulate in a warehouse and then puts out the list at the end of the month. Thus, a list of summer tires would be available over the next few weeks.

In a transmission dated November 13, 1998, Corby wrote to Chappell:

"The situation is as I explained yesterday, there are no summer tyres available at all but, if, and a very big if, this deal goes ahead we will get all surplus stocks at the end [of] each qu[arter] from now on, but if this deal does not go, then I know we can kiss any future offers good buy [sic]."

On November 20, 1998, Corby faxed Chappell a list of summer tires available for immediate shipment, but the listed units were not priced, were composed of many small "odd ball sizes" unmarketable in the United States, and did not approach the 50- to 70,000-range in aggregate quantity. In his cover letter, Corby assured Chappell that "I have of course been in contact with Michelin regarding the list of summer tyres" and "they have confirmed that in the next three/four weeks we have exclusive to us the new list of Michelin summer tyres, quantity unknown as yet, but they believe to be anything from 50,000/70,000 tyres, which would not be too bad for Jan sales." The letter also stated that Michelin was offering the tires at "the price of $1.50 per tyre more than the M & S tyres * * * based on taking the whole lot."

On November 23, 1998, Corby faxed the following letter to Jenkins:

"Subject: Michelin Tyre Programme.

"Dear F.A.

"I would just like to confirm our current position with the Off-Shore marketing company that have been authorised to sell all Michelin factory 'Over Stock' tyres. That is, from now on the tyres will only be offered for sale to us through PTZ Trading Ltd., these tyres will come available every two/three months which I have been informed by my contact the next large consignment (not including the current stock of winter/summer tyres) will be in the next three/four weeks time of around 50,000/70,000 tyres.

"If our business with the winter tyres goes well, then I see this as [an] extremely excellent opportunity to tap into large consignments of tyres direct from the factory on a regular long term basis.

"Just to confirm once again, I have been assured by PTZ Trading who are acting on behalf of the factory that we will have exclusivity to all tyres that come available from now on."

On December 1, 1998, Evans faxed a letter and "pro forma invoice" (an invoice that sets out in rough terms what the eventual invoice will look like) to Jenkins. The letter stated, "We understand from Gary Corby that you are now about to open the Letter of Credit for the Michelin M&S Tyres."

However, Chappell and Jenkins were hesitant to have Hine proceed with the financing for the winter tires because they had not yet received concrete information as to the cost and availability of the initial 50,000 to 70,000 summer tires. As Chappell and Jenkins held out for the list of summer tires, Corby and Evans pressed for the LC. While continually assuring Chappell and Jenkins that large stocks of Michelin summer tires will be made available in a short time, Corby and Evans became increasingly insistent about conditioning the offer of summer tires upon the issuance of an acceptable LC in favor of PTZ for the winter tires.

From early December 1998, through late January 1999, Corby made repeated, often daily, telephone calls to Chappell insisting that Jenkins confirm the issuance of the LC or forfeit the deal entirely. During this time, Corby also sent a number of faxes to Chappell, each one proclaiming that without confirmation of the LC by the end of the day, the offer for the winter tires would be withdrawn and there would be no future offers for winter or summer tires.

In addition, Evans faxed two messages to Jenkins on January 7, 1999. In the first, Evans wrote:

"There are large stocks of Michelin summer pattern tyres being made available within the next 7/10 days and we will be pleased to offer these to you when an acceptable Letter of Credit is received for the winter pattern tyres. We will be very happy to work with you on Michelin tyres on a long term basis and give you first option on offers.

"May we once again stress the urgency of letting us have the Letter of Credit for the Michelin winter tyres so that we can commence business on a long term basis."

In the second message, Evans informed Jenkins:

"Further to our fax of today we understand that you would like clarification on future offers made by PTZ Trading Ltd. of Michelin tyres.

"As we have already indicated we wish to commence a long term business relationship with Jenco Marketing Ltd. [Sic.] We assure you that we will not offer any Michelin tyres that we obtain to any other party in the United States of America provided Jenco Marketing Inc. agree[s] to purchase in a reasonable time."

D. The Issuance of the LC

By the end of January 1999, Jenkins and Hine were convinced that they had to open the LC for the winter tires as a show of good faith towards the quarterly acquisition of summer tires and that, upon doing so, PTZ would honor its end of the bargain.

Effective February 1, 1999, and expiring in Guernsey, Channel Islands, on April 2, 1999, First National issued an irrevocable credit at Hine's request in favor of PTZ and for the account of Mid-America in the amount of $517,260.33. The LC provided, among other things:

"COVERING SHIPMENT OF:

"14,851 MICHELIN TYPES AT USD 34.83 PER TIRE IN ACCORDANCE WITH SELLER'S PROFORMA INVOICE 927-98 DATED 11-19-98

"SHIPPING TERMS: EXWORKS ANY EUROPEAN LOCATION

"* * *

"THE CREDIT IS SUBJECT TO THE UNIFORM CUSTOMS AND PRACTICE FOR DOCUMENTARY CREDITS (1993 REVISION), INTERNATIONAL CHAMBER OF COMMERCE - PUBLICATION 500."

E. Events Following the Issuance of the LC

Over the next month, Corby and Evans pushed for shipping arrangements under the supporting LC for the winter tires, while Chappell and Jenkins continued to insist on a conforming price list for the summer tires. As the final LC shipping date approached, and several nonconforming lists of summer tires emerged, the negotiations grew increasingly volatile until they were hostilely terminated.

A week after the issuance of the LC, Chappell wrote to Corby, "Without the list and pricing [for the summer tires], we are at a standstill with the clock ticking on the winters. Please make every effort to send list during your workday, so we can compile our list for combined sales of both winter and summer units." Corby then faxed Chappell a list of summer tires but, as before, this list contained no prices and fell considerably short of 50,000 units. When Chappell complained, Corby sent another list, which he noted to be six out of 15 sheets of an "original list from Michelin." The other nine sheets, however, were never sent. In any event, this list once again failed to contain the promised quantities of tires, and a considerable number of the listed units were snow tires. Although this list did set forth unit prices, those prices were represented in French francs, and when the French francs were converted into United States dollars, it became apparent that the prices for these units were equal to or in excess of the maximum market prices for a like product in the United States.

On the morning of February 17, 1999, Evans telephoned Jenkins to inform him that no price list for summer tires would be sent until Barclays Bank received the LC for the winter tires. This caught Jenkins by surprise, as the LC had been in place since the first of the month and all information pertaining thereto had previously been sent to Evans, but Jenkins nevertheless faxed Evans the LC confirmation number. Throughout that day, Evans made repeated requests for Jenkins to provide him with shipping instructions and orders to release the winter tires. Jenkins responded with several letters that he faxed to Evans on February 17. In these letters, Jenkins informed Evans that he would not authorize the shipment of any winter tires in the absence of a conforming list of summer tires, that any attempt by Evans to ship the winter tires without Jenkins's written consent would be met with legal action, and that the deal would be voided and the LC recalled unless a complete list of competitively priced summer tires arrived in Jenkins's office by February 19.

On February 19, 1999, Evans faxed the following message to Jenkins:

"We appreciate your feeling of frustration at the delay in giving you the price for the Summer Tyres but assure you it is only in your best interests to obtain the most favourable prices.

* * *

Further urgent negotiations are due to take place with Michelin on Monday February 22nd 1999 to see if we can arrive at an acceptable packaged price but of course the final desission [sic] is yours.

In the meantime in the interests of all concerned please do not give a specific time for completion if you want us to obtain the most favourable price."

On February 23, 1999, Corby faxed Chappell another list of summer tires, but this list was illegible in places and irreconcilable with the previous list. Chappell complained and Corby sent another list the following day. However, once again, this list fell well short of 50,000 units, contained many European sizes not used in the United States and various tires not manufactured by Michelin, and stated prices that were often higher than the cost of purchasing the tires one at a time from most United States dealers. The list also provided that, in addition to the stated prices, appellants were required to pay all shipping, handling, duty, and freight charges. Moreover, Jenkins was now informed that he could no longer pick and choose from among the listed tires, but instead must purchase the entire lot or none at all.

On March 1, 1999, Jenkins wrote to Evans, "We are with drawing [sic] our offer effective immediately to purchase the snow package, as PTZ has failed to meet their agreed commitment on the Michelin summer tire offer." (Emphasis deleted.) Jenkins stated that the listed prices for the tires are "not competitive" and "TOTALLY UNACCEPTABLE," and that "[w]e have gone from a reported 50,000 tires to a total offer of about 12,000 tires of which approximately 2,500 of those are TRX tires not sold in this country."

Between March 1 and March 5, 1999, Chappell and Jenkins discovered that it was Doumerc, not PTZ, who all along had the direct and exclusive relationship with Michelin to sell all of its overstock and blem tires. They also discovered that Corby had misrepresented the "DA/2C" designation, which attached to many of the tires on the summer lists as well as on the original winter list. Rather than indicating the warehousing location for those tires, "/2C" actually meant that the Department of Transportation serial numbers had been buffed off those units, rendering them illegal for import or sale in the United States.

During this time, Jenkins informed Evans that he would notify the United States Customs Service if the DA/2C tires were shipped, and Evans confirmed that he would not ship those tires to the United States. Also, Chappell informed Doumerc of the entire course of events, and Doumerc agreed not to ship the tires until Chappell and Jenkins had the opportunity to come to France, inspect the tires, and resolve the situation.

Chappell and Jenkins made arrangements to fly to France, but when they called Doumerc on March 11, Sievers answered the phone. They explained the entire matter to Sievers and offered to extend the LC expiration date in order to allow for a peaceful resolution. Sievers rejected the offer, however, stating that the winter tires belonged to him, not Doumerc, that he did not care what Doumerc had agreed to, and that "I have a letter of credit and I am shipping the tires."

The following day, Mid-America instituted the present action to enjoin payment under the LC. The complaint was later amended to add Jenco as a plaintiff. The trial court granted a temporary restraining order on March 16, 1999, and a preliminary injunction on April 8, 1999.

On July 14 and 15, 1999, a trial was held on appellants' motion for a permanent injunction. In a final judgment entry dated October 8, 1999, the trial court granted a permanent injunction against honor or presentment under the LC pursuant to R.C. 1305.08(B). In its separate findings of fact and conclusions of law, the trial court found that the documents presented to Barclays Bank on behalf of PTZ appeared on their face to be in strict compliance with the terms and conditions of the LC. However, the court also found by clear and convincing evidence that PTZ, acting through Evans and Corby, fraudulently induced appellants to open the LC, and that such fraud was sufficient to vitiate the LC. In this regard, the trial court was "satisfied that fraud in the inducement of the issuance of a letter of credit is grounds for a court to grant injunctive relief against the payment of such letter of credit to the beneficiary who perpetrated such fraud."

In a split decision, the court of appeals reversed the judgment of the trial court. In so doing, the majority noted that the LC in this case is expressly made subject to the Uniform Customs and Practice for Documentary Credits (Rev.1993), International Chamber of Commerce, Publication No. 500 ("UCP"). Thus, in this case the UCP's terms replace those of R.C. 1305.08(B) with respect to the issues of whether and under what circumstances honor may be enjoined on the basis of fraud. The majority then found that the UCP embodies the "independence principle," under which the issuing bank's duty to honor a conforming presentment is independent of the underlying transaction. Because the UCP is silent as to any fraud exception to the independence principle, the majority concluded that the UCP necessarily precludes the enjoinment of LC honor on the basis of fraud in the underlying transaction.

The appeals court also examined cases decided under former UCC 5-114, which provided an exception to the independence principle where "there is fraud in the transaction." Based on these decisions, the court of appeals recognized that LC honor may be enjoined by a court when the beneficiary commits a fraud so extensive as to vitiate the entire transaction. However, the majority felt that this exception should be narrowly construed to require that the beneficiary's fraud occur in the credit transaction. Thus, the court decided that injunctive relief may be granted on the basis of a beneficiary's presentation of forged or fraudulent documents under an LC, but that such relief may not be granted on the basis of the beneficiary's commission of fraud solely in the underlying sales transaction. After finding that the invoice and shipping documents presented to Barclays Bank on behalf of PTZ conformed strictly to the LC in this case, the majority held the exception inapplicable and injunctive relief inappropriate.

The cause is now before this court pursuant to the allowance of a discretionary appeal and cross-appeal.

II. ISSUES FOR REVIEW

The issue generally presented by both appeals is whether the trial court abused its discretion in granting a permanent injunction against LC honor under the facts and circumstances of this case.

* * * *

III. MID-AMERICA AND JENCO'S APPEAL
A. Inadequate Legal Remedy

PTZ argues, and the court of appeals held, that appellants should be denied injunctive relief under R.C. 1305.08(B) because they have an adequate remedy at law. Appellants claim that the common-law requirement of irreparable injury is not one of the prerequisites for injunctive relief under R.C. 1305.08(B) and that, in any event, Mid-America does not have an adequate legal remedy.

It is well settled that an injunction will not issue where there is an adequate remedy at law. (Citations omitted).

However, there is one exception to this rule. "It is established law in Ohio that, when a statute grants a specific injunctive remedy to an individual or to the state, the party requesting the injunction 'need not aver and show, as under ordinary rules in equity, that great or irreparable injury is about to be done for which he has no adequate remedy at law.'" *Ackerman v. Tri-City Geriatric & Health Care, Inc.* (1978), 55 Ohio St.2d 51, 56, 9 O.O.3d 62, 378 N.E.2d 145, *quoting Stephan v. Daniels* (1875), 27 Ohio St. 527, 536, 1875 WL 203. (Citation omitted).

* * * *

[T]he court of appeals correctly noted that one of the stated requirements for injunctive relief under R.C. 1305.08 is that "[a]ll of the conditions to entitle a person to the relief under the law of this state have been met." R.C. 1305.08(B)(3). By virtue of this language, the General Assembly has incorporated into the statute all of the burdens usually imposed upon parties seeking equitable relief, including the requirement that a person seeking injunctive relief must establish the lack of an adequate remedy at law. *See* 6B Hawkland & Miller, UNIFORM COMMERCIAL CODE SERIES (Rev.2001) 5-155, Section 5-109:3, fn. 5, and 5-161, Section 5- 109:4 ("Irreparable injury is an oft stated requirement for injunctive relief"); 7A LAWRENCE'S ANDERSON ON THE UNIFORM COMMERCIAL CODE (Rev.2001) 595, Section 5-109:32.

We hold, therefore, that in order for a court of competent jurisdiction to enjoin the issuer of a letter of credit from honoring a presentation under R.C. 1305.08(B), the court must find that the applicant has no adequate remedy at law.

In actions to enjoin honor on the basis of fraud, courts usually find that the applicant has an adequate remedy at law where the alleged injury is capable of being measured in pecuniary terms. While there is some authority to the contrary, most courts find that the availability of a monetary damage award for fraud in the underlying contract constitutes an adequate legal remedy, even if the applicant must travel overseas and submit to the uncertainties of foreign litigation in order to obtain it. On the other hand, the availability of a damage award is usually held to be inadequate where resort to foreign courts would be futile or meaningless, where the beneficiary is insolvent or may abscond with the money drawn, where honoring a draft would likely force the applicant into bankruptcy, or where the determination of damages would be difficult or speculative. (Citations omitted).

* * * [W]e find it necessary to stress that the determination of whether an available legal remedy is adequate must be made in accordance with the equitable principles as developed in each respective jurisdiction, and that those principles should not be applied any more liberally or strictly in LC cases than in other cases. Courts should not attempt to alter or manipulate an equitable requirement that is designed for broad-based remedial application in order to advance their personal views of whether and to what extent the legislature should or should not have recognized a fraud exception to the independence principle. R.C. 1305.08(B) already contains a legislative determination that the requirements for equitable relief "under the law of this state," in combination with the other statutory conditions for enjoining LC honor, strike the proper balance between preserving the integrity of the independence principle and preventing fraudulent practices by beneficiaries. Thus, there is neither reason nor legislative directive to apply the inadequate-legal-remedy requirement differently in LC cases than in other cases.

* * * *

In order to be considered adequate, the legal remedy must "be of such a nature that full indemnity may be recovered without a multiplicity of suits." (Citation omitted). "'It is not enough that there is a remedy at law; it must be plain, adequate and complete; or in other words, as practical, and as efficient to the ends of justice and its prompt administration, as the remedy in equity.'" *Culver v. Rodgers* (1878), 33 Ohio St. 537, 545, 1878 WL 23, *quoting Boyce v. Grundy* (1830), 3 Pet. 210, 28 U.S. 210, 215, 7 L.Ed. 655. (Citation omitted). Thus, in determining the propriety of injunctive relief, adequate remedy at law "means that the legal remedy must be as efficient as the indicated equitable remedy would be; that such legal remedy must be presently available in a single action; and that such remedy must be certain and complete." *Fuchs v. United Motor Stage Co., Inc.* (1939), 135 Ohio St. 509, 14 O.O. 399, 21 N.E.2d 669, paragraph four of the syllabus.

The adequacy of the putative legal remedy is also dependent upon whether "damages might be reasonably estimated." *Id.* at 521, 14 O.O. 399, 21 N.E.2d 669. Thus, injunctive relief will not be denied on this basis when " '[t]he damages which might be sought to be recovered in a court of law would be practically impossible of ascertainment, because of the difficulty of determining in advance the quantity of the commodities which will be used.' " *Id.* at 523, 14 O.O. 399, 21 N.E.2d 669, *quoting Hendler Creamery Co. v. Lillich* (1927), 152 Md. 190, 203-204, 136 A. 631.

In the present case, an action to recover damages for fraud would not be an adequate legal remedy because it would not be as prompt, efficient, and practical as the injunction issued by the trial court, and would not provide appellants with certain and complete relief in a single action. The pursuit of such a remedy would likely entail a multiplicity of suits against a number of defendants in several jurisdictions. The damages that appellants might seek to recover in an action for fraud would be difficult to estimate because of the near impossibility of determining the quantity of winter and summer tires that could or would have been seasonally marketed together and separately, the quantity of the "DA/2C" and other tires not marketable in the United States that could have been sold overseas, and the appropriate market conditions, cost/price differential, and quantity of offered or promised units. While it may be true, as PTZ argues, that appellants accepted some risk of pursuing damages in another nation's courts, it cannot be found that appellants assumed the risk of having to pursue an inadequate legal remedy.

Moreover, even if we agreed that appellants could obtain complete and prompt relief in a single action for fraud, we consider it contrary to the expeditious administration of justice to require that appellants now pursue such a remedy. PTZ did not raise the issue of an adequate legal remedy by motion, pleading, or otherwise, at any time prior to trial. Instead, after extensive discovery and a full trial on the merits, PTZ claimed that appellants had an adequate legal remedy for the first time in a post-trial brief. Under these circumstances, and in the interest of eliminating delay and unnecessary expense, PTZ must be found to have waived the issue. (Citation omitted).

Thus, we find that injunctive relief should not be refused in this case on the basis that Mid-America has an adequate remedy at law. Accordingly, the judgment of the court of appeals is reversed as to this issue.

B. Governing Law

R.C. Chapter 1305 is Ohio's version of Article 5 of the Uniform Commercial Code ("UCC"). It was enacted in its current form, effective July 1, 1998, to reflect the 1995 revision of Article 5, and is applicable to any LC that is issued on or after its effective date. See 1997 H.B. No. 338, uncodified Section 4.

Although R.C. Chapter 1305 is the primary source of law governing LCs in Ohio, it "is far from comprehensive." UCC 5-103, Official Comment 2 (1995). It is designed to cover only "certain rights and obligations arising out of transactions involving letters of credit." R.C. 1305.02(A). It is intended to be supplemented by various principles of law and equity that will often apply to help determine those rights and obligations. R.C. 1301.03. And subject to certain exceptions, it allows the parties to vary the effect of its provisions "by agreement or by a provision stated or incorporated by reference in an undertaking." R.C. 1305.02(C). *See, also,* R.C. 1301.02(C).

The parties in this case have specifically adopted the UCP as applicable to the present undertaking. In fact, "[m]any letters of credit, domestic and international, state that they shall be governed by the UCP." 3 White & Summers, UNIFORM COMMERCIAL CODE (4th Ed.1995) 122, Section 26-3. "When rules of custom and practice are incorporated by reference, they are considered to be explicit terms of the agreement or undertaking." UCC 5-103, Official Comment 2.

The question that naturally arises from such an incorporation is whether and to what extent R.C. Chapter 1305 will continue to apply to the undertaking. In other words, when a particular LC states that it is subject to the UCP, what is the resulting relationship between the UCP and R.C. Chapter 1305 with regard to that transaction?

* * * *

This is not a situation where one complete set of rules is substituted for another. The scope of the UCP is basically different from that of Article 5. "Because of their different scope, Article 5 [of the UCC] covers some important areas not covered by the UCP, and the UCP covers some important areas not covered by Article 5." 6B HAWKLAND & MILLER (Rev.2001), at 5-46 to 5- 47, Section 5-103:3. Each of these bodies of rules will apply to govern the undertaking in their respective areas of coverage, and both will apply concurrently in the event of any overlapping consistent provisions. Id. at 5-47, Section 5-103:3. *See, also,* 7A Lawrence (Rev.2001) 431, Section 5- 101:25.

It is only when the UCP and R.C. Chapter 1305 contain overlapping inconsistent provisions on the same issue or subject that the UCP's terms will displace those of R.C. Chapter 1305. Thus, when a particular LC states that it is subject to the UCP, the UCP's terms will replace those of R.C. Chapter 1305 only to the extent that "there is a direct conflict between a provision of the UCP and an analogous provision of R.C. Chapter 1305." *Mantua Mfg. Co. v. Commerce Exchange Bank* (1996), 75 Ohio St.3d 1, 661 N.E.2d 161, paragraph one of the syllabus. In other words, "the UCP terms are permissible contractual modifications under [R.C. 1301.02(C) and 1305.02(C)] * * * when a rule explicitly stated in the UCP * * * is different from a rule explicitly stated in Article 5." UCC 5- 103, Official Comment 2.

Thus, the fact that the credit in this case was expressly made subject to the UCP is not dispositive. Instead, the determinative issue is whether a direct conflict exists between the UCP and R.C. Chapter 1305 as to the availability of injunctive relief against honor where fraud is claimed.

R.C. 1305.02(D) provides:

"Rights and obligations of an issuer to a beneficiary or a nominated person under a letter of credit are independent of the existence, performance, or nonperformance of a contract or arrangement out of which the letter of credit arises or which underlies it, including contracts or arrangements between the issuer and the applicant and between the applicant and the beneficiary."

R.C. 1305.07(A) provides:

"Except as otherwise provided in section 1305.08 of the Revised Code, an issuer shall honor a presentation that * * * appears on its face strictly to comply with the terms and conditions of the letter of credit."

R.C. 1305.08(B) provides:

"If an applicant claims that a required document is forged or materially fraudulent or that honor of the presentation would facilitate a material fraud by the beneficiary on the issuer or applicant, a court of competent jurisdiction may temporarily or permanently enjoin the issuer from honoring a presentation."

The UCP also adopts the independence principle, but does not provide for a fraud exception. Article 3(a) of the UCP states:

"Credits, by their nature, are separate transactions from the sales or other contract(s) on which they may be based and banks are in no way concerned with or bound by such contract(s), even if any reference whatsoever to such contract(s) is included in the Credit. Consequently, the undertaking of a bank to pay, accept and pay Draft(s) or negotiate and/or to fulfill any other obligation under the Credit, is not subject to claims or defences by the Applicant resulting from his relationships with the Issuing Bank or the Beneficiary."

Article 4 explains, "In Credit operations all parties concerned deal with documents, and not with goods, services and/or other performances to which the documents may relate."

* * * *

In adopting the UCP, "the International Chamber of Commerce undertook to fill in operational details for documentary letter of credit transactions by stating a consensus view of the customs and practice for documentary credits." 6B Hawkland & Miller (Rev.2001), at 5-44, Section 5-103:3. Because "the UCP 'is by definition a recording of practice rather than a statement of legal rules,' [it] does not purport to offer rules which govern the issuance of an injunction against honor of a draft." *Intraworld Indus., Inc. v. Girard Trust Bank* (1975), 461 Pa. 343, 355, 336 A.2d 316, *quoting* Harfield, PRACTICE COMMENTARY (McKinney's Consol.Laws of N.Y., 1964), Comment 38. Thus, the UCP's silence on the issue of fraud "should not be construed as *preventing* relief under the 'fraud in the transaction' doctrine, where applicable law permits it." (Emphasis sic.) *Wyle v. Bank Melli of Tehran, Iran* (N.D.Ca.1983), 577 F.Supp. 1148, 1164.

In fact, the overwhelming weight of authority is to the effect that Article 5's fraud exception continues to apply in credit transactions made subject to the UCP. These courts hold, in one form or another, that the UCP's failure to include a rule governing injunctive relief for fraud does not prevent the applicant from obtaining such relief under Article 5. Stated variously, these courts recognize that there is no inherent conflict between the UCP's statement of the independence principle and Article 5's remedy against honor where fraud is charged. Instead, this is merely a situation where Article 5 covers a subject not covered by the UCP. (Citations omitted)

* * * *

We hold, therefore, that when a letter of credit expressly incorporates the terms of the UCP, but the UCP does not contain any rule covering the issue in controversy, the UCP will not replace the relevant provisions of R.C. Chapter 1305. Since the UCP does not contain any rule addressing the issue of injunctive relief where fraud occurs in either the credit documents or the underlying transaction, R.C. 1305.08(B) remains applicable in credit transactions made subject to the UCP.

Accordingly, the rights and obligations of the parties in this case are governed by R.C. 1305.08(B), and the judgment of the court of appeals is reversed as to this issue.

C. Establishing Fraud Under R.C. 1305.08(B)

Having determined the applicability of R.C. 1305.08(B), we must now consider its boundaries. In this regard, we have been asked to decide whether an issuer may be enjoined from honoring a presentation on the basis of beneficiary's fraud in the underlying transaction and to characterize the fraudulent activity justifying such relief.

1. Fraud in the Underlying Transaction

May the issuer be enjoined from honoring a presentation under R.C. 1305.08(B) on the basis of the beneficiary's fraudulent activity in the underlying transaction? The short answer is yes, since R.C. 1305.08(B) authorizes injunctive relief where "honor of the presentation would facilitate a material fraud by the beneficiary on the * * * applicant." To fully appreciate the import of this language, however, it is necessary to review some of the history leading to its adoption.

Before the independence principle was ever codified, its parameters were set in the seminal case of *Sztejn v. J. Henry Schroder Banking Corp.* (1941), 177 Misc. 719, 31 N.Y.S.2d 631. In that case, the applicant-buyer contracted to purchase a quantity of bristles from the beneficiary-seller, but the seller shipped 50 crates of cow hair and other rubbish. The court concluded that these facts, if established, could support an injunction against honor. In so doing, the court explained that the independence principle applies "in cases concerning alleged breaches of warranty," but does not extend to a case "involving an intentional fraud on the part of the seller." *Id.* at 722, 31 N.Y.S.2d 631. In other words, the fraud defense actually " 'marks the limit of the generally accepted principle that a letter of credit is independent of whatever obligation it secures.' " *E & H Partners,* 39 F.Supp.2d at 285, *quoting Rockwell Internatl. Sys., Inc. v. Citibank, N.A.* (C.A.2, 1983), 719 F.2d 583, 588.

As originally drafted in 1955, UCC 5-114 provided that a court of appropriate jurisdiction may enjoin honor only if there was forgery or fraud in a required document. (Citation omitted). In 1957, the drafters added language providing that the court may enjoin such honor where "a required document * * * is forged or fraudulent *or there is fraud in the transaction*." (Emphasis added.) UCC 5-114(2). This rule represents a codification of the *Sztejn* case. (Citations omitted).

One of the major disputes surrounding former UCC 5-114(2) centered on whether the "transaction" meant only the credit transaction per se or encompassed the underlying transaction as well. As White and Summers explain:

> "[W]hat is the 'transaction' in which the fraud must have been committed to give rise to the 5-114(2) defense? Must fraud be in the letter of credit transaction, or can it be in the underlying transaction? The courts and commentators are split on the issue whether 'transaction' refers only to the letter of credit transactions or also to the underlying transaction. Those in the 'credit transaction' camp would limit the 'fraud in the transaction' exception to those situations in which the beneficiary has committed fraud on the issuer or has submitted false documents to the issuer. Proponents of this view would argue that the fraud committed in the *Sztejn* case [177 Misc. 719, 31 N.Y.S.2d 631] equals fraud in the credit transaction because the documents the beneficiary presented to the issuer actively misrepresented the underlying transaction.

> "In contrast, advocates who argue that the word 'transaction' refers to the underlying transaction read *Sztejn* as a case in which the fraud existed in the underlying sales transaction because the buyer was going to receive rubbish instead of the goods he contracted for. Under this reading of the *Sztejn* case--and consequently under section 5-114(2)--an applicant has the right to enjoin the issuer's payment of a draft if the beneficiary has committed fraud on the applicant in the underlying transaction."

> (Footnotes omitted.)

Id. at 179-180, Section 26-10.

UCC 5-114(2) was adopted verbatim in Ohio under former R.C. 1305.13(B). In *State ex rel. Barclays Bank PLC v. Hamilton Cty. Court of Common Pleas* (1996), 74 Ohio St.3d 536, 540, 660 N.E.2d 458, fn. 4, the court acknowledged but declined to determine "the question of whether 'fraud in the transaction' in R.C. 1305.13(B) refers to fraud between the customer and the beneficiary in the underlying investment transaction or to fraud in the separate transaction of presentment of a draft for payment."

R.C. 1305.08(B) (UCC 5-109[b]) now provides that a court of competent jurisdiction may grant injunctive relief where "honor of the presentation would facilitate a material fraud by the beneficiary on the issuer or applicant." In so doing, R.C. 1305.08(B) refocuses the court's attention away from the particular transaction in which the fraud occurred and toward the level of fraud committed. *See* 3 WHITE & SUMMERS at 184, Section 26-10. It clarifies that the beneficiary's fraud in either transaction will suffice to enjoin the issuer from honoring a presentation, provided the fraud is material.

Thus, UCC 5-109, Official Comment 1, states:

"This recodification makes clear that fraud must be found *either* in the documents *or* must have been committed by the beneficiary on the issuer or applicant. See *Cromwell v. Commerce & Energy Bank,* 464 So.2d 721 (La.1985)." (Emphasis added.)

In *Cromwell,* the court explained:

"As illustrated in the foregoing cases the independence principle is a strong influence in the decision of cases throughout the country. Adherence to that basic principle is necessary in order to protect the commercial utility of letters of credit.

"Nevertheless, the jurisprudence and literature recognize and illustrate the need to extend the meaning of 'fraud in the transaction' at least a step beyond fraudulent documentation. The strongest reason for such an extended interpretation is to deny rewarding fraudulent conduct by letter of credit beneficiaries. One author writes:

" 'Notwithstanding dictum to the contrary in some of the cases, the holding of the court in *NMC Enterprises, Inc. v. Columbia Broadcasting System, Inc.* [(N.Y.Sup.1974), 14 U.C.C. Rep.Serv. 1427, 1974 WL 21758] that fraud in the underlying transaction is sufficient to justify relief is the better rule. Since the issuer's obligation on a letter of credit is generally completely independent of the underlying transaction, the customer who obtains a letter of credit assumes the risk that payment may be made when the beneficiary has not properly performed the underlying contract. Moreover, the beneficiary may have required the letter of credit in part to assure that a dispute regarding performance of the underlying contract would not delay payment. By obtaining a letter of credit, however, the customer should not be required to assume the risk of making payment to a beneficiary who has engaged in fraudulent conduct in the underlying transaction. Furthermore, a rule that precludes injunctive relief where the fraud is in the underlying transaction will compensate the beneficiary for wrongful acts in situations where the customer will not have an effective legal remedy for the fraudulent conduct and thus tend to encourage fraud, a policy that should be avoided. As the court said in *Dynamics Corp. of America v. Citizens & Southern Nat. Bank* [(N.D.Ga.1973), 356 F.Supp. 991, 1000], there is as much public interest in discouraging fraud as in encouraging the use of letters of credit.'" (Emphasis deleted.)

Id., 464 So.2d at 733, *quoting* 6B Hawkland, at 5-236 to 5-237, Section 5-114:9.

In *NMC Ent.*, NMC agreed to purchase a large quantity of stereo receivers from CBS and opened an LC to secure its underlying obligations. In seeking a preliminary injunction to restrain the issuer from honoring the LC, NMC made a prima facie showing that CBS had misrepresented the performance specifications for the receivers, particularly with regard to their continuous power output ratings. In granting the injunction, the court held, "If the sales contract is tainted with fraud in its inducement, then any document or signed certificate which the letter of credit requires CBS to submit * * * is equally tainted." *Id.*, 14 U.C.C. Rep. Serv. at 1430.

Moreover, UCC 5-109, 1995 Comment 3 addresses so-called "clean" or "suicide" LCs, which are LCs calling only for a draft and no other document. The comment explains that it would be difficult for there to be fraud in the presentation under these LCs and that courts should be skeptical of such claims. Nevertheless, the comment states that even under these kinds of LCs, "[i]f the applicant were able to show that the beneficiary were [sic] committing material fraud on the applicant *in the underlying transaction,* then payment would facilitate a material fraud by the beneficiary on the applicant and honor could be enjoined." (Emphasis added.)

We hold, therefore, that material fraud committed by the beneficiary in either the letter of credit transaction or the underlying sales transaction is sufficient to warrant injunctive relief under R.C. 1305.08(B). Accordingly, the judgment of the court of appeals is reversed as to this issue.

2. Measure of Fraud

Another controversy that surrounded the "fraud in the transaction" language of UCC 5-114(2) involved the degree or quantity of fraud necessary to warrant injunctive relief. As noted in *Cromwell,* 464 So.2d at 734, "There is more than one measure of 'fraud' in the various jurisdictions in the United States." In fact, manifold tests were devised for establishing fraud under UCC 5-114(2). *See, generally,* 7A Lawrence (Rev.2001) 353-354, Section 5-114:67; 6B Hawkland & Miller (Rev.2001), at 5-239 to 5-248, Section 5- 114:9; 3 White & Summers, at

181-182, Section 26-10.

However, UCC 5-109(b) (R.C. 1305.08[B]) clarifies that only "material fraud" by the beneficiary will justify an injunction against honor. UCC 5-109, Official Comment 1 explains:

"Material fraud by the beneficiary occurs only when the beneficiary has no colorable right to expect honor and where there is no basis in fact to support such a right to honor. The section indorses articulations such as those stated in *Intraworld Indus. v. Girard Trust Bank,* 461 Pa. 343, 336 A.2d 316 (1975), *Roman Ceramics Corp. v. People's Nat. Bank,* 714 F.2d 1207 (3d Cir.1983), and similar decisions and embraces certain decisions under Section 5-114 that relied upon the phrase 'fraud in the transaction.' Some of these decisions have been summarized as follows in *Ground Air Transfer, Inc. v. Westate's [Westates] Airlines, Inc.,* 899 F.2d 1269, 1272-73 (1st Cir.1990):

" 'We have said throughout that courts may not "*normally*" issue an injunction because of an important exception to the general "no injunction" rule. The exception, as we also explained in *Itek [Corp. v. First Natl. Bank of Boston* (C.A.1, 1984)], 730 F.2d [19] at 24-25, concerns "fraud" so serious as to make it obviously pointless and unjust to permit the beneficiary to obtain the money. Where the circumstances "*plainly*" show that the underlying contract forbids the beneficiary to call a letter of credit, *Itek,* 730 F.2d at 24; where they show that the contract deprives the beneficiary of even a "*colorable*" right to do so, id., at 25; where the contract and circumstances reveal that the beneficiary's demand for payment has "absolutely no basis in fact," *id.; see Dynamics Corp. of America,* 356 F.Supp. at 999; where the beneficiary's conduct has "so vitiated the entire transaction that the legitimate purposes of the independence of the issuer's obligation would no longer be served," *Itek,* 730 F.2d at 25 (*quoting Roman Ceramics Corp.* [supra], 714 F.2d [at] 1212, n. 12, 1215 (*quoting Intraworld Indus.,* 336 A.2d at 324-25)); *then* a court may enjoin payment.' " (Emphasis sic.)

As another court adhering to this standard explained, the applicant must show that the letter of credit was, in fact, being used by the beneficiary "as a vehicle for fraud," or in other words, that the beneficiary's conduct, if rewarded by payment, "would deprive the [applicant] of any benefit of the underlying contract and * * * transform the letter of credit * * * into a means for perpetrating fraud." *GATX Leasing Corp.,* 657 S.W.2d at 183.

Thus, we hold that "material fraud" under R.C. 1305.08(B) means fraud that has so vitiated the entire transaction that the legitimate purposes of the independence of the issuer's obligation can no longer be served.

The court of appeals actually did rely on *Sztejn,* 177 Misc. 719, 31 N.Y.S.2d 631, *Intraworld Indus.,* 461 Pa. 343, 336 A.2d 316, and *Roman Ceramics Corp.,* 714 F.2d 1207, to establish its so-called "vitiation exception," but construed the exception so narrowly as to preclude relief where the beneficiary's fraudulent conduct occurs solely in the underlying transaction. Thus, the court of appeals relied on the right cases for the wrong reasons. As a consequence, the court of appeals declined to address the issues of agency and fraud in the underlying contract, holding instead that the trial court should not even have taken evidence on these issues.

Accordingly, the judgment of the court of appeals is reversed on this issue as well.

3. PTZ's Actions

The trial court found the following facts to have been established by clear and convincing evidence:

"6. Gary Corby represented to F.A. Jenkins that PTZ Trading, Ltd. was in fact the sole distributor for surplus Michelin tires and that there was a direct relationship between PTZ Trading, Ltd. [a]nd Michelin. Corby further represented to Jenkins that there would be 50,000 to 70,000 summer tires available to Jenco per quarter at a price 40 to 60 percent below the U.S. market price within weeks of Jenco showing good faith by purchasing in excess of five hundred thousand dollars worth of mud and snow tires currently offered by PTZ Trading, Ltd.

"7. The Court further finds that John Evans, as agent for PTZ Trading, Ltd., was aware that Corby was making such representations to Jenco and that such representations were false. Mr. John Evans, as an agent for PTZ, knew that Jenco considered the purchase of the summer tires to be necessary in order to make the winter snow and mud tires saleable in the U.S. market. Mr. Evans did nothing to correct Mr. Corby's misrepresentations. Mr. Evans affirmed the misrepresentations and attempted to buttress them in correspondence with Jenco.

"8. Mr. Evans conveyed this information to Mr. Sievers who also acknowledged that he understood that the purchase of the summer tires by Jenco was critical to the conclusion of the sale of the mud and snow tires and without which the winter tire sale would not occur.

"9. John Evans and Aloysius Sievers also knew that a large portion of the mud and snow tires they were attempting to sell were not capable of being imported into the United States or sol[d] here because the United States Department of Transportation identification number had been 'buffed' off of such tires. Both Sievers and Evans knew that Jenco and Mid America Tire intended to sell the snow tires in the United States, but neither advised Jenco or Mid America Tire of the existence of the 'buffed' tires.

"10. Prior to the issuance of the letter of credit, John Evans knew Mid America Tire, Inc. and Jenco were operating under intentionally false and inaccurate representations made by Corby and reinforced by John Evans."

* * *

"12. The Court finds, specifically, that the representation that PTZ had a direct relationship with Michelin Tire, the representation that PTZ was the exclusive distributor for surplus Michelin Tires, the representation that a substantial quantity of between fifty and seventy thousand tires would be available quarterly on an exclusive basis to Jenco and Mid America Tire, Inc. at 40 to 60 percent of the U.S. market price were all material statements inducing Plaintiffs to issue the underlying letter of credit and were in fact false and made with knowledge of their falsity."

Whether or not this court would have made the same factual findings is irrelevant. This court does not resolve questions of fact. We are constrained to accept these facts as established because the trial court sat as factfinder in this case and because the record contains ample evidence to support them.

Given these facts, we are compelled to conclude that PTZ's actions in this case are sufficiently egregious to warrant injunctive relief under the "material fraud" standard of R.C. 1305.08(B). The trial court's findings demonstrate that PTZ sought to unload a large quantity of surplus winter tires on appellants by promising a large number of bargain- priced summer tires, without which the winter tires would be virtually worthless to appellants. Keenly aware that appellants would not agree to purchase the winter tires without the summer tires, PTZ made, participated in, and/or failed to correct a series of materially fraudulent promises and representations regarding the more lucrative summer tires in order to induce appellants to commit to purchasing the winter tires and to open an LC in PTZ's favor to secure payment. Dangling the prospect of the summer tires just beyond appellants' reach, PTZ sought first the issuance of the LC, and then shipping instructions, in an effort to cash in on the winter deal before appellants could discover the truth about the "DA/2C" tires and PTZ's lack of ability and intention ever to provide summer tires at the price and quantity represented. Indeed, when appellants learned of PTZ's fraud after opening the LC, and PTZ was no longer able to stall for shipping instructions with nonconforming lists of summer tires, Sievers proclaimed, "I have a letter of credit and I am shipping the tires."

Under these facts, it can truly be said that the LC in this case was being used by PTZ as a vehicle for fraud and that PTZ's actions effectively deprived appellants of any benefit in the underlying arrangement. In this sense, PTZ's conduct is comparable to the shipment of cow hair in *Sztejn,* 177 Misc. 719, 31 N.Y.S.2d 631, the shipment of old, ripped, and mildewed boxing gloves in *Cambridge Sporting Goods,* 41 N.Y.2d 254, 392 N.Y.S.2d 265, 360 N.E.2d 943, and the failure to disclose nonconforming performance specifications for the stereo receives in *NMC Ent., Inc.,* 14 U.C.C. Rep.Serv. 1427.

PTZ's demand for payment under these circumstances has absolutely no basis in fact, and it would be pointless and unjust to permit PTZ to draw the money. PTZ's conduct has so vitiated the entire transaction that the only purpose served by invoking the independence principle in this case would be to transform the LC into a fraudulent seller's Holy Grail, which once obtained would provide cover for fraudulent business practices in the name of commercial expedience. Accordingly, we reverse the court of appeals' judgment as it bears on this issue.

* * * *

Judgment reversed.

Problem 7-2

Notes

Reconsider Problem 7-1. Assume that Acme Computer has learned via a source that Computer Parts is in desperate financial shape. Acme Computer fears that Computer Parts will ship substandard parts and try to collect on the letter of credit. If Computer Parts ships substandard parts, is that fraud which justifies a dishonor or an injunction against honor? What is the difference between fraud and breach of contract?

Review

Problem 7-3

Jane Engineer, owner of Design, Inc., wanted to buy some equipment from Int'l Design Equipment. Int'l demanded as a condition of sale that Jane provide a letter of credit to pay for the equipment. Jane asked Finance Bank to issue the letter of credit. Finance Bank agreed to do so if Jane signed a promissory note to pay for the credit. Jane signed a promissory note that provided:

> "The undersigned promises to pay to Finance Bank or its order the sum of $100,000 plus interest at 10% per annum on demand. This note is secured by a security interest as provided in the security agreement dated Feb. 1, 2007. The undersigned also promises to give additional collateral if Finance Bank deems itself insecure."

The note was dated Feb. 1, 2007, and signed on the bottom right hand corner "Design Inc. by Jane Engineer" and signed on the back "Bob Smith." Bob is Design Inc.'s vice president. On Feb. 10, 2007, Finance Bank sold the note to State Bank. Finance Bank signed the note on the back as follows: "Finance Bank without recourse."

On Feb. 2, 2007, Finance Bank issued an irrevocable letter of credit for $100,000 with Int'l Design as the beneficiary and sent an advice of credit to Int'l Design. The letter of credit required a negotiable bill of lading showing shipment of the equipment to Design Inc. and presentation of a sight draft drawn on the buyer and signed by the seller. The letter of credit stated it expired on March 1, 2007.

Int'l Design was short of cash and could not make the shipment to Design Inc. by March 1, 2007. Int'l Design's president decided to forge the bill of lading and presented the forged bill of lading and the sight draft to Finance Bank on February 20, 2007. Finance Bank paid Int'l Design $100,000. Design Inc. never received the equipment. State Bank presented the note to Jane and demanded payment. Jane refused to pay the note as she never received the equipment from Int'l Design.

Explain fully all of the parties' rights and liabilities.

Notes

CHAPTER 8
ELECTRONIC FUNDS TRANSFER

A. Overview

As we increasingly operate in an environment where electronic devices proliferate, the idea of a payment system tied to a tangible item becomes less attractive.* This area is constantly evolving as the players in the system invent new methodologies for increasing the efficiency of the payment systems and lowering

---

* *See Symposium, Negotiability in an Electronic Environment*, 31 IDAHO L. REV. 679 (1995); Uniform Electronic Transactions Act § 16 (1999) (allowing electronic documents of title and negotiable notes); Electronic Signatures in Global and National Commerce Act (E-Sign) (codified at 15 U.S.C. §§ 7001–31) (allowing for electronic negotiable promissory notes secured by real property). Each of these acts depends upon implementation of a control concept which functions as the equivalent of indorsement and possession of a comparable paper instrument. The extent to which these electronic equivalents will be used depends upon whether technological systems are developed that comply with the control concept. *See* Report, *Framework for Control Over Electronic Chattel Paper–Compliance with UCC § 9-105*, 61 BUS. LAW. 721 (2006); Jane Kaufman Winn, *Clash of the Titans: Regulating the Competition Between Established and Emerging Electronic Payment Systems*, 14 BERKELEY TECH. L.J. 675 (1999). For an evaluation of the U.S. approach against the European Union and Australian approaches, *see* Olujoke E. Akindemowo, *Electronic Money Regulation: A Comparative Survey of Policy Influences in Australia, the European Union and the United States of America*, 11 J.L. & INFO. SCI. 61 (2000/02).

In 2002, The Clearing House study "The Remaining Barriers to ePayments and Straight-Through Processing" (available at http://www.nych.org) cited concerns about security and fraud, unwillingness to allow debit transactions as opposed to credit transactions, failure to receive necessary information to make electronic payments, the loss of float, and the incompatibility of computer systems for accounting and payments. *See also* Jane K. Winn, *Making XML Pay: Revising Existing Electronic Payments Law to Accommodate Innovation*, 53 SMU L. REV. 1477 (2000) (discussing incompatible technology systems). A 2002 Federal Reserve study, "The Future of Retail Electronic Payments Systems: Industry Interviews and Analysis" (available at www.federalreserve.gov/paymentsys.htm.) identified additional concerns such as the inability to make electronic payments in "real time" which increases risk of nonsettlement of payments and lack of a business case that convinces participants that the electronic system is cheaper and more reliable than the paper system. The continuing question is whether these barriers to electronic processing are being eliminated as the technology improves. Recent documentation of the increasing use of electronic payments methods indicates that these methods are gaining popularity. *See* Geoffrey R. Gerdes et al., *Trends in the Use of Payment Instruments in the United States*, FEDERAL RESERVE BULLETIN 180 (Spring 2005).

the cost of settlement of payments. This Chapter addresses electronic payment systems that are governed by the Electronic Funds Transfer Act (EFTA) (codified at 15 U.S.C. §§ 1693–93r), the EFTA implementing regulation, Regulation E (12 C.F.R. pt. 205), or U.C.C. Article 4A.

To start thinking about electronic funds transfers, consider some commonplace uses of electronic funds transfers: automatic deposit of paychecks (not really a check at all); automatic deduction of regular monthly bills from a deposit account; using a debit card to pay for items from a retail store; using an ATM machine or telephone to transfer funds from one bank account to another; or a commercial party instructing its bank to transfer funds to another bank for the benefit of another party. In each of these examples, the value is funneled through the banking system.

Other examples of using electronics to make payment are stored value cards or e-cash systems where value is deposited with a non-bank entity. An example of a stored value card is a card used to make copies at a photocopy machine in a library. Some universities are issuing such cards to use for buying all types of goods and services on campus. Other merchant networks, such as VISA, may issue stored value cards. Gift cards are another example of a type of stored value system. The value available for use with the card may be encoded on the card itself or may be accessed when the card is run through a reader. E-cash is a type of system where the provider takes deposits of value into a web based account and the user can then spend that value at various merchant web sites. An example of this type of system is http:/www.paypal.com. Both of these systems (stored value and e-cash) are not settled through the banking system. In other words, the entity with which value is deposited is not a bank.

What all these transactions have in common, whether funneled through the banking system or through non-bank entities, is that funds transfer takes place electronically and does not depend on paper or other tangible items as evidence of or a mechanism for transfer of funds.

One of the continuing tensions in this area is the extent to which the existing regulatory systems found in U.C.C. Articles 4 and 4A, the EFTA, and Regulation E should be expanded or revised to govern the evolving electronic payment mechanisms. We previously confronted this when we looked at the coverage of Article 4 and the issues of check truncation. As you work your way through these materials on the EFTA, Regulation E, and Article 4A, consider what types of transactions are covered by these statutes and regulations and whether transactions that are not currently covered by them, should be so covered.

The mechanics of a funds transfer are deceptively simple. The originating party executes an instruction to a third party holding the originating party's fund to debit that fund and credit the fund of another. This is known as a "push" transaction, or in Article 4A terms, a credit funds transfer. That is, the instruction is to credit another's account. The originating party is pushing value from its fund to someone else's fund. A simple example of this is a person with a deposit account at a bank instructing the bank to transfer value to a payee to pay a monthly bill, such as a utility bill.

Another type of funds transfer is known as a pull transaction. In a pull transaction, the person that "owns" the value on deposit with a third party authorizes a payee to instruct the third party to "pull" value from a fund and transfer that value to the payee. This is known as a debit funds transfer. A simple example of this type of transaction is when a person authorizes an insurance company to take a monthly draw from the person's bank account to pay an insurance premium.

Electronic funds transfer as a payment system has the same four concerns as the other payment systems we have studied so far: (i) the mechanics of value transfer, (ii) incurring and satisfying the obligation to pay, (iii) enforcing the obligation to pay, and (iv) allocating the risks of errors and wrongdoing. The rules that govern these four concerns are based upon a combination of contracts between the parties, common law tort principles, statutes, and regulations.

Regulation E governs both push (credit) and pull (debit) transactions that involve a consumer's deposit account. U.C.C. Article 4A, however, governs only credit funds transfers, that is, a push transaction, through the banking system. **Read the Prefatory Note to Article 4A and the definition of "funds transfer" in U.C.C. § 4A-104.** Our study of funds transfers will focus on the EFTA, Regulation E, and Article 4A. We start with the EFTA and Regulation E.

B. EFTA and Regulation E

1. Scope

The first thing to determine is what transactions are covered by the EFTA and Reg. E and what transactions are covered by Article 4A. **Read Reg. E., 12 C.F.R. § 205.3 and the relevant definitions in 12 C.F.R. § 205.2.** Official staff interpretations of Regulation E found in Supplement I to Regulation E may be helpful in understanding the application of the regulation. These interpretations are set forth following the regulation in 12 C.F.R. pt. 205. **Read U.C.C. § 4A-108 regarding the relationship between the EFTA and Article 4A.** If the EFTA and

Regulation E do not apply to the transaction, does Article 4A apply? **Read U.C.C. §§ 4A-102, 4A-103, 4A-104.**

Problem 8-1

Notes

a) When Olive was in the bank at the teller's window depositing some checks, she requested the bank teller transfer funds from her checking account to her daughter's savings account at another bank. The bank teller has Olive fill out a funds transfer slip, indicating the account number of her daughter's account and the recipient bank's name and address. Does Article 4A or Reg. E apply to this transaction?

b) Olive logged on her home computer, accessed her bank account information and instructed her bank to transfer money to her daughter's account at another bank. She filled in the online form indicting the bank name and address and her daughter's account number. Does Article 4A or Reg. E apply to this transaction? What other information do you need to know to answer that question?

    What if Olive made her request by calling the bank on the telephone instead of logging onto her home computer? What if the transfer occurred automatically every month?

Notes

c) Mary owns a small business and has authorized her property and liability insurer to draw the amount of the premium from the business checking account each month. The insurer does so by an automated instruction to the bank holding the business checking account. Does Article 4A or Reg. E apply to this transaction?

d) At the grocery store, Sarah gave the clerk a check to pay for the groceries. The clerk scanned the check and keyed in the amount. The clerk returned the check to Sarah. The information from the check and the keyed in amount were transmitted to Sarah's bank and her account was debited. Does Article 4A or Reg. E apply to this transaction? Any difference if Sarah used a debit card instead of a check? How about if she used a credit card? *See* 12 C.F.R. § 205.12.

e) Bigtime Inc. decided that to pay its employees, it would set up an account at its bank and give each employee a card to access the amount of the employee's net pay. The employee could access the salary funds through any ATM machine. Does Article 4A or Reg. E apply to the employee's withdrawal of funds from the account?

Notes

f) Sarah has automatic overdraft protection to transfer money from her savings account to her checking account to cover checks or other withdrawals from her checking account. When the bank makes a transfer between those accounts, does Article 4A or Reg. E apply? Would it make any difference if the transfer was not automatic but Sarah made a monthly transfer between accounts using an ATM machine or by calling the bank on an automated phone line?

2. Regulation of the Bank-Customer Relationship

As we learned when we studied Article 4, a bank and its customer will enter into an agreement governing use of the account. Generally this agreement will address the rights and liability of the customer in making electronic funds transfers from or to the account. The EFTA and Regulation E are not directed at regulating the obligations of the parties in the funds transfer except as between the consumer and the depositary bank holding the consumer's deposit account. Regulation E does not require terms in the bank-customer agreement concerning when the customer is obligated on the funds transfer and how the funds transfer obligation is satisfied. Regulation CC, however, does provide when funds from an electronic funds transfer must be made available to the customer. **Reg. CC, 12 C.F.R. § 229.10(b)**. Thus, in any particular electronic funds transfer governed by the EFTA and Regulation E, the terms of the bank-customer agreement determine when a customer is obligated to pay the bank for the amount transferred and how the customer's obligation to pay the bank is satisfied. Similarly, the bank's obligation to the customer in terms of carrying out the funds transfer is also governed by the bank-customer agreement. If either party fails to comply with the bank-customer agreement, the remedy for that failure is a breach of contract action. The effect of an electronic funds transfer on the underlying obligation is also not addressed in the EFTA or Regulation E.

If a funds transfer is governed by the EFTA and Regulation E (and thus not U.C.C. Article 4A), and the issue is not governed by the parties' agreement, or not required by Regulation E or Regulation CC, it may be appropriate to apply other common law principles to resolve a dispute between the parties. In addition, funds transfer system rules may provide an avenue for recovery against other participants in the funds transfer. *Security First Network Bank v. C.A.P.S., Inc.*, 47 U.C.C. Rep. Serv. 2d 670 (N.D. Ill. 2002) (an account holder could maintain a breach of warranty action based on the NACHA (National Automated Clearing House Association) rules against a bank that originated an allegedly unauthorized ACH (Automated Clearing House) debit from the account holder's bank account).

The EFTA and Regulation E require disclosure to the consumer of many of the terms that govern making a funds transfer. For example, the bank must disclose the consumer's rights regarding unauthorized funds transfers, the fees for the funds transfer, any limitations on the ability to make a funds transfer, the ability to stop a funds transfer, and the bank's liability for failure to comply with its duties under the EFTA and Regulation E. Reg. E, 12 C.F.R. § 205.7. The bank must disclose the terms information required by Regulation E in clear and understandable terms and in a form that the consumer may keep. **Reg. E, 12 C.F.R. § 205.4.** The terms described in **Reg. E, 12 C.F.R. § 205.7** must be given at the time the consumer contracts with the bank regarding electronic funds transfers. If the terms are going to change, the bank must give advance notice of those changes in most circumstances. **Reg. E, 12 C.F.R. § 205.8.** If the consumer uses an electronic terminal, such as an ATM, the bank must make a receipt available. **Reg. E, 12 C.F.R. § 205.9(a).** The bank must also make available periodic statements with information concerning funds transfers noted thereon. **Reg. E, 12 C.F.R. § 205.9(b).** Fees for using ATMs must also be disclosed. **Reg. E, 12 C.F.R. § 205.16.** In some circumstances, the disclosures required may be communicated electronically. **Reg. E, 12 C.F.R. § 205.17.** If there is a combined credit and debit card, the bank must comply with the disclosure requirements of both Regulation Z, 12 C.F.R. pt. 226, and Regulation E. **Reg. E, 12 C.F.R. §§ 205.12, 205.4.**

As we saw in our look at credit cards under Regulation Z, the bank is also prohibited under Regulation E from issuing unrequested, validated access devices such as a debit card. **Read Reg. E, 12 C.F.R. § 205.5.** We also saw in our look at Regulation Z there was a billing error resolution process. There is also an error resolution process for funds transfer errors. **Read Reg. E, 12 C.F.R. § 205.11.**

Problem 8-2

Deb has a personal checking account at National Bank and a cash and debit card to access the account. On her monthly bank statement, she noticed that an ATM deposit of $1,000 was not reflected.

Notes

a) How can she get the deposit credited?

b) How long does National Bank have to investigate?

c) What must National Bank do in its investigation?

d) Suppose National Bank decided no error occurred. What must it do? What are Deb's rights if she disagrees with the bank?

e) Suppose National Bank decided an error did occur. What must it do?

f) Assume Deb paid for a new chair with her cash and debit card. The price was $500. Her bank statement reflected a charge of $700. Deb sent a notice of error to the bank. How long does the bank have to investigate?

The EFTA and Regulation E also address the consumer's rights concerning preauthorized funds transfers. **Read Reg. E, 12 C.F.R. § 205.10.**

Problem 8-3

John has both a savings and a checking account at National Bank. Both accounts are for his personal use.

Notes

a) Every quarter, John has a dividend payment deposited automatically in his savings account. Every two weeks, he has his paycheck deposited automatically in his checking account. Does the EFTA and Regulation E apply to these transactions? What are National Bank's obligations to John regarding these transfers? When do the funds have to be available to John? *See* Reg. CC, 12 C.F.R. § 229.10.

b) John has a life insurance premium paid monthly by a direct withdrawal from his checking account. Does the EFTA and Regulation E apply to this transaction? What are National Bank's obligations to John regarding these transfers?

c) Same facts as (b) above. If John decided to cancel his life insurance policy, how does he stop the withdrawal? If the bank failed to honor his timely stop order, what is the Bank's liability? If the life insurance premium is paid by a monthly preauthorized negotiable draft on his account, does the EFTA and Regulation E apply?

d) Same facts as (b) above. The computer at National Bank had a total systems failure. As a result, the payment of the premium to John's life insurance company was two days late. The insurance company attempted to cancel the policy due to the late payment. Can it do so under the EFTA and Regulation E?

e) John's employer requires that all employees have their paychecks deposited directly to their bank accounts. John does not want direct deposit. What are his rights? Can he refuse direct deposit of his paycheck?

3.   Unauthorized Transfers

The major function of the EFTA and Regulation E, other than disclosure requirements, is to allocate losses when something goes wrong. **Read Reg. E, 12 C.F.R. § 205.6 and § 205.11.**

Problem 8-4

State Bank issued Amy a cash card to access her personal checking account at State Bank.

a)   Amy threw the cash card away because she did not want it. Jane picked the cash card out of the trash, went to the bank, impersonated Amy and received a PIN number to use to access Amy's account. Jane withdrew $1,000 over the course of five days ($200 per day). Amy discovered the theft when several of her checks drawn on the account bounced.   Must State Bank recredit Amy's account with $1,000?

b)   Assume Amy lost the card after she had received the PIN number. Amy had written the number on the card so that she would not forget it.   Jane found the card and withdrew a total of $1,000 from Amy's account, $200 each day for five days. What is Amy's liability?

c)   Same facts as (b) above. Amy noticed she lost the card on the same day that she actually lost the card. What is Amy's liability if she notified the bank of the loss of the card three days later? Would your analysis change if Amy did not notice she had lost the card for a week after she actually lost the card and then immediately notified the bank?

Notes

d)   Same facts as (b) above.   What is Amy's liability if she notified the bank after she received her periodic statement on which the five transfers were reflected?

e)   Amy lent her cash card to her daughter to withdraw $50, who withdrew $200. Is that an unauthorized transfer?

f)   Assume that State Bank issued a validated access card without Amy's request. This card is not a renewal of an existing card. Harry intercepted the card in the mail and used it to withdraw $3,000 from Amy's account. State Bank refused to recredit her account. What can she do to get the money back from State Bank?

C.   U.C.C. Article 4A

1. Scope

Reread the Prefatory note to Article 4A.   That note provides a simple explanation of the electronic funds transfer that is the subject of Article 4A. **Read the comment to U.C.C. § 4A-102** which sets forth the policy behind Article 4A.[*]

---

[*] For discussion of international funds transfers, see PEB Commentary No. 13 and the UNCITRAL Model Law on International Credit Transfers (1992). *See also* Carl Felsenfeld, *The Compatibility of the Uncitral Model Law on International Credit Transfers with Article 4A of the UCC*, 60 FORDHAM L. REV. S53 (1992).

As we have explored through the problems above, if any part of the funds transfer is covered by the EFTA, Article 4A does not apply to the transaction. U.C.C. § 4A-108. Article 4A also applies only to "credit" funds transfers, that is, where the originator's instruction is to credit a beneficiary's account. Debit funds transfers, where the originator's instruction is to debit someone else's account, are not covered by Article 4A.

Article 4A may be varied by Federal Reserve regulations and operating circulars. **Read U.C.C. § 4A-107.** Regulation J, 12 C.F.R. pt. 210 governs funds transfers that go through the federal reserve system, Fedwire, and the Federal Reserve has issued Operating Circular 6 for Fedwire funds transfers.**Read Reg. J, 12 C.F.R. § 210.25**.

Article 4A also recognizes that parties to funds transfers may vary the rights and obligations stated in Article 4A and that associations may promulgate rules for funds transfers between members of the association. **Read U.C.C. § 4A-501.** Two examples of such funds transfer rules are those issued by the National Automated Clearing House Association (NACHA) covering ACH (Automated Clearing House) transactions and by The Clearing House covering CHIPS (Clearinghouse Interbank Payments System). Participants in a funds transfer system agree to abide by the rules of the system.[*]

The number and dollar amount of transactions that take place through these networks is staggering. NACHA reports that during the second quarter of 2006, three billion in transactions worth more than 6.5 trillion dollars took place through the ACH network. CHIPS reports that it transfers on average 1.57 trillion dollars daily. Fedwire reports that for 2005, its daily transfer volume was almost 528,000 transactions, with an average value of 3.92 million dollars per transfer.

2. Incurring the Obligation to Pay

Once you have determined that Article 4A applies to the transaction, the next step is to determine the rights and obligations of the various parties in the transaction. Unlike the EFTA and Regulation E, U.C.C. Article 4A regulates the parties' obligations to pay, although the parties may alter the rights and obligations

---

[*] The NACHA Operating Rules and Guidelines are available in a yearly publication. The most current publication is the 2007 ACH Rules: A Complete Guide to Rules and Regulations Governing the ACH Network, available by order from http://www.nacha.org. The Federal Reserve has also issued Operating Circular 4 to govern ACH items. The Rules and Administrative Procedures for CHIPS are available at http://www.chips.org.

created under Article 4A unless prohibited from doing so by a provision in Article 4A. **U.C.C. § 4A-501.** As we saw in other payment systems, consulting the bank-customer agreement is critical to a determination of the parties' rights. The parties' obligations as to each part of the funds transaction differs depending on the various roles the parties are fulfilling. Thus it is important to understand the terminology of Article 4A. **Read the definitions in U.C.C. §§ 4A-103, 4A-104, 4A-105.**

Consider the following example. Acme Corp. owed Supply Co. a debt for goods shipped for use in Acme's business. Acme instructed First Bank to send $100,000 to Third Bank to be credited to Supply Co.'s account at Third Bank. First Bank issued that instruction to Second Bank and Second Bank issued that instruction to Third Bank. Third Bank credited the Supply Co. account. Acme Corp. is a sender and an originator. First Bank is an originator's bank, a receiving bank, and a sender. Second Bank is a receiving bank, an intermediary bank, and a sender. Third Bank is a receiving bank and a beneficiary bank. Supply Co. is the beneficiary.

As you can see from reading the definition of "payment order" in U.C.C. § 4A-103, a payment order is an instruction to pay money to a beneficiary. Using the example above, Acme Corp. sent a payment order to First Bank. First Bank accepted that payment order by executing its own payment order to Second Bank. Second Bank accepted First Bank's payment order by executing its own payment order to Third Bank. Third Bank accepted Second Bank's payment order by crediting the account of the beneficiary, Supply Co. This process of sending and receiving the payment order is distinct from actually paying the payment order.

Once the payment orders are made and accepted, payment by virtue of credits and debits must be made. Using the example above, when First Bank accepted the payment order from Acme Corp., Acme Corp. became obligated to pay First Bank. Generally that payment would take place by First Bank debiting Acme Corp.'s account at First Bank. When Second Bank accepted First Bank's payment order, First Bank became obligated to pay Second Bank. The payment would generally take place by either a debit to First Bank's account at Second Bank or a credit to Second Bank's account at First Bank. Payment could also take place through some other payment mechanism, such as a check. When Third Bank accepted Second Bank's payment order, Second Bank became obligated to pay Third Bank. Second Bank would make payment by debits or credits to bank accounts or by some other payment mechanism, such as a check. When Third Bank accepted the payment order, Third Bank became obligated to the beneficiary, Supply Co. Payment to the beneficiary generally takes place by crediting the beneficiary's bank account.

Thus, it is helpful to divide an electronic funds transaction into three distinct conceptual parts: (i) sending the payment order; (ii) accepting the payment order; and (iii) paying the payment order.

Now reread the definition of payment order in U.C.C. § 4A-103. The payment order must be to pay a fixed amount of money to a beneficiary and there must not be any condition to the payment other than the time of the payment. The key to the funds transfer system is having clear and definite instructions without conditions. The system is intended to be a low cost and efficient system for moving value. The drafting of Article 4A was designed to give clear rules to facilitate that operational presumption.

a.   Obligations of a Receiving Bank Other Than a Beneficiary Bank

As you can see, a funds transfer starts when someone issues a payment order to a bank. To determine the rights and liabilities of the participants in this system, it is generally advisable to start at the beginning of the series of payment orders. The first question is often whether the first sender had authority to issue the payment order. **Read U.C.C. § 4A-202.** We will consider the effect of an unauthorized payment order when we consider errors and wrongdoing regarding funds transfers.

Once a receiving bank receives a payment order, it has to decide whether to accept or reject the payment order. There are several questions that must be asked and answered. First, must the receiving bank accept the payment order? Second, if the receiving bank is going to accept the payment order, how does it do so? Third, if the receiving bank is going to reject a payment order, how does it do so? **Read U.C.C. §§ 4A-209, 4A-210, 4A-212.** These questions are answered in those sections.

If the receiving bank accepts a payment order, it must execute that order. How does a receiving bank execute the payment order? When must the receiving bank execute the payment order? **Read U.C.C. §§ 4A-301, 4A-302, 4A-305, and 4A-106.**

The following problem should help you flesh out the obligations of a receiving bank, other than a beneficiary's bank, when it receives and executes a payment order.

Problem 8-5

On Monday June 1, Acme Inc. instructed its bank, First Bank in New York, by telephone to transfer $100,000 to Paradise Sellers, Inc. in payment for a piece of investment real estate. Paradise Sellers, Inc. maintains its account at State Bank in San Francisco. Pursuant to the agreement between Acme and Paradise, the payment must be credited to Paradise's account by the end of the day, Thursday, June 4.

Notes

a) What are First Bank's obligations once it receives Acme's instructions? Is it obligated to act on Acme's instruction?

b) How would First Bank reject Acme's instruction? Does it have any liability if it rejects Acme's instruction?

c) What happens if First Bank does nothing when it receives Acme's instruction?

d) Assume First Bank decided to execute Acme's instruction. When must First Bank execute the payment order? Does it matter if Acme's instruction was given at 3 p.m. and First Bank has a 12 noon cutoff time for payment orders?

e) Same facts as (d) above. What route must First Bank use in executing Acme's instruction? Assume First Bank instructed the Federal Reserve Bank of New York to make payment to the Federal Reserve Bank of San Francisco in order to then make payment to Paradise's account at State Bank. Is that a permissible course of action?

Notes

f)   Assume Acme told First Bank to use Second National Bank, located in Minnesota, to execute the transfer. Does First Bank have to use Second National Bank?

g)   What method of communication must First Bank use to execute the transfer? Assume Acme said to use a wire transfer. Must First Bank use that means?

h)   First Bank executed the order but does not act in time to get the payment to Paradise by June 4. What is First Bank's liability for that failure?

i)   Assume First Bank executed Acme's payment order by properly issuing a payment order to Second Bank on June 2, containing the instructions to credit Paradise's account at State Bank in San Francisco with $100,000 by June 4. What are Second Bank's obligations?

b. Beneficiary Bank's Obligations

When a receiving bank executes a payment order, the purpose of the payment order is to communicate to the beneficiary bank that the beneficiary bank should credit the beneficiary's account at the beneficiary bank with the amount of the payment order.

Now we turn our attention to the actions of the beneficiary bank. The beneficiary bank has to decide whether to accept or reject the payment order it has received from its sender. **Read U.C.C. §§ 4A-212, 4A-209, 4A-210**. Is the beneficiary bank obligated to accept the payment order? How does the beneficiary bank accept the payment order? How does the beneficiary bank reject the payment order? If the beneficiary bank accepts the payment order, what are the consequences of that acceptance? **Read U.C.C. §§ 4A-404, 4A-405 and Reg. CC, 12 C.F.R. § 229.10**.

Problem 8-6

On Monday June 1, Acme Inc. instructed its bank, First Bank in New York, by telephone to transfer $100,000 to Paradise Sellers, Inc. in payment for a piece of investment real estate. Paradise Sellers, Inc. maintains its account at State Bank in San Francisco. Pursuant to the agreement between Acme and Paradise, the payment must be credited to Paradise's account by the end of the day, Thursday, June 4. On June 2, First Bank properly executed Acme's instruction by issuing a payment order to Second Bank instructing payment to Paradise's account at State Bank in San Francisco on June 4. Second Bank properly executed a payment order to State Bank on June 3 at 3 p.m. to credit the account of Paradise Sellers, Inc.

Notes

a) Must State Bank accept the order to credit Paradise's account?

b) If State Bank does not want to accept the order, what must it do?

c) What may happen if State Bank does nothing when it receives Second Bank's payment order?

Notes

d)   Would your answers change if State
      Bank has a cutoff time of 12 noon for
      funds transfers?

e)   Assume State Bank accepted the
      payment order.   What are its
      obligations to Paradise?

f)   What risk is State Bank taking when
      it accepts the payment order?

c.   Canceling or Amending a Payment Order

Once a payment order is issued, it may be canceled or amended. **Read U.C.C.
§ 4A-211.** What are the risks to the parties in the funds transfer when a sender
wants to cancel or amend its payment order?

Problem 8-7

On Monday June 1, Acme Inc. instructed its bank, First Bank in New York, by telephone to
transfer $100,000 to Paradise Sellers, Inc. in payment for a piece of investment real estate.
Paradise Sellers, Inc. maintains its account at State Bank in San Francisco. Pursuant to the
agreement between Acme and Paradise, the payment must be credited to Paradise's account
by the end of the day, Thursday, June 4.

Notes

a)   Assume Acme decided not to go
      through with the transaction with
      Paradise. Acme called First Bank to
      cancel the payment order. Can Acme
      cancel the payment order?

b)   Assume First Bank told Acme that it has already executed the payment order by sending a payment order to State Bank. Acme called State Bank and asked it not to credit Paradise's account. What result?

c)   Assume First Bank had not executed the order when Acme called to cancel the payment order. What result?

d)   Assume Acme's cancellation of the payment order is timely but First Bank mistakenly executed the order and State Bank credited Paradise's account. Was Acme's payment order authorized? What result?

e)   Assume First Bank has already executed Acme's payment order. Under what circumstances can Acme still cancel the payment order?

f)   Assume that on June 1, after giving the initial payment order to First Bank, Acme filed bankruptcy. Can First Bank still execute that payment order? *See* 11 U.S.C. § 362.

3. Satisfying the Obligation to Pay

a. Payment of Accepted Payment Orders

The acceptance and execution of payment orders must be followed by a settlement of the payment order. The actual value must move in some way from the originator to the beneficiary through a series of debits and credits between the banks in the transaction. Under the Article 4A scheme, this process is called payment of the payment order. It is the way in which the obligation to pay that is created by an acceptance of a payment order is satisfied. **Read U.C.C. §§ 4A-401, 4A-402, 4A-403, 4A-404, 4A-405**.

Problem 8-8

On Monday June 1, Jill Investor instructed her bank, First Bank in New York, by telephone to transfer $200,000 to Bill Seller to purchase a painting. Jill is an art dealer and her account at First Bank is used for her business. Seller is an artist and has an account at State Bank in San Francisco. Pursuant to the agreement between Investor and Seller, the funds must be in Seller's account by the end of the day, Thursday, June 4. First Bank issued a payment order to Second Bank. Second Bank issued a payment order to State Bank. State Bank accepted the order.

Notes

a)   What are State Bank's obligations to Seller?

b)   What are Second Bank's obligations to State Bank?

c)   What are First Bank's obligations to Second Bank?

Notes

d)　What are Jill's obligations to First Bank?

e)　How are the various payments to be made?

f)　Assume State Bank did not accept the payment order. What are the parties' obligations?

b.　Satisfying the Underlying Obligation

Most payment orders are given in order to settle an underlying obligation. The beneficiary bank's acceptance of a payment order has an effect on the originator's underlying obligation to the beneficiary. **Read U.C.C. § 4A-406**. Notice that the underlying obligation is satisfied even if the settlement of the payment order does not take place.

Problem 8-9

On Monday June 1, Acme Inc. instructed its bank, First Bank in New York, by telephone to transfer $100,000 to Paradise Sellers, Inc. in payment for a piece of investment real estate. Paradise Sellers, Inc. maintains its account at State Bank in San Francisco. Pursuant to the agreement between Acme and Paradise, the payment must be credited to Paradise's account by the end of the day, Thursday, June 4. On June 2, First Bank properly executed Acme's instruction by issuing a payment order to Second Bank instructing payment to Paradise's account at State Bank in San Francisco on June 4. Second Bank properly executed a payment order to State Bank on June 3 at 3 p.m. to pay Paradise Sellers, Inc. State Bank accepted the payment order and notified Paradise of the receipt of that order.

Notes

a)　What is the effect of that acceptance on Acme's obligation to Paradise?

Notes

b)   If Paradise refused the payment, does
     that change the effect of State Bank's
     acceptance of the payment order on
     Acme's obligation to Paradise?

c)   Can Paradise argue that the obligation
     has not been discharged if the amount
     credited to its account is $20 short
     due to fees charged by First Bank and
     Second Bank?

4. Funds Transfers and Rights Related to the Deposit Account

Just as in Article 4, the timing of credits and debits to an account can be
critical. Article 4A has its own provisions on this issue. **Read U.C.C. §§ 4A-502,
4A-503, 4A-504**.

Problem 8-10

Best Rugs issued a payment order to First Bank for $100,000 identifying Textile Corp.,
which has an account at National Bank, as the beneficiary. Best Rugs' account has a
$150,000 credit balance. One of Best's creditors served a garnishment summons on First
Bank to enforce a judgment for $200,000 against Best.

Notes

a)   Assume First Bank accepted the
     payment order. Must First Bank hold
     the money for the creditor?

b)   Assume First Bank did not accept the
     payment order. Must First Bank hold
     the money for the creditor?

Problem 8-11

Best Rugs issued a payment order to First Bank for $100,000 identifying Textile Corp., which has an account at National Bank, as the beneficiary. Best Rugs' account has a $150,000 credit balance. First Bank issued a payment order to National Bank. Prior to National Bank's acceptance of the payment order, Textile Corp.'s account had a credit balance of $50,000. Textile owed National Bank $100,000. One of Textile's creditors served a garnishment summons on National Bank to enforce a judgment against Textile for $200,000.

Notes

a) National Bank wants to accept the payment order for $100,000, credit Textile's account, then set off its $100,000 debt against the account, before it honors the creditor's garnishment. Assuming National Bank is entitled to exercise its setoff rights, is that a permissible course of action?

b) If Textile's creditor served a garnishment summons on First Bank, would that action be successful to intercept the funds before National Bank accepted the payment order?

c) May Textile's creditor obtain an injunction against any bank in the funds transfer to stop payment of the payment order to Textile?

d) On the day that Best Rugs issued its payment order, First Bank received checks totaling $70,000, drawn against Best Rugs' account. Must First Bank accept the payment order and dishonor the checks?

5. Funds Transfers Through Fedwire

Funds transfers do not always go directly from one bank to another bank. Often the banks will use funds transfer intermediaries. As previously mentioned, those intermediaries may be private associations of banks or may be the Federal Reserve System. **Read U.C.C. §§ 4A-206, 4A-501, 4A-107, and Reg. J, 12 C.F.R. pt. 210, Subpart B**.

Problem 8-12

Plumbing Supply Company issued a payment order to State Bank in New York to pay $100,000 to Wholesaler's account held by National Bank in San Francisco. State Bank issued a payment order to the Federal Reserve Bank of New York.

Notes

a) Must the Federal Reserve Bank accept the payment order?

b) If the Federal Reserve Bank accepts the order, when is State Bank obligated to pay the order?

c) Can State Bank require the Federal Reserve Bank to use Second National Bank as an intermediary bank?

d) If State Bank identified National Bank in San Francisco by number and name, but the number is wrong, can the Federal Reserve Bank rely on the name or the number in executing the payment order?

Notes

e)   Federal Reserve Bank of New York issued a payment order to the Federal Reserve Bank of San Francisco. Federal Reserve Bank of San Francisco issued a payment order to National Bank. How will the Federal Reserve Bank of San Francisco make payment of its payment order? When will it make its payment?

6. Allocation of the Risks of Error and Wrongdoing

The funds transfer system is designed to be a low-cost, efficient system of transferring value. In order to fulfill that goal, Article 4A was drafted to clearly allocate the risk of errors. One of the tensions is whether other principles, such as conversion and negligence, can be used to supplement the loss allocation principles in Article 4A. The relationship between common law causes of action, equitable principles, and the UCC is set forth in U.C.C. § 1-103. Reread the comment to U.C.C. § 4A-102 which suggests that the use of common law and equitable principles should not be used to subvert the allocation of risk as set out in Article 4A. For examples of courts wrestling with this issue, see *Schlegel v. Bank of America, N.A.*, 628 S.E.2d 362 (Va. 2006); *Fitts v. AmSouth Bank*, 917 So. 2d 818 (Ala. 2005); *Regions Bank v. The Provident Bank, Inc.*, 345 F.3d 1267 (11th Cir. 2003).

When determining who bears the risk of errors and wrongdoing, organize your analysis by the type of problem that has taken place.

a. Unauthorized Payment Orders

As with other payment systems, one type of problem that must be addressed is fraudulent payment orders.[*] **Read U.C.C. §§ 4A-201, 4A-202, 4A-203, 4A-204.** What is the difference between an authorized and a verified payment order? *See*

---

[*] J. Kevin French, *Article 4A's Treatment of Fraudulent Payment Orders–The Customer's Perspective*, 42 ALA. L. REV. 773 (1991).

Hedged Investment Partners, L.P. v. Norwest Bank Minnesota, N.A., 578 N.W.2d 765 (Minn. Ct. App. 1998).

Problem 8-13

Sam, an employee of Acme Corp., called First Bank and instructed the bank to transfer $100,000 from Acme's account to Jill Gray. First Bank required Sam to identify both Acme's account number and Jill's account number, and to give Acme's authorization code.

Notes

a) Has First Bank used a commercially reasonable security procedure?

b) Assume this is a commercially reasonable security procedure and Sam was not authorized to order transfers on behalf of Acme Corp. If First Bank executed the payment order and that order is accepted by the beneficiary bank, must Acme Corp. pay the amount of the order?

c) Assume this is a commercially reasonable security procedure and Sam is not an employee of Acme Corp. Sam broke into Acme's office building and ordered First Bank to transfer the money using Acme's computer system. If the funds transfer is completed by the beneficiary bank's acceptance of the payment order, must Acme pay the amount of the order?

Notes

d)   Assume Acme Corp. negotiated an agreement with First Bank that stated Acme Corp. is not responsible for any unauthorized payment orders. Answer questions (b) and (c) above.

e)   Assume in each case above that the procedure followed by First Bank was not a commercially reasonable security procedure and Sam is not an employee of Acme Corp. Sam's order was unauthorized. Must Acme pay the amount of the payment order?

f)   Same facts as (e) above. Assume Acme paid the amount of the payment order and later discovered the order was unauthorized. Acme requested First Bank to refund the money to Acme. Must First Bank refund the money? Assume Acme notified First Bank of the unauthorized transfer 30 days after First Bank notified Acme that the order was accepted. Does that effect Acme's right to a refund of the money? Can First Bank enforce an agreement stating that Acme bears all the risk of unauthorized payment orders?

b. Errors in Transmission

In any process involving multiple parties, mistakes during the process are inevitable. Article 4A was designed to clearly designate who bears the risk of errors made along the way without getting into factual disputes about the degree of fault of any party. In addition to problems with authorization of a payment order, other types of errors may occur. Sometimes there is a security procedure designed to detect error. *See* U.C.C. § 4A-201. **Read U.C.C. § 4A-205**.

Typical errors are misdescription of the beneficiary, misdescription of an intermediary or beneficiary bank, executing payment orders in the wrong amount, issuing duplicate payment orders, failure to follow instructions in executing the payment order, and delay in executing the payment order. **Read U.C.C. §§ 4A-207, 4A-208, 4A-303, 4A-304, 4A-305, 4A-505**.

**FIRST NATIONAL BANK & TRUST CO. V.
BRANT (IN RE CALUMET FARM, INC.)
398 F. 3d 555 (6th Cir. 2005)**

Gilman, Circuit Judge

This case arises out of a botched electronic wire transfer from Calumet Farm, Inc. to Peter M. Brant and White Birch Farm, Inc. (collectively, White Birch). On Friday, March 8, 1991, Calumet initiated the wire transfer of $77,301.58 by a payment order to its bank, First National Bank & Trust Company. This amount was calculated by Calumet as a payment of interest on its outstanding debt of over $1 million due to White Birch. When Calumet received written confirmation of the wire transfer from First National on the following Monday, March 11, 1991, it learned that $770,301.58, rather than $77,301.58, had mistakenly been transferred. White Birch refused to return the additional $693,000, and Calumet subsequently declared bankruptcy.

First National is now seeking restitution from White Birch for the excess payment. Both the bankruptcy court and district court ruled in favor of White Birch. The key issue on appeal is whether White Birch established the elements of the "discharge-for-value" defense to First National's restitution claim. For the reasons set forth below, we reverse the judgment of the district court and remand the case for the entry of judgment in favor of First National.

I. BACKGROUND

Most of the facts of this case were previously set forth by this court in *In re Calumet Farm, Inc.*, No. 95-5953, 1997 WL 253278, at *1-2 (6th Cir. May 14, 1997) (unpublished), as follows:

White Birch is a thoroughbred horse farm in Connecticut owned by Peter Brant. In 1986, Calumet purchased a one-half interest in the thoroughbred stallion

Mogambo from White Birch and executed a $6,500,000 promissory note ("the Mogambo note") evidencing the obligation. On October 31, 1990, Calumet defaulted in making its annual principal payment of [$1,300,000] on the debt. Brant and J.T. Lundy, president of Calumet, reached an agreement whereby Calumet would make the payment on or before March 15, 1991. Calumet also defaulted in making several intervening interest payments and, as of March 7, 1991, owed White Birch approximately $103,057.50 in interest and penalties.

On March 8, 1991, Lundy instructed Calumet's bookkeeper, Angela Holleran [properly, "Hollearn"], to pay the interest due to White Birch as of January 31, 1991, amounting to $77,301.58. Holleran thereupon called First National to arrange payment by wire transfer, and also called White Birch to inform it that a wire transfer payment was forthcoming; however, the substance of these conversations is disputed as to the amount that White Birch was to receive. The wire transfer, referenced as "MOGAMBO INT," was made to White Birch's account at Citibank in New York on March 8, 1991.

On March 11, 1991, Holleran received written confirmation of the wire transfer from First National and realized that $770,301.58, rather than $77,301.58, had been transferred. Holleran notified First National of the mistake and First National contacted Citibank to request reversal of the wire transfer. Because the money already had been credited to White Birch's account, Citibank refused to reverse the wire transfer. Thereafter, First National requested that Brant return the additional $693,000 erroneously transferred to him, but Brant refused to return the money unless First National acknowledged in writing that it had made the error in transferring the funds.

On March 27, 1991, Calumet filed suit against First National in Scott County Circuit Court alleging negligence and breach of contract with respect to the mistaken wire transfer. Because of Calumet's precarious financial condition, Calumet and First National reached a partial settlement whereby First National agreed to lend Calumet $500,000, secured by Calumet's interest in the Mogambo note. Calumet also assigned to First National any right of recovery that it might possess against White Birch and agreed to release First National from any liability arising from the wire transfer. Although First National and Calumet had partially settled the state court action, First National filed an answer and counterclaim [actually, a third-party complaint] on April 4, 1991, asserting claims against White Birch. In the meantime, White Birch filed a complaint against Calumet in the United States District Court for the Eastern District of Kentucky, seeking the principal and interest due on the Mogambo note.

On June 11, 1991, Calumet filed a bankruptcy petition in the United States

Bankruptcy Court for the Eastern District of Kentucky. In October 1991, the state court actions were removed to the Bankruptcy Court as adversary proceedings, and on December 12, 1991, the district court action was referred to the bankruptcy court.

Upon cross-motions for summary judgment, the bankruptcy court entered partial summary judgment in favor of White Birch on December 22, 1993. The court held that First National lacked standing to assert a restitution claim against White Birch, reasoning that the amount of a wire transfer, once debited from a depositor's account, belongs solely to that depositor; accordingly, the court held that only Calumet possessed standing to recover the transferred funds from White Birch. However, because Calumet owed White Birch a sum well in excess of the amount of the wire transfer, the court held that White Birch had not been unjustly enriched and was not obligated to make restitution. The court then denied First National leave to file a second amended counterclaim to include claims for conversion and intentional interference with a contract, but allowed First National to assert other state-law claims.

On September 6, 1994, the bankruptcy court entered summary judgment in favor of White Birch on all remaining claims and entered its final order on October 27, 1994. [As part of the final settlement, First National agreed to pay Calumet $50,000 in addition to the $500,000 loan, which Calumet never repaid.] First National appealed the bankruptcy court's grant of summary judgment in favor of White Birch and the court's denial of leave to amend its counterclaim. The district court affirmed the bankruptcy court's decision in its entirety on June 13, 1995.

In May of 1997, this court reversed the grant of summary judgment in favor of White Birch, but also affirmed the denial of First National's motion for leave to amend its counterclaim. The case was remanded to the district court with instructions to return the matter to the bankruptcy court for further proceedings. This court held that "the bankruptcy court should make additional factual findings as to whether White Birch had notice that the funds transfer had been made in error and, thus, determine whether White Birch [could] successfully assert [the 'discharge-for-value'] defense to First National's restitution claim." 1997 WL 253278, at *5.

In resolving cross-motions for summary judgment, the bankruptcy court determined on remand that there was insufficient evidence in the record to support a finding that White Birch had notice of the error in the amount transferred before the funds were credited to its account at Citibank. It therefore held that White Birch had satisfied the required elements of the discharge-for-value defense to First National's restitution claim. Accordingly, the bankruptcy court granted summary judgment in favor of White Birch and denied the cross-motion filed by First National. In March of 2003, the district court affirmed both determinations. First National now appeals, claiming that the lower courts failed to properly interpret and apply the discharge-for-value defense asserted by White Birch.

II. ANALYSIS
* * * *

B. The discharge-for-value defense

In its earlier opinion, this court held that First National had standing to assert a claim for restitution under U.C.C. § 4A-303(a) (enacted as § 355.4A-303(1) of the Kentucky Revised Statutes and incorporated into Federal Reserve Regulation J, 12 C.F.R. §§ 210.25-31, which governs funds transfers). . . . This provision authorizes a bank to seek restitution from the beneficiary of the excess payment if the bank committed an error in executing the payment order. In the prior opinion, this court noted that § 4A-303(a) incorporates the discharge-for-value defense. 1997 WL 253278, at *4. The RESTATEMENT OF RESTITUTION defines the discharge-for-value defense as follows:

> A creditor of another or one having a lien on another's property who has received from a third person any benefit in discharge of the debt or lien, is under no duty to make restitution therefor, although the discharge was given by mistake of the transferor as to his interests or duties, *if the transferee* made no misrepresentation and *did not have notice of the transferor's mistake.*

RESTATEMENT OF RESTITUTION § 14(1) (emphasis added). Thus, when a creditor receives what appears to be a payment on a debt from someone other than the debtor, the creditor becomes a bona fide purchaser and may keep the mistaken payment if the creditor discharges the obligation of its debtor prior to becoming aware of the mistake.

Section 14(1) of the RESTATEMENT, however, does not specify the point in time by which notice of the mistake must be received. Nor did this court's prior opinion in the present case address the issue. And the two other appellate courts that have concluded that the discharge-for-value rule applies to wire transfers also failed to focus on the timing question. *See Gen. Elec. Capital Corp. v. Cent. Bank*, 49 F.3d 280, 284 (7th Cir.1995) (GECC); *Banque Worms v. BankAmerica Int'l*, 77 N.Y.2d 362, 568 N.Y.S.2d 541, 570 N.E.2d 189, 196 (1991).

Isolated language in both of the above cases, however, indicates that the notice must occur before the funds arrive. *See GECC*, 49 F.3d at 284 (holding that "a creditor should be able to treat funds credited in apparent payment of a debt as irrevocably his, unless news of the error precedes arrival of the funds"); *Banque Worms*, 568 N.Y.S.2d 541, 570 N.E.2d at 196 (explaining that "[w]hen a beneficiary receives money to which it is entitled and has no knowledge that the money was erroneously wired, the beneficiary should not have to wonder whether it may retain the funds; rather, such a beneficiary should be able to consider the transfer of funds as a final and complete transaction, not subject to revocation"). But the question in each case (as in this court's prior decision) was whether the discharge-for-value rule applies in this setting, not how it applies. Nor, at any rate, does the quoted language squarely address the point. In a wire transfer setting, is the relevant event when the beneficiary's bank receives the money, or when the beneficiary learns that the money is in its account, or when the beneficiary credits the money to the debtor's account? Neither this court's prior decision, *GECC*, nor *Banque Worms* purports to consider the question, much less answer it.

Traditionally, the U.C.C. provides that payment in discharge of an obligation occurs under the first option-"at the time a payment order for the benefit of the beneficiary is accepted by the beneficiary's bank in the funds transfer." U.C.C. § 4A-406(a). But this approach does not square with the notice exception to the discharge-for-value rule. Application of this U.C.C. definition of discharge would mean that the entity that must receive notice (here White Birch) is an entity other than the entity to whom the funds were wired (here Citibank). To divide the "receipt of payment" and "notice of error" elements between different entities makes little sense and at any rate is a recipe for reading the notice exception out of the rule.

Equally unpersuasive is the argument that the discharge-triggering event necessarily occurs only when the beneficiary has actual notice that funds have been placed in its account. Such notice may not connect the funds to a given debtor or to the size of the debtor's outstanding obligation. Furthermore, while actual notice of a mistake may of course be independently disclosed by the originator to the beneficiary, constructive notice of a mistake may also occur simply as a result of the size of the transfer when considered in connection with the name of the originator. In this case, for example, White Birch assuredly would have had constructive notice of the mistake if the transfer had been, say, for $7.7 million-if, in other words, First National had made a two-digit error rather than a one-digit error in transmitting Calumet's payment order. Any sensible application of the discharge-for-value rule in this unique setting must account for constructive as well as actual notice of a mistake.

That leaves what seems to us to be the most desirable option-that the discharge-for-value defense will apply unless the beneficiary receives notice of a mistake before the beneficiary of the transfer credits the debtor's account. In addition to aligning the entity that receives notice of any mistake with the entity that receives the payment, and permitting constructive notice to trigger the rule, this approach is consistent with one of the underlying principles of the discharge-for-value rule; namely, that the creditor has given value for the mistaken payment. Nor, despite White Birch's suggestion to the contrary, will this approach undermine the discharge-for-value rule on the theory that the rule will kick in only after the beneficiary on its own terms makes an accounting of how the transfer should be credited. The time value of money being what it is, most commercial recipients of such transfers can be counted on to promptly credit the debtor's account. As in most settings, at any rate, the rule applies only to commercially reasonable accountings.

We note that a district court decision directly on point followed a similar analysis. In *NBase Communications v. American National Bank & Trust*, 8 F.Supp.2d 1071 (N.D. Ill.1998), the court held that notice was sufficient so long as the beneficiary of the payment learned of the mistake before recovering the check from a lock box. In reaching that conclusion, the court noted that the creditor must give value for the mistaken payment-by crediting the debtor's account-before receiving notice of the mistake in order to invoke the discharge-for-value defense. *Id.* at 1076-77. Checks and wire transfers, we acknowledge, do not offer a perfect analogy. The former are governed by state law, the latter by federal law, and the two are governed by different sections of the U.C.C. But in the unique setting of applying the notice exception to the discharge-for-value rule, the reasoning of *NBase* aptly respects the principles of the rule and the realities of applying it to checks and wire transfers: "[I]t is difficult to see what is unfair about requiring a bank to return money if it was notified of the mistaken payment before it gave value for the payment. For example, only after the crediting would it be unfair to require the innocent creditor to make restitution." *Id.* at 1077 (emphasis in original). So it is here.

Both the bankruptcy court and the district court, in taking up the case on remand, erred in focusing on when White Birch received the funds rather than on when White Birch credited Calumet's account. In doing so, both courts effectively wrote out the element of "discharge" from the discharge-for-value defense. The undisputed record shows that White Birch did not credit the funds to Calumet's account until the afternoon of March 11, 1991. First National offered the testimony of Calumet employee Angela Hollearn to prove that White Birch was aware well before then that Calumet had intended to wire only $77,301.58 to White Birch for the payment of accrued interest. The bankruptcy court ruled against First National on the basis that Hollearn's testimony was equivocal on the issue of to whom she spoke and what was said on March 8, 1991 when she allegedly conveyed to White Birch the fact that a wire transfer had been sent, the amount of the transfer, and how that amount had been calculated.

The district court likewise dismissed Hollearn's testimony on this point as too speculative. It therefore determined that First National had not established that White Birch had notice of the error before receiving the funds. Without deciding whether the lower courts erred in excluding the disputed testimony as a matter of law, . . . , we note that there is no dispute that Hollearn notified White Birch of the error on the morning of March 11, 1991.

Furthermore, White Birch's behavior establishes that it was aware of the error as soon as it was informed of the wire transfer by its own bank. When White Birch discovered on the morning of March 11, 1991 that Citibank had credited its account for $770,301.58, it immediately transferred the additional $693,000 to Brant's personal account at Citibank, ostensibly so that "everything could be sorted out." It did not apply that amount to reduce Calumet's debt on the Mogambo note until later that day. If White Birch did not know or at least suspect that it had erroneously received the additional funds, it would have had no reason to segregate them into its owner's personal account. The fact that it segregated the precise amount of the overage, moreover, is strong evidence that White Birch knew exactly how much it was supposed to receive from Calumet. Even the wire transfer itself, after all, was referenced as "MOGAMBO *INT.*" (Emphasis added.)

Thus, even if the bankruptcy court and district court correctly determined that White Birch did not have notice of the error before receiving the funds, White Birch certainly had notice before crediting Calumet's account. We therefore hold as a matter of law that White Birch had prior notice of the mistake in the funds transfer for purposes of the discharge-for-value rule and cannot avail itself of that defense. First National is therefore entitled to restitution from White Birch.

Under normal circumstances, the amount of restitution would be the $693,000 overpayment. But here First National was able to settle Calumet's claim against it for a total of $550,000. First National conceded at oral argument that this is the true extent of its loss, and thus the measure by which White Birch has been unjustly enriched at the bank's expense. Although White Birch has argued that $500,000 of the bank's claim was in the form of a loan to Calumet, the record makes clear that First National credited this amount to Calumet's account solely to settle the lawsuit filed against it as a result of the mistaken wire transfer. If the bank has in fact recovered any of this "loan" in the Calumet bankruptcy proceedings, the district court on remand can take this into account in rendering the final judgment against

White Birch. The district court is also free to consider whether First National is entitled to prejudgment interest on its restitution claim.

As a final point, we note that allowing White Birch to keep funds that no one intended for it to have when it received them would constitute a windfall to White Birch at the expense of First National. Returning the $550,000 paid out by First National to extricate itself from its transmission error will, however, put the parties in the same position that they would have been in had the error in transferring the funds not occurred. Although these equitable considerations do not trump the discharge-for-value defense in situations where the defense is applicable, they are pertinent here. White Birch should, in fact, consider itself fortunate that it is having to return only $550,000 of the $693,000 excess it received because First National was able to settle with Calumet for less than the amount of the mistaken transfer.

III. CONCLUSION

For all of the reasons set forth above, we reverse the judgment of the district court and remand the case for the entry of judgment in favor of First National.

Problem 8-14

Assume that this transaction is not covered by the EFTA. Bob ordered State Bank to transfer $10,000 from his account to Sue White's account at National Bank. Bob and State Bank have agreed that all transfers of an amount greater than $5,000 will have the letter B preceding the amount. Bob's order did not have the letter B preceding the amount. Bob really meant to order State Bank to transfer $1,000. State Bank instructed National Bank to credit Sue's account at National Bank for $10,000.

Notes

a)   Must Bob pay $10,000 to State Bank?

b)   Must State Bank pay $10,000 to National Bank? Can State Bank recover from National Bank or from Sue White?

Notes

c) Assume State Bank sent a notice to Bob that his account had been debited $10,000. Sixty days later, Bob told State Bank that the transfer was supposed to be for $1,000. Can Bob recover the money from State Bank?

Problem 8-15

Assume that this transaction is not covered by the EFTA. Jim ordered State Bank to transfer $1,000 to Supply Company's account at National Bank. To execute that order, State Bank sent a payment order directly to National Bank. State Bank's employee mistakenly identified Supply Company as Supply Corporation in the payment order to National Bank. National Bank accepted the payment order and credited Supply Corporation's account. Supply Company and Supply Corporation are two different, unrelated entities.

Notes

a) Must Jim pay his payment order?

b) Must State Bank pay its payment order?

Problem 8-16

Assume that this transaction is not covered by the EFTA. Jim ordered State Bank to transfer $1,000 to Supply Company's account at National Bank. Jim identified Supply Company as the beneficiary and gave State Bank the account number of 12345 as Supply Company's account. Supply Company's correct account number is 12347. State Bank executed that order by issuing a payment order to National Bank to credit account number 12345, beneficiary Supply Company.

Notes

a) Can National Bank accept that payment order?

Notes

b)   Can National Bank rely on the name
     or the number in accepting that
     payment order and paying the
     beneficiary?

c)   Must Jim pay his payment order?

d)   If National Bank credits account
     number 12345, can anyone recover
     the money from the holder of that
     account?

Problem 8-17

Best Rugs ordered National Bank to pay $100,000 to Textile Corporation's account at First
Bank. National Bank sent a payment order of $1,000,000 to First Bank to credit Textile's
account.

Notes

a)   Must Best Rugs pay its order? Must
     National Bank pay its order?

b)   If Best Rugs has already paid the
     order for $1,000,000 because
     National Bank has debited Best Rugs'
     account, does Best Rugs get a refund
     from National Bank, First Bank, or
     Textile Corp?

REGATOS V. NORTH FORK BANK
838 N.E.2d 629 (N.Y. 2005)

Rosenblatt, J.

The United States Court of Appeals for the Second Circuit, by certified questions, asks us whether a commercial bank customer can recover funds that the bank improperly transferred out of his account, even though he did not notify the bank of the unauthorized transfer until well after the time limit stated in his account agreement. This issue requires us to decide whether the one-year period of repose in our Uniform Commercial Code § 4-A-505 may be modified by agreement. We also resolve whether UCC 4-A-204(1) requires the bank actually to send the customer notice of an unauthorized transfer in order to trigger the running of a "reasonable time" within the meaning of that section, or whether a private agreement to hold a customer's mail can allow constructive notice to start that period. These are questions of first impression in this Court, and apparently in every other court of last resort in states that have adopted the relevant statutes.

In accord with the United States District Court for the Southern District of New York, we hold for the customer on both questions. The one-year period of repose in UCC 4-A-505, governing the customer's time in which to notify the bank of the unauthorized transfer, may not be modified by contract. Furthermore, both the one-year statute of repose and the "reasonable time" referred to in section 4-A-204 (1), which determines the customer's ability to recover interest on the misallocated money, begin to run when the customer receives actual notice of the improper transfer.

I.

Tomáz Mendes Regatos held a commercial account with Commercial Bank of New York, the predecessor to North Fork Bank. His agreement with the bank required him to notify the bank of any irregularity regarding his account within 15 days after the bank statement and items were first mailed or made available to him.[1]

---

[1] The relevant part of the account agreement stated that

"[t]he depositor will exercise reasonable care and promptness in examining such statement and items to discover any irregularity including, but not limited to, any unauthorized signature or alteration and will notify the Bank promptly in writing of any such discovery, and in no event more than fifteen (15) calendar days subsequent to the time that such statement and items were first mailed or available to the

(continued...)

The agreement did not provide for notice to him of electronic funds transfers, except to the extent those transfers appeared on his monthly statements. The bank adopted a practice of holding Regatos's bank statements rather than mailing them to him, and expected him to request the statements when he wanted to see them.

On March 23, 2001, the bank received a funds transfer order from someone it believed to be Regatos, but failed to follow agreed security procedures[2] to confirm the order. Without authorization, the bank then transferred $450,000 out of his account. On April 6, 2001, the bank received another transfer order, again failed to follow its security procedures and without authorization transferred an additional $150,000 out of his account. Together, these transfers represented most of the value of the account.

Regatos did not learn of the unauthorized transfers until he checked his accumulated account statements on August 9, 2001. The transfers were reflected on statements issued on March 23, 2001 and April 25, 2001, but the bank held these statements until he asked for them, following its standard practice in relation to him. He informed the bank of the unauthorized transfers on the day he learned of them, August 9, 2001.

When the bank refused to reimburse Regatos for the lost funds, he sued in the United States District Court for the Southern District of New York. In a comprehensive, well-reasoned opinion, District Judge Shira Scheindlin denied the bank's motion for summary judgment and held that the one-year statute of repose may not be shortened by agreement. The court ruled that, in any event, the 15-day notice period set by the account agreement was unreasonable and invalid. The Federal District Court further held that the UCC 4-A-505 period to notify the bank began to run when Regatos received actual notice of the error on August 9, 2001

---

[1] (...continued)
depositor. In those situations in which the depositor has authorized the Bank to hold his correspondence, this section shall apply as if the depositor received such statement on the date shown on the statement."

[2] The security procedures here involved nothing more than checking Regatos's signature against the signature on the faxed transfer order and calling him to confirm (cf. UCC 4-A-201 ["Comparison of a signature on a payment order or communication with an authorized specimen signature of the customer is not by itself a security procedure"]). Apparently, the bank did not require any password, even for large sums. Here, the bank compared the signature on the fax to its signature on file, but did not realize that the fax signature had been forged. The jury found that the bank did not telephone Regatos to confirm that the order was legitimate.

(*Regatos v. North Fork Bank*, 257 F. Supp.2d 632 [S.D.N.Y.2003]).

A federal jury found in favor of Regatos. Following UCC 4-A-204, the court awarded him both the principal ($600,000) and the interest from the date the bank improperly transferred the funds.

The bank appealed, and the United States Court of Appeals for the Second Circuit determined that the legal issues necessary to dispose of the case were novel, important questions of New York law. (Footnote omitted) The Second Circuit certified to this Court, and we accepted, the following questions:

"[1] Can the one-year statute of repose established by New York U.C.C. [ ] 4-A-505 be varied by agreement? If so, are there any minimum limits on the variation thereof (such as 'reasonable time') that estop [the bank] from denying Regatos recovery in this case? ...

"[2] In the absence of agreement, does New York U.C.C. Article 4-A require actual notice, rather than merely constructive notice? If so, can this requirement be altered by agreement of the parties and was such achieved here?" (*Regatos v. North Fork Bank*, 396 F.3d 493, 498-499 [2005] [Wesley, J.].)

We answer the first part of the first question "no," rendering the second part academic. We answer the first part of the second question "yes" and the second part of the second question "no."

II.

UCC 4-A-204 establishes a bank's basic obligation to make good on unauthorized and ineffective[4] transfers and, with one exception, forbids any variation of that obligation by agreement. * * * *

Regatos argues that the one-year statutory period [provided in UCC 4-A-505] is an integral part of the bank's "obligation ... to refund payment" under UCC 4-A-204(1) and so, pursuant to UCC 4-A-204(2), "may not ... be varied by agreement." The bank and its supporting amici point out that the notice provision is in section 4-A-505, not section 4-A-204(1), and rely on UCC 4-A-501(1), which declares that "[e]xcept as otherwise provided ... the rights and obligations of a party to a funds transfer may be varied by agreement of the affected party."[5] The bank maintains

---

[4] Ineffective transfers are those in which the bank has not properly executed security procedures (UCC 4-A-202).

[5] In support of this position, the amici urge that article 4-A is not a consumer protection statute, especially considering that it applies solely to presumably sophisticated commercial

(continued...)

that the customer's duty to notify the bank of the error before recovering misallocated funds is an "obligation" separate from that created by section 4-A-204(1) and therefore modifiable.

We agree with Regatos's reading of the statutes. In context, the policy behind article 4-A encourages banks to adopt appropriate security procedures. Only when a commercially reasonable security procedure is in place (or has been offered to the customer) may the bank disclaim its liability for unauthorized transfers (UCC 4-A-202). Permitting banks to vary the notice period by agreement would reduce the effectiveness of the statute's one-year period of repose as an incentive for banks to create and follow security procedures.

While the issue is close, we cannot accept the bank's argument that the customer's responsibility to notify the bank of its error is modifiable. UCC 4-A-204(1) states that "[t]he bank is not entitled to any recovery from the customer on account of a failure by the customer to give notification as stated in this section." (Footnote omitted) Accordingly, a bank has an obligation to refund the principal regardless of notice, provided such notice is given within one year in accordance with UCC 4-A-505 (*see* 3 JAMES J. WHITE AND ROBERT S. SUMMERS, UNIFORM COMMERCIAL CODE § 22-4 [4th ed.]). Moreover, as the District Court pointed out, section 4-A-505 (the one-year notice period) appears in the "Miscellaneous Provisions" part of the article, not the parts touching upon substantive rights and obligations (*Regatos*, 257 F.Supp.2d 632, 644 n. 19 [2003]). The period of repose in section 4-A-505 is essentially a jurisdictional attribute of the "rights and obligations" contained in UCC 4-A-204(1). To vary the period of repose would, in effect, impair the customer's section 4-A-204(1) right to a refund, a modification that section 4-A-204(2) forbids.

Article 4-A was intended, in significant part, to promote finality of banking operations and to give the bank relief from unknown liabilities of potentially indefinite duration (*see Banque Worms v. BankAmerica Intl.*, 77 N.Y.2d 362, 371, 568 N.Y.S.2d 541, 570 N.E.2d 189 [1991]). This legislative purpose does not suggest that those interests alter (or should alter) the statute's fine-tuned balance between the customer and the bank as to who should bear the burden of unauthorized transfers.

---

[5] (...continued)
parties. While this is true to some extent, the provision in section 4-A-204 refusing to allow parties to modify the bank's basic obligation to refund unauthorized transfer funds contradicts the amici's argument because the provision clearly protects consumers, even commercial consumers, from bearing the burden of this type of bank error.

Therefore, we hold that the one-year repose period in section 4-A-505 cannot be modified by agreement. By notifying the bank on August 9, 2001, the day he received actual notice, and four or five months after the statements were available, Regatos acted either way within the year-long period of repose. This clearly satisfied the statutory requirement and he is entitled to recover at least his $600,000 principal.

III.

The Second Circuit next asks whether actual notice is required under article 4-A (or whether mere constructive notice will do) and, consequently, whether Regatos is also entitled to recover interest on the misdirected funds.

The bank made Regatos's monthly account statements available for his review, but waited for him to request them rather than send them to him. According to its agreed security procedures, the bank was to reach him by telephone immediately after it received a funds transfer order, to confirm that he had actually authorized the transfer. Other than that call, which the jury found was never made, the only notice available to him would come from his own perusal of the account statements.

In his earlier dealings with the bank, Regatos tended to check his statements regularly. By 2001, however, he reviewed the bank's statements only intermittently. In that year, he asked to see his statements some time before the unauthorized transfer on March 23, 2001 and did not ask again until August 9, 2001, after the bank had generated statements on March 23, 2001 and April 25, 2001. These two statements revealed the unauthorized transfers, but the bank continued to hold the statements until Regatos asked for them. As discussed, he immediately notified the bank of its error when he discovered it on August 9, 2001.

The bank argues that Regatos obtained constructive notice of the transfers on March 23, 2001 and April 25, 2001, when the statements disclosing them were first generated. UCC 4-A-204 requires a customer seeking to recover interest on funds lost due to an unauthorized transfer "to notify the bank of the relevant facts within a reasonable time not exceeding ninety days after the date the customer received notification from the bank that the order was accepted." We agree with Regatos that this requirement may not be waived.

Under the bank's reading of the statute, an agreed 15-day notice period could run before a bank statement was even available for the customer's review. If the burden of checking whether the bank has wrongfully transferred funds out of the customer's account were to fall on the customer, as it would under a constructive notice interpretation, the customer's duty to check would presumably arise as soon as the data became available for review. In electronic funds transfers, the bank would be able to inform an inquiring customer of the transfer well before the formal monthly statement is compiled. Conceivably, the crucial information could be sitting in the bank's possession for weeks, awaiting discovery by the customer. If the customer did not inquire, and the agreement's 15-day period ran, the customer would lose the transferred funds even though the error was entirely the bank's. This seems to us both the logical consequence of a constructive notice system and an unreasonable view of actual banking relationships. Because interpretation of the UCC is always conducted with an eye toward business realities and the predictable consequences of legal rules, we reject a statutory interpretation that conflicts with reasonable business practices.

Policy arguments support an actual notice requirement. An invariable statutory rule provides a bright line for banks and their customers, bringing reliability and certainty to these dealings. Constructive notice is far less exact, leaving too much room for varying interpretation and disorder. If the bank had complied with its security procedures, it would have called Regatos the same day it received each purported transfer order, thereby providing him with actual notice of the events.

Even where customers enter "hold mail" agreements with their banks, the actual notice rule still applies. Just as the one-year notice limitation is an inherent aspect of the customer's right to recover unauthorized payments, the actual notice requirement provides the bedrock for the exercise of that right. Permitting banks to enforce "agreements" to accept constructive notice would defeat article 4-A's guarantee of recovery for unauthorized payments.

In response to the second certified question, we answer that article 4-A requires actual notice, and that this requirement cannot be varied by a "hold mail" agreement, neither to begin the statute of repose, nor to begin "reasonable time" under the account agreement. Regatos notified the bank of his loss within an indisputably reasonable time after receiving actual notice, and is therefore entitled to recover the interest on his lost principal (UCC 4-A-204).

Accordingly, the first part of certified question 1 should be answered in the negative and the second part not answered as unnecessary, and the first part of certified question 2 should be answered in the affirmative and the second part in the negative.

Should the reasoning in *Regatos* be applied to U.C.C. § 4-406? Do you think the *Regatos* court came to the correct result in interpreting Article 4A?

Problem 8-18

Best Rugs ordered National Bank to pay $100,000 to Textile Corporation's account at First Bank. National Bank sent a payment order of $1,000,000 to First Bank to credit Textile's account. National Bank sent Best a notice that its account was debited $1,000,000 instead of $100,000. Best notified the bank 60 days later that an error had occurred.

Notes

a) Is Best precluded from getting a refund of the excess amount from National Bank?

b) Assume Best did not object to National Bank's debit of its account for two years. Can Best get a refund of the excess amount of the payment order?

c) Assume that the agreement between Best and National Bank provided that Best must object to all errors in funds transfers within 30 days of receipt of notice of the transfer. Can Best get a refund of the excess amount of the payment order?

Problem 8-19

Notes

Best Rugs ordered National Bank to pay $100,000 to Textile Corporation's account at First Bank. National Bank executed a payment order for $10,000 to First Bank, instead of $100,000. Must Best pay its order?

Problem 8-20

Best Rugs issued a payment order to First Bank for $100,000 identifying the beneficiary by the correct account number of 678910 at Third Bank. Third Bank's correct identifying number is 134. First Bank sent a payment order to Second Bank.

Notes

a)   Assume First Bank's payment order to Second Bank identified Third Bank only by number 143. Second Bank sent a payment order to bank number 143, Finance Bank, identifying the beneficiary's account as 678910. Finance Bank credited the amount of the order to account 678910. Do Best Rugs, First Bank, and Second Bank have to pay the amount of their payment orders?

b)   Same facts as (a) above except assume First Bank's payment order provided "Third Bank, #143." Does that change the analysis?

c)   Same facts as (a) above except assume Best is the sender who gave the wrong number for Third Bank. Does that change the analysis?

Problem 8-21

Plumbing Supply Company issued a payment order to State Bank in New York to pay $100,000 to Wholesaler's account with National Bank in San Francisco. State Bank issued a payment order to Federal Reserve Bank of New York. Federal Reserve Bank of New York issued a payment order to National Bank. National Bank accepted the payment order, crediting Wholesaler's account. Plumbing Supply Company's original order was completely unauthorized and Plumbing Supply Company and State Bank had no security procedure in effect. Plumbing Supply Company discovered the unauthorized order 45 days after its account was debited.

Notes

a)   Must State Bank refund the money to
      Plumbing Supply?

b)   Must the Federal Reserve Bank
      refund the money to State Bank?

D.   Regulation of Evolving Payment Systems

Now that we have come to the end of our study of the regulation of payment systems, you should have a good sense of the policy concerns inherent in this area of the law. You can also see that there are significant gaps in regulation, particularly with electronic methods of payment. For instance, we know that debit funds transfers that are not covered by the EFTA and Regulation E (because they do not involve a consumer account) are also not covered by Article 4A. The only body of regulation for those debit funds transfers are the private rules made by the entities that carry them out, such as the CHIPS or NACHA rules cited earlier in this Chapter. Should payments law leave some types of payments regulation to private agreement and association rulemaking?   What are the risks inherent in that approach?

Some types of payment mechanisms, such as gift cards, are not systematically regulated at all. Rather, some states have enacted laws dealing with some aspects of gift cards, focusing on end user protection, but not regulating them as a system of payments.[*]

---

[*] *See, e.g.*, Mark T. Gillett, et al., *Developments in Cyberbanking*, 61 BUS. LAW. 911 (2006).

Problem 8-22

You are on the study commission working for the National Conference of Commissioners on Uniform State Laws. A proposed uniform law on regulation of stored value cards, including gift cards, has been proposed. Answer the following questions.

Notes

a) Should either the federal or state government act to regulate this type of payment system? If so, who should regulate and why?

b) How would you deal with the four concerns of payment systems that we have repeatedly encountered in the payment systems we have discussed?

Review

The following problem provides you with an opportunity to review not only issues concerning electronic funds transfers, but also issues arising from use of other payment systems we have studied. The key to working your way through this long problem is to take the payment mechanisms one by one in the order the incidents occurred and play the "pass the loss" game we learned in an earlier chapter.

Problem 8-23

Assume all banks are within the same federal reserve district.

Lou is an accountant. He is an independent contractor who periodically does work for Best Construction. Tim, Best Construction's treasurer, has Lou work on tax issues and do some of the quarterly tax filings for the company. On June 1, Lou was in Tim's office going over some items in preparation for second quarter filings. Lou saw Tim sign checks on behalf of Best Construction in payment of invoices.

Supply Company is an existing company that sells construction supplies to Best Construction. As a condition of doing business with Best Construction, Supply Company required Best Construction to supply a letter of credit for $50,000 to guarantee payment for supplies if Best Construction did not pay invoices within 30 days of the date on the invoice. Third Bank, Best Construction's bank sent the original letter of credit on February 1 in the amount of $50,000 to Supply Company. The letter of credit provided that payment would be made if Supply Company presented the original letter of credit, a copy of an invoice for supplies delivered to Best Construction dated at least 45 days previous to the presentation, and a letter stating "Best Construction has not paid this submitted invoice within 30 days of its issuance." The letter of credit also provided that Supply Company had to present a sight draft drawn on Third Bank in an amount no greater than the amount of the invoice.

Lou persuaded his friend Joe, who worked in the mail room at Best Construction, to intercept Supply Company's invoices and substitute fake invoices with Joe's home address at the top of the fake invoice. Joe sent a fake invoice for $4,000 in the name of Supply Company to Best Construction as a bill for nails shipped to Best Construction in June. Tim knew that Supply Company supplies construction material to Best Construction and did not notice the different address at the top of the fake invoice. Tim signed a check for $4,000 on behalf of Best Construction payable to the order of Supply Company and drawn on Third Bank. Tim then sent the check to the address on the top of the invoice Joe sent to Best Construction. Joe turned the check over to Lou. Lou signed the back of the check as follows "For deposit only, Supply Company by Joe, president." Lou deposited the check on Friday, June 30 in an account at First Bank. Lou and Joe previously opened that account in the name of Supply Company, showing both Lou and Joe as authorized signatories on that account. First Bank sent the check to the Federal Reserve Bank that evening. The Federal Reserve Bank had the check at the beginning of the day on Monday, July 3. That evening the Federal Reserve Bank sent the check to Third Bank. On Wednesday July 5, Third Bank debited Best Construction's account. That check was returned to Best Construction in the July 30 bank statement.

On August 1, Lou was in Tim's office and when Tim left to talk to someone else, Lou took three checks from the bottom of the pack. These checks have Best Construction's name imprinted on the top left hand corner of the check. Lou, having seen Tim's signature many times, expertly forged Tim's signature on the drawer's signature line on the three checks. Lou made the checks payable to Supply Company in the amount of $450 each. Lou knew from his work with the company that the company did not require an invoice for items less than $500. Once a month for the next three months (on August 1, September 1, and October 1), Lou took the checks to Check Cashing Inc., having signed them on the back "Supply Company." Each time Check Cashing deposited the checks in its account at Second Bank and Second Bank forwarded the checks directly to Third Bank. Third Bank received the checks on August 4, September 4, and October 4 respectively. Each time, Third Bank debited Best Construction's account that same day. The August 1 check was returned to Best Construction in the August 30 bank statement. The September 1 check was returned to Best Construction in the September 30 bank statement. The October 1 check was returned to Best Construction in the October 30 bank statement.

On September 1, emboldened by his success so far, Lou persuaded Joe to call up Tim and demand a wire transfer of funds in payment of an invoice that was supposedly overdue. Tim searched for the invoice but could not find it. Joe threatened to stop supplying goods to Best Construction if Tim did not execute the transfer for $10,000 to Supply Company's account at First Bank, account # 4213-56-7890. It was not an uncommon occurrence for creditors to call Tim and threaten to cut off the company from further supply if he did not pay up immediately. Tim was somewhat puzzled by the demand for a wire transfer given the letter of credit issued to Supply Company. Nonetheless, Tim instructed Third Bank to send $10,000 to account # 4321-56-7890 at First Bank. Third Bank did not want to conduct the transfer because Best Construction was in precarious financial condition. After Tim pleaded with the bank officer, the bank officer at Third Bank agreed to conduct the transfer if Tim signed a note for $20,000. Tim requested that the bank officer not transfer the note to anyone else. The bank officer agreed. Tim signed the following note:

September 4, 2006

The undersigned promise to pay to the order of Third Bank on October 1, 2006 the sum of $20,000 plus interest at 2% over published 90 day Treasury bill rate. At any time Third Bank deems itself insecure, the undersigned promises to provide security to secure the repayment obligation hereunder. All parties to this note waive presentment and notice of dishonor.

Best Construction
Tim Best, Treasurer.

After Tim signed the note on the front as shown and on the back "Tim Best", Third Bank credited $20,000 to Best Construction's account. Third Bank then instructed Federal Reserve Bank to transfer $10,000 to account #4321-56-7890 at First Bank, Bank # 5789. The Federal Reserve instructed Bank #5789, which was really State Bank, to credit account #4321-56-7890. State Bank did so. That account is held by ZigZag Co.

On September 15, Lou and Joe sent another invoice to Best Construction ostensibly from Supply Company, this time for $6,000. On September 20, Tim issued a check payable to the order of Supply Company for $6,000 and sent it to the address on the false invoice. This time, Joe signed the check on the back "Supply Company" and took it to Third Bank, asking a teller to pay the amount of the check to him in cash. The teller asked for identification and

Joe presented a driver's license. The teller checked Best Construction's account balance and determined that the account did not have enough money in it to cover the check and refused to pay the money to Joe. Joe then took the check and deposited it in the account in Supply Company's name at First Bank on September 23. The check arrived at Third Bank on September 25. Third Bank debited Best Construction's account creating an overdraft and then re-credited the account and returned the check on September 26 directly to First Bank.

On September 24, Lou and Joe withdrew all of the funds from the Supply Company account at First Bank by having First Bank certify a check drawn on that account for $11,350 payable to the order of Lou and Joe. Both Lou and Joe indorsed it in blank and gave the check to Qantas Airlines in payment of two first class tickets to Australia.

On September 30, Tim discovered the three missing check blanks and issued three stop payment orders on those three checks by telephoning Third Bank. Third Bank sent a form for Tim to fill out and return to the bank to confirm the oral stop orders. Tim returned the forms to the bank properly filled out on October 10.

On October 15, the real Supply Company drew on the letter of credit by presenting an invoice for $15,000 that was 50 days past due, the original letter of credit and a sight draft for the amount of the invoice. Supply Company also presented a letter stating "Best Construction has not paid this invoice within 45 days of the invoice being sent." Third Bank paid $15,000 to Supply Company on October 18 and debited Best Construction's account for $15,000 creating an overdraft. Third Bank demanded that Best Construction satisfy the overdraft. Because of the overdraft, Third Bank returned checks drawn on the account that Tim had signed to pay other suppliers. Those suppliers threatened to sue Tim and Best Construction.

On November 1, Finance Bank demanded payment of the $20,000 note. Finance Bank had purchased the note on October 15 from Third Bank for $18,000. Third Bank had indorsed the note on the back "Third Bank, without recourse." Third Bank had sold the note to Finance Bank because it was concerned about Best Construction's ability to pay. Third Bank did not communicate that concern to Finance Bank. Tim refused to pay the note. Finance Bank threatened to sue both Best Construction and Tim.

Tim told you the whole story on the telephone and is sitting in your office on December 1. Your commercial paper instructor is not available for a quick consult. She is enjoying the white sand beaches and the crystal blue water of the Caribbean. What are you going to do to help Tim? Explain all of the rights and liabilities of all of the parties. Clearly state any factual assumptions that you make in your explanation. After you have explained everything to Tim, recommend a course of action to Tim and explain why you think that is the best course of action.

Notes